Document Design
A Guide for Technical Communicators

Document Design

A Guide for Technical Communicators

Miles A. Kimball

Texas Tech University

Ann R. Hawkins

Texas Tech University

Bedford/St. Martin's

Boston ◆ New York

For Bedford/St. Martin's

Executive Editor: Leasa Burton
Developmental Editor: Joanna Lee
Editorial Assistant: Sarah Guariglia
Production Editor: Ryan Sullivan
Production Supervisor: Andrew Ensor
Marketing Manager: Karita dos Santos
Art Director: Donna Lee Dennison
Text Design: Claire Seng-Niemoeller
Copy Editor: Books By Design, Inc.
Indexer: Books By Design, Inc.
Cover Design: Kim Cevoli
Composition: Books By Design, Inc.
Printing and Binding: Haddon Craftsmen, Inc., an R.R. Donnelley & Sons
  Company

President: Joan E. Feinberg
Editorial Director: Denise B. Wydra
Editor in Chief: Karen S. Henry
Director of Marketing: Karen Melton Soeltz
Director of Editing, Design, and Production: Marcia Cohen
Manager, Publishing Services: Emily Berleth

Library of Congress Control Number: 2007931378

Manufactured in the United States of America.

2   1   0   9   8   7

f   e   d   c   b   a

For information, write: Bedford/St. Martin's, 75 Arlington Street,
Boston, MA 02116   (617-399-4000)

ISBN-10: 0-312-43699-8
ISBN-13: 978-0-312-43699-5

Acknowledgments

*Acknowledgments and copyrights appear at the back of the book on pages 375–76, which constitute
an extension of the copyright page.*

Preface

To become successful professionals today, students must learn to communicate visually just as well as they learn to write. Whether students go on to work as document designers, web designers, interaction designers, information designers, or even user experience designers, many of the new paths for technical communicators focus squarely on visual communication and require a working knowledge of digital tools and formats that didn't exist just a few years ago. Given the complexities of both visual and digital work environments, understanding the fundamentals of document design is more important than ever. Even students who plan careers in business, medicine, industry, or government will find themselves communicating visually through documents in their workplaces.

Document Design: A Guide for Technical Communicators introduces students to the basic principles and theories of design, combining practical advice about the design process with a foundation in visual rhetoric and usability. In this preface, we lay out a few of the considerations that form our approach to teaching document design and to writing this book.

A Balance of Theory and Practice

Most books on document design lean toward either theory or practice. We offer a balanced approach — theoretically informed practice — that introduces a working vocabulary to help students become reflective practitioners, able not only to create effective and usable designs, but also to explain why and how they made their design choices.

The book's structure works to reinforce this balance. **Unit One, Principles**, introduces students to the practical terms, principles, and theories at the heart of good design. These concepts are then integrated throughout the book in discussions of the choices that designers make as well as in analysis of the sample documents. The theoretical lenses — visual perception, visual culture, and visual rhetoric — are also carried throughout *Unit Two, Processes*, in brief introductions to each chapter's topic. Each chapter in Unit Two focuses on a single important aspect of document design, including format, page layout, typography, graphics, and color. A final chapter in Unit Two guides students in designing those indispensable parts of many technical documents: lists, tables, and forms. *Unit Three, Practices*, will help students succeed in some of the more practical aspects of professional document design, including managing projects strategically, from user and needs analysis to invention, prototyping, and usability testing. Unit Three also includes a chapter on print production, covering the vocabulary students will need to speak effectively with professional printers.

Drawing from the most current research and best practices in the field today, we hope to give students the foundation they need to make decisions like designers in any rhetorical situation. Students will learn to negotiate between the needs and desires of both users and clients. Not every design situation calls for a beautiful and intricate document design. In some situations, a cheap and fast document will meet the needs of both clients and users more effectively than something more visually sophisticated. In others, an impressive and expensive design is absolutely essential for the document to fulfill its purposes. *Document Design* will help students make choices about what level of design investment is appropriate for the situation at hand, given the time, money, and resources available, as well as the client's goals and the users' needs.

Up-to-Date Advice about Digital Tools, Processes, and Formats

The impact of digital technologies on document design is profound. Whether creating websites or more traditional paper documents, document designers today must work through digital technologies. And more often than not, designs must work in multiple media and formats. For example, the designers of the Amtrak schedules in Chapter 1 (p. 8) needed to create information that could be delivered simultaneously in print, on the Web, and in PDF.

Recognizing that almost all documents today are at least born digitally, *Document Design* helps students understand the dynamics and possibilities of both screen and print media. We offer accessible advice about using technology throughout the design process, such as how to choose typefaces for the screen, how to manipulate bitmap and vector graphics, when to use RGB or CMYK color, and how to use color pickers. We discuss both print and screen media because we want to help document designers make practical, theoretically informed choices about what medium or mixture of media to use for the particular design projects they face.

However, this book is not a book on web design, of which there are many excellent examples on the market. We firmly believe that paper documents will be with us for a long time to come. As technologies, paper and printing form a convenient, usable, and economical medium for conveying technical information in many situations. To give students a range of flexible design skills necessary for them to succeed professionally, *Document Design* discusses how to create designs for print production through digital tools.

A Book That Shows the Principles of Good Design in Action

We are very proud of the careful design and the variety of real-world examples we use throughout the book. Most of the examples were culled from our own surroundings at home, at work, and in our travels. Rather than including the snazziest documents or creating artificial ones, we have tried to find the real examples that best illustrate the principle we are discussing, and present them as we found them. We hope this approach helps students recognize the documents that permeate their own lives.

However, we recognize that some concepts need good visualizations for students to understand, so the book also includes line art to help students see important ideas about design. We have designed the line art to be as minimalistic and clear as possible. In a number of cases, line art accompanies the scanned examples and helps explain to students what they are seeing.

We believe this book practices the principles it preaches. For this we thank the book's designer, Claire Seng-Niemoeller, who has years of experience creating successful textbooks that meet the needs of users. Every page visually reinforces rhetorically informed design practices, and students will find the format of the book helps make it a reference they can return to as they develop careers.

In addition to sample documents and illustrations, the book includes several helpful reference features:

- *Design Tips* throughout the text offer practical advice for students to apply to their own designs.

- *More about . . .* boxes delve deeper into topics related to chapter discussions to give students a broader understanding of the history and practice of document design.

- *An 8-page full-color insert* is integrated into Chapter 8, "Color," to illustrate color principles and tools, with several sample documents.

- *Sample documents are also featured in color on the companion website*, http://bedfordstmartins.com/documentdesign. The site also includes links to other useful document-design sites, tools, and pedagogical materials.

Acknowledgments

We would like to thank the many thorough reviewers of this book, including Diana Ashe, University of North Carolina Wilmington; Susan Codone, Mercer University; Gordon Scott Gehrs, Illinois Institute of Technology; Craig J. Hansen, Metropolitan State University; Suguru Ishizaki, Carnegie Mellon University; Carolyn Rude, Virginia Polytechnic Institute and State University; Jennifer Sheppard, New Mexico State University; and Ronald Shook, Utah State University. Your insights and suggestions have made this a much better book.

We would also like to thank the many folks who worked on this book at Bedford/St. Martin's. Thanks in particular to Leasa Burton for her good humor, support, and kindness in helping us envision the project, and Joanna Lee for her patience and grace in helping us develop and bring the book together. We are extremely grateful to the hardworking and skillful production team whose professionalism made this book possible: manager of publishing services Emily Berleth, project editor Ryan Sullivan, Nancy Benjamin of Books By Design, and production supervisor Andrew Ensor; designers Claire Seng-Niemoeller and Anna Palchik; and permissions editor Martha Friedman. Kim Cevoli designed a beautiful cover, and Cate Kashem designed and produced the book's website. Karita dos Santos and Nikkole Meimbresse continue to market and promote the book enthusiastically. We also thank Joan Feinberg, president; Denise Wydra, editorial director; and Karen Henry, editor in chief, for their early and continued support.

Thanks as well to our friends, colleagues, and students, whose support has made a long road seem short. At Texas Tech, they include Locke Carter, Becky Rickly, Craig Baehr, Rich Rice, Sean Grass, Iris Rivero, Jill Patterson, Scott Baugh, and many others. We also owe thanks to our good friends Carol Brobeck at the Folger Shakespeare Library, Carl Fischer and Vlatka Velcic at California State University, Long Beach, and Richard Porter at the *Plainview Daily Herald*. Finally, many thanks to our families for their support and understanding.

Miles A. Kimball and Ann R. Hawkins

Brief Contents

Contents

UNIT TWO   # Processes

UNIT THREE

Practices

10   **Projects**   309

Document Design
A Guide for Technical Communicators

What Is Document Design?

Take a look around and notice the documents in your life. You will probably discover more than you anticipated — in your office, your desk drawer, your car, your wallet. Documents from the U.S. Constitution to the manual for your cell phone surround you every day, guiding and shaping your interactions with the world. In fact, you're very likely *wearing* some documents right now (see Figure 1.1).

Documents help us interact with technology by giving us clear instructions on how to use computers, equipment, and vehicles. They help us travel by supplying information about where to go, how to get there, and what to do when we get there. Our government provides documents that guide our social lives, and organizations such as corporations and schools produce documents that shape our relationships. Documents give us the opportunity to communicate, convince, persuade, and express our identity and community. It's no exaggeration to say that documents are the foundation of organized society, a practical mechanism for mediating human action within and among communities, nations, and cultures.

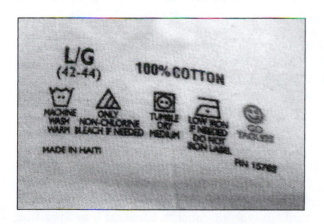

Figure 1.1 A document you wear. Clothing tags are a humble but essential example of how document design affects people's lives. This document was designed with careful attention to usability across cultures: all of the instructions include an international symbol that conveys important information to people who don't speak English, and the document provides sizing information in U.S. terms (L for large), as well as in French, Spanish, and German terms (G for grande or for groß). And, most important, the document is designed for comfort and durability: it needs to work well both while being worn and after being washed.

Ironically, documents are so ubiquitous that at times they seem to be invisible—just a part of the landscape of human society. But if we think about them, it is easy to see how tightly documents are entwined throughout our daily lives.

Documents like the clothing tag in Figure 1.1 do a small but necessary job. They help us as consumers to know whether the clothes will fit, what materials the clothes are made of, where the clothes came from, and how to launder and care for them. Clothing tags also help manufacturers to track clothing models and styles and to advertise their products. Sometimes the tag itself is a selling point. In 2003 the Hanes underwear company used Jackie Chan and Michael Jordan to advertise the comfort of their printed-on (rather than sewn-in) undershirt labels. And some labels, like those for Levi's jeans, appear on the *outside* of the clothes, showing consumers (and their friends!) how cool the clothes are while helping the manufacturer to sell even more clothes. So although they may be a humble example of documents, clothing tags must be readable, understandable, comfortable, and convincing to be effective.

Behind each of these documents stands a team of professionals: document designers. Even designing something as simple as a clothing tag requires dealing with some difficult challenges. How do you display essential information clearly in such a small space? How can you communicate effectively with people who speak many different languages? How do you design a document that is both comfortable to wear and easy to understand? And finally, how do you design a document that can survive the washer and dryer—not just once, but many times?

In this book, you will practice some of the techniques designers use to solve the challenges of successful document design. You will learn essential skills for communicating in the complex, intercultural world of technology and community. And you will learn how to analyze human communication situations so you can create documents that solve human problems. You'll find not only practical techniques and helpful information but also important theories about how to communicate through documents. Having a theoretical awareness as well as practical skills will help you make smart decisions about the documents you design, whatever the situation.

In the rest of this introduction, we'll dig a bit further into the question of exactly what document design *is*. This will help you understand the practical and theoretical information that comes later.

Document Design as Information Design

Document design is one part of the broader activity of *Information Design (ID)*. ID is still an evolving concept. Some see it as a practice;

others consider it a professional field in which information designers work. Still others consider it an academic discipline of study. The American Institute for Graphic Artists (AIGA) defines ID as "a highly specialized area of design that involves making large amounts of complex information clear and accessible to audiences" (AIGA Design Forum). Visual communication guru Robert E. Horn has defined ID as "the art and science of preparing information so that it can be used by human beings with efficiency and effectiveness" (15). More specifically, noted scholar Saul Carliner has suggested that ID works on three levels:

- *Physical:* ID helps users find and use information by providing a meaningful visual and physical design to communication products, including the design of pages and screens, writing, and production.

- *Cognitive:* ID helps users understand information by structuring and presenting it in ways that help solve problems.

- *Affective:* ID motivates users by gaining their attention and convincing them to act. (45)

What these definitions share is a sense that ID involves more than just creating pretty packaging for information. ID's scope is more profound: it deals with the relationships among people who create the information, people who use the information, and people's cultures, societies, and environment. Information designers create artifacts that define and build these relationships by helping people solve real problems they face.

In this sense, information design is as old as writing, or even older. The first person who carved an arrow into a tree trunk to mark a path for travelers was an information designer. So is a member of a team today who creates a complex website for customers of an international corporation who need to access purchase orders or shipping records. Both took up the task of making information "clear and accessible to audiences." Both used tools and systems of understanding, like writing and visual design, to convey meaning so it can be used by other people to solve specific problems in specific situations.

Horn later suggests that ID applies in three areas: designing documents, designing computer interfaces, and designing three-dimensional spaces. Because this book deals with the training of technical communicators, who for the most part work to convey ideas through documents, we concentrate on the first of Horn's areas: document design. Document design focuses information design principles and practices on the crafting of documents. Document designers work to understand the problems and situations of information users and information providers and then craft documents that help solve those problems within those situations. They also constantly assess whether the products of their efforts are working successfully and try to improve the quality of their information products.

The Document in Document Design

So document designers design documents. But what exactly *are* documents?

In previous centuries, it might have been easier to answer this question: documents were meaningful marks inscribed, incised, pressed, painted, or scratched on something, whether it was stone, clay, leaves, bark, wood, leather, or paper. These marks might be handwriting, numbers, pictures, or all three, but together marks and surfaces were combined to preserve and convey meaning. Documents of this sort include everything from simple records (receipts, bills of sale, deeds, birth, death, and marriage certificates) to more complex ones (letters, memos, reports, proposals, instructions, documentaries, manifestos, regulations, laws) to great works of art (novels, poems, plays, films, music). In a chaotic and changing world, we still use such tangible documents to fix information so it can be retrieved for later use. Documents like these are the glue that holds together most societies today. They are the objects we use to create more stable relationships between citizens and governments, accusers and defendants, producers and consumers, buyers and sellers, employers and employees, students and teachers.

But the rapid expansion of electronic media like the Internet and the Web has made us rethink this earlier definition of *document*. Does the word still mean anything when the digital networks that support something like a website are so changeable? Are websites and other electronic forms of communication documents?

Many have argued that because the Web is so dynamic and fluid, it does not convey "documents" so much as rapidly changing, rearranged, and repurposed "content." David M. Levy has countered this idea by emphasizing the similarities of all documents, paper or electronic:

> Attractive and popular though it may be, this understanding of the difference between paper and digital forms is, quite simply, wrong. What it fails to grasp is that paper documents — and indeed all documents — are static and changing, fixed and fluid. It also fails to see the importance of fixity in the digital world. There is a reason why text and graphics editors have a Save button, after all. (36)

Levy's comments suggest that although electronic documents might collect millions of bits of information on the fly, these random pieces of information are still assembled for a user to see. At that moment, a document is whatever is available and evident to the user's eyes and hands. Whether the user sees a web page or a printed page, at the moment of use, many factors behind the scenes combine to present information in a meaningful way. With electronic documents, those factors include the networks of computers, electrical power, and international standards that make it possible to create on one computer what can be viewed on another. With paper documents, those factors include the networks of paper and ink manufacture, printing, transportation, commerce, and archiving that must work together to bring a document into our view.

When we look at a document, whether paper or electronic, these myriad factors combine temporarily, settling into something we can use. After we obtain the information we are looking for, we might click to a different web page or turn to a different page in a printed document or go to a completely different document, but the visual field for that moment provides users with a framework for consuming information and an interface for working with that information.

Of course, electronic documents are more fluid than documents inscribed on paper, wood, or stone. We expect a web page to change from day to day, but we usually expect paper documents to remain the same for a longer period of time. The idea of the document, however, remains useful despite this impermanence. This is one reason digital artifacts follow many print conventions, even though they don't have to (what David Bolter and Richard Grusin call *remediation*). We commonly refer to many kinds of electronic communication as documents, including web pages, websites, word processing documents, spreadsheets, slide shows, Flash animations, and blogs, and we treat them as if they have coherence and boundaries, just as paper documents are bounded by their covers and shapes. Even when they break from print conventions, digital artifacts such as websites have quickly settled into a relatively stable set of conventions — for example, site navigation links are almost always at the left or top of each web page.

Arguably, in electronic documents, the permanence of digital information has simply shifted from the interface to the database or network. For example, we expect the appearance of our online bank statement to be different each time we look at it, but we certainly hope that the bank will permanently document our payments, deposits, and other transactions. So while the information within the electronic statement may change, the *concept* of a bank statement — a document — remains.

So for our purposes, documents are not bound by any particular medium. Instead, documents are best understood as a site where one person can mark information for the use of another. Document design, then, is the practice of creating these sites of interaction in such a way

Document design, then, is the practice of creating these sites of interaction in such a way that they respond effectively to the needs of both information producers and information users.

that they respond effectively to the needs of both information producers and information users.

From Document to Design

Because all documents, whether fixed permanently on paper or fixed temporarily on a screen, are presented to the user's field of view, in this book we focus specifically on how document designers make meaning through the *visual* features of documents.

Consider an example probably very familiar to you: the academic essay. Your instructors probably had specific requirements for some visual aspects of the text, such as the width of margins. For the most part, you probably complied with those requirements without giving them much further thought (except perhaps about the pickiness of teachers).

In document design terms, however, the academic essays you prepared were designed for a specific user: the instructor. Your instructor's requirements for formatting were intended to make his or her job — reading and evaluating your essays — easier and more convenient. Such requirements were probably mostly visual, including the following:

- *Double-spaced text*, to give the instructor room for corrections and interlinear comments.

- *Margins of a particular width*, to place a boundary between the text and the rest of the world, buffering the instructor's attention and helping her to focus on the text, as well as providing an area to write longer comments.

- *Paragraph indentations*, to help the instructor recognize when you intended to shift to a new topic.

- *Titles and headings*, usually bigger or bolder than the paragraph text, to allow the instructor to skim for structure.

- *Page headers or footers with page numbers*, to help the instructor keep the pages in the right order.

- *A staple, paper clip, or binder*, to keep all the pages of your document together.

- *A particular typeface or size of text*, to help the instructor get through a stack of grading without undue eyestrain.

These visual features are very familiar, so we might not pay much attention to them in writing or reading essays. But in other kinds of documents, visual features can become very important indeed. Visual features serve as the user interface of a document, helping users realize a number of important things:

- What kind of document they are reading, and what they might find in it
- How the document is structured
- Where they are in the document
- What's more important in the document, and what's less important
- How to find what they need

Together, these visual aspects of a document have a huge impact on how well the document works.

Let's look at a more complex example: the System Timetable (see Figure 1.2 on page 8), a 132-page document published by Amtrak, the national rail service, opened to the page for the Empire Builder train service from Chicago to Seattle.

Both the designers and the users of this document face difficult challenges. The travelers who are using the document face the complex task of planning trips by rail. They need convenient and economical transportation, but they also need clear information, including exactly what train they should take, where they can get off, when the train will depart and arrive, and what amenities are available on the train, such as dining and sleeping cars. They want to find this information easily, quickly, and accurately. Travel in itself makes people feel stressed and dislocated. If passengers also feel confused or frustrated about the information they receive in this schedule, they might well consider using a different mode of travel on their next trip.

The designer's task is perhaps even more difficult. Train schedules can be pretty complicated, and Amtrak is the biggest passenger rail system in the country. The designer must take into account all of the many possible users of the document and accommodate the travel plans of many different people. The document designer must also respond to Amtrak's needs. Amtrak wants its passengers to ride its trains and pay fares so the company can bring in a profit. Amtrak needs passengers to show up at the right time and place for the right train and to feel good about their trip-planning experience so they will travel with Amtrak again. Efficient and cost-effective documents can help accomplish these goals.

A document designer would approach this situation by considering all of these needs (both user's and client's) and by crafting a document that meets as many of them as possible. The designer must convey

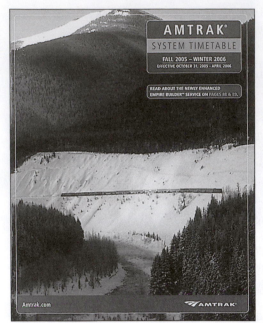

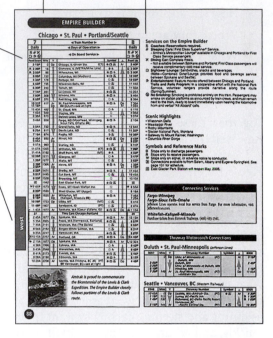

Headings tell the user what train the schedule table describes (the Empire Builder) and what cities it travels between.

Symbols encode complex information in the table, and a key to the symbols is placed beside the table.

Tables organize the train route schedule between Chicago and Portland/ Seattle in both directions.

A bleed index on the outside edges of the page helps users find trains in the region they wish to travel.

Figure 1.2 Communicating information visually.   Note how the designers used visual communication features that allow the user to navigate the document much as he or she might navigate the country. In addition, the cover and the "Empire Builder" page help build a sense of excitement and adventure about rail travel.

Amtrak, "Amtrak System Timetable, Fall 2005–Winter 2006."

accurate information, but, more important, he or she must design that information to meet the specific needs of Amtrak and its passengers as effectively as possible. With these needs in mind, the designer must make decisions not only about the visual design of text, tables, images, and pages, but also about the medium and physical size, format, and production of the document. The designer must pay attention to how the document actually works, constantly testing and improving its effectiveness in solving the communication problem. Moreover, the designer must also work within a team of professionals such as advertising designers, writers, and copy editors to produce the document on time and under budget.

In fact, to accommodate the complex needs and agendas of both Amtrak and its passengers, a designer might develop multiple documents in different formats and even different media. Figure 1.3 shows the dynamic, database-driven Amtrak website, where travelers can input the departure and arrival dates of their trip and receive a person-

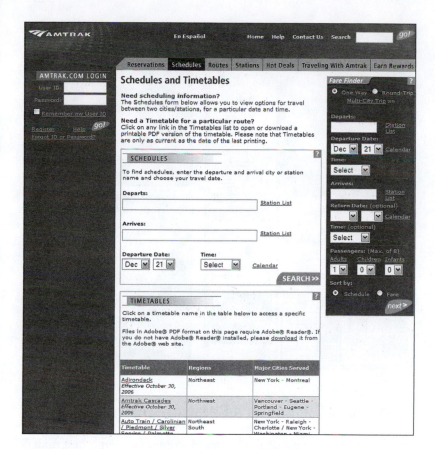

Figure 1.3 The web version of a print document.   The "Schedules and Timetables" form allows users to access what might be represented as a single page in the printed schedule. The "Fare Finder" form (on the right) provides an option for creating a customized schedule for your specific trip. Visual elements such as color, page layout, and typography help users recognize these forms as separate but parallel options.

Amtrak, <www.amtrak.com>.

alized schedule — an electronic version of the traditional paper time-table. Figure 1.4 (page 10) shows a hybrid document that straddles both electronic and paper media: an Adobe Portable Document Format (PDF) version of the Empire Builder's schedule, an electronic version of a folio pamphlet available in Amtrak stations. This version of the document might be useful to users who want to access a schedule on-line and also print it out to take with them on their trip. It is also convenient for Amtrak, which can provide one version of the document that will be accessible in two different media (print and electronic).

In all three of these versions of Amtrak's train schedule, document designers have developed the document's visual interface (whether paper, electronic, or hybrid) and therefore helped shape the user's experience with that interface. This is not to say that all three of these documents work the same way or offer the same capabilities to Amtrak or its passengers, but all three are most definitely documents, crafted to solve particular problems in particular situations.

Figure 1.4 Delivering a document in multiple formats. The Amtrak Empire Builder pamphlet is available on screen (as PDF) and in hand (as paper). The electronic format allows users to print out a schedule from the website that looks like the one they would see in an Amtrak station. It also helps Amtrak save money by using the same document two ways.

Amtrak, "Empire Builder" pamphlet, <www.amtrak.com>.

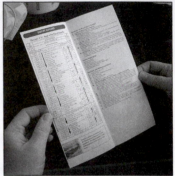

Document Design as a Relationship

As the Amtrak example demonstrates, document design is best understood as a complex relationship between you as a designer and two sets of people: those who ask you (and hopefully pay you) to design documents and those who will use the documents you design. We typically call the former group *clients* and the latter group *users*. The relationship between all three parties is diagrammed in Figure 1.5.

Clients

Your client forms one node of this three-part relationship. Sometimes as a designer you might be a permanent employee of the client; other times, you might work as a design consultant working on contract. You might even be both the client *and* the designer, creating something for your own purposes. In any of these situations, it is essential that you understand why, what, and how the client wants to communicate—and to whom.

Clients ask designers to create documents for specific reasons, usually because they want certain things to happen—what we call an *agenda*. Documents cost money, so clients want documents that fulfill their agenda efficiently.

Often, the client's agenda initiates what kind of document will be created. But you will often find that the client's agenda is based on his or her perception of user needs and desires. For example, the client who suspects that employees won't be enthusiastic about a new training seminar might ask you to design a document that encourages participation and makes it clear to employees why, when, and where to show up.

Client agendas can also be more general and complex. A client might want to reaffirm the user's choice in buying a product and give the user a positive experience so he or she will recommend the product to others, thus increasing sales. To fulfill this set of agendas, a designer might propose a variety of different documents, from a manual to a quick reference guide to a dynamic customer forum hosted on the client's website.

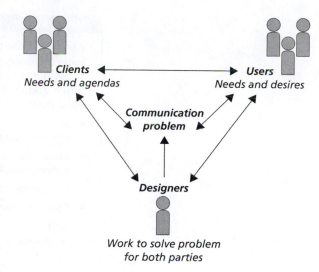

Figure 1.5 Designers, clients, and users.   Document design is a relationship between the designer, clients, and users.

To gain a clear understanding of your client's agenda, you must ask many questions, especially since clients sometimes aren't entirely clear about their own motivations (see Chapter 10 for more on researching client agendas). Asking questions will help you build a picture of what the client wants the document to *do* — an awareness that will make a strong foundation for your design project.

Users

Finding out about the client may be relatively easy because you can usually identify your clients readily and speak to them frequently. But the second node of the design relationship — users — can be harder to pin down. Nonetheless, every successful document designer invests time to analyze users and their situations, needs, and desires.

Finding out about users is an essential step in creating a successful design. No two users or design situations are the same, so it is important to consider who will use each particular document you create. Perhaps the best way to find out about users is to meet them and talk to them about their interests, biases, and concerns, or to watch them and observe the challenges they face. Or you can conduct other kinds of research, such as demographic studies, to find out more about users (see Chapter 10 for more about user research).

Users are complex and unique. What works for one user won't always work for another, what works for most won't work for all, and

---

> **MORE ABOUT . . . THE TERM *USERS***
>
> Why do we use the term *user* rather than just *reader* or *audience*?
> Some designers still refer to people who use documents as readers,
> but that makes it sound as if reading is the only thing people do
> with a document. Think about all of the other things you do with
> documents:
>
> - Scroll or flip quickly through a document, checking to see if it is
>   one you want to look at more closely
> - Search for particular information you need by looking at the
>   index or table of contents
> - Skim paragraphs or sections that look interesting or useful
> - Compare one part of the document to another
> - Stick a document in your pocket or book bag for easy reference
>   on the road, or bookmark it in your browser for later reference
>   online
>
> People do these and many more things with documents, so they are
> more accurately classified as users than as simply readers.

what works one time might not work the next time. To begin understanding users, however, we can start with four general characteristics
that apply to most:

- *Users are real people with real problems to solve and real situations to face.* As a result, users look at the documents we design
  to fulfill their own goals, not ours. Good design can help users
  solve their problems successfully.

- *Users do not want to* read *documents; they want to* do *things.*
  Users often approach documentation only as a last resort —
  when they have already failed at all other attempts to complete
  the tasks they face. Good design can help users do what they
  want to do.

- *Users often approach documents already feeling frustrated, wor-
  ried, or lost.* Because documents are often the last resort to solve
  a pressing problem, users already feel stressed when they pick up
  a document to look for solutions. Good design can help alleviate that stress by helping users solve their problems quickly and
  easily.

- *When users do read documents, they rarely read all the way
  through.* Instead, users tend to be hunter-gatherers, culling
  visually through a large landscape of data to look for the small
  pieces of information that will mean something in their current

situation. Good design helps users gather what they need efficiently and quickly.

Taken together, these characteristics paint a picture of users as unique, self-motivated people. As a document designer, you will need to spend time *for each document you design*, finding out more about these people and their situations, needs, and desires.

Designers

Finally, there is *you*: the document designer. It's your job to negotiate the needs of both clients *and* users. Clients have things they want to happen, problems they hope to solve, people they wish to communicate with through documentation. Users have their own individual problems, needs, and desires, depending on their situations and motivations. As a document designer, you'll need to find ways to make both groups happy with the documents you create. Fortunately, the client's ultimate goal is often to give the user a positive experience, which makes meeting both groups' agendas a little more manageable.

As the mediator between clients and users, you have some significant responsibilities. Although you must strive to please your employers (as all professionals must), you must also stand up for the rights and interests of users. Document designers often struggle through ethical dilemmas in completing design projects. When does spinning the client's product in a positive light become simply misleading users? What information is okay to leave out of a document? How do you decide what things users don't need to know, especially if those things paint the client in a bad light? What responsibilities do you have to make your client look good in situations where users might be getting hurt? Legal and professional guidelines can provide some help in resolving these dilemmas, but ultimately the designer holds responsibility to represent both clients and users. (See Chapter 3 for a broader discussion on ethics in design.)

Levels of Design

Understanding the relationship between clients, users, and you as designer can help you prioritize projects to determine how much effort to put into a design. Without this prioritization, it's difficult to create documents that meet needs efficiently.

In a perfect world, every document would be beautiful. But this is not a perfect world. Design always costs money and always takes time. The less money the client has to spend, the less of the designer's time

In a perfect world, every document would be beautiful. But this is not a perfect world.

he or she can pay for. The tighter the schedule and the smaller the budget, the less elaborate the design can be to meet project deadlines. Despite our best intentions to create beautiful documents, factors like time, cost, and production methods will limit how aesthetically pleasing we can make our designs.

In addition, depending on the client, the users, and the situation, some documents are simply worthy of a higher design investment than other documents. This leads us to the concept of *levels of design*, which we derive from the well-known concept of levels of edit in technical editing practices (see Van Buren and Buehler). By *a higher level of design*, we mean a document that deserves the investment of more time and more money in its visual design. By *a lower level of design*, we mean a document that does not deserve a significant investment in time or money in its design.

The level of a design can be described broadly by how elaborate the design is — literally, how much *labor* is invested in the design. We can define the amount of labor in a document through two sets of indicators:

- *Polished versus rough production values:* Some production materials are more costly and difficult to work with than others, and some production methods create a more polished document than others. Photocopying a document on standard letter-size paper and binding it with staples has a low production value but requires relatively little labor. Sending a document out to a professional printer for four-color printing and binding has a high production value and thus more labor.

- *Customization versus consistency:* The more the design takes advantage of off-the-shelf elements, like clip art or very conventional formats and layouts, the less labor it takes to produce. The more we customize the graphics, colors, or format of a document, the greater the labor required. For example, creating a simple text-based web page requires little customization — the browser does all the work in determining how the text will be displayed. But creating a dynamic, graphically intense website with complex computer scripting to allow user accounts, comments, or user-customized content would take significantly more work.

Most projects will fall somewhere between these extremes, as you can see graphically in Figure 1.6.

The difficulty is that we must determine as wisely and strategically as possible what labor investment our particular project deserves in this spectrum. Several interlocking factors can help us determine what level of design is justified by a particular project:

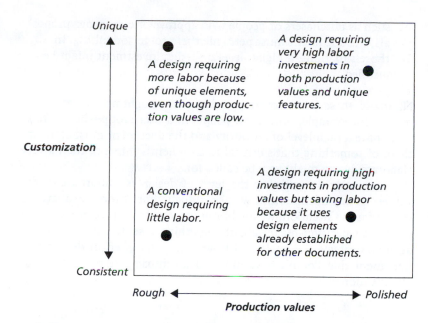

Figure 1.6 Levels of design. The greater the level of labor required or justified by a project, the higher the level of design. A particular project could fall anywhere within this field, depending on the situations of the client and users.

- *Ephemerality:* How long is the document supposed to last? If you want it to last a long time, a higher level of design might be justified. If it will go out of date next week, it might not be worth a high design investment. For example, an annual report is usually intended to be distributed throughout a whole year, if not longer, justifying a more elaborate document. A memo or e-mail about the company picnic, however, is likely valid only for a very short time and so justifies a simple document.

- *Relationship to the client's mission:* Is the success of the document critical to the client's mission — his or her agenda, strategies, or goals? Every document should respond to a real need, but some needs are more important than others. If the document is essential to a client's mission, a higher level of design investment might be justified. If it's less essential, a lower level of design might do.

- *Reach:* How many people will see the document? If the document will reach only a few people, a lower level of design investment might be warranted. If it's going to be seen by many people, it might deserve a higher level of design.

- *User authority:* How much decision-making power will the users of the document possess, and how hard must the document work to persuade them? If the users are important decision-makers, such as purchasers or people who approve or disapprove proposals, the document must persuade them to do something. In those situations, a higher level of design investment might be justified.

Naturally, these factors overlap. A document might have a very small reach — for example, only a few people in a user group — but if those users have a high level of authority and the document must convince them of something that's critical to the client's mission, then a very elaborate design might well be called for.

Accurately determining the level of design is important to the success of any document. If we aim a document at too low a level of design for the situation, we might miss an opportunity to convince an important decision-maker about something essential to the client's agenda, strategies, or goals. But if we exert a lot of effort designing a document that doesn't have much of an impact, we're wasting our client's money.

Design, Rhetoric, and Emotion

As this description of the relationships involved in the design process suggests, much of the success of a design depends on how people *feel* about the document. If people feel good about using a document, they're more likely to use it successfully, fulfilling the client's goals — and making the client happy.

As Donald Norman argued in his influential book *Emotional Design*, users do react to documents emotionally, including the documents we design. These reactions can range from delight at seeing a document that answers an urgent question to annoyance at having to look at a document in the first place to being impressed by the professionalism of the organization that published the document.

Because people often have such immediate emotional reactions to what they see, design gives us an important opportunity to shape how users will feel about the document. Doing so is an important aspect of usability. Even if a document is accurate and *could* be used successfully, it might actually fail if users have negative reactions to the document, the authors, or the subject.

Try to think about shaping two kinds of emotional impressions in document design: the user's impressions of the client who is "speaking" through the document and the user's feelings about the document itself and its subject. In rhetoric, the user's impression about the speaker is called *ethos*, and an invocation of the user's feelings is called **pathos**.

The design of a document can very directly imply an ethos for the speaker and pathos for the subject. For example, a company trying to attract the attention of a young audience might employ a design that makes the company sound fun and interesting. In the website in Figure 1.7, LeapFrog Enterprises, Inc., used bright colors, cartoon backgrounds, and photographs of young, attractive spokespersons to put an appealing face on their company while telling potential users (adolescent boys and girls) about a new product: the FLY Pentop Computer. The design speaks for the company by implying an ethos of teenage coolness. In turn, the design encourages potential buyers to feel a positive pathos by associating the pen with their desire for fun — for example, the pen can be used to make music (FlyTones) and play games (FlyBall).

However, the same company might want to project an entirely different ethos and pathos for a different audience or purpose, such as with the annual report in Figure 1.8 (page 18). Here, the document puts a different face on Leapfrog, Inc. — that of the CEO and the chairman of the board — to encourage investors to put their money into a solid, profitable, well-run corporation. This ethos is created visually with traditional text and page layout, as well as with a photograph of the well-dressed CEO and chairman. The design hopes to encourage users to feel reassured and confident about the subject of the document: the financial probity and success of the company. In an application of pathos, invoking this feeling of confidence responds to the user's desire for financial security.

Figure 1.7 Appealing to an audience of consumers. This web page implies a certain ethos for the company offering the product, a computerized pen designed for teenagers. The designers included teenage students to "speak" for the company, giving it a voice the company hopes users will find appealing.

LeapFrog Enterprises, Inc., "FLY Pentop Computer," <www.flypentop.com>.

Figure 1.8 Appealing to an audience of investors. This corporate annual report is from the same company that produced the website in Figure 1.7. Instead of teenagers, however, the designers chose to include pictures of the CEO and chairman of the board to "speak" for the company, presenting a different ethos for a different audience: investors.

LeapFrog Enterprises, Inc., "Annual Report 2004."

Visual Design

As a document designer, your primary tools for helping clients create a positive experience for users are visual. Document designers create clear visual patterns that help readers see the relationships between different pieces of information. The rest of this book concentrates on this visual aspect of document design. Chapter 2 gets you started by outlining some consistent principles of design.

Exercises

1. Find a document whose client was someone you know or can talk to. For example, you might look for a document produced by your employer or at your school. Interview the client about the document, focusing on these questions:

   - What were your goals in having this document designed? What did you want the document to *do*?

   - Who did you think the audience of this document would be?

   - How was the document intended to fulfill the audience's needs?

   - What parts of the document worked best? What parts didn't work so well?

2. Find someone who might have used the document you examined in exercise 1 and interview him or her. Consider asking questions like these:

   - What did you find useful about the document?

   - What did you find not so useful about the document?

   - What things, if any, do you think the document designers did not understand about people like you who would be using this document?

3. Find a document you can examine and discuss in class. Form small groups and share your documents with each other. Select one document and choose two members of your group to role-play to the rest of the class — one acting as the document's client, one as the document's user. The client should explain to the user what he or she wanted the document to do. The user should respond by explaining how the document actually works (or does not work) for users. Afterward, discuss the dialogue as a class:

   - In what areas do the client and user seem to have overlapping agendas or goals?

   - What disagreements do you see between the two roles?

   - How could the document designer have better mediated this relationship?

Works Cited

AIGA Design Forum. "Document Design." N.d. <http://designforum.aiga.org/content.cfm/df_informationdesign>. Accessed 29 March 2006.

Carliner, Saul. "Physical, Cognitive, and Affective: A Three-Part Framework for Information Design." *Content and Complexity: Information Design in Technical Communication.* Ed. Michael J. Albers and Beth Mazur. Mahwah, NJ: Lawrence Erlbaum, 2003. 39–58.

Horn, Robert E. "What Is Information Design? Information Design as an Emerging Profession." *Information Design.* Ed. Robert Jacobson. Cambridge, MA: MIT Press, 1999. 15–33.

Levy, David M. *Scrolling Forward: Making Sense of Documents in the Digital Age.* New York: Arcade, 2001.

Norman, Donald. *Emotional Design.* New York: Basic Books, 2004.

Van Buren, Robert, and Mary Fran Buehler. *The Levels of Edit.* Pasadena, CA: Jet Propulsion Laboratory, 1980.

Further Reading

Bolter, Jay David, and Richard Grusin. *Remediation: Understanding New Media.* Cambridge, MA: MIT Press, 2000.

Slack, Jennifer Daryl, David James Miller, and Jeffrey Doak. "The Technical Communicator as Author: Meaning, Power, Authority." *Journal of Business and Technical Communication* 7.1 (January 1993): 12–36.

CHAPTER 2

Principles of Design

When we use documents, we often don't consciously pay attention to the actual marks on the page or screen. Instead, we usually rely on our experience and understanding of conventions to understand what a document means. As you read this chapter, for instance, you probably aren't thinking consciously about the individual letters on the page or the relationship between the different parts of the page spread— headers, footers, page numbers, headings, words, sentences, paragraphs, margins, and so on. You're probably concentrating more on what you're reading than on the visual display of the page.

As designers, however, we must develop a height-ened awareness of these individual marks, as well as the power of combining them. To help you develop that awareness, look at Figure 2.1. Of course, you'll notice right away that the document in Figure 2.1 is upside-down. We placed it that way to short-circuit your experience as a user of documents—your prac-ticed, conventional, unconscious ability to decipher meaning from marks on a page. But because you can no longer *read* the marks on the flyer easily, there's a good possibility that you can see the marks as they are in themselves—shapes and arrangements of shapes on a visual field. Designers often use this technique of looking at a document from a differ-ent perspective to help them see the separate ele-ments. Developing a sensitivity to marks as marks will help you become more conscious of how you use marks to create meaning.

In this chapter, we'll discuss two important concepts based on this awareness of the rich and varied characteristics of the marks we can make on

Figure 2.1 Looking at a document upside-down.
Don't try to *read* this upside-down flyer for a university alcoholism-awareness campaign. Instead, try just to *look* at it as a collection of marks arranged into patterns in a visual field. What do you notice when you look at the document upside-down? What objects seem promi-nent or important? How do the objects relate to each other visually?

Texas Tech University Student Health Services, 2006.

a page or screen: ***design objects*** and ***principles of design***. Thinking of those marks as design objects that can be moved and manipulated will keep our approach to design flexible. Principles of design guide the way we combine design objects to create patterns of meaning for users. Understanding these two concepts will help you become a more successful designer because it will give you power over design objects and ways to combine them to create meaning. You'll also find that the concepts introduced here will be referred to throughout the book, so this chapter will provide you with a helpful framework as you go on to more detailed chapters.

Design Objects and Their Characteristics

You're probably already familiar with the concept of design objects if you've ever used a computer drawing program, a page layout program, or even the drawing function in a word processing program. In such programs, you can typically access a toolbar of different objects that you can insert into a document. For example, the Drawing toolbar from Microsoft Word allows users to insert a variety of objects, including different styles of lines, various shapes, and text boxes.

Design objects include any mark or group of marks that can be seen and manipulated on a page. They can be simple marks such as dots, lines, shapes, or background shadings, each of which carries some kind of meaning or function in the design. For example, designers often use a simple printer's bullet (•) to mark the beginning of each entry in a list.

Design objects also include the marks we use to make **text**, including letters, numbers, and punctuation. We sometimes think of text as primarily verbal, but in document design, text is a system of visual marks that stand for linguistic expressions. Text is just as visual as any other kind of design object.

Design objects can also be *combinations* of individual marks that are treated as one visual unit. For example, single letters can combine to create words, words combine to create a line of text, and lines combine to make a paragraph or a column of text. In the same way, a combination of lines, shapes, and letters could be manipulated as a single graphic — a bar graph, for example. Similarly, a combination of composite objects (paragraphs, graphics, headers, footers) can make up a whole page or a screen.

All of these objects mark a ***positive space*** on the page, but a design object can also be formed by a ***negative space***. Positive space includes the marks actually made on a page or screen, such as the text or a photograph. Negative space is the space *between* and *around* positive space.

> Design objects include any mark or group of marks that can be seen and manipulated on a page.

For example, the margins on a page are a negative space. Positive and negative space can be equally important to users for conveying meaning and fulfilling a function in the design. For example, the negative space between a graphic and the text wrapped around it marks a boundary, encouraging users to look at the two objects separately.

This example also clarifies what kinds of meaning design objects can carry. The meaning associated with a design object can range from simple to complex. The negative space around the graphic is a relatively simple meaning, conveying to users only that the graphic and its surrounding text should be considered as two separate, though related, objects. Other design objects are richer in meaning—the graphic itself, for example, might convey complex data visually. The objects carrying the most complex meanings are likely the marks we use to convey language—letters, words, sentences, and paragraphs.

A considerable and growing tradition of object-oriented thinking, derived from cognitive psychology and computer science, supports this way of thinking about design objects. In essence, cognitive psychologists have suggested that we tend to think of our surroundings in terms of objects and their qualities. (For a summary, see Mark Johnson's book, *The Body in the Mind: The Bodily Basis of Meaning, Imagination, and Reason.*)

Of course, the term *design objects* as we use it here is a metaphor—but a very useful one. Computer programs can make it look as if we're picking up and moving objects as if they were children's blocks on a table, but we're not actually moving anything in three dimensions. We know that pages really have only two dimensions: width and height. On a page, all we see are some inked areas and some uninked areas, all on the same plane; on a screen, we see only some pixels turned on (possibly at different levels of intensity) and others turned off.

But design objects allow us to think of pages as three-dimensional—letting us arrange, combine, or overlap different objects for different effects. Thinking of marks as design objects also allows us to manipulate their qualities and characteristics with great precision. Semiotic theorist Jacques Bertin (1983) suggested that there are seven **visual variables** we can use to manipulate objects in two-dimensional design:

- Shape
- Orientation
- Texture
- Color
- Value
- Size
- Position

These variables intersect and combine to give design objects their individuality, recognizability, and meaning.

Shape

Shape refers to the two-dimensional area covered or enclosed by an object. As Bertin points out, "the universe of shapes is infinite," even in two dimensions (95). Shapes can be regular or symmetrical, like geometric figures. But they can also be irregular or asymmetrical — letters, for example, are complex, mostly asymmetrical shapes.

Even the tiniest objects have a shape if we look closely enough. Periods, for example, are probably the smallest mark used in typography. But different typefaces have differently shaped periods, as you can see in Figure 2.2.

Times New Roman   Verdana   Fairfield Medium   Script MT   Goudy Old Style

Figure 2.2 Differently shaped periods in different typefaces. The possible variations in shape are nearly endless, even with something as prosaic and conventional as a period, shown here at 72 points.

Shapes can carry meaning either by convention or by resembling something. The letters of the English alphabet don't actually look like sounds, but by training in standard conventions, we associate them with sounds. Similarly, some shapes are associated with conventional meanings (see Figure 2.3). Other shapes actually resemble something we might recognize (see Figure 2.4), and some shapes might do both, such as the hand shapes in Figure 2.5 (though their meaning is culturally specific).

One important shape often used in document design is the *line* (also known in printing as a *rule*). In geometry, lines have only one

No   Thinking

Figure 2.3 Objects with conventional meaning. Some objects carry meanings based on *convention*— that is, society implicitly agrees on what these objects mean by using them repeatedly in similar ways.

Scissors   Phone

Figure 2.4 Objects with representational meaning. Objects can have representational meanings in that they actually look like what they're meant to indicate.

Good   Bad

Figure 2.5 Objects with both representational and conventional meaning. Sometimes even representational shapes can have conventional meanings. These are representations of hands, but by convention in North America a thumbs-up hand means "good," while a thumbs-down hand means "bad."

dimension: length. But in design, lines must have two dimensions to be seen: length and width. By definition, lines are longer than they are wide — but that still leaves a lot of room for variation (see Figure 2.6). Lines can be wider or thinner, consistent or irregular, curved or angled. Curved and angled lines often imply connection and dynamic relationships. Lines can also differ in the shape of their ends. Such lines are often used to imply a relationship or connection between different objects, as on a flowchart. Arrowed lines, for example, imply direction of flow, causality, or chronology.

Lines can also be implied rather than drawn. For example, most of us easily recognize a dotted or dashed line, such as the curved one in Figure 2.6. Dotted or dashed lines, however, are composite objects formed by small shapes placed close enough to each other in a row so that they *imply* lines. All of these differences in lines are based on the variable of shape. By the same token, any kind of design object — letters, words, graphics, shaded fields, and so on — can have countless variations of shape.

Orientation

If lines are important and useful objects, then the directions in which they point — their ***orientation*** — must be important, too. Each of the

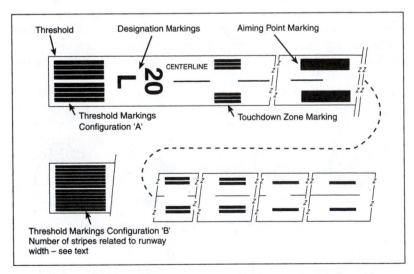

Figure 2.6 Lines with variations in shape. This diagram from a manual on aviation uses many different shapes of lines — straight, curved, dashed, arrowed, with different widths — to show pilots what kinds of markings to expect on an airport runway. Interestingly, an actual runway is also a document with lines that tell pilots how and where to land.

Federal Aviation Administration, *FAR/AIM 2005.*

lines we have just seen clearly has an orientation, but other shapes can have orientations, as well. Text in English is arranged in a horizontal orientation that leads users to read along each line left to right. Text in Japanese, on the other hand, traditionally has a vertical orientation to aid reading top to bottom. And individual shapes, like the hand in Figure 2.7, also can have implicit orientations.

Figure 2.7 Implicit orientation. Some shapes imply an orientation inherently. Most people would describe this pointing hand as being oriented or pointed to the right.

Texture

Texture refers to any pattern applied to an object. Obvious repeating patterns such as cross-hatching are often used for information graphics printed in black and white—for example, to distinguish between bars in a bar chart printed in black and white (Figure 2.8).

But textures can also include other kinds of patterns, such as applying an image to an object. Examples include using a background image or watermark on a page, a PowerPoint slide, or the desktop interface of your computer (Figure 2.9). Such applications of textures can reduce readability, but they're very common.

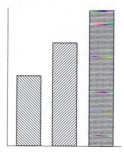

Figure 2.8 Using texture in a bar chart.   This bar chart uses textures to indicate that the different bars stand for different sets of data.

Color

Color is an increasingly common variable in design objects because in recent years color reproduction technologies have become cheaper and more convenient. For paper documents, color inkjet and laser printers are readily available. And for electronic documents, nearly all computers and most portable devices like cell phones now use color monitors. These factors have increased the likelihood that designers will use color to modify design objects. See Chapter 8 for more about using color.

Value

Value refers to the *relative* lightness or darkness of a design object compared to its surroundings, including other objects near it and the background. High-value objects are those that contrast most with their surroundings; low-value objects are those that blend in with their surroundings.

On a mostly light background, such as white paper, a dark object typically has a higher value and greater visual density than a lighter object, so the darker object will likely be more prominent. This effect is reversed on mostly dark backgrounds, such as we often see on websites (see Figure 2.10 on page 26).

Value is often used for emphasis, as high-value objects tend to get more immediate attention than low-value objects.

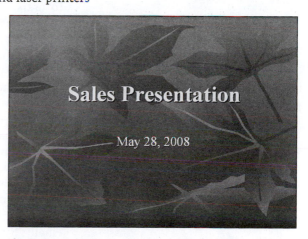

Figure 2.9 Using texture in a PowerPoint slide.   Default PowerPoint slide templates often have a background texture to give a three-dimensional effect to the design.

Figure 2.10 Contrast and value.
Value is determined by the contrast between objects and their backgrounds. The more contrast, the higher the value.

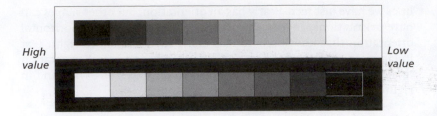

Size

However, the impact of value for emphasis also depends on the object's *size*: a very small, dark object on a white page will carry less emphasis than a larger dark object on the same page.

We can control the size of objects with many variables, but two aspects of size are most important: ***absolute size*** and ***relative size***. Absolute size refers to the dimensions of an object in relation to a standard, such as the centimeter or the inch. Document designers often use these measurement units, as well as less familiar ones such as ***picas*** and ***points***. A pica is one-sixth of an inch; a point is one-twelfth of a pica, or one seventy-second of an inch (1 inch = 6 picas = 72 points). Using accurate absolute measurements is essential in design because it allows us to be precise and consistent in our use of design objects.

To users, however, absolute size doesn't really mean much; we don't often see them pulling out a ruler to measure a design object. But users can visually discriminate between the size of one object and that of another—that is, they can recognize objects as being relatively *bigger than* and *smaller than* with great sensitivity. Designers frequently use this discrimination of relative size to convey two important meanings: that one object is more important than another or that one object contains another. Users often assume that a larger object is more significant than a smaller object—for example, the title of a document is usually larger than its first-level headings, which in turn are larger than the second-level headings. But larger objects can also imply a relationship of ownership over the smaller objects they "contain." A single line in a graph, for example, is considered as "belonging to" the larger object that contains it (the graph itself).

Finally, the size of design objects is also relative to the boundaries of the visual field. These boundaries are easy to recognize: they're the edges of the paper or the screen that define the two-dimensional space in which we work. This might seem pretty obvious, but working within the available space can be remarkably difficult, requiring a careful balancing of different elements, especially in terms of their size. On most pages, some elements are more important than others and so deserve more space. But there's only so much space to go around, and even minor objects — if they're important enough to include — must get their fair share.

Position

We can control the position of objects on the plane in two dimensions: width and height. Most layout and drawing programs let us specify the position of an object with great accuracy.

In keeping with the object metaphor, we can also position objects on top of each other — for example, positioning a pull-quote on a shaded field to distinguish it from the surrounding text. Of course, the objects aren't *really* on top of each other. The printer or screen actually stops printing gray when the black of the text begins, but we assume that the gray continues under the text, forming a consistent field. (See Chapter 3 for more information on this phenomenon.)

> We can also position objects on top of each other — for example, positioning a pull-quote on a shaded field to distinguish it from the surrounding text.

Six Principles of Design

Carefully controlling the qualities of individual design objects is an essential first step in creating good designs. But how do we show relationships *between* design objects? Using a welter of terms and ideas, many designers and scholars have tried to articulate the basic principles by which we create these relationships. As you can imagine, nobody entirely agrees on what *the* principles of design are; instead, they propose many possible ways of describing basic principles. One fascinating book — William Lidwell, Kritina Holden, and Jill Butler's *Universal Principles of Design* — proposes over a hundred design principles! Despite this ambiguity and disagreement, however, a limited set of basic design principles can help you focus your design thinking. Principles of design serve as rules of thumb to help you make good decisions about your designs.

In this book we'll use six basic principles of design that we think govern most visual relationships between design objects:

- Similarity
- Contrast
- Proximity
- Alignment
- Order
- Enclosure

Ideally, the *visual* relationships between design objects should echo and reinforce the *logical* relationships between them. The principles of design work together to build a system of relationships so users can see how all of these design objects work together.

These principles are not exclusive. Frequently, objects will be related by multiple principles at the same time, the principles working together visually to create complex meanings. And different designers might use different terms to describe these ideas, depending on their training and background. But employing each of these principles consciously will enable you to create designs that guide and help users through using a document. Moreover, you can use these principles to create a ***design system*** — a coherent and consistent set of visual elements in a document that helps users use the document in ways that fit their needs.

Understanding the principles of design will make you more conscious of the visual relationships between objects when you design. Ideally, the *visual* relationships between design objects should echo and reinforce the *logical* relationships between them. The principles of design work together to build a system of relationships so users can see how all of these design objects work together.

Similarity

Use similarity to show that design objects are alike in kind or in function. Users naturally assume that design objects that *look* similar *are* similar — that they do something alike, that they belong together somehow, or that they are parallel in function or kind. The more consistently a design applies similarity to similar objects, the faster users will be able to discern patterns and use the document efficiently. Similarity is essential for showing relationships of connection, such as coherence and consistency.

We can control similarity very precisely by paying attention to the qualities of design objects: shape, orientation, texture, color, value, size, and position. Objects can be similar in any combination of these variables. For example, print documents often use similarity in their design of page numbers. To work efficiently, page numbers need to be similar in these visual variables:

- *Shape:* all in the same typeface
- *Size:* all in the same size
- *Color:* all in the same hue
- *Value:* all the same relative density (all boldface or none boldface)
- *Position:* always in a consistent, predictable position on the page — for example, the bottom outside corners of each page

Any inconsistency in these visual variables will make it more difficult for users to predict where to find the page numbers — or more difficult for them even to recognize the numbers as page numbers.

Users may still be able to use the document successfully but less efficiently, and probably less happily, than they might if the page numbers were all similar.

Contrast

Use contrast to show difference and create emphasis. Just as objects can be similar in terms of the visual variables, design objects can differ from or contrast with other design objects by having different visual characteristics. Users typically assume that a difference in appearance means a difference in function or meaning.

Similarity and contrast are closely connected: Designs often employ both in concert as two sides of the same coin. In fact, it's impossible to show contrast without a comparison to something else; contrast means something only in the context of similarity. For example, a word in bold can stand out only in a field of words in regular text; if all the words are in bold, none stands out individually.

Contrast is a valuable tool for emphasizing important design objects, such as notes, safety warnings, or cautions. Without adequate contrast from the surrounding text, users might not notice such important information. So designers typically make these objects stand out from the regular or *basal* text of the document in these ways:

- *Shape:* a different typeface; a conventional icon such as a stop sign or warning triangle; a border surrounding the warning

- *Size:* a larger point size than the surrounding text

- *Color:* often, a use of red or yellow in an otherwise black-and-white document

- *Value:* a greater density or higher value than the surrounding objects, created by bolding text or adding a gray field behind the text

- *Position:* separate from the text — for example, a consistent position in the margin of the document

However, to be successful, safety warnings must also be consistently recognizable: all safety warnings should look the same throughout a document. So once again, contrast and similarity work hand in hand.

Taken together, similarity and contrast can also be very powerful tools for communicating relationships of *structure* between objects. One of the most obvious ways to express similarity and contrast in this way is with headings, which imply a hierarchical structure for a document and thus echo its logical organization. The key is to make the levels of heading different enough to recognize easily while retaining consistency in multiple iterations of the same level of heading.

Figure 2.11 Contrasting headings.
Notice that the contrast and similarity must work as a coherent system. Different levels need enough contrast to seem visually distinct, but not so much that the first-level headings end up too large or the basal text too small.

Level 1 Heading
Basal text …
Level 2 Heading
Basal text …
Level 2 Heading
Basal text …
Level 1 Heading
Basal text …
Level 2 Heading
Basal text …
Level 3 Heading
Basal text …
Level 3 Heading
Basal text …
Level 2 Heading
Basal text …

Level 1 Heading
Basal text …
Level 2 Heading
Basal text …
Level 2 Heading
Basal text …
Level 1 Heading
Basal text …
Level 2 Heading
Basal text …
Level 3 Heading
Basal text …
Level 3 Heading
Basal text …
Level 2 Heading
Basal text …

For example, the first heading design in Figure 2.11, although very consistent, doesn't include adequate contrast between the different levels of heading and basal text, making it hard to make out the logical hierarchy of the document. The second heading design, however, uses size, value, shape, and position to identify different heading levels, while maintaining consistency each time a heading level appears. This heading system visually implies a set of important relationships. Each higher level is different enough (bigger, denser, differently shaped) to convey the relationship of ownership over the subsections it "contains." At the same time, the visual similarity of headings at the same level—for example, the level 2 headings—implies that these headings and the text that follows them are parallel, equal parts of the document.

Finally—and at the most basic level—contrast is essential simply for distinguishing objects as separate from the background. For example, websites with dark or patterned backgrounds sometimes use relatively dark type as well—like the purple commonly used to indicate followed links. In those designs, users have trouble distinguishing between the background and the foreground objects (the text) because they are too close together in value or pattern. This effect is also known as *inadequate figure-ground contrast* (see "Figure-Ground Discrimination" on page 42).

Don't be afraid to use contrast to make something stand out. Of course, there are limitations—you still want the design to work well as a whole system—but for the most part, more contrast makes for

Same **Different**   Same   *Really different*

Figure 2.12 Building contrast.
The example on the left employs contrast in just one variable: font size. The example on the right demonstrates that we can build contrast in multiple visual variables simultaneously: not just font size, but also color, typeface, and position.

easier usability. To show contrast strongly, consciously apply differences *in multiple variables* — instead of just making something you want to emphasize bigger, make it bigger, denser, a different color, *and* a different shape (Figure 2.12).

Proximity

Use proximity to show grouping and belonging. Users typically assume that design objects that appear in close proximity belong together. Conversely, design objects that are relatively distant from each other imply that they don't belong together.

We can see this principle at work in Figure 2.13. Chances are, you see the group of squares on the left as vertical columns and the group on the right as horizontal rows. Why do you think you see the objects this way? The answer has to do with *proximity*. If the squares are closer together vertically than horizontally, we tend to see groupings that make vertical composite objects — columns. If the squares are closer together horizontally than vertically, we see groupings that make horizontal composite objects — rows. Note also that the squares are grouped not just by *absolute* proximity — the measured distance between them — but also by *relative* proximity. In other words, they build relationships not just by being close, but also by being *closer* in one dimension than in the other.

We can use this principle to make larger, composite design objects out of smaller, individual ones — in effect, grouping related design objects to show their logical relationship of belonging together. For

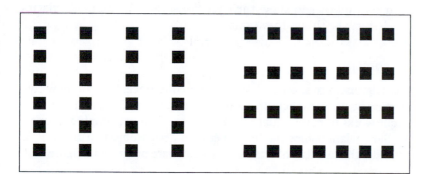

Figure 2.13 Proximity relationships determine grouping.   Because the squares on the left are closer together vertically than horizontally, we see them as four vertical lines, or columns. Conversely, because the squares on the right are closer together horizontally than vertically, we see them as four horizontal lines, or rows.

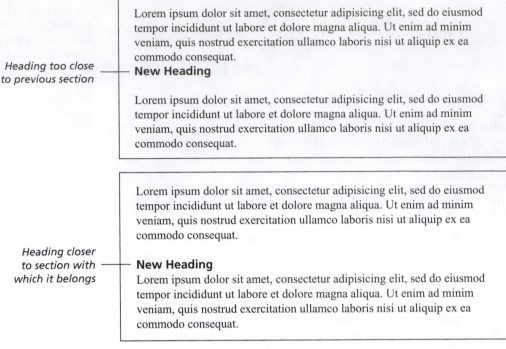

Heading too close to previous section

Lorem ipsum dolor sit amet, consectetur adipisicing elit, sed do eiusmod tempor incididunt ut labore et dolore magna aliqua. Ut enim ad minim veniam, quis nostrud exercitation ullamco laboris nisi ut aliquip ex ea commodo consequat.

New Heading

Lorem ipsum dolor sit amet, consectetur adipisicing elit, sed do eiusmod tempor incididunt ut labore et dolore magna aliqua. Ut enim ad minim veniam, quis nostrud exercitation ullamco laboris nisi ut aliquip ex ea commodo consequat.

Heading closer to section with which it belongs

Lorem ipsum dolor sit amet, consectetur adipisicing elit, sed do eiusmod tempor incididunt ut labore et dolore magna aliqua. Ut enim ad minim veniam, quis nostrud exercitation ullamco laboris nisi ut aliquip ex ea commodo consequat.

New Heading
Lorem ipsum dolor sit amet, consectetur adipisicing elit, sed do eiusmod tempor incididunt ut labore et dolore magna aliqua. Ut enim ad minim veniam, quis nostrud exercitation ullamco laboris nisi ut aliquip ex ea commodo consequat.

Figure 2.14 Using proximity for headings.   Headings should be in closer proximity to the text they introduce than to the text they follow.

example, designers often mark paragraphs by including more vertical space between paragraphs than between individual lines of text. As a result, each paragraph appears as a single composite unit. Using the same technique, we typically place a heading closer to the section that follows it — the section it introduces — than to the section that precedes it. That way, relative proximity makes the heading visually connect to the paragraph that follows it (see Figure 2.14).

Proximity also makes a natural tool for grouping like concepts together. It's common in information graphics to place related objects near one another to show their relationships — for example, placing labels near the things they explain.

Alignment

Use alignment to show connection and coherence. We can show connection by using explicit lines (as we saw in Figure 2.6), and this technique works in many situations. But we can also use simple alignment to show relationships implicitly between design objects. For example, consider the two lists of features for a software program in Figure 2.15.

Product features: active updating; synchronous data transmission; updated user interface; accessibility kit; backup software; import and export functions	**Product features** • Active updating • Synchronous data transmission • Updated user interface • Accessibility kit • Backup software • Import and export functions

Figure 2.15 Alignment and bulleted lists. The alignment emphasizes each element of the list and makes it clear that they are all parallel.

Both lists contain the same information, but the list on the left takes more time and effort to read because none of the features align. The bulleted list on the right, however, aligns each feature on the same implied vertical line, making it easier for users to skim down the entries to see if they're interested in buying the product and to compare different features. In fact, the bulleted list uses several different vertical alignments to emphasize its "listness"—the alignment of the heading, the alignment of the bullets, and the alignment of the list text all contribute to the effect. Each level of vertical alignment (or indentation) implies a further step down the hierarchy of the information, from main idea ("Product features") to subitems (the features list).

We can see alignment applied more fully in Figure 2.16 (page 34), a website for a note-taking program. The design of this site aligns a number of design objects both horizontally and vertically to show their relationship as *belonging to* or *parallel with*. Used carefully, alignment can help organize the different parts of a page, making it easier for users to manage the many different design objects that can appear by creating a unified system of page design. Typically, designers use a page layout grid to manage such alignments (see Chapter 5 for a discussion of grids and page layout).

Order

Use order to show sequence and importance. Order refers to most users' tendency to assume that what they see first on a page is more important than things they see later on. We can use this tendency to provide information in an order that makes sense for the user and for the information a document design presents.

Most users have encountered thousands of documents in their lifetimes, so they're very experienced and practiced in using them. This experience creates certain patterns of use that readers apply to new documents they encounter. As we will discuss in more depth in Chapter 5, one of the most powerful patterns in western hemisphere readers is that we tend to read languages written from left to right and from top to bottom. When we encounter a page, we tend to look first at the top, then in a series of zigzags across and down the page. This pattern leads

The "v" in EverNote aligns with the boundary between the navigation area (left) and the content area (right).

The main site navigation area aligns horizontally.

This axis aligns the feature descriptions.

This axis aligns the product screen thumbnails.

The top of EverNote aligns with the bottom of the slogan.

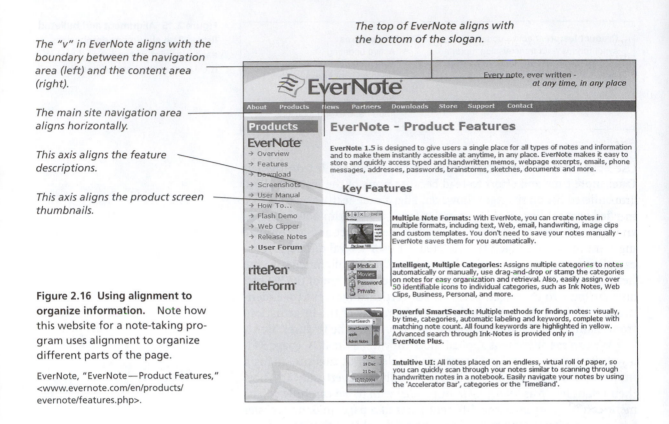

Figure 2.16 Using alignment to organize information.   Note how this website for a note-taking program uses alignment to organize different parts of the page.

EverNote, "EverNote—Product Features," <www.evernote.com/en/products/ evernote/features.php>.

us to focus more immediately, frequently, and intently on the top and the left side of a page than on the bottom or the right side.

Designers take advantage of this tendency by ordering pages so that the most important information is positioned at the top, followed by information of decreasing importance as the reader moves down the page. (Unscrupulous designers sometimes use this technique to emphasize positive information and deemphasize negative information. Sadly, the small print is usually at the bottom of the page rather than at the top.)

This is not to say that readers always create order on the page from top to bottom and from left to right. Eye-tracking research suggests that the typical pattern of reading websites on-screen is somewhat different: users tend to scan the page more holistically, hunting for what seems most important to their current task first and then moving on to less important or more detailed items. And more complex designs might encourage users to navigate through a page or screen in a different order than simple top-down, left-right. We can use other principles of design such as alignment and contrast to draw the user's eye to the most important information first and then lead the user through the document in a logical order.

We should also recognize that users create their own order as they encounter documents, depending on their own purposes and situations. If a user is looking for a picture, he or she might not pay attention to the text, even if it's at the top of the page. Still, ordering design objects carefully can help create meaningful relationships between those objects.

Enclosure

Use enclosure to show separation and to group complex objects. Finally, we can use positive or negative elements to enclose objects or groups of objects, setting them apart from their context. Positive elements of enclosure include lines, borders, and shadings that surround an individual or complex object and distinguish it from the surrounding objects on the page or screen. Figure 2.17 includes a number of examples of enclosure.

In this web page design, enclosure is mostly formed positively, with lines and borders. But enclosure can also be formed simply by negative

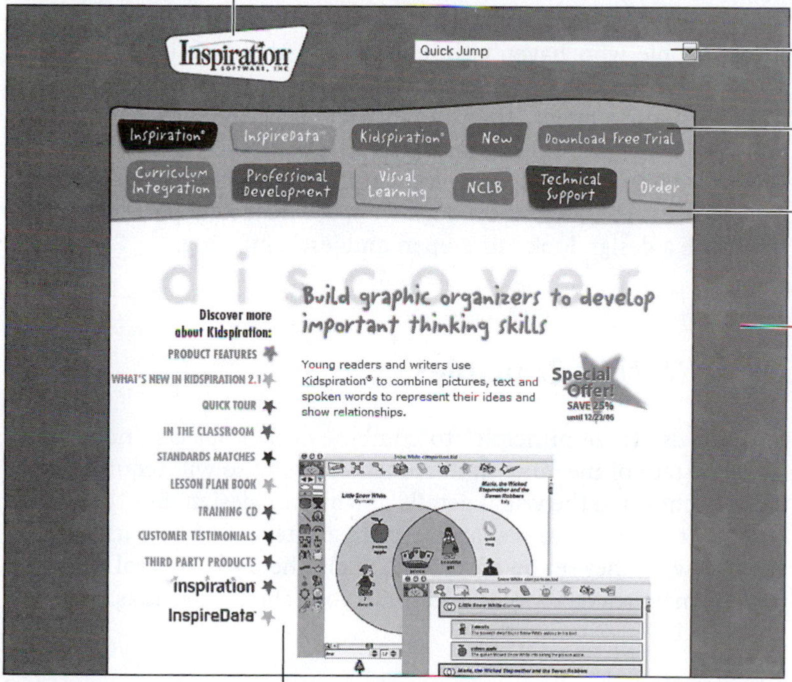

An oblong shape encloses the company logo.

A rectangular box encloses a drop-down menu.

Various shapes enclose each navigation button.

This area encloses all of the navigation buttons, separating them from the content area.

A background pattern encloses the entire product page.

Negative space encloses the page navigation table.

Figure 2.17 Using enclosure to show separation.   This website uses enclosure in several ways to separate areas of interest.

Inspiration Software Inc., "Kidspiration," <www.inspiration.com/productinfo/ kidspiration/features/index.cfm>.

Figure 2.18 Two versions of a table from a municipal water quality report.   The first table relies on borders to enclose the cells and form rows and columns; the second relies on negative space (and alignment) to do the same thing.

SUBSTANCE	MCL	HIGHEST LEVEL	MCLG	RANGE	SOURCES OF CONTAMINATION
Beta/photon emitters	50 pCi/L	11.9 pCi/L	0	N/A	Decay of natural and man-made deposits
Alpha emitters	15 pCi/L	8.1 pCi/L	0	N/A	Erosion of natural deposits
Combined radium	5 pCi/L	1.3 pCi/L	0	N/A	Erosion of natural deposits
Arsenic	50 ppb	4.7 ppb	N/A	N/A	Erosion of natural deposits
Barium	2 ppm	0.2 ppm	2 ppm	N/A	Erosion of natural deposits
Fluoride	4 ppm	0.9 ppm	4 ppm	N/A	Erosion of natural deposits
Nitrate	10 ppm	1.05 ppm	10 ppm	N/A	Runoff from fertilizer use
Turbidity	TT = 5 NTU	0.20 NTU	0	N/A	Soil runoff
Total organic carbon	TT	2.3 ppm	TT	2.0–2.8 ppm	Naturally present in environment
Diethylhexylphthalate	6 ppb	4.12 ppb	0	0–4.12 ppb	Rubber and chemical factories
Chloramines	MRDL = 4 ppm	3.0 ppm	MRDLG = 4 ppm	0.4–3.0 ppm	Water additive used to control microbes

SUBSTANCE	MCL	HIGHEST LEVEL	MCLG	RANGE	SOURCES OF CONTAMINATION
Beta/photon emitters	50 pCi/L	11.9 pCi/L	0	N/A	Decay of natural and man-made deposits
Alpha emitters	15 pCi/L	8.1 pCi/L	0	N/A	Erosion of natural deposits
Combined radium	5 pCi/L	1.3 pCi/L	0	N/A	Erosion of natural deposits
Arsenic	50 ppb	4.7 ppb	N/A	N/A	Erosion of natural deposits
Barium	2 ppm	0.2 ppm	2 ppm	N/A	Erosion of natural deposits
Fluoride	4 ppm	0.9 ppm	4 ppm	N/A	Erosion of natural deposits
Nitrate	10 ppm	1.05 ppm	10 ppm	N/A	Runoff from fertilizer use
Turbidity	TT = 5 NTU	0.20 NTU	0	N/A	Soil runoff
Total organic carbon	TT	2.3 ppm	TT	2.0–2.8 ppm	Naturally present in environment
Diethylhexylphthalate	6 ppb	4.12 ppb	0	0–4.12 ppb	Rubber and chemical factories
Chloramines	MRDL = 4 ppm	3.0 ppm	MRDLG = 4 ppm	0.4–3.0 ppm	Water additive used to control microbes

space. People who haven't thought much about design sometimes assume that borders are essential to enclose objects — for example, when designing tables, they might include borders by default. But many well-designed tables use negative space instead of positive borders to enclose each cell, row, and column and set them off from the rest (Figure 2.18). Relying on negative space instead of positive borders can make a design look more open and less confusing.

Using Design Principles

You can use these principles to combine design objects and create a visual system of meaning in documents. Doing so will require paying close attention to the visual details of what you design. But that attention to detail will give you an intimate awareness of how users make sense of what they see on a page. It will also help you control how your designs meet readers' needs and fulfill your clients' agendas.

Exercises

1. Collect a handful of documents so you can explore their designs. You should be able to find documents easily. Try looking at home, at school, at work, or at any public facility, such as a doctor's office, a museum, a library, or the local chamber of commerce. Look not just for advertisements and magazines but also for documents that convey important information to users, such as pamphlets, booklets, manuals, newsletters, and sets of instructions.

2. Interview someone who designs documents as part of his or her job—or even as a profession. Ask what principles the designer uses as rules of thumb in creating document designs. Do the principles seem similar to those described here? What terms does the designer use that are different from those here?

3. Take one of the documents you gathered in exercise 1, and look at it more closely.

   a. Choose one page of the document. How many different kinds of objects can you identify? Remember, sometimes objects are composite objects made up of other objects. Describe six of these objects in terms of their visual variables: shape, orientation, texture, color, value, size, and position.

   b. Examine the same page for its use of principles of design: similarity, contrast, proximity, alignment, order, and enclosure. How many uses of the principles can you see? (Not all of the principles may be used or used effectively on the page you chose.) What principles would you apply to improve the page's design?

4. Design your own business card. Be sure to employ as many of the design principles as possible in creating your design. Include at least the following information on your card:

- Your name
- Your phone number
- Your e-mail address
- Your mailing address
- Your slogan (make one up!)

You can use a word processing program, a drawing program, or just a sheet of paper and a pencil.

Works Cited

Bertin, Jacques. *The Semiology of Graphics.* Madison: University of Wisconsin Press, 1983.

Johnson, Mark. *The Body in the Mind: The Bodily Basis of Meaning, Imagination, and Reason.* Chicago: University of Chicago Press, 1987.

Lidwell, William, Kritina Holden, and Jill Butler. *Universal Principles of Design: 100 Ways to Enhance Usability, Influence Perception, Increase Appeal, Make Better Design Decisions, and Teach through Design.* Gloucester, MA: Rockport, 2003.

Nielsen, Jakob. How to Conduct a Heuristic Evaluation. <www.useit.com/papers/heuristic/heuristic_evaluation.html>.

Further Reading

Berger, Arthur Asa. *Seeing Is Believing: An Introduction to Visual Communication.* 2nd ed. Mountain View, CA: Mayfield, 1998.

Kostelnick, Charles, and David D. Roberts. *Designing Visual Language: Strategies for Professional Communicators.* New York: Longman, 1997.

Schriver, Karen A. *Dynamics in Document Design: Creating Texts for Readers.* New York: John Wiley & Sons, 1997.

Swann, Alan, and David Dabner. *How to Understand and Use Design and Layout.* 2nd ed. Cincinnati, OH: HOW Design Books, 2003.

White, Allen W. *The Elements of Graphic Design.* New York: Allworth, 2002.

Williams, Robin. *The Non-Designer's Design Book.* Berkeley, CA: Peachpit, 1994.

CHAPTER 3

Theories of Design

Figure 3.1 Explaining how a design works. This leaflet introduces young museum visitors to art by asking them to be "art detectives." We can explore how this document works through visual perception, visual culture, and visual rhetoric. For example, one panel, perforated into four clue cards, asks children to find the detail pictured on the front by following the clues on the back. Doing so requires perceptual skills such as pattern recognition. The repeated use of magnifying glasses takes advantage of common cultural awareness about detective fiction, all the way back to Sherlock Holmes.

The J. Paul Getty Museum, "Be an Art Detective."

Sometimes visual design seems simple: We look at a document and feel immediately whether it looks good or has something wrong with it. With practice, some designers develop what is called a "good eye" for design: an intrinsic, habitual, instinctive feeling for what will probably work, based mostly on their own experience.

But, as designers, our feelings about what looks "good" may not match the users' feelings. Rather than relying on feelings, a master designer should be able to *explain* what works and why. Theory is an attempt to provide those explanations—ultimately, to discover and convey fundamental principles of the human experience that can be applied to new design situations.

Finding these explanations can be a difficult but illuminating challenge, primarily because there are so many ways to explain how people interact with documents. Consider the example in Figure 3.1.

We can look at this document through a myriad of angles, but three general approaches are most common:

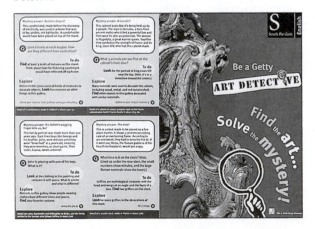

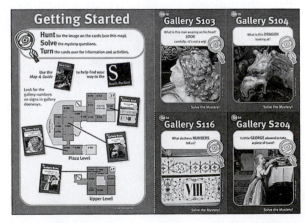

- Visual perception
- Visual culture
- Visual rhetoric

Theories of visual perception concentrate on using psychology and biology to explain how all human beings experience the world through their sense of vision. Understanding how users perceive documents helps us create easy-to-use documents that attract users' attention. So, for example, the leaflet in Figure 3.1 is printed in bright colors designed to attract a child's attention, and it asks children to interact with the document and their surroundings by matching what they see on the cards to what they see in the museum. Theories of visual culture tend to explain visual design by recognizing how societies and groups establish what visual perceptions *mean*. In the case of the museum leaflet, the images employed represent the European cultures that created the art the museum preserves. The concept of being a detective is also reinforced by the visual mark of the magnifying glass repeated throughout the leaflet; people know the link between detectives and magnifying glasses from their cultural experiences. Finally, theories of visual rhetoric borrow from both perception and culture to create visual designs that meet specific needs for specific people. This leaflet encourages children to be interested in and excited about the details of art by guiding an interactive activity with the art collection.

Among these three general approaches, scholars and designers have proposed many individual theories. Naturally, these theories do not all agree with each other, and they each have their strengths and weaknesses. Researchers and practitioners from many fields — including physiology, psychology, rhetoric, communication, art, and design — are still trying to figure out exactly how visual experience works.

So rather than trying to reconcile all of these different viewpoints, we will present a framework for understanding them, examining how they work together and where they disagree. Besides, recognizing the breadth of competing theories about visuality will make you a more thoughtful designer than simply choosing one theory and applying it formulaically.

Visual Perception

Humans are highly visual animals — in the way we experience the world, describe what we experience, and think about our experiences. In fact, our **visual perception** is so central to our personal experience that we often don't think consciously about what we see.

Imagine yourself watching a sitcom on television — let's say *Gilligan's Island*. Are you conscious of the flashing lights on a sheet of glass mounted in a plastic box, or do you just see the Skipper and his Little Buddy getting into trouble again? Obviously, on some level you know that there is no deserted island; that the people aren't real castaways, but actors on a soundstage; and that you're watching a video recording created and displayed with technology. But are you consciously aware of all that while you laugh at Gilligan's problems? And most of us *do* laugh, even though we are only seeing patterns of lights on a screen. Somehow our visual perceptions allow us to take these shifting lights and turn them into a compelling visual experience.

This ironic gap between what we *sense* as biological entities and what we *experience* as seeing humans is a central question in understanding visual perception. Gestalt psychologist Kurt Koffka summarized his and others' attempts to understand this irony with the question "Why do things look as they do?" This question may seem simple, but it has proven remarkably difficult to answer, leading to widely different theories of how we perceive visually.

In this section, we'll discuss some of the most influential theories of visual perception. Understanding these different approaches to Koffka's question will help you better understand how users create meaning out of the documents we design.

"Why do things look as they do?" —Kurt Koffka

Neurophysiology

Neurophysiology explains visual perception by exploring how organisms, and particularly their nervous systems, respond to visual stimuli. In making this exploration, neurophysiologists have discovered features of the human vision system that have a direct effect on how we see the world.

One example is the neurophysiological explanation of how we see colors. For centuries, scientists and philosophers such as Sir Isaac Newton and Wolfgang Goethe theorized about ways to systematize our perception of colors, producing remarkably persuasive accounts of how colors work together. It was only in the twentieth century, however, that scientists could finally explain how the biology of our nervous system creates the sensations we perceive as colors. They did so primarily by subjecting the nervous system to experiments, such as shining a pure light into a subject's eyes and measuring the chemical or bioelectrical response. Collectively, experimental techniques like this are called **psychophysics**.

Neurophysiologists discovered that humans have specialized nerve cells on their retinas known as **rods** and **cones**. These cells have different but complementary responses to light. Rod cells start a nerve response related to the *amount* of light cast on the retina through the lens of the eye—in other words, the intensity of the light transmitted or reflected into the eye. As a result, they are very sensitive to the edges and shapes of objects. Cone cells, however, invoke a nerve response related to the *wavelength* of light received. Together, the responses of rods and cones create the physical sensations we think of as color. From the responses of our cones, we perceive different wavelengths of light as different **hues** of color, and from the responses of our rods we perceive different intensities of light as different **saturations** or **brightnesses** of color. (For more information on color perception, see Chapter 8.)

Neurophysiology offers powerful explanations of many aspects of visual perception because it concentrates on human beings as biological creatures who have developed through evolutionary changes. For example, neurophysiologists also discovered that rods are more numerous and sensitive than cones. This discovery explains why as light recedes at twilight, the color seems gradually to fade away from the objects we view. Under these conditions, our rods are still working at detecting brightness, edges, and shapes, but the smaller number of cones have too little visual stimulus to invoke the hue response. This mechanism also makes sense in evolutionary terms. Early humans who could make out the shadowy forms of predators in dim shadows or the dark of night survived more often than those who had less sensitive perceptions of edges and shapes. The survivors passed on this skill; as a result, evolutionary forces encouraged the development of a multitude of rod cells for sensitive light response. Color, however, became more useful in daylight as a means for early humans to discriminate between what was edible and what was not. Good color perceivers were more likely to distinguish an edible mushroom from a poisonous one or ripe fruit from unripe and thus to survive and pass on this ability to their offspring.

This kind of research into the basic building blocks of sensation is neurophysiology's specialty. Neurophysiologists call these building blocks **primitives**, including basic sensations such as brightness, hue, edges, and patterns. Primitives combine into more complete sensations called *percepts* — for example, the recognition of shapes.

These neurophysiological aspects of experience are important to document design because they help us understand how users respond biologically to what they see. Neurophysiology helps us understand how users detect the shapes they see on pages, and so it is the basis of many technologies of document production, including color monitors and color printing. For example, the realization that the neurophysiology of color perceptions is based on experiences of red, green, and blue led to the development of color monitors, which use tiny red, green, and blue lights to create a wide range of colors.

Despite its usefulness and explanatory power, neurophysiology still has its limitations. Neurophysiology tends to focus on biological *mechanisms* of perception rather than on the *psychology* of perception. It explains how visual stimuli affect our nervous system, but it doesn't explain very well how we make meaning out of these stimuli. It makes perception seem a passive biological response, rather than something people do actively. Neurophysiology also implies that our experience of the world is mostly indirect — almost as if our consciousness is hidden deep inside our neural system, weighing and assembling what we sense but never coming into direct contact with anything.

Gestalt

One approach that counters neurophysiology's focus on isolated neurological responses is **Gestalt theory**. While acknowledging what neurophysiology tells us about human perception, Gestalt attempts to create a more comprehensive version of human perception, contending that experience is more than the sum of its parts. Gestalt suggests that we don't just see edges, colors, brightnesses, and shapes — we see fruit, or a tree, or a dog. In other words, we experience what we see as a *whole* — which is also the meaning of the German word *Gestalt*.

The primary figures in Gestalt psychology's heyday (between about 1890 and 1940) were the Frankfurt University psychologist Max Wertheimer (1880–1943) and his students Wolfgang Köhler (1887–1967) and Kurt Koffka (1886–1941). These scientists argued that we should try to answer Koffka's question "Why do things look as they do?" by concentrating on the phenomena of perception as experienced by a naive, uncritical observer. They identified a number of phenomena that are stable across different people and cultures; these phenomena have become known as the **Gestalt laws of perception**, the most significant of which are these:

- Figure-ground discrimination
- Laws of grouping
- Good figure

These laws have been particularly influential on document design. In fact, you'll probably notice several connections between the following sections and the principles of design in Chapter 2.

FIGURE-GROUND DISCRIMINATION

One of the most basic laws Gestalt psychologists identified was that we tend to organize the visual world into two categories: figure and ground. **Figure** is what we perceive as an object, and **ground** is what we perceive as the object's context. Figure-ground discrimination describes how we tell the difference between the two. This Gestalt law has a direct application to document design: it helps us predict how users will recognize design objects (figures) on a page (the ground).

We use a variety of cues to determine what is figure and what is ground. For example, we typically recognize the *smaller* continuous parts of a visual field as figures and the *larger* parts as the ground. Consider the first graphic in Figure 3.2, a white square and a black circle. Simply by recognizing these marks as "objects," you have made some judgments about figure and ground. If we take the square as the visual field, then most of us would identify the black circle as a figure in that ground because it is smaller than the surrounding white space. But if we take the entire page as the visual field, then we recognize both the square and the circle as figures on the ground of the page. We also tend to see the black circle as being "on" the paper, when it could just as easily be a hole through the paper (see the discussion of continuation on page 44).

One application of this principle to document design is the concept of *figure-ground contrast*. If the figure and the ground look different, users have an easier time distinguishing one from the other than if the figure and the ground look similar. For example, in Figure 3.2, it's easier to make out the black circle on the white square than it is to make out the light gray circle on the dark gray square. As these graphics suggest, figure-ground contrast can be formed with brightness (different values), hue (different colors), or saturation (different purities of color). In addition to the contrast of the figure to the ground, good figure-ground contrast relies on the consistency and distinctness of the figure's edges. Figures with fuzzy edges are harder to recognize because they have poor figure-ground contrast. The last graphic in Figure 3.2 shows the same size circle and square but with a pattern applied to each that makes it hard to see where the figure ends and the ground begins.

One of the more general applications of figure-ground contrast is in camouflage, which works by blurring the distinction between figure and ground. But camouflage is rarely a good idea in document design, where *inadequate* figure-ground contrast is a common problem, making documents harder to read. Documents that use background images,

Figure 3.2 Figure-ground contrast. Black and white are highly contrastive, making it easy to see the black circle against the white square. The gray square and circle contrast significantly less. The patterned gray circle is difficult to make out against the patterned gray square.

patterns, or watermarks often provide too little contrast between the ground and the design objects placed on that ground. Text, because it's made up of relatively small and intricate shapes, can easily get lost on a busy background.

GROUPING

Gestalt theory postulates several ways we group figures once we have recognized them through figure-ground discrimination. The most important grouping indicators are proximity, similarity, continuation, and common region.

Proximity and similarity.   The natural tendency of users to group figures can be very useful in document design. Designers rely on proximity and similarity as two of the six principles of design you read about in Chapter 2 (see Figure 2.13 on page 31). To summarize, the law of **proximity** suggests that we tend to group figures that are closer together, and the law of *similarity* suggests that we perceive similar figures as belonging together.

Continuation.   The law of **continuation** suggests that we will assume a connection between figures that are lined up, even if we don't have any direct evidence that they are connected. Consider the graphics in Figure 3.3. Most of us would recognize the first graphic as a circle obscuring the top edge of a rectangle, assuming that the rectangle's top edge continues behind the circle. But there is no real evidence that this perception is accurate. In fact, there could be a semicircular gap in the rectangle that the circle merely covers up. The law of continuation describes our tendency to see that upper line of the rectangle as continuing "behind" the circle, despite the lack of visual evidence that this is so.

Continuation also explains our tendency to see shapes where they do not exist. For example, the "Pac-Man" shapes in Figure 3.4 might seem unitary and separate when arranged randomly. But when arranged differently, the same shapes make us see something that's not explicitly there: a triangle. Continuation also makes us see things as

Figure 3.3 The law of continuation. Our sense of continuation "behind" an object is an important tool for recognizing objects, but it can also be misleading.

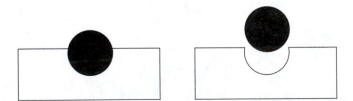

Figure 3.4 Creating shape through continuation.   Continuation can create shape perceptions and groupings. Here, the three shapes can be arranged to imply a triangle through continuation, even though there is no triangle explicitly marked. This continuation also makes the three shapes look connected to each other.

groups, even when there isn't any positive connection between them. We see the three black objects that form the implied triangle as "belonging together" because the acute angles they contain seem to form lines that continue across the gap.

Continuation is the foundation of alignment, another principle of design discussed in Chapter 2. When we align design objects on a page, we suggest to users that those objects are connected by an implied continued line. For example, we almost always align individual letters of text on a consistent, implied line (the baseline). Readers naturally group the letters along this implied line into lines of type, words, sentences, and paragraphs.

D₀ing o₁herwise m₄kes rea₄ing h₄rder.

Common region.   The law of common region is the foundation for the design principle of enclosure, as discussed in Chapter 2. **Common region** claims that people see objects sharing a common space as belonging together (Palmer). For example, consider the three sets of objects in Figure 3.5. The first set of objects seems to be grouped several ways: by continuation (rows of shapes), by similarity (circles and triangles), and by proximity (the triangles are closer to each other than to any circle, and vice versa). All of these groupings suggest two distinct groups: the line of circles on the left and the line of triangles on the right.

Yet if we draw boxes around some of the shapes, we form a common region that now pairs each circle with a triangle. This enclosure overpowers the principles of continuation, similarity, and proximity in

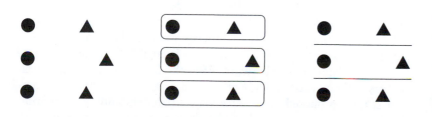

Figure 3.5 Forming a common region.   A common region can be formed explicitly by drawing boundaries completely around grouped objects or less explicitly by using dividing lines or even negative space.

grouping the objects. Even simple lines drawn between each pair of shapes will invoke a common region because they imply a horizontal connection between the object pairs. Negative space can imply common region, too, if it is not overpowered by other principles.

Document designers use common region all the time—for example, to set off design objects from the text, such as graphics, notes, caution and warning statements, headers, and footers. In electronic documents, common region leads designers to create buttons for important links or commands, such as those in a website navigation bar.

GOOD FIGURE

Gestalt suggests that figures that use proximity, similarity, continuation, and common region consistently are stronger, more stable, and more recognizable than those that don't. For example, examine the two sets of objects in Figure 3.6. Both use the laws of proximity and continuation to imply a complex object (lines) built out of simpler objects (diamonds). But because the line on the bottom is straighter (continuation), more regular (similarity), and more consistently spaced (proximity), it makes a better figure than the line on the top.

Users typically recognize good figures in document designs more readily than weaker figures. Logically, if we want users to recognize something important, we should make it a strong figure. This application leads many document designers to create simple, rather minimalistic documents that focus on visual clarity, good alignment, and obvious groupings of related information. With the graphic possibilities of software, it's easy to create fancier, more visually complex designs that don't form good figures. These designs might get more initial attention, but they might also be less easy or efficient to use.

GESTALT AND DOCUMENT DESIGN

As you might have guessed by now, Gestalt had an enormous influence on document design, if only because its principles are so easy to apply to documents. In fact, many Gestalt experiments involved asking subjects to look at shapes printed on cards—very similar to what we do when we look at a document on paper or on a screen. Although this parallel has been a boon for document designers, some critics claim that Gestalt works better in the laboratory than in the real world.

In addition, despite how convincing and useful Gestalt principles may be, Gestalt psychologists have never been able to explain successfully *why* Gestalt principles work. After the first half of the twentieth century (when Wertheimer, Koffka, and Köhler were active), perception studies proposed alternative ways of understanding perception that more successfully explained why perception works as it does,

Figure 3.6 Creating a good figure. We perceive good figure particularly when Gestalt laws are followed completely. Here, for example, the aligned row of diamonds makes a better figure than the haphazard row.

but these newer theories don't necessarily work well with Gestalt. For example, Gestalt does not always mesh well with neurophysiology, which focuses on finding the explanations for perception that Gestalt fails to supply. Finally, although the Gestalt principles provide good indications of how a *general, universal human being* might respond to a document, they don't always predict how individual users or particular groups of users might respond. Users come in many shapes and sizes, and they come from many different cultures and backgrounds; individual users or particular groups of users often respond differently to the same documents.

So although Gestalt is perhaps the most popular and useful theory of perception among designers, it's wise to take its principles with a grain of salt, recognizing that other explanations of perception have something to add to our understanding as well.

Constructivism

Another explanation of perception is constructivism. Imagine you are backing your car out of a garage (see Figure 3.7). Before you start to move, you glance quickly in several different directions: in the side mirrors to your left and right, and in the central rearview mirror. You even crane your neck around left and right to check for anything that might

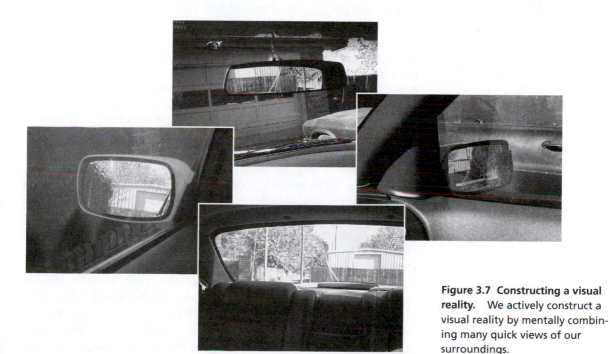

Figure 3.7 Constructing a visual reality.   We actively construct a visual reality by mentally combining many quick views of our surroundings.

be behind the car. Once you're satisfied that the coast is clear, you back out, still constantly adjusting the course of the car with additional glances forward over the fenders, as well as backward in the mirrors and over your shoulder. If you're an experienced driver, you perform all of these actions quickly, efficiently, and almost unconsciously.

So what have you done here perceptually? You haven't looked at *every* aspect of the world around you—even the mirrors and your backward glances can't reach everywhere behind the car. Instead, you have used your fragmentary perceptions to *construct* a model of the visual world that fills the gaps in your perception. You also constantly test that model against additional observations, building a more and more accurate idea of your surroundings.

Constructivist theories explain this kind of scenario particularly well. Like Gestalt, constructivist theories find neurophysiology unsatisfying because it implies that people are mostly passive receivers of stimuli. But unlike Gestalt, which posits that we understand the whole visual scene at a glance, constructivist theories propose that human beings perceive the world in fragments from which they actively construct a visual reality. Constructivist theories focus on explaining how we use the limited building blocks of sensation and perception to create bigger concepts of the visual world we live in.

Most constructivist research focuses on how we build a visual world by *sampling* the visual ecology by taking in perceptions a bit at a time—what John M. Findlay and Iain D. Gilchrist have called *active vision*. When we look at an object, constructivism suggests, we don't see it all at once; instead, we take multiple visual snapshots, looking at different aspects of the object. These snapshots are called *fixations*, and the fast eye movements between fixations are called *saccadic movements*. According to constructivism, we use repeated fixations on different parts of the visual field to build up a picture of what we perceive.

As a result, we never actually see the entire visual field precisely or completely—rather, we put together our perceptions dynamically, filling in the gaps with memory and experience. Even in the perception of a single visual field, we must use short-term memory to remember what we saw in the previous fixation and add it to what we see in the next. Long-term memory and general experience affect our perceptions as well. One experiment, for example, found that when children were asked to estimate the physical size of coins shown to them, they overestimated the size of the coins of higher value: the higher the value of the coin, the greater the overestimation of size. The children's knowledge of the relative monetary values of the coins, in other words, influenced their ability to estimate size visually (Gibson 128).

Constructivist theories suggest that humans start with hypotheses about how the world works. For example, the children in the coin experiment started with the general idea that bigger things are often more valuable than smaller ones. But we constantly seek out and absorb additional information about the world, and we just as constantly readjust our hypotheses. In fact, constructivism suggests that we have to stay on this constant search for visual information because our visual apparatus doesn't really provide enough data for our minds to create a sense of the world. Instead, our minds supply most of our mental model of our surroundings, using incomplete and fragmentary sensations to build more and more accurate mental models. This explains how we can make our way through a familiar room blindfolded, but in an unfamiliar room, we must watch carefully where we're going, taking in lots of visual snapshots to build a mental model of our surroundings. In this regard, while acknowledging the importance of neurophysiology, constructivism moves the locus of perception even further into cognition and psychology, but away from biology.

Constructivism has been influential in document design, particularly as researchers have used eye-tracking equipment to record how users look at a document. As we mentioned in Chapter 1, eye-tracking research has found that for most printed documents, readers of English and other left-to-right languages fixate first at the upper left-hand corner of a document. Then, in a series of saccadic movements and fixations, users move their eyes in a Z pattern down the rest of the page, scanning for the information they need. The more consistently the text on the page fits this pattern, the more likely that users can make clear connections between their fixations as they build a picture of the visual field and its contents. (See Chapter 5 for further discussion of this observation.)

Constructivist theories of perception reveal the importance of giving users clear visual cues about the structure and content of documents. For example, obvious headings, labels, and titles for text and graphics give users' eyes somewhere to rest momentarily as they build a mental model of the page, spread, or screen. Without these cues, users must slog their way through the entire document, rather than using their natural fixations and saccadic movements to build up a concept of the document's structure and contents efficiently and dynamically.

Ecological Perception

Like neurophysiology, however, constructivism implies a separation between people and the world that some scientists and philosophers find troubling: it suggests a fragmentary and incomplete world we can never fully comprehend. Ecological perception counters constructivism by suggesting that we perceive a full and rich world of sensory data directly and immediately, without the intervention of discrete neurological responses or prior hypotheses—a phenomenon called *direct perception*.

Psychologist James J. Gibson, the major proponent of ecological perception and direct perception, argued that rather than perceiving the world as tiny, discrete sensations or percepts that we build into bigger *concepts*, we experience the surrounding world or *ecology* simultaneously, in a rush of available data that we interact with dynamically and unconsciously. But unlike Gestalt, which focuses on a mostly stationary viewer, ecological perception notes that we do not stand still while we look at our ecology. Without much thought, we cock our heads to the side to get a better angle of view, we move closer or farther away from an object, and we walk around and look at the back side of whatever we're examining.

According to ecological perception, we also consider the relationship of objects to our own bodies and recognize how we might *use* objects. For example, we might recognize an object as something we can grasp, twist, pull, push, climb on, walk across, pick up, or throw. The qualities of objects that allow us to use them in some way are called *affordances* (Figure 3.8). The object's relationship to our bodies determines what extent of graspability, sitability, or walkability it affords.

In document design terms, we must provide affordances in documents so users understand what they can use to work with the document. In designing the physical document, we can provide tabbed indexes, convenient bindings, and other physical features that make a document easy to use. In terms of page design, we can provide clear and definite navigational cues, such as links, buttons, and form fields that users can easily recognize as design objects they can *do* something with. This recognition of the importance of affordances is one reason why the cursor in most web browsers turns into a small, pointing

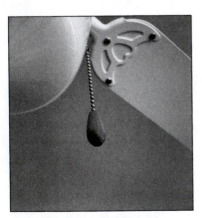

Figure 3.8 Examples of affordances. We recognize affordances as tools for interacting with things around us—here, by pulling a chain, turning a doorknob, or flipping a switch. Documents can include similar affordances, helping users manipulate and work with information.

hand when we place the mouse over a link. The hand implies that the link is something that can be *touched*, if only remotely through a mouse-click.

This focus on affordances in the world that surrounds us fits in particularly well with discussions of **usability** in document design. Usability studies can take into account all aspects of the user experience — not just the surface of the page, but the back of the page, its size and shape, even its materials — to find how users interact with the objects in their ecology (for more information on usability, see "Visual Rhetoric as User-Centered Design" on page 66). The idea of affordances has also been very influential on **interface design** for software and websites. Designers create visual-spatial cues to suggest to users what affordances the interface offers — that is, what can be clicked, dragged, pushed (as in buttons), or otherwise manipulated. So promising is this connection that designers have begun to think of design much more holistically as part of the user's ecology, labeling their efforts **interaction design** (IXD), or even more broadly, **user experience design** (UX).

However, if constructivism implies that too many things (such as values and preconceptions) come between people and the world, ecological perception implies that there is nothing between people and the world. Ecological perception's emphasis on direct perception without the intervention of cognition moves us farther away from the mind and back into the senses. For this reason, although many have found the concept of affordances useful, Gibson's concept of direct perception has found fewer supporters.

Theories of Visual Perception Influence Document Design

Because theories of visual perception such as neurophysiology, Gestalt, constructivism, and ecological perception concentrate on explaining human beings' basic interactions with the world, they have had a great influence on document design. Documents, after all, are part of the world we live in and interact with. If our designs do not take the basic dynamics of users' visual experience into account, they may be unsuccessful or even inaccessible to users.

All of the theories of visual perception we have discussed attempt to explain how we recognize objects. Object recognition is simultaneously all of these things:

- A fundamental part of our neural apparatus for seeing (neurophysiology)
- A technique we use to mark the boundary between one object and its surroundings (Gestalt figure-ground discrimination and good figure)

- A way to recognize how we might interact with our environment (ecological perception, constructivism)

All of this insight into object recognition helps us design usable documents. For example, consider Figure 3.9, an epigraph quoted at the top of an academic journal article that has been scanned and saved as a PDF (portable document format). When it was first designed as a paper document, this journal article was easy to read. But it lost a lot of clarity after it was scanned to PDF for on-screen viewing, and it becomes even fuzzier when it is printed out again, as it is here.

It's easy to see what's happened here. In the translation of the printed article to PDF for distribution through an online database, the page image had to be downsampled to a lower resolution, both to prepare it for viewing on a screen (which has coarser resolution than a printed page) and to make it small enough as a file to transmit quickly through the Internet. Unfortunately, these constraints lead to a document that users will find hard to read, whether they attempt to do so on the screen or print out the document. The letters have blurry edges, and they are not particularly dark, so they don't have good contrast against the white paper; they also have halos of extraneous gray smudges around them.

We know this almost by instinct, but theories of visual perception provide us with good reasons why these characteristics make a document hard to read. Neurophysiology tells us that our rod cells are sensitive to boundaries between one pattern and the next. If the boundary isn't clear, we'll have to look at it more closely to see it. Gestalt suggests that we can distinguish figure from ground more easily if the figure is "good"; the letters in Figure 3.9 are hazy and not clearly aligned, making it hard to tell figure from ground. Both constructivism and ecology suggest that we gather information from the environment to interact with it; if the information is vague or hard to discern, how can we do so effectively?

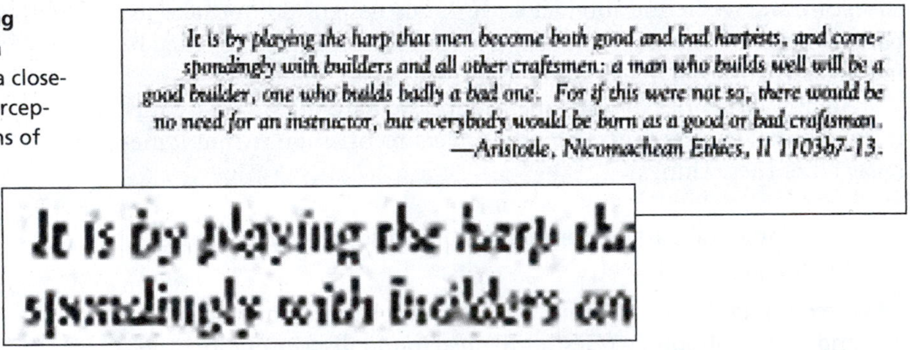

Figure 3.9 A document lacking clarity.   This epigraph from a scanned PDF document (and a close-up) shows how theories of perception can help explain problems of reading.

It is by playing the harp that men become both good and bad harpists, and correspondingly with builders and all other craftsmen: a man who builds well will be a good builder, one who builds badly a bad one. For if this were not so, there would be no need for an instructor, but everybody would be born as a good or bad craftsman.
—Aristotle, *Nicomachean Ethics*, II 1103b7-13.

However, as we've noted particularly for Gestalt, most theories of visual perception focus on human beings in a general, universal sense. This focus is a strength because it gives us basic principles, like the Gestalt laws, that should apply well to most communication situations. But it's also a weakness because it doesn't allow well for the effect of our *nurture* as well as our *nature*. In other words, theories of visual perception don't always give adequate weight to the influence of our cultural and social experience on what we see.

Visual Culture

A set of approaches tries to fill this gap by focusing explicitly on **visual culture**. To understand the role of visual culture, let's return to an earlier example, the sitcom *Gilligan's Island*, where we pointed out the irony of being amused by flashing lights on a screen. People who are interested in theories of visual perception (such as neurophysiology, Gestalt, constructivism, and ecological perception) would probably analyze this situation by trying to explain how we perceive shifting lights as images.

But of course, not everyone would laugh. They might not laugh because they aren't familiar with American culture and don't understand the jokes, many of which are based on visual cues about the identities of the characters (Figure 3.10). For example, viewers might not be able to infer that the Skipper and Gilligan are sailors from seeing their hats. Or if viewers do recognize such visual markers as meaning "sailor," they might also take Mr. Howell for a sailor, since he wears a yacht club jacket. Viewers also might not recognize the visual markers that mean "wealthy people," such as Mr. and Mrs. Howell's fancy clothes. They might find neither Maryann nor Ginger particularly attractive, or they might find one more attractive than the other, depending on their cultural notions of beauty. Even if the viewers are natives of the culture that created the sitcom, they might find the visual objectification and oversimplification of these women characters offensive rather than funny. (As a further case, if you've never watched *Gilligan's Island* before, you might not find our discussion here very engaging because you don't know what we're talking about!)

Figure 3.10 Recognizing visual culture cues. Understanding the humor in *Gilligan's Island* depends on our ability to recognize visual culture cues about class, society, gender, and money.

These aspects of visual communication start with our visual perceptions, but they focus more fully on the connections we make between those perceptions and our culture or the culture of those who created the program. Visual culture influences how we ascribe *meaning* to what we see. When we watch something as visually complex as a sitcom, we don't rely just on our visual perceptions—we use the web of associations, connotations, and connections that our visual perceptions evoke.

The same thing applies to the documents we use, which are complex *cultural* objects as well as physical and perceptual ones. Visual culture is particularly important to document design because documents are not just part of our natural visual environment. Instead, someone who comes from a particular cultural background designs the documents. And the documents are *used* by people with their own unique and varied cultural backgrounds. Both the designer and the user rely on a complex field of conventions to convey meaning. For example, the size (or *font*) of the type used for different design objects in this book conveys a particular meaning. We use the largest fonts for chapter titles and headings; we use a smaller font for basal text; and we use an even smaller font for captions to the figures. The contrast between these sizes helps convey the book's structure. Simply put, in hierarchical terms the bigger parts (chapters, sections) are marked with bigger type, while smaller parts are marked with smaller type. This use of fonts to show structure isn't an accident—it's a result of strong visual conventions with which designers consciously guide users.

Visual Language

In some ways, visual communication can convey as much as written communication, forming in effect a **visual language**. For an example of this, let us consider driving a car.

When we drive, we rely not only on our own perceptions to guide the vehicle but also on the "rules of the road." We must learn these rules before we are permitted to drive, and we are penalized when we break those rules. Driving laws govern not only our own actions but also those of other motorists to keep them from running into us. After we have been driving awhile, we internalize these rules and do not have to think much about them. This internalization reduces our cognitive load, allowing us simply to follow the conventions without giving them much thought.

But if we visit a country where the rules are different, our cognitive load increases dramatically. Then we must constantly remind ourselves of the simplest things, such as what side of the road to drive on (see Figure 3.11).

Figure 3.11 Considering cultural conventions.   All conventions have a cultural element—some drive on the left side of the road, some on the right. The conventions of visual design are no exception.

This example parallels in some ways our use of language. When we are young children, we think about our language a lot, constantly acquiring new words and rules for combining them into expressions. After a while, though, we stop thinking about the words themselves and simply speak. It's only when we try to learn a new language that we must think about language rules again. In other words, languages work by conventions, such as the shared agreement on what words mean (semantics), how they are spoken (phonetics), and how they can be combined (syntax).

Similarly, visual language supposes that people within a culture have well-developed general agreements or *conventions* about what images can mean, how they can be presented, and how they interact. For example, Charles Kostelnick and Michael Hassett have discussed at length the visual convention of the arrow and similar pointers (see Figure 3.12 on page 56). Arrows are exclusively *visual* marks—we can't read an arrow out loud the way we can read a written word. Yet users from many cultures recognize arrows as meaning something—usually "look here," "go this way," or "do something with this." Some scholars have labeled our ability to "read" visual images as **visual literacy**. According to Paul Messaris and Sandra Moriarty, visual literacy is "the viewer's awareness of the conventions through which the meanings of visual images are created and understood" (481).

Figure 3.12 Considering visual conventions. Pointer marks can come in many shapes and sizes, but visual conventions help us understand that they mean similar things.

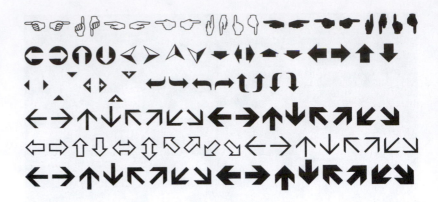

Intercultural Communication

Moreover, these conventions are determined by individual cultures. One often-used example is the meaning of *red*. In most Western cultures, red signifies danger—that's why our stop signs and stop lights are red. But in Japan, China, and other Asian countries, red often means happiness, joy, and celebration.

So in document design terms, a document designed for one culture's conventions of visual language might not work for another culture. With this realization comes a big problem, since we live in a global community with international businesses and organizations. How can a global business create a document that will work successfully in the visual languages of all of the cultures with which it must communicate?

Two general approaches hope to solve this problem of intercultural communication: *globalization* and *localization*. Designers using a global approach try to create documents (usually in simplified English, the most common language on the planet) that they hope most people can understand. By avoiding colloquialisms, metaphors, local expressions, and local visual conventions, globalization attempts to create a document that will succeed for most people in most cultures. Globalized documents, however, can never hope to speak successfully to people of all cultures, and this approach often produces oversimplified, unsuccessful documents.

Localization takes the opposite approach: rather than creating one very basic document, it creates different versions of a document for each set of users in different cultures. Localization often involves translating documents into a different language, and it can also involve creating new designs for documents using local visual conventions.

When localizing a document, designers typically try to take into account all they know about the particular culture that will use it. For example, designers might try to categorize the target culture according to Edward Hall's concepts of **high context** or **low context**. High-context cultures tend to rely less on explicit documents and more on the social relationships and unspoken norms of their culture to determine how to act. Low-context cultures tend to rely more on explicit rules and extensive documentation. So a document designer localizing a set of instructions to a high-context culture might try a more visual or narrative approach — even designing something like a documentary video or a story, rather than a written manual.

Ideally, localization helps designers create culturally sensitive documents. But localization inevitably costs more than globalization, making some organizations reluctant to invest in this practice except for their most mission-critical communications. Localization projects also sometimes depend on superficial cultural stereotypes, such as "Asians don't like to do business with strangers." Although such a stereotype may have some general truth, many Asians actually like working with new people. So a deep familiarity with the target culture and even individual members of that culture is necessary for localization to succeed.

Semiotics

Given the complexity of visual communication (to say nothing of intercultural visual communication), theorists have tried to find more accurate ways to describe how people ascribe meaning to visual language. One common approach comes from **semiotics**, the study of signs and sign-systems. Its most influential early proponent, the anthropologist Ferdinand de Saussure (1857–1913), suggested that a **sign** is actually a complex formed by the relationship between two components: the **signifier** (the mark we see) and the **signified** (the concept the mark points to). The signifier can be any visual mark, including images and letters. However, this relationship is ambiguous and unsettled; it depends on people's willingness to accept it to make it real. In other words, we rely on convention to link a signifier (such as the written word *bird*) and its signified (the concept of bird) and make meaning.

Charles Saunders Peirce (1839–1914) proposed a way to understand signs with even greater discrimination. Although Peirce (pronounced *purse*) used different terms than Saussure, he suggested that there are three kinds of signs, depending on the tightness of the signifier's connection to the signified:

- **Icons** are signs that *look like* the thing they signify. Most representational images — photographs, for example — are icons.
- **Indexes** are signs that have a clear connection to whatever they signify (that is, they *indicate* something). Peirce's example was a

signpost, which indicates the road to the destination written on the sign.

- *Symbols* are signs that have an *arbitrary* relationship to whatever they signify; Peirce described them as signs that "have become associated with their meanings by usage." Examples include written letters, words, and texts, as well as signifiers that don't have a direct relationship to whatever concept they signify. For example, signifiers such as #, *, and $ have only conventional relationships to the concepts "number," "note," and "money."

So in Figure 3.13, the photograph of a house is an icon because it *looks like* or *represents* a house. The sign pointing to a restroom does not look like a restroom, but it carries meaning as an index because it *indicates* the restroom's location and function. And an *arbitrary* mark like the international "no" or "prohibition" sign is a symbol because it has no direct connection to anything except the connection we've collectively decided upon.

Of course, the category into which a sign falls depends entirely on how we use the sign. A picture of a house can be an icon when it's used to mean *this particular house*. But it could also be used more generally to signify the general concept of home, which is why we still see it used in the toolbars of most web browsers to mark a link to the user's home page (Figure 3.14). Used this way, this mark would be an index because it points to a *metaphorical* home on the Web: the base page the user wants to see upon first opening the browser. However, this mark doesn't represent any particular house (as an icon would), and it isn't entirely arbitrary (as a symbol would be).

Moreover, semiotics reminds us that conventional signs are not stable or unitary. Rarely can we assume that a mark means only one thing; more often, it can mean several or many possible things. This parallels spoken language, where a word might have one *denotative* meaning (like a dictionary definition) but many *connotative*, or implied, meanings—a concept known as **polysemy**. Denotatively, the word

Figure 3.13 Examples of icon, index, and symbol.   C. S. Peirce's concepts of icon, index, and symbol can help us understand how people find and create meaning from what they see.

father means an organism that offers genetic material to create offspring; connotatively, *father* can have many implied meanings, from positive (warmth, nurture) to negative (control, discipline). Roland Barthes (1915–1980), in particular, brought to our attention the relationship between signs and connotations. The constellation of possible meanings that surround a sign relies almost entirely on culture, society, and usage.

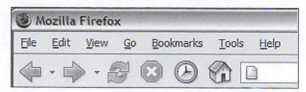

Figure 3.14 Indexes versus icons.   In this context, a web browser toolbar, the image of the house acts as an index rather than an icon because it points a user to his or her *home page*, not an actual house.

An awareness of the complex, imprecise, and sometimes arbitrary nature of signs helps document designers because it makes us sensitive to the many ways users might interpret the marks on a page. Often, users latch on to a denotation or connotation we didn't intend. As document designers, we must be on the watch for marks that users might interpret differently than we intended. We also need to *ask* users what they think something means by testing the usability of our designs.

Visual Culture and Power

As we've seen, signs can act as a visual language; we even use signs, in the form of letters, to signify our spoken language. And the meaning of those signs is mostly conventional and culturally derived. But this observation begs a question: *who* decides what signs mean?

In some cases, signs come to mean what they do organically, from the habit of usage by many people across the years. Alternately, the meanings of signs are established by an authority, such as a government or an international standards body. For example, the design of stop signs in the United States is determined by the U.S. Department of Transportation.

But in many cases, power plays a role in how meaning gets attached to signs. People who have the money and freedom to speak louder and broadcast their ideas through the media are more likely to establish the meaning of a sign than those who are poor, isolated, or silenced. One example of this dynamic is the use of corporate logos, such as the Nike symbol, the Coca-Cola logo, or McDonald's Golden Arches. Each of these corporations has spent billions of dollars on advertisements that constantly stress positive associations between these symbols and the company and its product. They've been so successful in doing so that it's hard to find a place in the world where someone *won't* recognize these symbols as meaning what the corporations wish them to mean. If these corporations didn't have the money to advertise their logos on such a large scale, we would not recognize them so easily. The Nike symbol would be a meaningless squiggle, we might think Coca-Cola was a brand of hot cocoa rather than soda, and we might take the Golden Arches to just look like a stylized letter *M* (which, of course, it is — polysemy again!). In the meantime, these corporations have so successfully wielded their brand power that they have probably pushed out of existence many smaller businesses that might make a better pair of shoes, a tastier drink, or a more palatable hamburger.

Scholars interested in *cultural studies* focus on these issues of power as they relate to visual communication. The power of some people or organizations to set the meaning of signs in such a society can amount to what Antonio Gramsci (1891–1937) called *hegemony*, the tendency of particular ideas, usually associated with powerful people, institutions, or even general cultures, to limit and even control the ways we interact and communicate — in a sense, to write and enforce the rules of discourse. This power has positive benefits. For example, we wouldn't want people to make up their own rules for voting in public elections. But it also makes individuals conform in their meaning-making. For example, many U.S. citizens find the term *socialism* unappealing, even though some U.S. allies, such as Britain, Sweden, and Italy, have more or less socialist governments. In its most basic form, socialism refers to collective ownership and action. Even in the United States, we use socialism for some aspects of our system, such as publicly owned electric power plants, Social Security, and national parks. But the common wisdom that socialism is dangerous, emphasized repeatedly by U.S. politicians and powerful social groups, limits our ability to use the term without raising people's fears through the specter of Stalinist communism, fascism, and war.

Of course, corporations and governments can never entirely control language or visual communication. Even powerful organizations must try to speak to users in a language they can understand and respond to. As a result, people also have a certain amount of power to determine the terms in which they're spoken to.

Visual Culture and Ethics

From this recognition of the relationship between visual culture and power, document designers have grown much more aware of their ethical role in working with both clients and users. As we discussed in Chapter 1, most document designers serve as the representatives of clients who can pay them for their work (we hope). But when you rely on the client for your income, you may encounter pressure to act in ways that are good for your client, but not so good for the people who use the documents you design.

As a document designer, you will often encounter situations in which you must decide how to balance the agendas of your clients with

the needs of users. You must also find appropriate compromises between your own ethical values and the client's objectives. For example,
imagine you are hired to work on the website design for a firearms manufacturer, like the one in Figure 3.15. Depending on your ethical perceptions about guns, you might have a variety of ethical qualms about
working on this project. If you don't agree with the prominence of guns
in U.S. culture, you clearly must find a way to negotiate between your
ethical values and the client's need to sell the product. You may ultimately find that you cannot ethically work on the project, even if it
means losing money or even your job. On the other hand, if you do not
object to guns, you might still have ethical problems with the image
of the waving U.S. flag on the website. Does this design cheapen the
meaning of the flag by using patriotism to sell a product? Does it con-
flate patriotism with the right to bear arms?

Consider a different scenario: you're asked to produce a brochure
for a pharmaceutical company. The client wants a cover photo of happy,
healthy people to emphasize the company's commitment to community service. But you discover that the company has been indicted in
lawsuits for rushing unsafe drugs into the market. Is the planned design an unethical manipulation of users' feelings? If you continue to
work on the project, are you involving yourself in that manipulation?

These questions are thorny and difficult to resolve. What is most
important is to make a conscious, informed decision about your
actions in document design, striving to create coherence between the
ethical standards you hold and the work you do.

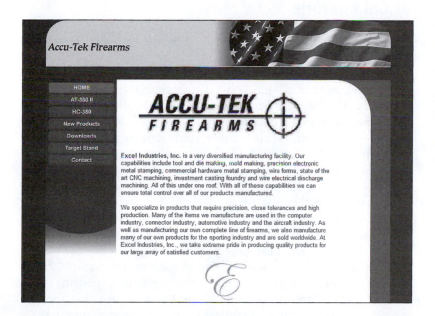

Figure 3.15 Raising ethical questions.   Design projects always involve ethical questions, regardless of the designer's personal views. Depending on your social values, professional values, and moral sense, you might consider the red, white, and blue color scheme and a waving American flag either acceptable or unethical.

Accu-Tek Firearms, <www.accutek.com>.

> **DESIGN TIP**
>
> ## Making Ethical Decisions in Document Design
>
> Thinking of visual design in cultural terms requires that we also think about the ethics of our designs. Document designers must make decisions about issues such as these:
>
> - How do we design documents that meet the needs of users when those needs might be at odds with those of our clients?
>
> - In emphasizing the positive features of the client's agenda in our designs, are we obscuring the more negative aspects?
>
> - Do our designs represent the world (whether information about a service, program, product, or policy) accurately, without distortion? For example, in what ways might our charts and graphs distort the data they're meant to convey—either by presenting data inaccurately or by omitting data that contradicts the client's aims?
>
> - Does our work forward ideologies or ends with which we can't agree? How do we manage to make a living while standing up for our own ethical principles?
>
> None of these questions is easy to answer. And the answers depend on many competing sets of moral values, including your society's values, your profession's values, and your own values. The answers you come up with will also depend very much on the particular situation you find yourself in, making it difficult to make black-and-white pronouncements about what's right or wrong.

Visual Rhetoric

Thus far in this chapter, we've discussed theories of visual perception and theories of visual culture. But you may have noticed that both sets of theories tend to focus on *describing* how people respond to the visual world they live in—either the natural ecology or the artificial one created by culture. These descriptions are valuable, but how do we use them when we design a document?

One way to address this problem is to focus on a third set of theories, which we'll categorize under *visual rhetoric*. You may have heard the word *rhetoric* used before to describe empty or cynical communications—for example, one politician saying that another's words are "just rhetoric," rather than honest facts. But rhetoric has a much broader scope: Paolo Valesio has defined rhetoric as "all of language, in its realization as discourse" (7). Generally, most theories of rhetoric use the term to discuss how people try to influence each other through human communication. Kenneth Burke, for example, called rhetoric "the use of language as [a] symbolic means of inducing cooperation" (43). More specifically, Wayne Booth argued that rhetoric is most concerned with a "rhetorical stance" negotiated among three essential elements: "the available arguments about the subject itself, the interests and peculiarities of the audience, and the voice, the implied character, of the speaker" (141). Rhetoric, in other words, focuses on the relationships among a speaker or *rhetor*, the rhetor's goals, and the people to whom he or she is speaking.

Rhetoric has long been used to analyze these relationships in written communication, especially the relationships between writers, their goals, and the audiences to whom they write. This analytical process also helps rhetors to plan and create communications that will fulfill rhetorical goals with particular audiences.

Visual rhetoric extends rhetorical theory by taking into account the visual design of a document, as well as its words. In this regard, it synthesizes and applies what we have discovered about visual perception and visual culture. Visual rhetoric is a way of understanding the relationship among clients, users, and designers. It takes advantage of what theories of visual perception tell us about the nature of human viewing in general and what theories of visual culture tell us about how people from different cultures view created objects. Visual rhetoric applies our understanding of both perception and culture to speak convincingly and effectively to users.

In the sections that follow, we'll discuss two aspects of visual rhetoric. First, we'll discuss it as a collection of strategies for persuading users. This aspect of visual rhetoric focuses on the client's goals and the designer's attempts to represent those goals visually to an audience. It also includes the question of visual ethics. Then, we'll discuss visual rhetoric in terms of *usability*, a term that brings the focus of the rhetorical stance to the user and his or her needs.

Visual Rhetoric as Persuasion

Much of the research on visual rhetoric has focused on advertisements, where the need for the client to persuade the viewer is paramount. But visual rhetoric also applies to the design of more "neutral" documents, such as manuals, reports, and proposals. Of these, proposals seem to rely the most on persuasion. When we write a proposal, we are by definition putting forward an idea to someone who can make a decision to accept or reject it. That proposal might be to convince someone to allow us to do a variety of things:

- To perform a service, such as offering to design a website (a services proposal)
- To provide a product at a particular cost and under certain conditions (a sales proposal)
- To do a project that someone finds worthy of financial support (a grant proposal)

In all of these situations, we must convince the decision-maker to allow us to do the work or provide the goods. We must also convince the decision-maker that our proposal is better than that of any competitor. What we say in our proposal is obviously important, but the visual design of our proposal can play a role in convincing the decision-maker that our proposal is the best. A proposal with a clear, usable, smart-looking design is often more convincing than one that looks confusing, awkward to use, or clumsy. In other words, a well-designed proposal reflects on us, making us look like we know what we're doing.

But do we need to convince a user of anything when we design a report or an instruction manual? Often, we do. Corporate annual reports, for example, often have a persuasive mission as well as a reporting mission. They not only report on the financial performance of the company, but they also make stockholders feel confident about the corporation so its stock price goes up. And corporations also hope their annual reports will encourage potential stockholders to buy stock in the corporation.

Even something as seemingly value-neutral as a set of product instructions must also convince users of a variety of things. For example, the instructions must convince users that the instructions are worth reading. The instructions must convince users that the instructions are authoritative and trustworthy. And they must convince users that the product the instructions explain was worth the cost of purchase. Finally, a well-designed set of instructions can persuade users that they should buy more products from the company.

With websites, it's particularly easy to see visual rhetoric at work. The Mint website (Figure 3.16) is a good example. Mint's product is a software tool that captures user information from a website that analyzes how many users visit the site, which pages they go to, and how much time they spend there. But many people who own websites might find statistical analysis intimidating. Mint's website counters this potential attitude toward statistics by offering an easy-to-use, clear, and stylish design. The designers used a sans serif typeface to make the design look open and inviting. They also used color to direct users to important information, like the main benefit of the software printed in green reverse text ("Mint helps you identify where the most interest is being generated and over what"). A few casually scattered screenshots give a sense of the graphical approach to statistics the software provides. In sum, the design of the website reiterates the main point of the software itself, making statistics look easy, interesting, and clear, rather than complicated and intimidating. This reinforcement helps potential users feel good about the product.

One way to look at the rhetorical strategies at work on this website is to separate them into three aspects of rhetoric first identified by Aristotle:

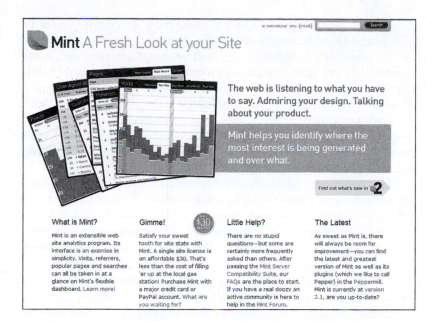

Figure 3.16 Persuading users with a friendly design. This website has a persuasive as well as informational purpose. It sells the product by making users happy with their purchase.

Shaun Inman Design & Development, Inc., <haveamint.com>.

- **Ethos** refers to the sense the user gathers of the speaker's character (or in our terms, the client's character).
- **Pathos** refers to aspects of the document intended to evoke an emotional response in the user (see pages 16–17).
- **Logos** refers to the logical or factual information conveyed by the document.

This rhetorical framework makes it easy to analyze how a document's visual rhetoric works and how well it works. In the case of the Mint website, the clear and simple design supplies useful information about the product (logos), encourages people to think Mint is cool (ethos), and makes people feel good about the prospect of purchasing the product (pathos). By itself, the visual design of the website can't compensate for a product that doesn't work well. But the design of the website at least contributes to a rhetorical argument for the product and the company.

Of course, this is only one rhetorical theory—there are many other alternatives, some more suited to specific document designs and situations. Kenneth Burke's rhetorical theory, for example, works particularly well in helping us understand how images can influence users. Burke analyzed rhetoric in terms of what he called the **pentad** of act, scene, agent, agency, and purpose.

Figure 3.17 (page 66) shows the privacy policy leaflet from the banker Wells Fargo, with a highly cropped photograph on the cover. From the photograph—and from knowing about Wells Fargo's origins

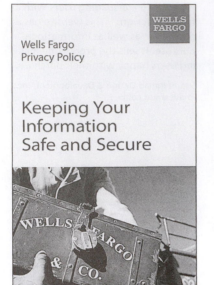

Figure 3.17 Influencing users through a photograph. This leaflet uses visual rhetoric to convince customers that the bank will keep information as secure as it once kept money and shipments in the Old West.

Wells Fargo & Company, "Keeping Your Information Safe and Secure."

as a shipping agent in the nineteenth-century American West—we understand that the *scene* is next to a stagecoach (which also serves as the company's branded imagery). The *agents* are the two people handling the strongbox. The *act* is that of the agent on the ground handing the strongbox up carefully to the agent on the wagon. The *agency*— the means by which the act is completed—is the strongbox itself, with its sturdy construction, prominent lock, and equally prominent label. The purpose for the agents' care in handling the box is clearly to safeguard whatever the box contains—keeping it locked up and handing it directly to someone trustworthy.

This application of Burke's rhetorical theory helps us understand what the designers were thinking when they chose this image for this design. Together, the Burkean elements in this dramatic scene imply that Wells Fargo employees today will guard our privacy from theft as carefully as their predecessors handled letters, papers, and currency shipped through the company across the dangerous western frontier.

In fact, this rhetorical analysis reveals that the designers probably *created* the image specifically for this purpose. The photograph is not a nineteenth-century original, but a photograph staged for this document (or similar documents that hinge on the idea of safekeeping). The analysis allows us to think about how we can create or use images in our own designs to reinforce the rhetorical purpose of the documents we create.

Visual Rhetoric as User-Centered Design

User-centered design recognizes that successful visual rhetoric requires not just a convincing visual presentation, but a design that helps users fulfill their own needs and agendas rather than just those of the client. This focus on the user is inherently rhetorical. As Robert R. Johnson argued, rhetoric is closely tied to user-centered design because it foregrounds the need for communicators to understand their audience.

Document designers have increasingly come to realize their responsibility to represent the interests of users in the visual rhetoric they create. But user-centered design is also smart from the client's perspective: it's easier for a client to convince a user of something if designers create a design that meets the user's needs and expectations. A successful user-centered design is said to have good **usability**.

To understand user-centered design more fully, we can turn our attention to one of its most prominent proponents: Jakob Nielsen. Although Nielsen's work has focused mostly on website design, it applies equally well for other kinds of document design. Nielsen suggests that usability can be defined through five variables:

- *Learnability:* The quality of the document that allows users to figure out how to use it. Users are likely to find more success with documents that are easy to learn.

> **DESIGN TIP**
>
> ## Designing through Visual Rhetoric
>
> When planning the visual rhetoric of your document design projects, think about how you want ethos, logos, and pathos to come into play:
>
> - **Ethos:** What image of the client should the document put forward? Does the client want to appear cool, hip, respectable, mature, solid, or something else?
> - **Logos:** What information will the document convey? What is the structure of that information? What's most important about the information, and what's less important?
> - **Pathos:** How do you want users to feel about the document — and by extension, about the product and the client?

- *Efficiency:* The ease and speed with which users can use the document. A document users find efficient to use is one they'll probably use more effectively.

- *Memorability:* How well the document helps users become habituated to its means of use. A memorable document is more likely to be used and used effectively.

- *Error avoidance:* How well the document helps users avoid errors — particularly navigational errors — and recover gracefully when they happen.

- *Subjective satisfaction:* How well the document convinces users of its utility. If the document fulfills a need, users will trust it and use it repeatedly.

These variables are only one way of looking at usability and user-centered design, but they foreground the importance of designing documents that meet users' needs and expectations.

Finding out what those needs and expectations are, however, can be a challenge. The most important impact of the user-centered focus in document design has been a growing attempt to understand users better. Designers do so by using two primary approaches: user research and usability testing (for more on these topics, see Chapter 10). They conduct **user research** to find out more about the users, employing a variety of techniques. For example, user researchers (or document designers wearing their "user-research hats") might conduct surveys to find out about the users' background, education, and other demographic information. Or they might conduct focus groups by gathering a group of potential users and asking their opinions about different subjects related to the document or about a draft of the document itself.

Rather than just asking users what they *think*, designers also conduct **usability testing**, asking users to perform a series of tasks with a document—for example, finding the customer service phone number on a website or following one procedure in an instruction manual. To provide more data for analysis, usability researchers often ask users to narrate their thoughts as they perform the tasks. The researchers record the user's attempts and study the recordings to find out where the document went wrong—that is, where the user had trouble completing the task. The goal is not to test the user, but to test the document against the user's real-world responses.

The goal of user research and usability testing is to explore how real users might use and feel about the documents we design. Employed together, these methods help us gauge how to respond to users' situations, in terms of both their visual abilities and their attempts to use a document within the context of all the other documents they have used—in other words, in terms of both visual perception and visual culture. For visual perception, user research in particular can help us understand whether potential users of a document have a perceptual limitation. If you're designing a document for a group of senior citizens, for example, you might want to find out how well most senior citizens can see. Or if you're designing a document primarily for men, you might want to know what effect color-blindness might have on their perceptions (about 8 percent of men have some impairment of color perception, as opposed to 0.5 percent of women). User research can also help us understand the cultural attitudes and conventions user groups bring to their interactions with documents. Usability tests can reveal whether the designs we create work, visually, as we intend them to. They can help us recognize where our designs fit in with users' cultural or conventional expectations and how we need to redesign documents to better fit their expectations.

From Theory to Practice

In this chapter, we discussed a variety of ideas about how users perceive their visual environment, both through their biological and psychological equipment and through their cultural and social expectations. Together, these two aspects of understanding how users see the world help us make good design decisions that fit both our clients' objectives and our users' needs through visual rhetoric.

Of course, we have scarcely touched upon many important theories. No one chapter—in fact, no one book—could provide a full account of all the theories of visual perception, visual culture, and visual rhetoric. But we encourage you to read further about these and other theories that might give your work as a document designer a stronger foundation.

Exercises

1. Find a document that you think is visually interesting for some reason. Then ask two people from different cultures to look at the document and tell you their responses. What do they like? Dislike? What elements do they find interesting or boring? Listen carefully to what they say and how they express it. Then write a report in which you describe the background of your two "viewers," outline what they noticed, and write a reflective comment in which you think about how their comments fit into (or don't) visual perception, visual culture, and visual rhetoric.

2. Choose a document or a website and discuss it from two of the perspectives we examined in this chapter. For example, you might analyze a web page from the perspective of visual perception and visual culture, or from the perspective of visual rhetoric and visual culture. What aspects of the design would the perspectives you have chosen explain differently? What aspects of the design would the perspectives you have chosen explain similarly? What insights did you gain from looking at this artifact from different perspectives?

3. This exercise will help you start thinking visually. Using only one page and no more than three abstract shapes, create a sign that expresses an idea. Try *not* to use any letters or words. Here are some ideas, but feel free to think of your own:

   > descend, flip, slow, accelerate, celebrate, move, dance, attend, avoid, enter, no, yes, pick up, drop, throw, push, pull

   After you've created your sign, write a cover memo for your classmates or your instructor in which you explain how your design will influence users, basing your argument on the concepts about perception presented in this chapter. How would people of different backgrounds or cultures respond to your design? In what situations would your design work best?

Works Cited

Boothe, Ronald G. *Perception of the Visual Environment*. New York: Springer, 2003.

Burke, Kenneth. *A Rhetoric of Motives*. New York: Prentice-Hall, 1950.

Findlay, John M., and Iain D. Gilchrist. *Active Vision: The Psychology of Looking and Seeing*. Oxford and New York: Oxford University Press, 2003.

Gibson, James J. *The Ecological Approach to Visual Perception*. Boston: Houghton Mifflin, 1979.

Hall, Edward T. *Beyond Culture*. New York: Anchor/Doubleday, 1971.

Hoffman, Donald D. *Visual Intelligence: How We Create What We See*. New York: Norton, 1998.

Johnson, Robert. *User-Centered Technology: A Rhetorical Theory for Computers and Other Mundane Artifacts*. Albany: State University of New York Press, 1998.

Kostelnick, Charles, and Michael Hassett. *Shaping Information: The Rhetoric of Visual Conventions*. Carbondale: Southern Illinois University Press, 2003.

Messaris, Paul, and Sandra Moriarty. "Visual Literacy Theory." *Handbook of Visual Communication: Theory, Methods, and Media*. Ed. Ken Smith et al. Mahwah, NJ: Lawrence Erlbaum, 2005. 481–502.

Nielsen, Jakob. *Designing Web Usability: The Practice of Simplicity*. Indianapolis: New Riders Publishing, 2000.

Palmer, S. E. "Common Region: A New Principle of Perceptual Grouping." *Cognitive Psychology* 24 (1992): 436–47.

Peirce, Charles Saunders. "What Is a Sign?" Chapter 2 of *The Essential Peirce*. Ed. Nathan Houser and Christian Kloesel. Bloomington: Indiana University Press, 1998. <www.iupui.edu/~peirce/ep/ep2/ep2book/ch02/ep2ch2.htm>. Accessed July 19, 2006.

Valesio, Paolo. *Novantiqua: Rhetorics as a Contemporary Theory*. Bloomington: Indiana University Press, 1980.

Further Reading

Barthes, Roland. *Elements of Semiology*. New York: Hill and Wang, 1977.

Booth, Wayne C. "The Rhetorical Stance." *College Composition and Communication* 14 (1963): 139–45.

Bruner, J. S., and C. C. Goodman. "Value and Need as Organizing Factors in Perception." *Journal of Abnormal and Social Psychology* 42 (1947): 33–44.

Debord, Guy. *The Society of the Spectacle*. Trans. Donald Nicholson-Smith. New York: Zone Books, 1995.

Gordon, Ian E. *Theories of Visual Perception*. New York: John Wiley & Sons, 1989.

Gramsci, Antonio. *The Antonio Gramsci Reader: Selected Writings, 1916–1935*. Ed. David Forgacs and Eric J. Hobsbawm. New York: New York University Press, 2000.

Handa, Carolyn. *Visual Rhetoric in a Digital World: A Critical Sourcebook*. New York: Bedford/St. Martin's, 2004.

Hill, Charles A., and Marguerite Helmers, eds. *Defining Visual Rhetorics*. Mahwah, NJ: Lawrence Erlbaum, 2004.

Jenks, Chris, ed. *Visual Culture*. London and New York: Routledge, 1995.

Meggs, Philip B. *A History of Graphic Design*. 2nd ed. New York: Van Nostrand Reinhold, 1992.

Mirzoeff, Nicholas, ed. *The Visual Culture Reader*. London and New York: Routledge, 1998.

Saussure, Ferdinand de. *Writings in General Linguistics*. Oxford: Oxford University Press, 2006.

CHAPTER 4

The Whole Document

Imagine you've just bought a car. You probably have questions about how to work some of the features, like the radio, lights, and so on. To find answers, you'll probably refer to the owner's manual at least a few times as you get to know your car.

But think for a moment about where that owner's manual must live and work. Normally, it's kept in a pretty dark and dangerous place (for documents, at least): the glove box, where it has to contend with not only gloves but a flashlight; a wad of napkins, straws, and ketchup packets from the last drive-thru you visited; a handful of assorted pens and pencils; and perhaps even a screwdriver and a pair of pliers. All sorts of objects tailor-made to poke, bend, rip, crease, and otherwise mess up a typical document. Then there are the conditions under which it's used in the car. It has to stand up to the abuse of being repeatedly pulled out and tossed into the glove box. Plus, it has to help you find information quickly, when you need it. It can't be too big to use while you're sitting in the driver's seat. But it has to be big enough to

Figure 4.1 A manual designed to work in a difficult environment. The designers of this brochure had to think carefully about the conditions in which it would be stored and used.

Mazda3 Quick Tips manual, 5½" × 4⅝". Used with permission.

Mazda3 manual in a user's hands.

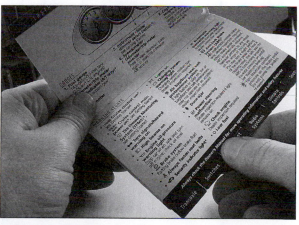

Using a tab to open to a page.

contain a lot of important information. And ideally, because we sometimes drive at night, it should be something you can make out easily by a dome or map light. On top of all that, it has to serve a rhetorical purpose: to make us feel good about having bought the car, so we might do so again someday or recommend the brand to our friends. Altogether, that owner's manual must do a tough job in a difficult environment.

Figure 4.1 on page 71 shows how one car manufacturer addressed this difficult job. This quick reference manual for a Mazda is a handy size, easy to flip through, and convenient to use in the car. Rather than being bound conventionally on the left, it's bound at the top edge to encourage easy flipping. To facilitate that pattern of use, it features a special trim on the bottom (outside) edge of each page to create a tabbed index. New owners of the Mazda3 can use the tabs to flip exactly to the point they wish to read. To manage that tough environment of the glove box, the manual is printed on heavily coated and varnished paper.

This example suggests that designing a document requires thinking not only about two-dimensional layout, colors, typefaces, and so on, but also about how the document will perform as a physical, three-dimensional object in a particular environment. As Charles Kostelnick has pointed out, aspects of the **whole document** (which he calls "**supra-textual elements**") have a significant effect on the way users interact with documents. So we need to think about the whole document and its place in users' lives.

What do we mean by the *whole* document? In Chapter 2, when we discussed design objects as a way to think about the marks we put on pages or screens, we noted that thinking of these marks as "objects" is simply a useful metaphor. But the *whole* document really is a physical object. Thinking about the whole document adds a third dimension to design: the document as a tangible, physical object with a front, back, depth, and weight, as well as two-dimensional width and height. In this chapter we consider the whole document as the physical aspects of any document design: the size of the document, its binding, the technologies used to produce it, the paper on which it's printed or the screen on which it's presented.

You might think it would be better when producing a document to begin with something smaller than the whole document, such as typography or page design. And sometimes designers *do* start with one feature — a color scheme, a typeface, a logo, an image, or even elements that show brand identity with the client's other products or publications. But the decisions you make about the whole document provide the context for all the decisions about the smaller parts. Addressing the big decisions first can help make those smaller decisions more manageable and efficient.

We'll begin this chapter by discussing the whole document through the perspectives of perception, culture, and rhetoric. Then we'll discuss two important whole-document design decisions: **medium** and **format**.

Throughout, we'll provide plenty of examples to help you make these decisions effectively in your own document design projects.

Three Perspectives on the Whole Document

Perception

People experience documents not just as two-dimensional visual fields, such as pages or page spreads, but also as three-dimensional objects they can touch. Printed documents have a weight and a relationship to the hand that can make them feel either natural or awkward to use. Even electronic documents take on the physical features of the hardware that embodies them, from the glowing pixels of the monitor to the software interface to the keyboard, mouse, or trackball we use to navigate the document.

Considering the whole document requires that we pay attention to senses other than just our vision: touch, hearing, and even smell. (Taste doesn't often come into play once users get old enough to read documents rather than to chew on them!) The sensation of touch can be affected by the quality and kind of paper and binding. The sense of hearing can help users navigate flipping through a printed document, and auditory clues (like clicks and beeps) can give users feedback in electronic documents. Even the smell of a printed document can have an effect on users, as some find that certain inks and papers have a strong odor.

These physical features of the whole document aren't just nuisances — they're integral aspects of our experiences with documents. To use what some scholars call **visual-spatial thinking**, users *need* these physical cues to understand the structure and content of a document (see Johnson-Sheehan and Baehr). You've probably used this kind of thinking when looking for something you had read earlier in a document. You might not remember the exact page number, but your spatial senses help you remember that it's near the end of the document or on the top of a right-hand page. Or you might even have changed your document physically for easy reference: adding a sticky note, dog-earing a page, or highlighting a passage in a document or bookmarking a page on a computer screen.

Culture

As three-dimensional, physical objects, documents have had a significant effect on culture. Entire academic fields, such as history of the book, bibliography, and print history, focus on exploring the history of printing, its key technologies, its products, and their effect on culture. Oxford bibliographer D. F. McKenzie referred to these studies as the "sociology of the book"—an examination of the web of people surrounding the creation and consumption of books, including authors, designers, printers, booksellers, and readers.

But a book is only one kind of document, and perhaps not the most culturally influential one today. For most people, the number of books they read pales against the number of other kinds of documents they encounter every day—what they receive in the mail (either snail-mail or e-mail); what they use to understand how to do their work; what they read as they browse the Internet. In many ways, Western culture has transitioned from the age of the book to the age of the document, a broader category that includes the many other kinds of document we live with. These documents have a significant and growing effect on what we do and on how we see ourselves, both individually and as members of a culture.

As a result of this ubiquity, even people who seldom think consciously about documents can have a very well-developed sense of document conventions. Although they might be hard pressed to name what characteristics make a document a technical manual, users typically know a technical manual when they see one. Conventions about the whole document can be very strong, which works both to our advantage and to our disadvantage. If we create a technical manual that firmly meets users' conventional expectations, they'll immediately recognize the manual for what it is, but it might not stand out very much. An unconventional manual might attract users' attention more quickly, but they might consider it annoying or off-putting because it flouts established conventions, and they might even resent having to learn how to use something new.

Rhetoric

The rhetoric of the whole document arises from its place in the user's life and experiences. In this sense, what matters isn't just the document itself but the ecology in which it's used—the physical environment of the user. Two ecological factors are especially important:

- *The occasion of use:* When will users use the document? Will they refer to it repeatedly, read it through only once, or use it some other way? What circumstances will motivate them to use the document?

- *The conditions of use:* Will the document be used in an office, a car, an airplane cockpit, a factory floor? Will the conditions be dry, wet, windy? Can users lay the document on a flat surface, or must they hold it in their hands? Will the document be fixed to a surface, displayed on a stationary screen, or appear on a portable screen such as a personal digital assistant or a cell phone?

Understanding these factors will help us create a document that is both convincing and usable in the user's specific environment.

More broadly, the physical design of the whole document can have a significant effect on how users respond both to the document itself and to the client who commissioned its creation. A document bound expensively with valuable materials gains an ethos of luxury, exclusivity, and professionalism. One bound cheaply — perhaps only stapled — carries a rhetoric of disposability. Sometimes disposability is appropriate, depending on the level of design the document merits. But on other occasions, a fancier whole-document design is crucial to convincing the user that it's valuable and important.

Making Decisions about Media

In simple terms, *media* (singular: *medium*) refers to the means by which a document is conveyed to readers. However, media are not neutral conduits; the medium of a document places significant constraints on its design, as each medium has different capabilities and limitations.

In document design, the two most significant media are **print** and **screen**. Print incorporates any document marked in some kind of ink on a physical page, usually made of paper, cardboard, or plastic. Screen incorporates any document conveyed to readers through an electronic viewing interface, such as a computer monitor or digital projector.

Making good choices about what medium to use for a given document design project can be a complex task. In this section, we'll discuss the following factors that affect decisions about medium:

- Conventions
- Human factors
- Transformation
- Cost

We'll also discuss single-sourcing, a technique for using more than one medium.

Conventions

When choosing the medium in which to produce a document, one factor to consider is the experiences users have had in receiving similar documents. These experiences can build very strong conventional expectations. If we break those conventions thoughtlessly, we risk creating a document that will make users uncomfortable, or even a document that users won't recognize.

Consider the humble memorandum, the long-standing embodiment of interoffice communication. For a century, memos were printed on paper and routed through an organization's mail system. To expedite writing memos, companies sometimes used a memo form, with blanks for the sender (From) and the receiver (To), as well as the date and subject. This convention of using the paper medium for memos is still common today, even though most companies use e-mail instead.

However, e-mail encountered resistance when it was first introduced primarily because it presented interoffice communication in an unfamiliar, unconventional medium — the then-high-tech green or amber text on a black computer screen. E-mail system designers overcame this problem by creating e-mail program interfaces that follow the conventions of traditional paper memo forms. Look at your own e-mail application, and you'll likely see the traditional fields for routing information (To, CC, Bcc) and a subject line, followed by a space in which to write the memo (Figure 4.2). Only the Date and From lines are omitted because the computer supplies this information automatically.

Figure 4.2 E-mail message form. An e-mail message form contains many conventions left over from paper memo forms, such as blanks for the receiver and the subject. The date and the sender are filled in automatically, making these blanks unnecessary.

If you do choose to use a medium different from what users expect, be prepared to explain the advantages of the new medium so users will be willing to give it a try. In recent years, users have often felt uncomfortable about documents that have transferred from print to screen. But increasingly, users complain just as loudly about documents on paper if they have become used to the additional functionalities of screen documents, such as search capability. In most cases, design documents to meet your users' expectations.

Design documents to meet your users' expectations.

Human Factors

User conventions are just one aspect of making a decision about medium. Sometimes the physical qualities of a medium make a big difference in users' abilities to use the medium effectively in their ecology.

Users experience a document's medium physically, as part of their tangible lives. We often think of media as being somewhat ephemeral, transitory, hard to grasp in a physical sense; pages decay, and screens change. At the very least, we might think of them as entirely two-dimensional spaces with only width and height. But print and screen media both involve users in multiple dimensions, incorporating depth (or the illusion of depth) and the passage of time. Paper has a thickness and a heft that users respond to, and users encounter paper documents sequentially, one page or spread at a time. Users' terminology reaffirms this sense of physical experience in time. In paper documents, we speak of a section of a document as being "before" or "after" another section; in websites, we use "back" and "forward" buttons to move through the sequences of pages we have viewed.

The same physical multidimensionality applies to screen documents because users encounter these documents on interface devices such as computers, which have depth and weight (as anyone who has juggled a notebook computer through an airport security check can attest). Good designers pay attention to the *human factors* of use regardless of what medium they choose.

Many human factors come into play in document design, but three particularly important ones can significantly affect our choice of medium: the medium's interaction with light, its resolution, and its manner of transmission.

INTERACTION WITH LIGHT: REFLECTIVE OR TRANSMISSIVE

All vision involves light, but light is generated differently in print and on screen. In print documents, light comes from some other source (the sun, a desk lamp, fluorescent overhead lights) and *reflects* off the page to our eyes. In screen documents, the screen itself *transmits* light to our eyes by turning on a pattern of glowing pixels.

This distinction is important because we must take into account the situations in which users will use a document. In low-light conditions — such as in a submarine or a mine — a document that transmits its own light might make more sense than one requiring a separate light source. In brightly lit conditions the opposite might make more sense: a paper document is easy to read in bright light, while too much light can make seeing a screen more difficult.

In addition, not all users have the same visual capacity; some can see better than others. Depending on their vision, users might prefer paper documents to screen documents. Or if their technological setup permits digital magnification, the opposite might be true. We must accommodate users by providing the document in a medium they can see easily.

> We must accommodate users by providing the document in a medium they can see easily.

RESOLUTION: HIGH TO LOW

To make good decisions about media, we also must consider the different resolutions of print and screen. *Resolution* is the fineness of detail that the medium can provide to viewers. Screens usually have a much lower resolution than print. Most screens are limited in their resolution by the size of the glowing, square pixels that make up the screen image. Computer monitors typically have a pixel size of less than 100 pixels per linear inch (ppi) — making each pixel 1/100 of an inch, easily visible to most human eyes. (Look closely at a computer monitor when it's displaying an image; you should see a grid of tiny squares, each of which is an individual pixel.) As a result of this relatively low resolution and the square grid of pixels, screen images are often jagged around the edges, particularly on curves or angled lines. Even the technological approaches to solving this problem have their own usability issues. Some computer systems, for example, smooth (or *dither*) the edges of letters to provide a gradient between the letter and the surrounding space — but in the process, they can make text look indistinct or even fuzzy. This fuzziness makes text less legible because it provides inadequate figure-ground contrast and poor edge discrimination.

Printed documents, even those produced on a garden-variety laser or inkjet printer, typically have a resolution of 300 dots of ink per inch (dpi) or better. So a printed document has a resolution almost ten times higher than the typical screen document: 300 dpi equals 90,000 dots in a square inch (300 wide × 300 tall), whereas a common screen resolution of 96 ppi equals only 9,216 pixels in a square inch (96 wide × 96 tall). The resulting dots in a printed document are usually difficult to see with the naked eye. Because the dots are made from microscopic blobs of ink, they also aren't square, allowing them to blend together more smoothly than do pixels on a screen.

The higher resolution of print is one of the biggest reasons users print screen documents before reading them, even if the documents aren't intended to be printed. A common user complaint with electronic documents is eyestrain, particularly for documents intended to be read at length. Designers also often choose print over screen when conveying information that requires fine detail, such as high-quality photographic images. But when it comes to documents that will be used only for brief periods, such as reference materials, users will gladly give up higher resolution in favor of convenient electronic searching or hyperlinked content. (For more information on image resolution, see Chapter 6.)

TRANSMISSION AND ACCESS

Deciding whether to produce a document in print or on screen involves accepting widely different means for getting the document to users. For the most part, print documents must be physically carried from one place to another, usually through shipping, mail, or direct distribution. Screen documents, however, can be broken down into electronic bits and bytes and transmitted through the Internet.

Each medium's method of transmission has advantages and disadvantages. But the biggest distinction is that documents produced in print are usually more **portable** than those produced for the screen, whereas those produced for screens are more easily **networked**.

Documents produced in print are usually more *portable* than those produced for the screen, whereas those produced for screens are more easily *networked*.

By *portability*, we mean the quality of a document that allows users to take it with them, to consult at any time they want. Books are a technology thousands of years old, but one of the reasons they remain popular is their portability. Users often appreciate a document they can stick in a pocket or shove in a briefcase, especially documents they might use as a reference. This is why we still call some documents *handbooks* or *manuals* (literally, "by hand").

This quality of portability means that print documents must be designed to fit comfortably in people's hands—not only the user's but also those of others who must handle the document, including sellers and shippers. For example, many print documents must fit into a package for shipping, and many leaflets and brochures are designed to carry postage and address information so they can be delivered through the mail. This dynamic gives many print documents a natural affordance to the human body: they're designed to fit *us*. Fortunately, print documents are also very durable, and they can still be read easily even after all the wear and tear they suffer because of their portability.

However, not all information fits us easily. What about a document that's too long to carry around physically or to find information in easily? That's where screen documents come in. Screen documents specialize not so much in portability as in *networkability*—the quality that allows users to access them over long distances through a network. This quality also allows screen documents to be linked to one another. A paper document might refer to another paper document, but the user must follow the reference manually—by physically getting the other document, either personally or by proxy (asking someone else to send it). But because most screen documents today are digital, they can be associated with each other easily, usually through a system such as the Web that allows searching, automatic indexing, and hyperlinks.

This networkability comes at the expense of portability and therefore of access. We might be able to access a screen document from many different networked screens, but taking the screens themselves around with us can be inconvenient. Even devices such as portable digital assistants (PDAs), cell phones, or notebook computers typically sacrifice ease of reading to increased portability (one reason that electronic books have thus far failed to capture a market). And although it might sound obvious, obtaining networked documents requires access to a network with its entire infrastructure, including sources of electrical power and wired or wireless data transmission. (How many times have you heard, "Sorry! The network is down"?) Despite today's wired world, a good one-third of U.S. residents don't have convenient access to the Internet, and fewer still have constant access. Outside of the United States and Europe, only a minority of people have access to consistent electrical power, much less the Internet. In contrast, print documents are always on, always ready to be used.

Transformation

These physical factors (light, resolution, and transmission) are important considerations when determining what medium is best for a given document. But screen and print documents also have an essential difference in their ability to transform.

Documents in print are relatively *static*; once they're printed, they stay that way. For some kinds of documents, that static nature fits the purpose of the document—for example, a company's sexual harassment policy document should probably stay the same for many months or years. The static nature of paper documents can also convey a sense of solidity to the document, building an ethos of stability for the client. Although annual reports are now often distributed as both print and electronic documents, the glossy, printed annual report will be around for a long time yet.

Documents produced for the screen, however, are quite *dynamic*, with the potential of changing thousands of times per second. This dynamic nature gives screens the illusion of movement—for example, by showing a few dozen frames per second of a video clip, animation, or progress indicator. It also allows electronic documents to change quickly according to user input. So a website might remember your information from the last time you filled out a form and already have many fields completed before you fill it out again.

One advantage of this dynamic nature is that electronic documents can be updated quickly and inexpensively because an electronic document is typically saved in one location (a network or Internet server) and simply accessed by many users through their computers. Updating a printed manual requires printing the manual over again, in however many copies are required; updating an online help system requires making the change only once and resaving the file that users will access through the network.

However, this distinction between static and dynamic isn't firm. Even some print documents are dynamic in that they are designed to be changed or modified after production. Some printed signs are designed so letters, words, or entire sections can be updated or replaced, and printed forms are designed so users can add their own information. A leaflet from a natural gas company (Figure 4.3) even includes a place for readers to scratch the printed flame so they can experience what a natural gas leak smells like. We also know that users often change print documents for their own convenience by folding, tearing, or marking them. And nearly all print documents created in business, government, or education today at least *start* as electronic documents—that is, as electronic files that are printed onto paper as a last step in the production process.

Conversely, users can and often do print documents designed for the screen, even if the designers never intended the documents to be printed. Users can also save networked electronic documents locally on their own hard drive, creating a static version of a dynamic page by saving it as a PDF or an HTML file.

When deciding in which medium to produce a document, consider how the document should or could change once it's in the user's hands, as well as how frequently it may have to be updated. Certainly, if the document must be updated regularly — such as a product catalog — consider the screen medium, where documents can be updated simply by making a change and saving it. If solidity or consistency is more important, however, choose print.

Cost

In themselves, print documents usually cost more to produce than screen documents. If you want to provide a print document to a thousand users, you must pay for a thousand copies. But if you want to provide an electronic document to a thousand users, you must pay for only one copy, which most users can access on their own computer screens.

But print documents often cost less per copy the more you print. The expense usually comes with setting up printing in the first place; after you've printed a hundred copies, printing a thousand more isn't typically that much more expensive. (Photocopying and laser printing are exceptions: the last copy costs just as much as the first one.) We must also take into account the whole cost of electronic documents — including the expertise required to create them, the constant maintenance they demand, and the infrastructure of power and networks required to get them to users.

Producing a document in color is also much more expensive in print than on screen. Most computer monitors today can show thousands of colors as easily and cheaply as they can show black and white. But printing multiple colors actually requires printing a document in multiple inks, which increases the cost considerably. (See Chapters 8 and 11 for more information on color printing technologies.)

Regardless of the medium, documents cost money. In choosing a medium for your own designs, pay attention to what makes economic sense for the situation.

Single-Sourcing: Having It Both (or Many) Ways

Up to this point, we've distinguished media as an exclusive choice designers must make between print and screen. But new technologies

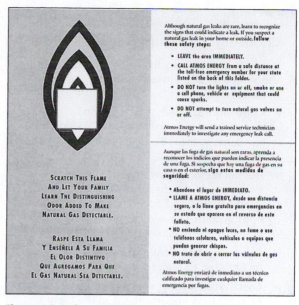

Figure 4.3 A dynamic paper document. Paper documents *can* be dynamic: this natural gas utility leaflet includes a scratch-and-sniff panel so users can learn what a natural gas leak smells like.

Atmos Energy.

DESIGN TIP

Choosing a Medium

Here are some factors to keep in mind when choosing a medium in which to produce a document.

- **Conventions:** In what medium do users expect the document to appear? What might the consequences be of going against those expectations?

- **Human factors:** How important is resolution to the use of the document? Do users most need a networked document or a portable one? Will they have access to a computer for an electronic document?

- **Transformation:** Will the document need to be updated frequently?

- **Cost:** What level of cost is justified by the project? How important is it to the client's mission? How many eyes will see it, and how important are they to impress?

allow designers and their clients to create documents that can take on print *and* on-screen forms, depending on the situation and the needs of users. This technique is often called ***single-sourcing***.

The basic idea behind single-sourcing is to create content once and then reuse it in multiple ways. For example, you might write the text and prepare the illustrations for a report separately and then use single-sourcing technologies to output that content to a website, a PDF, or a printed document, depending on user needs and demands. The train schedules in Figures 1.2, 1.3, and 1.4, pages 8–10, whether in print or on screen, were created from a basic set of consistent information: the actual schedule of train arrivals, departures, and routes.

In the most advanced forms of single-sourcing, the content is stored in a database or text file and assembled on the fly in whatever output medium the designers have planned for. To do so, the content is compiled in an ***eXtensible Markup Language*** (XML) file with ***metatags*** that describe each piece of content. For example, an XML file might include metatags to mark the title, author, date, headings, illustrations, captions, and paragraphs of a document. Metatags aren't visible to the user; they simply give computers a consistent way of identifying different elements in the document. Finally, a series of digital ***style sheets*** directs computers how to display each different kind of metatag when the document is ported to page or screen. For example, the style sheets might specify that when the title of a document is displayed on-screen, it will appear as 24-point Arial Bold, but that when the title is displayed in print, it will appear as 24-point Gill Sans. The advantage of this approach is that when you change the basic information in the XML file, those changes automatically cascade to all of the different kinds of output you have planned for.

As you might imagine, single-sourcing can be a complex task, and a full discussion of single-sourcing technologies is beyond the scope of this book (see Ann Rockley, Pamela Kostur, and Steve Manning's *Managing Enterprise Content* for more extensive coverage of this topic). But one very common technique for single-sourcing is to use simple Acrobat PDF files. As we mentioned earlier, PDFs already straddle the boundary between print and screen. They are an electronic file format that users can view on-screen either through the free Acrobat Reader program or through a web browser with the Acrobat Reader plug-in installed. But they can also be printed, coming out almost exactly like what was represented on-screen. So PDFs make for a nice compromise approach to single-sourcing if your client isn't up to the technological investment of more complex single-sourcing techniques.

Making Decisions about Format

Once you have decided what medium is best for your document design project, you must also determine what *format* will work best. By format, we mean all of the possible physical arrangements of documents within the medium, including size, shape, height, width, depth, texture, arrangement of pages and leaves, and so on. A document designer's primary goal in choosing or creating a format is to make the document's format fit its intended use and intended users.

Each kind of format has its own conventions and history, its own quirks and possibilities, its own manner of use that it suggests to users by its physical design. So in this section, we'll discuss how to make choices about what format might be best for your project.

Conventions in Format

Users often have well-developed conventional expectations about format, just as they do for medium. If you provide documents in an unfamiliar format, readers may feel uncomfortable using the document and either avoid using it or use it in a way you didn't anticipate.

Find out what format users expect to see for documents similar to the one you are designing. Then think carefully before choosing a format. Consider, for example, the experience of the mail order plant nursery White Flower Farm, whose catalog had been produced for more than 50 years in an unusual format: a 10½" × 8⅜", horizontally oriented booklet (see Figure 4.4 on page 84). The company decided to try a less expensive format, using a shape and size that has become common for many magazines: 7¾" × 10⅜" in a vertical orientation. But the earlier, horizontal format had *become* conventional for White Flower Farm's customers, who were frustrated by the new format.

Here's what the company had to say after it returned the catalog to its original shape and size:

Nostra Culpa

Last year at this time, we mailed our 53rd spring catalogue and the first ever in a vertical format. We made the choice for economic reasons, and, like many purely economic decisions, it turned out to be a mistake. We didn't like the way it looked or felt, and it wouldn't fit on the shelf with its predecessors. Worse, yet, it became impossible to find in the deluge of printed materials that swamps our desk.

> Find out what format users expect to see for documents similar to the one you are designing. Then think carefully before choosing a format.

Version A, landscape (horizontal) format, 10½" × 8⅜"

Version B, portrait (vertical) format, 7¾" × 10⅜"

Figure 4.4 Format and user expectations.   For more than 50 years, the White Flower Farm catalog used a horizontal format (version A). When the company switched to a cheaper, vertical format (version B), the new version broke customers' expectations, and they complained loudly.

White Flower Farm, Spring 2004, Spring 2003.

Judging by our correspondence, some of which was what the State Department calls "open and frank," you felt the same. So the natural order of things has been restored.

The title of this apology, which means "our fault" in Latin, suggests what a big mistake the company felt it had made in breaking the conventions it had established with users of its catalog.

This example shows the power of conventions. Users had come to expect something out of the company's information products — including a catalog distinguished from the many others in the market by its size and shape. The earlier format was also unusual enough to make it easy to find; the new format looked like all the other catalogs people constantly receive. Moreover, the new format didn't fit into the users' ecologies — the spaces (shelves, desks) where people kept the catalogs in their offices or homes.

Of course, you may determine that switching to an unconventional medium has so many advantages that defying convention makes sense.

An innovative format might meet users' needs so much better that it's worth the added time and expense to create something cool and new. There's also something to be said about the power of novelty to attract a user's attention. But be sure to *ask* users through usability testing what they think about an unusual format — preferably during the prototyping stage of the design project, so you can make changes *before* producing the document in its final form. (See Chapter 10 for more advice on useability testing.)

Formats in Print and Screen

With print, the number of available physical formats is vast. For example, in the print medium, we can create documents in formats like these:

- Brochures and pamphlets
- Leaflets
- Books
- Booklets
- Quick-reference cards
- Flyers
- Newsletters
- Signs

Why so many different formats? Because the essence of the print medium is *paper*, a material we can fold, cut, staple, stitch, punch, glue, and bind into a myriad of unique formats within the general categories above. Although most paper starts out rectangular, its flexibility — with its opportunities for folding, punching, perforating, trimming, and binding — makes the format possibilities almost endless.

It is also possible to create screens in many physical formats — that is, in different shapes, sizes, and arrangements. Early television screens were round; engineers are currently experimenting with screens that can be folded or rolled up; and a number of university media laboratories are experimenting with fully immersive interfaces — rooms with screens on the floor, the ceiling, and all four walls. A fascinating screen outside a downtown Chicago office building is 30 feet tall and twists like a ribbon down its length!

But for the vast majority of users today, all screens are in pretty much the same physical format: flat, rectangular, and wider than they are tall. This format places significant limitations on the possibilities for screen designs, constraining designers to what they can show in such a rectangular space. Of course, those limitations are balanced by the many flexibilities offered by a screen's dynamism as a medium, as we discussed earlier. Screens can display websites, digital kiosks, and touch-screen interfaces. They can be made in many sizes, from cell phone screens to Jumbotron sports scoreboards.

But because of the limitations of screen formats, in the following sections we'll focus on discussing a few of the many formats of print documents.

Variables in Print Formats

Choosing the right format involves weighing a number of factors, some of which are similar to those we considered in making a decision about what medium to use. The more complex your design, the higher the cost and the more time it will take to complete. So in the rest of this section, we'll discuss a number of common formats, moving from simple, fast, and cheap formats to more complex, time-consuming, and expensive ones.

Several variables come into play when designing a format for a document, but the most important are paper, folds, page shape and orientation, trims, and bindings.

MORE ABOUT . . . PHYSICAL AND ELECTRONIC FILE FORMATS

Although most screens have only one **physical format**, they can display many **electronic file formats**. An electronic file format is a computer standard for creating and reading files of some particular type, such as a word processing document, a page design file, or an image file. We can usually tell the electronic file format of a computer file by its **extension**—that is, the three or four letters after the period at the end of the file name (for example, .doc). However, these electronic file formats differ from physical formats in that they're essentially invisible to users and meaningful only to computers.

However, document designers use electronic files to *create* most documents today, whether they're to be printed or displayed on-screen. So to create effective documents through computer technologies, you need to explore the possibilities and limitations of the file formats you'll be working with.

For print documents, common electronic file formats include InDesign files (INDD), QuarkXPress files (QXD), and Microsoft Word files (DOC). These file types are usually either printed directly or translated to other file types for electronic delivery.

Other file formats are designed to stay electronic—most often, to be delivered through a web browser. The most obvious are web pages, which are formatted as HTML files. Some of these files are written as static documents; others start with a computer script in a file format such as Active Server Pages (ASP) or PHP Hypertext Processor (PHP), which take information from a database and assemble an HTML output on the fly. Electronic file formats also include those that require a browser plug-in or helper application, such as Flash and Shockwave (SWF) animations and Adobe Acrobat Portable Document Format (PDF).

PDF is also the most print-like of all electronic file formats, since a PDF file holds the electronic description of a printed page that can be sent directly to a computer printer. In fact, many print shops now ask that print jobs be delivered to them as a PDF, since that file format can include all information about typefaces, images, and layout in one file or a series of connected files.

DESIGN TIP

Choosing a Print Format

Consider the following issues when choosing a format for your document.

Client Issues

- **Rhetorical purpose.** What agendas does your client want to fulfill with the document?

- **Level of design and cost.** What level of design does your situation call for? Is this a mission-critical document that would benefit from expensive special features like unusual formats, trims, bleeds, or perforations (high-level design)? Or is it something more humble and basic, where extra expense would simply be wasted, calling for a low-level design?

- **Production capabilities.** What production capabilities do you have? Will you be working with just a desktop computer and a laser printer, a copy center, or a full-service print shop? The more complete the production capabilities, the greater flexibility you will have in deciding on a format.

- **Distribution.** Will the document be packaged in a particular-sized product box? Will it be mailed? If so, sizing it in a common postal size will keep costs down.

User Issues

- **Conditions of use.** How, where, and under what physical conditions will users use the document? How will they handle the document? Will they want to flip through it, lay it flat, or hang it on a wall? Will they use it in a wet or windy environment? What else will users be doing while they look at the document?

- **Interaction.** Will users want to write or mark on the document? Will the document incorporate a worksheet? Do you want them to fill out a form or survey and return it to you?

- **Conventions.** In what format will users expect the document to be presented? Expectations about formats can be very powerful; if you present information in an unexpected format, users might not recognize the document as something they need.

- **Storage.** Will users keep the document in a file drawer? Post it on a wall? Throw it in a toolbox?

- **Longevity.** Will users refer to the document frequently or read it only once and discard it?

PAPER

Paper can have a huge impact on document format. New designers often start with a sense that all paper is 8½" × 11" (letter size), but this couldn't be farther from the truth. Although it's more economical to stick with commonly available sizes, documents can be produced in nearly any dimensions a job requires, from business cards to billboards. The only limits are the original sheet size from the manufacturer and your print shop's cutting and printing capacity.

We can also take advantage of many different kinds of "paper" for special applications such as cover stock and packaging materials — everything from standard photocopy paper to high-tech plasticized sheets to cardboards.

Keep in mind what paper you intend to use for different purposes from the very beginning of the design process. (For more information on specifying paper for your designs, see Chapter 11.)

> Keep in mind what paper you intend to use for different purposes from the very beginning of the design process.

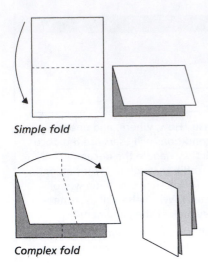

Simple fold

Complex fold

Figure 4.5 Simple and complex folds.

FOLDS

The size of a document ultimately depends both on the size of the original paper sheet and on how the paper sheet is folded. Sheets can be folded either with *simple folds*—one or more parallel folds—or with *complex folds*—one or more folds across a previous simple fold (Figure 4.5).

The finished, folded size of documents is often a consideration in design, since documents have to fit particular conditions of use and storage. Many documents are sized to fit in standard leaflet racks, for example, or to fit in product packaging. In general, the more folds incorporated into the format, the greater its flexibility as a space for accommodating different kinds of information. But with more folds comes greater complexity, particularly in terms of layout and production.

Folds break up the surface of the sheet into smaller pages or panels, which can be used individually or in combination to fit different kinds of content (Figure 4.6). Generally, *page* refers to one side of one *leaf* of a bound format. In a book, for example, each leaf would contain two pages: the front or *recto*, which is visible on the right when the book is held open, and the back or *verso*, which is visible on the left. *Panels* are the areas formed by folds on the same side of a sheet. A single sheet folded in thirds would have three panels on the inside and three on the outside. All of the pages or panels visible when you open a document out flat are collectively called a *spread*.

Pages, panels, and spreads serve as natural areas in which to divide and organize content. Content can be designed to stay within individual panels or to extend over two or more panels of a spread, lending great flexibility to the design.

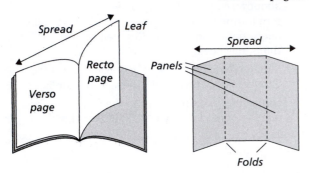

Figure 4.6 Pages, leaves, panels, and spreads.   Each leaf has two pages, recto and verso.

PAGE OR PANEL SHAPE AND ORIENTATION

Pages and panels are generally (although not always) rectangular. If the dimension of the document running parallel to the text is narrower than the dimension running perpendicular to the text, the document is said to have a *vertical* or *portrait* orientation. If it is wider than tall in relation to the text, we say it has a *horizontal* or *landscape* orientation. (See Figure 4.4 on page 84 for examples of these orientations.)

The relationship between the height and width of a page, panel, sheet, or even screen is also referred to as its *aspect ratio*, represented in terms of the numerical relationship between width and height, in that order. For example, the landscape version of the White Flower Farm catalog in Figure 4.4, at 10½" × 8⅜", has an aspect ratio of about 21:17. The portrait version of the catalog, at 7¾" × 10⅜", would have an aspect ratio of about 3:4.

It's particularly important to pay attention to page or panel orientation because of the constraints it places on text. Readability decreases if lines of text are either too long or too short. If pages or panels are oriented vertically, they might constrain text enough to decrease readability because the lines are too short. If the pages or panels are oriented horizontally, they might encourage us to use too long a line of text. In that case, you might have to divide the page or panel into columns of text. Large formats, such as tabloids, also need this treatment because even though they might be oriented vertically, they're still wide enough to make line length a potential problem. (See the discussion of grid systems in Chapter 5 for more information about laying out text on pages.)

TRIMS

Paper can also be trimmed to a special size before printing, or it can be trimmed after printing to its final size and shape. Most straight trims are made with a *guillotine* or *shear*—electrical or hydraulic machines that can cut cleanly through a thick stack of paper in one stroke.

Patterned trims are called *die-cuts* because they're created with a specially shaped cutter known as a *die* that presses through the sheets. The tabs on the Mazda booklet in Figure 4.1 on page 71 were die-cut so users can thumb to the section they want to consult.

Paper can also be trimmed after folding and binding (see the next section) to create many sheets from one larger sheet. Most books are created this way. Between 4 and 32 pages are printed on a large sheet. The sheet is then folded, bound, and trimmed on the top and front edges of the book to release the individual pages. This technique makes laying the pages out on the sheet rather complex, but fortunately, a print shop will take care of this aspect of your work for you (see Chapter 11).

BINDINGS

Binding allows us to use multiple sheets in the same document. Binding methods include stitching (stapling), sewing, gluing, and mechanical binding (see Chapter 11). Through binding, you can add a sturdy cover, if necessary, to protect the document from handling and extend its service life. Covers are also a great way to inform users about the document's contents and advertise its importance.

COMBINING THE VARIABLES

The variables of print format discussed in the previous sections interact to create the finished document. The document format — its general size and orientation — starts with sheet size but is then modified by how that sheet is folded and trimmed. This multiplies the options for document format tremendously. In the rest of this chapter, we'll discuss some of the more common print formats to give you a sense of some of these options.

To help keep track of these many variables, please refer to the table on page 91, which lays out some common formats in a range of complexities. The formats are grouped into two types: one-sheet formats and multiple-sheet formats.

Of course, this is a simplification of the most common formats — there are many others available, and a number of variations you should have in your toolkit of techniques. So after examining each of the formats in turn, we'll discuss a few special options that can add functionality or interest to document formats.

One-Sheet Formats

One-sheet formats are simple to design and easy to produce, so there are many common formats in this category. Because of their simplicity and economy, documents in these formats are useful for functions from basic office communications, such as letters and memos, to basic public communications, such as flyers, information sheets, product instruction sheets, and folded leaflets. Because they use only one sheet or leaf of paper, these formats are known as *leaflets*.

One-sheet formats are often produced on laser printers or photocopiers, so they often start from the standard letter-sized paper (8½" × 11") or legal paper (8½" × 14") that fits into these machines. But that doesn't mean that we have to use these sheet sizes with one-sheet formats. A full-service print shop can easily make unconventionally sized one-sheet designs. Even most standard office copiers and laser printers can accommodate European sheet sizes such as A4, which is slightly taller and narrower than the U.S.-standard 8½" × 11" letter-sized paper (see Chapter 11 for more information on paper sizes).

ONE SHEET, NO FOLDS

Documents formatted as one sheet with no folds are designed to fit either just one side or both sides of the sheet. They might be folded for distribution (for example, as business letters are often folded in thirds to fit into business envelopes), but these folds are not typically part of the visual layout of the document.

Simple to Complex Formats

Simple ⎯⎯⎯⎯⎯⎯⎯⎯⎯⎯⎯⎯⎯⎯⎯⎯⎯⎯⎯⎯⎯⎯⎯▶ *Complex*

One-Sheet Formats

NO FOLDS

For correspondence, flyers, information sheets, specification sheets, and signs.

SIMPLE FOLDS

One simple fold (folio): For simple brochures, pamphlets, and basic newsletters.

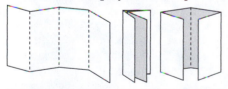

Two simple folds: For 3-panel brochures.

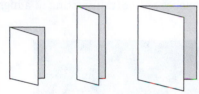

Three or more simple folds: For 4-panel brochures.

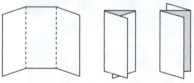

COMPLEX FOLDS

For information sheets and product instructions. Often folded to fit packaging or to promote a particular order of reading.

Multiple-Sheet Formats

STACKED SINGLE SHEETS

For basic reports, memos. Often stapled or drilled for three-ring binders, comb binding, or spiral binding. May also be glued for square-back (perfect) binding.

GATHERED FOLIOS

For pamphlets, booklets, and newsletters. Stitched (stapled) at fold.

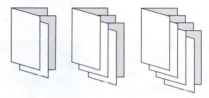

STACKED SIGNATURES

For long manuals, reports, and other square-backed books. Signatures in folio, quarto, octavo, and so on (see Chapter 11). Stacked, then sewn or glued into a binding.

Complex

No-fold one-sheet formats often work best where the entire sheet will be easily visible, such as flyers and information sheets intended to be posted on walls, bulletin boards, or other flat surfaces. These documents often serve a marketing purpose as well as an information-delivery purpose, so they can often involve a high level of design to attract the attention of passersby—as you can see from NASA's flyer promoting its new moon exploration initiative in Figure 4.7.

Because they might change frequently, no-fold one-sheet documents can also incorporate a relatively low level of design. And because documents with a low level of design can be produced very quickly, you'll often see them used for temporary signs or notices.

No-fold one-sheet formats are also used for standard business correspondence such as memos and letters because they're easy to distribute and require little design effort. These everyday documents also involve a low level of design because they are meant for a limited audience and deliver ephemeral (although sometimes important) information. But some business documents are worth investing in a higher

Figure 4.7 One sheet, no folds.
This flyer promoting NASA's new moon exploration initiative uses a high level of design to attract users' attention.

<www.nasa.gov>

Figure 4.8 Large single sheets can capture attention. This Chicago Transit Authority poster is sized to fit in the display rack of Chicago Transit Authority trains.

level of design; for example, it's not uncommon for a client to request a two-color or process-color stationery to impress readers.

Just because this format is used for business letters, however, doesn't mean that it's restricted to standard letter-sized paper. Larger sheets can be used to attract attention across greater distances or in specific local situations. For example, a poster encouraging Chicagoans to prevent children from falling out of windows (Figure 4.8) is sized precisely to fit in the curved display rack of a Chicago Transit Authority elevated train so that passengers can read it as they commute to work.

ONE SHEET, ONE SIMPLE FOLD

One-sheet formats with one simple fold are called *folio leaflets*. Folios (from the Latin for "leaf") expand the design and layout possibilities for a single-sheet document, giving us four panels or pages to work with — two on the outside and two on the inside. The front outside or cover panel is typically what the user sees first, so it's a good place for something important — a title or an attention-getting graphic. The back outside panel is useful for printing the user's address (if the document is to be mailed) or some background information about the client organization.

Remember, however, that a folio format requires some thought about the *imposition* of the panels — the way they're laid out on the sheet for printing. Because the sheet will be folded, the outside will hold panels 1 and 4, and the inside will hold panels 2 and 3 (see Figure 4.9 on page 94).

The size of the original sheet also makes a difference to the format, as does the orientation of the fold (see Figure 4.10 on page 94). Folios can also be large or small — anything from a credit card–sized folio that fits in a wallet to a newspaper tabloid size.

Figure 4.9 Folio impositions.

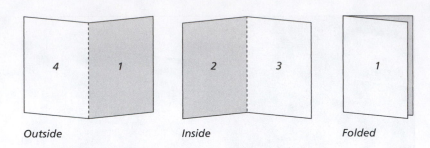

Outside   *Inside*   *Folded*

Figure 4.10 Folios in several sheet sizes and orientations.

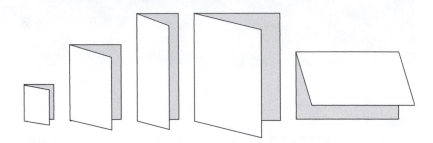

Folios can also be relatively tall and narrow or relatively short and broad, like the Dia de los Muertos leaflet in Figure 4.11, which is based on a full 8½" × 11" sheet folded across its length, resulting in a 5½" × 8½" finished format.

ONE SHEET, TWO OR MORE SIMPLE FOLDS

One-sheet formats can also incorporate two or more simple folds. Because multiple simple folds break up the page into multiple panels, these formats can increase the possibilities for design. For example, these formats allow for some interesting dynamics in how the panels become visible to users as they unfold the document.

Three-panel leaflets.   One of the most common such formats is the three-panel leaflet (see Figure 4.12 on page 96) — sometimes called a "trifold" leaflet, even though it actually uses two folds to make three panels on the outside and three on the inside.

Three-panel leaflets can be folded either in a *C-fold* or in a *zig-zag fold* (also known as an *accordion fold*). In a C-fold, the third leaf (panels 4|5) nests into the crease created by the first two leaves (panels 1|2, panels 3|6), so it must be sized a tiny bit narrower than the other two for the leaflet to fold flat. In this format, panels 1 and 6 almost always stand alone as the front and back of the folded leaflet. But the other panels can be combined into larger units: Panels 2, 3, and 4, the inside

Cover

Outside spread

Inside spread

Figure 4.11 A broad folio.   Notice how the designer extended content (the "In the Dead of the Night" event information and the picture of clouds) across both of the inside panels, tying them together into a visually unified spread.

Texas Tech University, "Dia de los Muertos" pamphlet (5½" × 8½" folded, on 8½" × 11" sheet).

Figure 4.12 Imposition of a three-panel C-fold leaflet. Two folds form three panels on each side. Leaf 4/5 must be slightly narrower than the other panels so it can tuck into the fold.

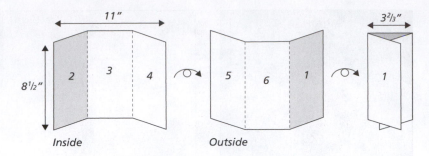

of the leaflet, can form either one large unit or two units (such as one spreading across panels 2 and 3 and a second taking up just panel 4). Zig-zag folded leaflets allow us to design spreads made from panels 2 and 3 and panels 5 and 6 (Figure 4.13).

Though a relatively simple and common format, three-panel leaflets can lead to both challenges and opportunities, primarily because we can never be sure in what order users will see the panels. Consider a typical C-fold leaflet (Figure 4.14). Users will usually look at panel 1 first—the "cover" of the leaflet (first view). But as users turn to look inside the leaflet, before completely unfolding it, they may pause to look at panels 2 and 5 (second view). We can design the leaflet so that 2 and 5 are seen as a unit or as separate content areas. If we design it as a unit, however, it still must make sense when users finally do open the leaflet all the way (third view). This flexibility of reading order provides a lot of opportunities for creative and interesting design, but it requires careful planning.

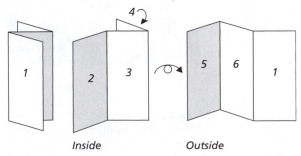

Figure 4.13 Zig-zag fold. A zig-zag fold offers different potential views to readers than a C-fold leaflet.

Figure 4.15 shows how a designer can unify two or more panels in a three-panel leaflet. Here, a colored field extends across the top of inside panels 3 and 4, and this design feature continues on the outside with panel 5. All three panels (3, 4, and 5) are thus made to look as if they are conveying information on a similar level—the details of three areas of content: "At Your Home or Office," "On the Go," and "At Your Service."

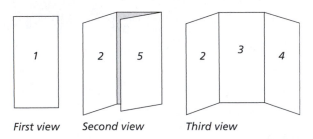

Figure 4.14 Revealing a three-panel leaflet. The way we fold a three-panel leaflet affects what readers see as they unfold the panels.

Four-panel leaflets. Of course, there's no rule restricting us to two simple folds in a sheet; designers often specify three or more folds. One common format is a four-panel leaflet, which starts from an 8½" × 14" legal sheet with three folds, making four panels on each side (Figure 4.16).

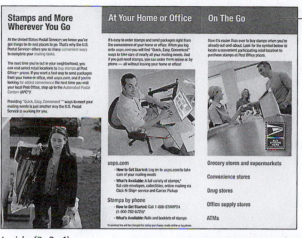

Inside (2, 3, 4)

Red field unifies panels 3 and 4

Red field continues on panel 5

Figure 4.15 Design features extending across panels.
This United States Postal Service C-fold leaflet uses a colored field on the inside spread to join panels 3 and 4, extending this field onto the outside on panel 5. The back (panel 6) is left for information about the publication and version information.

United States Postal Service Publication 611, April 2005, 3¾" × 8½".

Outside (5, 6, 1)

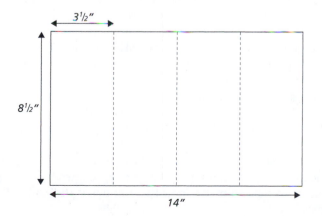

Figure 4.16 A four-panel leaflet.   Folds for a four-panel leaflet that will still fit in a three-panel leaflet rack.

3½"

8½"

14"

Figure 4.17 Folding patterns for four-panel leaflets.

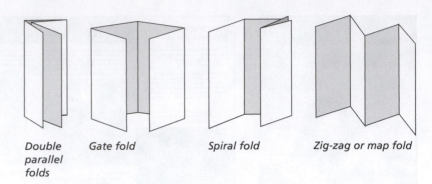

Double parallel folds   Gate fold   Spiral fold   Zig-zag or map fold

The advantage of this format when made from a legal sheet is that we get two more panels (front and back) than in a three-panel leaflet, yet the finished, folded size of the document is just a bit smaller than a three-panel leaflet built from a letter-sized sheet (14" divided by 4 panels = 3½"; 11" divided by 3 panels = 3⅔"). So both formats can fit in the same standard leaflet rack. Legal sheets can also fit in most office printers and photocopiers, keeping production costs low (and clients happy).

Four-panel leaflets can also be folded several different ways, which gives us a lot of flexibility of design (Figure 4.17). For example, the most common fold, *double parallel folds*, can use two different panels for the front cover. The first is similar to what we might see in a three-panel leaflet, with the cover set as the first panel on the outside (Figure 4.18).

This format gives users two options to see the interior of the leaflet: either turn just the first leaf (the cover) or turn two leaves (the cover leaf and the next leaf beneath it). Either way, the user must be presented with a logical display of information. If users turn only one leaf in the example in Figure 4.18, they will see two unrelated panels that nonetheless look visually unified ("Payments by Mail" and "Consumer Update Now Available in Spanish"). If they turn both leaves, users will see a coherent spread of two connected panels explaining "10 Easy Ways to Save Your Energy Dollars This Winter."

Alternately, double parallel folds allow one of the middle panels to serve as the "cover" panel, as you can see in Figure 4.19 on page 100. In this type of leaflet, users would open the cover panel to see the second view, two related panels providing information about the MallRide program. Users would then open these two panels to see the route map on three panels of the full inside spread. The final, back panel is reserved for contact information.

Of course, with these more complex formats, users are more likely to encounter a document in different ways than we expect. Arrange the panels in the format so that no matter how the user opens the leaflet, it will make sense.

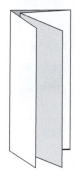

Figure 4.18 Leaflet in double parallel folds with cover on first outside panel.

Atmos Energy Corporation, "Consumer Update" pamphlet, 3⅜" × 6½" folded from 13" × 6½" sheet.

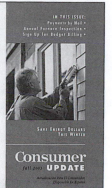

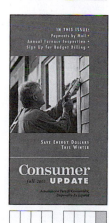

Cover

User opens one leaf to see two unrelated but visually unified leaves.

User opens two leaves to see two logically related panels.

Figure 4.19 Leaflet with double parallel folds. This format changes the viewing order of the panels.

Denver Regional Transportation District, "Free Mall Rides," (2608-04.01), 3½" × 8½" folded from 14" × 8½" sheet.

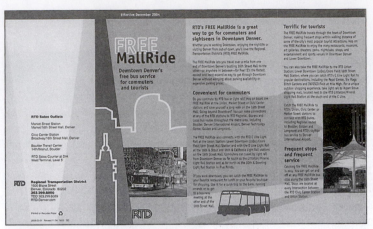

Outside spread

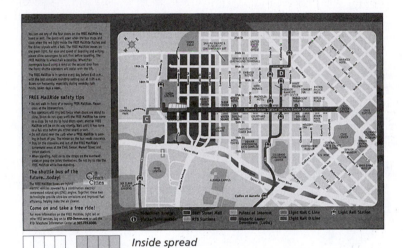

Inside spread

First view

Second view

ONE SHEET, COMPLEX FOLDS

Finally, we can use one sheet to make documents with complex folds (folds across a simple fold). You're probably most familiar with complex folds from highway maps, but complex folds are also used to format documents such as large instruction sheets that fold to fit product packaging. Besides using space efficiently, documents with complex folds end up with a natural grid that can be used to organize the content and affect what readers see as they unfold the sheet. (For more on grids in page design, see Chapter 5.) For example, the manual for a Palm handheld device in Figure 4.20 uses the complex folds to guide the user through the document.

First view

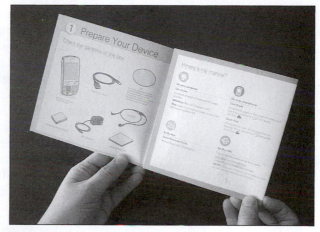

Second view

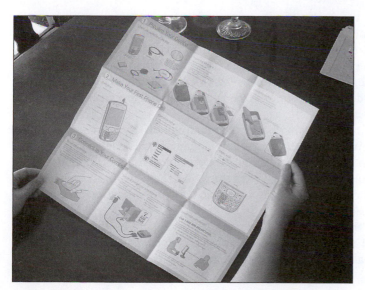

Third view

Figure 4.20　A complex fold document.

Palm, Inc. Trēo 680 smartphone: Read This First manual (5½" × 5½" folded, from 16½" × 16½" sheet).

The Palm manual starts from a 16½" × 16½" sheet, folded first with two horizontal folds and then with two vertical folds, resulting in nine panels on each side of the sheet. The resulting document measures 5½" square — the exact size of the CD-ROM envelope with which the manual is packaged. The designers draw users' attention to the cover panel by prominently displaying the name of the product (Trēo 680) and the title, "Read This First" (Figure 4.20, first view). Then when users flip the first fold open to see the interior of the leaflet, they are greeted with an equally prominent heading, "1: Prepare Your Device" (second view). Opening the leaflet further, they see groups of panels labeled for steps 2 and 3 (third view) — clearly a procedure the user must follow to set up his or her device.

However, it's equally easy to lead users astray by not paying attention to how they might interact physically with complex fold formats. Consider the example of a university bus route map in Figure 4.21. The route map starts with a standard 11" × 17" sheet, folded first in half to 11" × 8½" and then in thirds across the first fold to a finished size of 3¹¹⁄₁₆" × 8½" — small enough to fit in standard leaflet racks.

In most aspects, this format works very well. It provides clear information about the available bus routes, incorporating one combined route map and four individual route maps. But as the user unfolds the leaflet to read its contents (Figure 4.21, third view), one of the content areas — the combined route map, spreading across three panels — turns out upside-down from the user's perspective. This problem might not be fatal, but it makes the user flip the document upside-down to read the map correctly.

Multiple-Sheet Formats

Despite the wealth of options and advantages of single-sheet formats, some documents are simply too long to be delivered that way in print. There are also physical limits to the convenience of sheet size: we wouldn't want to design a single sheet that when unfolded was bigger than the user's desk or arm spread unless we had a very compelling reasons to do so (for example, when designing a large sign to be seen from a distance).

That leaves us with the dilemma of how to put together many sheets into one document. Early document designers managed this problem by stitching together sheets end-to-end, storing them either as a scroll or as a zig-zag folded stack. But these arrangements had definite usability disadvantages — particularly if the documents were ever dropped and unrolled!

So the scroll was superseded centuries ago by the *codex* format (plural: *codices*). A codex is simply a document formatted on multiple sheets, all bound together at a common spine at the left, right, top, or

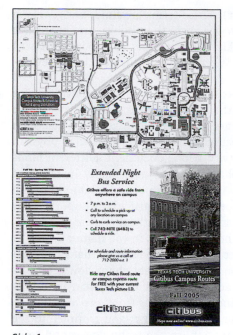

Side 1

Side 2

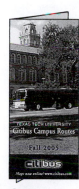

Cover

Figure 4.21 A confusing complex fold document.

Citibus, "Texas Tech University Citibus Campus Routes," Fall 2005 (3¹¹⁄₁₆" × 8½" folded, from 11" × 17" sheet).

First view: The user sees the cover of the Citibus route map pamphlet.

Second view: The user opens one flap of the pamphlet to see a bus schedule.

Third view: The user opens the second flap to find that the combined route map is upside-down.

bottom of the stack of sheets. The spine serves as a hinge allowing users to flip the individual leaves of paper back and forth. Naturally, over the centuries a lot of effort has gone into the design of this hinge, also known as a ***binding***. Together, the codex and its binding form an efficient, compact, and user-friendly package that is still the format of choice for lengthy documents, such as textbooks, long reports, or manuals.

Codices are more commonly termed ***books***, ***booklets***, ***pamphlets***, or ***brochures*** (from the French verb for "to sew," since codex bindings are often sewn or *stitched* together). These terms are fluid, but generally booklets and pamphlets have fewer pages than books, and brochures have even fewer pages than booklets or pamphlets. Any codex with hard covers (also known as *boards*) is generally considered a book, regardless of length.

In this section, we'll discuss several options for formatting documents as a codex, focusing on the different styles of binding available today. Some of these bindings are simple and cheap, others elaborate and expensive, but all are focused on meeting particular physical needs of users as they grapple with a long document. Different bindings have different usability characteristics, particularly in terms of durability and the ability to lie flat when open so users don't have to hold the document to use it. Opening flat is particularly important for instructional documents like manuals because the user's hands are usually occupied while following the instructions in the manual.

As we discuss multiple-sheet formats, keep in mind that we're talking about the format as the user handles it, not about how multiple-sheet formatted documents are actually created. In fact, many multiple-sheet formats are actually produced by printing from 4 to 64 pages on very large sheets, which are then folded, bound, and trimmed to the final page size. For more information on the technologies and techniques involved in this kind of approach, see Chapter 11.

STACKED SINGLE SHEETS

One of the most basic multiple-sheet formats is simply a stack of identically sized single sheets bound with some sort of simple mechanical binding, including paper clips, staples, three-ring binders, comb bindings, or spiral bindings. These bindings aren't fancy, but they are fast and cheap — sometimes fitting the constraints of a project perfectly.

Paper clips and staples.   Historian of technology Henry Petroski wrote in *The Evolution of Useful Things* that the staple and paper clip required significant technological development and went through many different forms before they were more or less standardized to the devices we know today. The styles we are most familiar with appeared only in the late nineteenth century; before that, people used straight pins, thread, or glue to hold together multiple sheets.

The ubiquity of paper clips and staples in offices today, even in the computer age, speaks to their success in meeting user needs by binding together a stack of paper quickly, cheaply, and conveniently. They also have the advantage of being removable (although paper clips are easier to remove than staples).

Naturally, paper clips and staples also have disadvantages. They have limited capacity — usually not more than 25 sheets, although some paper clips known as **binder clips** trade off a little convenience for a better grasp on thicker stacks. Because they are usually positioned at the top-left corner of the stack, paper clips and staples require the user to bend back the page over that corner rather than directly left as in a more substantial codex binding that extends down the whole spine. So paper clips and staples are hard on paper, either by design (the stapler punches holes) or by accident (paper clips rust or their ends snag on the paper as they are removed). Finally, paper clips must be applied manually, and staples require a stapler, which often jams and mangles the staples themselves.

But for low-level designs—those that need or deserve little investment in time, money, or personnel—the familiarity and utility of these devices make them indispensable. For short-run and ephemeral work, you can staple or paper-clip the sheets yourself, seeing your design through from inception to completion. For longer runs, some photocopiers include staplers, or you can ask a copy center or printer to staple a document for you. Printers and copy centers typically have machines that can staple pretty much anywhere on the sheet, and they can usually staple through three or four times more sheets than you can with a handheld stapler. However, they may balk at paper-clipping any long document runs, since doing so would require significant (and expensive) manual labor.

Binders. In the past two decades, many new binder designs have become available, with a variety of clips, grippers, and plastic sleeves to bind individual sheets into a codex. Many of them work well for small-run document design jobs, but they tend to be fussy, requiring lots of manual effort to get them on the sheets. Binders also tend to keep the document from opening flat because they grip about a half-inch of paper at the spine.

But one older binder technology still works well, even though it is just a step more elaborate than paper clips or staples: the **ringed binder**. You're probably very familiar with the standard three-ring binder, which comes in a variety of thicknesses and colors. As a technology, binders require a simple piece of office equipment to punch, or **drill**, holes through which the binder's rings extend to hold the sheets. These machines can drill either single holes or consistently spaced multiple holes. Or you can ask a copy center or printer to drill your document to your specifications.

Like staples and paper clips, ringed binders are a simple technology with many formatting advantages. Ringed binders also allow easy access to both sides of the sheet, they will lie flat, they're relatively sturdy, and users know how to use them. It's also easy to include tabbed dividers of cardboard or plastic to separate the sections of a document so users can access its contents easily. Ringed binders also work well for documents that must be updated occasionally. Reprinting the entire document would be too expensive, but if the document is in a ringed binder, outdated pages can easily be replaced. This time-honored technique requires careful version control; you must keep track not only of the correct version of the document but of each page, as well. It's still a workable system, though, especially if the document is one that wouldn't translate well to a computer screen. Binders are also pretty tough, so they're a good choice for reference documents.

However, ringed binders are hard on paper. Most hold each sheet by only three points, making it easy for a user to rip out a sheet inadvertently. Drilled holes, particularly on the first or last sheets, also tend to rip if the document is very thick or if it's crammed into a binder that's too small. Manufacturers are constantly looking for ways to make the holes stronger, but it remains a basic weakness of the format.

Comb and spiral bindings. A further step up the ladder of technological complexity brings us to *comb bindings* and *spiral bindings* (Figure 4.22).

Comb and spiral bindings extend the binder concept by using several holes instead of just three. Comb bindings insert a series of curved "fingers" through these holes, and as the name suggests, spiral bindings use a continuous spiral of wire or plastic inserted through the holes. Both types are available in wire or plastic, and both have the advantage of allowing a document to lie flat. But spiral bindings also allow users to bend the spine completely back.

Wire spiral bindings require an expensive machine to run the spiral wire through the row of drilled holes, so they're usually an option only if you are working with a professional printer. However, the equipment required for plastic and wire comb bindings is relatively inexpensive, and many offices and copy centers have those machines.

Perfect bindings. *Perfect binding* is the trade term for what are more commonly known as "paperback," "softcover," or "squareback" bindings. Perfect bindings use a hot-melt plastic glue to bind sheets together along the spine. Typically, the stacked sheets are fanned at an angle before the glue is applied to the spine. After they are straightened up again, placed in the cover, and clamped, a little bit of glue remains between each sheet, holding them all together and sticking them to the cover. Well-equipped print shops often have machines that can do all this in one pass.

Perfect bindings are durable and sharp-looking, but they're also more expensive than the other bindings we've discussed, primarily because they require special equipment and supplies. They also create a document that does not lie flat well, particularly if the cover stock

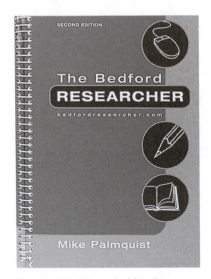

Figure 4.22 Wire spiral binding.

Mike Palmquist, *The Bedford Researcher.* 7¼" × 9½".

is very stiff. One compromise is to score the cover stock about one quarter-inch out from the spine, which creates a hinge point that allows the binding to fold open a bit more easily.

GATHERED FOLIOS

One simple way to bind multiple-sheet documents is to format them as gathered folios (Figure 4.23). As you'll recall, a folio is just a sheet folded in half. If we nest several folios together, they can be *stitched* with one or more staples in the fold to create a quick and inexpensive binding. This technique is also known as *saddle-stitching* because the nested folios are laid over an angled block that looks like a saddle for the staples to be inserted.

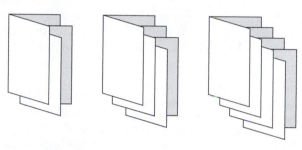

Figure 4.23 Gathered folios.

Gathered folios are a very usable format for mid-level design documents, including event programs, longer pamphlets or brochures, and mid-length instruction booklets (up to around 80 pages). The format lies open well, and it also allows us to use a cover stock of a somewhat thicker paper to increase the document's durability and raise its level of design. Because each folio is made from a different sheet, you can choose which sheets should be printed in color. It's common, for example, to use a color folio cover around an otherwise black-and-white document.

But gathered folios run into a couple of problems when the document gets very long. First, the more folios nested together, the more likely the document won't stay closed, particularly if the paper is relatively stiff. Second, because of the thickness of the paper, each nested sheet sticks out a little farther on the fore-edge than the previous sheet did, leading to a condition called *creep* (Figure 4.24).

Depending on the thickness of the paper, creep can become evident in as few as four or five gathered folios. The creeping edge is often trimmed off at the very end of the production process, but this can cause problems with the fore-edge margin, which gets smaller and smaller for the folios sticking out furthest (that is, those in the center of the gathering). Fortunately, most page layout programs can automatically adjust for creep to eliminate this problem.

Figure 4.24 Creep at the fore-edge of gathered folios. Creep happens when several folios are gathered together; each nested sheet sticks out a little farther on the fore-edge than the previous sheet did.

STACKED SIGNATURES

For longer documents, such as books, nested folios won't work as well as multiple stacked *signatures*—essentially, stacks of gathered folios that can be bound together. A signature is a single sheet with multiple pages printed on it—typically between 4 and 64 pages. After printing, the sheet is folded so that the pages line up in the correct order. Multiple signatures can then be stacked and bound before they're trimmed on the top edge, bottom edge, and fore-edge, releasing the individual leaves. After several signatures are stacked, bound, and trimmed, they are actually just a stacked collection of gathered folios, usually of two, four, six, or eight sheets each. (Chapter 11 discusses this production technique in more detail.)

A bound stack of signatures can also be glued into a square-back, perfect binding, just as in a perfect binding of single sheets. Or the bound stack can be inserted into a *case binding* (Figure 4.25). Case bindings are formed by binding together the signatures first, by either sewing or gluing. Then the bound signatures are glued into a previously prepared "case" composed of the hardcover boards, the spine, and the cover fabric. Most hardcover books have case bindings.

Case bindings are extremely durable and friendly to the users' hands. When closed, they stay closed, and they lie open more easily than perfect bindings. They are impressive, giving the document an air of importance. But they're also among the most expensive of all the bindings used in document design, and they definitely require the services of a full-fledged commercial print shop.

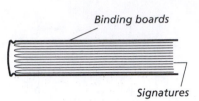

Binding boards

Signatures

Figure 4.25 Stacked signatures in a case binding, viewed from the top edge. The case is made of fiberboards covered in fabric or strong paper and joined together to cover the spine.

Special Features

For projects that merit a higher level of design, a variety of special features can add interest or functionality to a document's format. Most of these special features require the services of a commercial print shop, and although they add considerably to the unit price of the document, sometimes rhetorical or practical situations call for spending a little extra money. In this section, we'll discuss three special format features often used in document design: trims, perforations, and composite formats.

SPECIAL TRIMS

Special trims are typically performed after a document is printed on an oversized sheet. For example, if you want part of the design to extend all the way to the edge of the finished document (called a *bleed*), the document must be printed on a slightly larger sheet, leaving a half-inch or so of paper all around for the printing press to grab (Figure 4.26). The paper is then trimmed to its finished size to remove the unprinted edges. Naturally, this increases the cost of the printing because it requires larger, specially sized paper. To finish with a trimmed sheet of 8½" × 11", for example, you'd need to start with an original sheet size of about 9" × 11½".

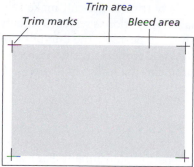

Trim area

Trim marks   Bleed area

Original sheet   *Trimmed sheet*

Figure 4.26 Trimming a bleed. If part of a document's design extends to the very edge of the page, it must be printed on a larger sheet and then trimmed to its finished size.

Other special trims can be much more elaborate. For example, the leaflet in Figure 4.27 is trimmed square on three edges but in a complex die-cut shape on the fourth. When the leaflet is folded, this die-cut makes the different images stack up, giving a dramatic, three-dimensional effect.

Side A

Figure 4.27 Die cutting. The special die-cut at the top edge of this leaflet gives a three-dimensional appearance to the images when the leaflet is folded.

Holiday Inn, 3 1/16" × 9", from 15 1/4" × 9" sheet, die-cut.

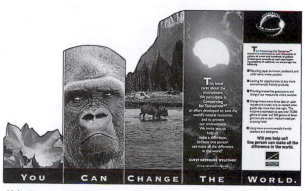

Cover, folded   *Side B*

But before deciding to use a specialty trim or die-cut, make sure that some rhetorical, practical, or usability function is served. Specialty trims are quite expensive, and they tend to decrease the durability of the document by creating unusual edges and corners that inevitably get bent back or torn. To counter this problem, the leaflet in Figure 4.28 is printed on heavily varnished paper.

PERFORATIONS

Perforations allow users to tear away a part of a document. For example, a leaflet from the Corcoran Gallery in Washington, D.C., explains the benefits of membership in the gallery and includes a two-panel tear-off membership application (Figure 4.28).

After tearing off the membership form and filling it out, users can fold the torn-off panels in half, lick a gummed area to stick them together, and pop the application in the mail using the prepaid postage. This format encourages a pattern of use: read the pamphlet to

Figure 4.28 Perforations. This leaflet for an art museum includes a perforated tear-off membership application form. The form can be filled out, folded, glued or taped, and sent in the mail, with the postal information and postage already provided.

Corcoran Gallery of Art, "Join" leaflet. 4" × 9¼" folded, from 9¼" × 23½" sheet.

Side A

Cover

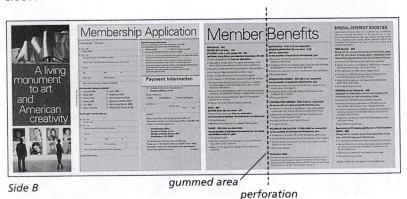

Side B

understand the benefits and then tear off, fill out, and mail the application to join — easy, useful, and user-oriented!

COMPOSITE FORMATS

Finally, you can combine some of the formats we have discussed to create documents with composite formats. An example of a composite document is a brochure from the Denver Museum of Outdoor Arts in Figure 4.29.

At first glance, it seems a simple gathered folio with a colored band printed on the cover. But on closer examination, the printed band is a much smaller folio stitched to the outside of the larger gathered folio.

Turning to the inside, the user finds only two folio sheets, but within the folio sheets is nestled a four-panel leaflet that folds out to show a schematic of the public art a pedestrian would see following a planned viewing walk. The leaflet is stitched into the folio at one of its folds, and the whole package folds up to a convenient 6" × 11"

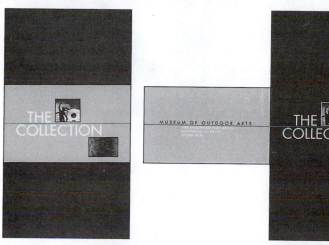

First view   *Second view*

Third view

Figure 4.29 A composite format: two sizes of folio and a leaflet. The outermost folio of this brochure is in a smaller format than the rest, adding some visual interest. The stitching holding the folios and the leaflet together is between the first two panels of the spread shown in the third view, with the other two panels folding out to show additional graphics and the map.

Denver Museum of Outdoor Arts, "The Collection" brochure. 6" × 11" folded, from three gathered folios and inserted four-panel leaflet.

Cover image: Edward Hopper, *Ground Swell*, 1939, oil on canvas, 36½" × 50¼". In the Collection of the Corcoran Gallery of Art, Washington DC, Museum Purchase, William A. Clark Fund.

size—just right for carrying with you as you go on your walk. In other words, this single document combines two formats of folios with a four-panel leaflet, making a flexible and interesting composite document.

Another example of composite formats is a booklet from the British Library advising patrons on how to order photocopies and other reproductions (Figure 4.30). Overall, it's a simple folio booklet with a card stock cover measuring 9" × 12". But the designers have designed a pocket in the inside back cover, which holds the appropriate forms to order reproductions of library holdings.

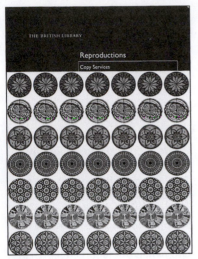

Cover

Figure 4.30 Another composite format: booklet and order form. The back cover of the stitched booklet has a pocket to hold an order form.

British Library, "Reproductions," 9" × 12".

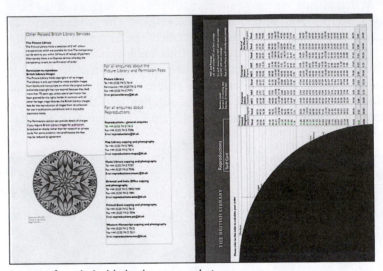

Request form in inside back cover pocket

Exercises

1. Observing how users use documents in their own ecology can be fascinating. Go to a workplace and explore how documents are physically used there. Workplaces other than offices can be particularly enlightening: consider places like construction sites, factories, police stations, or restaurants. Ask if you can talk to some of the employees about the documents they use and observe them during work for an hour or two.

   Ask them these questions during your visit:

   - What documents are essential to your work? (Remind interviewees that documents aren't just reports and memos but also signs, checklists, forms, websites, and so on.)

   - How often do you use these documents?

   - How and where do you use these documents?

   - How well do they stand up to use? What tends to mess them up?

   - Where do you keep them? Why?

   Write a memo to your instructor reporting your findings. In the memo, reflect on the documents' physical ecology, how well the documents are designed to that ecology, and how you'd improve the documents to fit their ecology better.

2. Find a document with an unconventional, unusual, or specialized format, and bring it to class. In groups, discuss the following about each of the documents your group members collected:

   - What needs was the document intended to meet?

   - Under what physical conditions would users likely use the document?

   - What factors led the designers to go to the extra effort and expense to create a document in this format? Was it worth the extra cost?

   - What has the document's physical life been like after it left the designer's hand and came to yours? Has it held up well?

   Choose what you think are the most and least successful documents in terms of format. Pre-pare a presentation to the rest of the class to explain your choices.

3. Take one of the documents from exercise 2 as a model, and try to replicate its format in whatever page layout or word processing software you have access to. Don't worry necessarily about replicating the model's page layout itself. Just set up a new document with the same page size as the model. Don't forget to take into account folds, trims, and bleed areas.

   - In word processing programs, your options will naturally be limited. But try to press against the boundaries of your word processor's capabilities to set up a document as close as possible to your model. (Hint: In Microsoft Word, go to File : Page Setup and experiment with the options available there.)

   - In most page layout programs such as InDesign, Quark, PageMaker, and Microsoft Publisher, you should be able to set up a document format very similar to your model.

   After you've created a document format as close as possible to your model, discuss with your classmates what you learned. What were the software's limitations and capabilities?

Works Cited

Johnson-Sheehan, Richard, and Craig Baehr. "Visual-Spatial Thinking in Hypertexts." *Technical Communication* 48 (2001): 22–30.

Kostelnick, Charles. "Supra-Textual Design: The Visual Rhetoric of Whole Documents." *Technical Communication Quarterly* 5 (1996): 9–33.

McKenzie, D. F. *Bibliography and the Sociology of Texts.* Cambridge: Cambridge University Press, 2004.

Petroski, Henry. *The Evolution of Useful Things.* New York: Vintage, 1994.

Rockley, Ann, Pamela Kostur, and Steve Manning. *Managing Enterprise Content: A Unified Content Strategy.* Upper Saddle River, NJ: New Riders, 2002.

Further Reading

Evans, Poppy. *Forms, Folds, and Sizes: All the Details Graphic Designers Need to Know but Can Never Find.* Gloucester, MA: Rockport, 2004.

CHAPTER 5

Pages

Figure 5.1 Pages as visual fields.
The concept of *page* as a visual field is useful across media and formats.

"Power in Numbers," Nucleus Gallery; "David Garrick (1717–1779), A Theatrical Life," Folger Shakespeare Library; "Countertops," Expo Design Center; "Have a Mint" home page, <www.haveamint.com>.

Panels

One of the most challenging and dynamic tasks a document designer will undertake is page design. The page is the space where a document comes together in the user's field of vision—everything from content to context, from the visual marks on page or screen to the material framework that surrounds and delivers them. Designing pages requires close attention to the shape and dimensions of the visual field, as well as to the characteristics of and relationships among the design objects we place there. It also must work dynamically within the medium and format you have chosen.

As a term, *page* has both general and specific meanings. Generally, a page is just a single coherent visual field in a document—whatever the user can see at once, without manipulating the document by turning a paper page or clicking to go to another web page (see Figure 5.1). But both print and electronic media add some specific twists to that visual field. In print documents, a page is only one side of one sheet of paper, but when we open a bound document, the visual field we see is a *spread* of two pages connected at the spine. And as we saw in Chapter 4, each *panel* in a folded document can be designed as a separate visual field or combined with other panels to create larger fields. Even electronic documents use the concept of page, such as a web page.

Page

Two-page spread

Web page

114

In this definition of page, **page design** is the process of placing design objects such as text, headings, and images consistently and effectively on the page, taking into account the actual visual field, the characteristics of the design objects, and the relationships implied among them by the principles of design.

To see what we mean, consider the design of a web page in Figure 5.2, from a promotional website for Altoids mints. Though primarily intended for entertainment, this web page is a good example of how pages serve as a frame, defining a particular visual field. This example does so by using the visual metaphor of a stage, complete with curtains and a carnival barker. This visual metaphor also provides a visual framework for the many design objects on the page, including navigational links across the top and previews to promotional videos and games. The designers used principles of alignment, enclosure, proximity, order, similarity, and contrast to organize the many design objects on the page into an understandable system, group together like information, and distinguish different types of information (for example, separating the entertainment features and games from traditional website navigation links along the top).

Figure 5.2 Pages on screen. This web page frames the content within a metaphorical stage, complete with curtains. This design emphasizes the frame provided by a page, which provides content within a unified visual field.

Altoids, <hugo.wddg.com/altoids/2006>.

Proximity. *The navigation links are closer together than they are collectively to the rest of the design objects below.*

Order. *Users will probably look first at the central feature, "Sweet & Cool," then at the other design objects radiating from it.*

Similarity. *All of the navigation links at the top are formatted in the same typography to show they do similar things.*

Enclosure. *Design objects are enclosed in three levels: individual frames, the larger composite frame with the scroll on top, and finally the theater curtains.*

Alignment. *Design objects line up in three horizontal rows—four, counting the navigation links at the top.*

Contrast. *The animated carnival barker seems to stand outside and in front of the page layout.*

This is a good example of how page design can bring order to the chaos of information within the primary visual field in documents: the page. Page design guides users through the myriad pieces of information in the visual field by using design principles to create clear relationships among design objects.

In this chapter, we'll discuss some of the many techniques for designing effective pages. First, we'll discuss pages through the three theoretical perspectives introduced in Chapter 2: perception, culture, and rhetoric. Building on these perspectives, you'll learn how to assess content for its structure and set up a grid system to organize content into logical and visually distinct spaces. Finally, you'll learn when to break the consistent system you've created to emphasize important content.

Three Perspectives on Pages

Perception

Take a minute to think about what you're seeing right now. On your desk or in your hands, you see a book. More specifically, because much of the book is obscured from view, you are looking at a two-page spread in a book. This view might seem very familiar. But think for a moment about *why* the pages are designed this way. Pages don't have to be rectangular, and they don't have to feature a nice symmetrical shape with strong edges and a frame of empty margins. So why *do* they?

As we learned in Chapter 2, Gestalt psychology suggests that one reason is our visual need to know where the page ends and the background begins. Gestalt theory posits that we perceive things with consistent edges as *figures* on a *ground*. The book you are holding illustrates that principle: the sharp and consistent edges identify the joined pages as an object within your field of vision, or a figure on a ground. When we read documents, we so trust the figure/ground distinction that we allow the rest of the visual field to recede from our awareness — the pages of the document make up all of the conscious visual field. (Have you paid any attention to the background *around* or *behind* this book while you've been reading it?)

But this is just the beginning. Just as the pages before you seem like figures on a broader visual field, you can also see figures (*design objects*, as we discussed in Chapter 1) within the page field. For example, there's a design object you recognize as where the text goes — the primary *text field*. Nested in the primary text field, you recognize smaller areas of coherent and separate text figures: *paragraphs* and *headings*. You can also see some areas in the text field that you take as coherent and separate *graphic elements*. And you see some other text fields at the top and bottom of the page: the *header* and the *footer*. Finally, you can tunnel down to even smaller design objects: sentences, words, and individual letters.

As an experienced reader, you're familiar with these design objects — so much so that you typically use them to organize your reading of the page without consciously thinking about them as figures on a ground, as we are here. But these objects are not random; they're the result of a document designer's careful work to assemble design objects into a coherent visual system. A great part of page design is creating a visual field filled with design objects and using users' perceptions to suggest clear relationships among those objects.

Culture

The designer's careful work, however, doesn't spring up from nothing. Part of design relies on cultural conventions — the long-standing but always-changing expectations users have about where some kinds of design objects will be located on a page and how those objects will look. Understanding such conventions involves more than simplistically applying page design rules to documents. Instead, it requires designing while keeping in mind the many cultural factors surrounding documents in the user's own experience.

For example, most people are familiar with the design objects in a typical formal letter — letterhead, address block, salutation ("Dear . . ."), text block, closing ("Sincerely"), and signature. But conventional elements, like those of a letter's page design, developed over time due to specific cultural influences.

Consider what letters have looked like under *different* cultural conditions. Today, the sender of a letter must pay for it to be delivered, usually by purchasing a postage stamp and pasting it to the letter. Before stamps were introduced in the mid-nineteenth century, however, the *receiver* of the letter had to pay the postage — and the more sheets in the letter, the higher the postage due. Sending a longer-than-necessary letter was wasteful, expensive, and rude.

So letter-writers found ways to conserve the amount of paper they used on letters. One technique was called *crossing* (Figure 5.3).

As you can imagine, crossing made reading the letter quite difficult because it consisted of two competing page designs set at 90-degree angles, with each

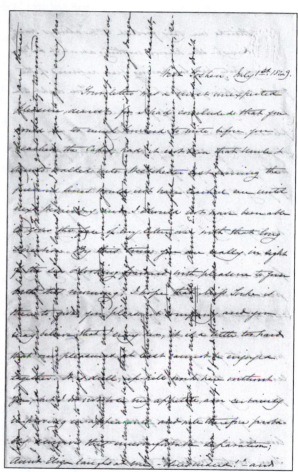

Figure 5.3 The page layout of a crossed letter.   Different cultural conditions often lead to different conventions of page layout, as you can see from this crossed letter. Because of the expense of postage, the writer would complete a page of the letter normally, then turn the sheet 90 degrees, and write a second page across the first set of text lines.

direction making the other less legible. Some readers were willing to accept this inconvenience in the name of economy, but others were less understanding. The narrator of one of Benjamin Disraeli's novels remarked that he appreciated a woman correspondent, "provided always that she does not *cross*" (112). At the time, however, cultural conditions made it somewhat acceptable to cross. Those social conditions have since changed, so crossing has fallen entirely out of use.

Page design conventions arise from the culture surrounding documents as much as from general perceptual principles. Sometimes those conventions can even overpower perceptual principles, producing document designs that are not ideal, but that work in their cultural context. By the same token, sometimes breaking well-established conventions can draw more attention to a document—but doing so always involves some risk.

Moreover, there is never just *one* culture surrounding documents, but many different cultures. Some are extremely local—for example, a company or work group can have its own cultural expectations. Others are broader, such as an immigrant culture or a professional culture within a nation. Still others are extremely broad, such as ethnic cultures, national cultures, or even continental cultures (European, South American, and so on). Smart designers pay attention to the power of culture on users' page design expectations, habits, preferences, and conventions.

Rhetoric

From the perspective of visual rhetoric, page design is important because it can further your goals as a page designer and meet the reader's needs. For example, page design can promote an ethos that reflects well on the client, matches the purpose, sets a tone for the document, and encourages users to use it. Consider the page design of two websites in Figures 5.4 and 5.5. Both page designs share the same format: the computer screen. And the topics of both are health oriented—the Medicare prescription drug benefit and quitting smoking.

Despite their similar topics, these web pages differ remarkably in their use of page design to impart a different sense of ethos to different audiences. These page layouts reflect the designers' anticipations of two different sets of users: one more mature and less interested in playing on websites, and the other younger and more interested in novelty. The page layouts also try to appeal to the interests and needs of each audience by building for the client organizations an ethos of responsibility and maturity for the web page on Medicare drug benefits, and an ethos of youth and cool for the web page on smoking. Both sites also use page design for an important ethical purpose: to get people interested in their own health.

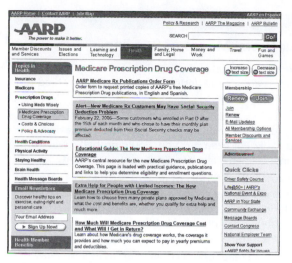

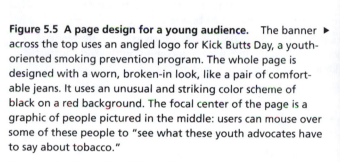

◄ **Figure 5.4 A page design for a mature audience.**   This web page uses a relatively traditional design, with clear navigational areas on the top, left, and right surrounding a content area, the focal center of the page. This central content area includes a lot of text, which suggests that its audience wants information quickly, clearly, and efficiently.

AARP, "Medicare Prescription Drug Coverage," <www.aarp.org/health/rx_drugs/med_d/>.

Figure 5.5 A page design for a young audience.   The banner ► across the top uses an angled logo for Kick Butts Day, a youth-oriented smoking prevention program. The whole page is designed with a worn, broken-in look, like a pair of comfortable jeans. It uses an unusual and striking color scheme of black on a red background. The focal center of the page is a graphic of people pictured in the middle: users can mouse over some of these people to "see what these youth advocates have to say about tobacco."

Campaign for Tobacco-Free Kids, "Kick Butts Day," <kickbuttsday.org>.

Viewing Pages

Before we discuss how to create a successful page design, we must address how and why users usually encounter pages as they do. Users typically engage in three modes of looking at documents:

- Sometimes they *skim* the document, looking for something that will catch their eye.

- Sometimes they *scan*, looking for particular information.

- Sometimes they settle down and *read* passages of text or images.

Users switch rapidly between these three modes, often within the same document. They might scan first, looking for some particular section that will help them solve a problem. When they find the appropriate section, they will likely slow down to read it carefully. Then they

DESIGN TIP

Reflecting Your Users' Modes of Reading

As a designer, you must anticipate what modes of viewing users will likely need, and create a page design that helps them to read the way they want. For example:

- If the user needs to find specific information quickly, like a procedure to follow to solve a problem, you'll want to create a document that scans easily. For example, you would probably want to make navigational elements like headings very prominent.

- If the user will want to look at lots of images, such as in a catalog, you'll need to design the pages with the images and accompanying text arranged in a consistent, regular framework. This arrangement will help users quickly find the images they want to look at more carefully.

- If the user will want to read long sections, such as in a formal business report, you'll want to create a document with consistent and comfortable blocks of text.

- If users will just skim the document—such as a newsletter, for instance—you'll want to create a document with vivid contrast to make each story attractive and engaging.

might skim the rest of the document to see if there's anything else interesting or helpful that they might want to check out. Or they might start with skimming, letting their eyes rest idly here and there until they find something that piques their interest enough to slow down and read. Or they might start by reading, find that the text is less useful than they thought, and skim through the rest of the document to see if anything looks more useful. It all depends on the users' needs and agendas when they encounter the document.

We should design pages that accommodate users in whatever mode makes sense for their situation—skimming, scanning, or reading. Doing so will foster users' interaction with the document, increase their comprehension, and help them complete the tasks that brought them to the document in the first place.

Creating Meaning with Page Design

It's easy to dismiss page design, believing either that it doesn't matter as much as text in the transmission of information or that it is primarily aesthetic. On one hand, as Rudolf Arnheim pointed out, for a long time our culture has privileged lexical meaning (conveyed in words) over visual meaning (conveyed in images), teaching us all at some time in our childhood to put down the crayons and pick up the pen — or later, the keyboard. On the other hand, even those who create page designs often consider their work an aesthetic act — the process of creating a beautiful wrapper for "content" — which again they see primarily as words. In either case, these attitudes suggest that any meaning we gain from visual cues is a mere adjunct or shell to the words themselves.

But in documents, we cannot even experience words without seeing them. And the way words and other design objects are arranged on the page conveys a significant amount of meaning to users. This meaning is often *metatextual* — about the text. Page design uses visual cues to create order among the chaos of words, to guide users through the information held in the document, and to help users get what they need out of the document. In short, good page design creates *meaning*.

Page design does this by implying a logical structure for documents, using the visual variables and principles of design to create design objects and define relationships among them (as we discussed in Chapter 2). Page design is the craft of developing a consistent system in the document for implying those relationships.

The possible relationships among design objects on pages are numerous, but for the most part they boil down to *connection*, *hierarchy*, *sequence*, and *balance*. In practice, these relationships can be deeply interrelated; any document can exemplify all four simultaneously, often using similar techniques to imply these relationships. But in the following sections, we'll discuss each individually, examining how we can use design objects and apply principles of design to show these relationships and create visual systems of meaning on pages.

> Good page design creates *meaning*.

Connection

The most basic relationship between page design objects is that of simple connection. Using visual cues, we can imply that one design object is somehow logically connected to other design objects, thereby reinforcing the logic of the page.

As we discussed in Chapter 2, relationships of connection are mostly governed by the principles of design: *similarity*, *contrast*, *proximity*, *alignment*, *order*, and *enclosure*. We can use these principles to break up content into manageable chunks and then group those chunks to show the relationships among them. For example, consider the layout in Figure 5.6 on page 122, a page from an elections guide for the board of a philanthropic organization. As the callouts describe, the page layout arranges content into design objects and uses alignment, similarity, proximity, and enclosure to show particular relationships between those design objects.

Horizontal alignment and the *similarity* of page objects implies that the three candidates are parallel, running for the same office.

Proximity implies that objects close together are connected. Here, the caption is close to the photo, creating a strong relationship between the candidate's photo and his or her name.

Order implies that what comes after is related to what came before—for example, that the text below the photo is connected to the photo.

By corollary, *negative space* implies that each of these objects is a separate page object. Each separate page object has a different task, and each kind of page object has a different task: headings introduce sections, paragraphs organize text, captions explain images.

Enclosure implies that what's inside is separate from what's outside. Here, content above the line is in the candidate's voice, while what's below the line is reported by the organization.

Figure 5.6 Principles of design create connection among design objects. Notice how the minimalist design of this page in an election guide for the board of a philanthropic organization follows the principles of design to present clear information.

National Trust, "Your Views Count," <www.nationaltrust.org.uk>.

Vertical alignment connects the various page objects vertically—each column representing one candidate's information.

candidates' statements

Janet Wootton (Nottinghamshire)

'A communicator with a regional voice and advocate for the Trust's work'

A voice for National Trust members, particularly in the Regions. Communication skills, gained from a career in journalism, public relations, government information and broadcasting, enables me to provide advocacy support and ensure accountability for the National Trust as it looks to the future and faces new challenges. I am an over-50s champion, being a non-executive director of Saga Radio in the Midlands and a mature university student in the Visual Arts.

Jane Kingsley (Oxfordshire)

'I am forthright in both my support and criticism of the Trust's work'

I have been an active member of the Trust's governance since joining the Finance Committee in 1998. However, my strongest contribution has been on the Nominations Committee which recently helped select the new Board of Trustees. As a Council member, I am known for being willing to speak out as both a supporter and critic of the Trust's work, but am fundamentally one of its greatest fans.

Richard Haslam (Hampshire)

'I'll help Council with architectural knowledge and nurture the Trust's intellectual traditions'

Contributing for 25 years to the acquisition and management of Trust properties – from hill farms and industrial sites in Wales, to visitor centres at its larger historic places – has convinced me of the importance to the Trust of cultural concerns.

In bringing this experience to the Council, I hope to add to its judgements on architectural and landscape issues, and to build on the Trust's intellectual traditions at its regional and country roots.

Born 1948

Member for 25 years

Career history

Journalist, Nottingham Evening Post. Press relations, Government Senior Information Officer (including an attachment to Prime Minister's Press Office). Head of Independent Television Commission in Midlands. Currently communications consultant and part-time student in Visual Arts. Non-Executive Director of Saga Radio in the Midlands. Member, Royal Television Society.

Involvement with the National Trust

Current member of East Midlands Regional Committee – now in second three-year term. Specialist knowledge of regional advocacy work.

Proposer: Mr Richard Moisey

Seconders: Mr John Anfield, Mrs Ann Howard

Born 1948

Member for 15 years

Career history

1978–2000 Russell Reynolds Associates, Executive Recruitment, including Managing Director of London Office, 1993–2000. Partner responsible for investment management practice.
1973–8 Citibank
Non-executive roles in Michael Clark Dance Company, Spectrum (executive recruitment), IDDAS (senior executive advisory firm) and on the Council of Cheltenham Ladies College.

Involvement with the National Trust

1998 to present: Finance Committee
2002 to present: Council member
2002 to present: Senior Management Remuneration Committee
2004/05: Nominations Committee (Chairman in 2005)
2005: Elected Senior Member of the Council

Proposer: Mr Michael Quicke

Seconders: Mr John Marsham, Mr Christopher Purvis

Number of Council meetings attended since 2002 election: 10 out of 13.

Born 1944

Member for 25 years

Career history

Working as an architectural historian in England, Wales and Italy includes writing articles for Country Life; two Pevsner Architectural Guides for Wales; and collaborating on Italian architecture and landscape projects. Member of the Historic Buildings Council for Wales (1980–98) and of the Royal Commission on the Ancient Monuments of Wales (1986–95); and of Dedalo Minosse Prize jury (1998 to present).

Involvement with the National Trust

Member of the Architectural Panel 1979 to present; of the Properties Committee 1985–2005; of the Committee for Wales 1980–8; and of Stowe Advisory Panel 1989 to present.

Proposer: Mrs Elisabeth Walters

Seconders: Mr Nicholas Cooper, Mr David Gentleman

11

Hierarchy

But what kind of connection should we show between design objects? Many kinds are possible, but the most common in document design is *hierarchy*. Smaller design objects build up into larger and larger *composite* design objects: letters make up words, words make up lines, lines make up paragraphs, paragraphs make up sections. Hierarchy even goes beyond the page, providing the most common organizational principle of all documents: subsections make up bigger sections, sections make up chapters, and chapters make up whole documents.

Showing these hierarchical relationships visually is a key part of page design, particularly in technical documents. But unfortunately, we often don't incorporate adequate visual cues to make the hierarchy obvious to users. Imagine that when you take your new answering machine out of the box, you find the product documentation sheet in Figure 5.7.

Not only is this document difficult to read, but it's also hard to understand. Using line breaks, it sets up a very basic set of sections: an introduction, Functions, Contents, and Setup. By themselves, however, these line breaks don't distinguish the sections adequately, much less show a hierarchical relationship among the sections. All of the different kinds of content on the page — titles, headings, sentences, and lists — are consigned to a single bland, indistinct, generic field.

For this document, we would need a visual system that shows at least four distinct levels of hierarchy:

- The document as a whole (title)
- Sections within the document (headings)
- Text within the sections (paragraphs)
- Specifics (items or steps)

We can use the visual variables and principles of design to show this hierarchy on the page by carefully managing typography and the positioning of elements (see Figure 5.8 on page 124). Clear visual cues help users distinguish the levels of hierarchy. They also enable users to scan the document to find the particular information they need, and they make skimming easy.

> Setup and Operating Instructions, Acme Answering Machine. Thank you for purchasing the Acme Answering Machine, model #3221-1448. Functions. The Acme Answering Machine has the following functions: 30-minute call memory; 100-message capacity; four separate mailboxes with individual security codes; remote answering; automatic fax cutoff; message counter display; audio memo function; caller ID window; room monitoring function; and emergency battery operation in the case of occasional power loss. Contents. The package holds the following materials: the answering machine; a 6-foot standard phone cord with RJ-11 modular plugs; an AC-DC power converter; and one 9-volt battery. Setup. To set up the Acme Answering Machine, first turn the machine face down on a table or similar surface. Then with a fingernail pry open the battery compartment cover. Draw out the battery cable and attach the 9-volt battery to it, matching the positive terminal with the positive battery receptacle.

Figure 5.7 Unclear visual hierarchy. This document is difficult to use because of the unclear hierarchy of page objects. All of the text looks the same, regardless of its level within the document hierarchy.

Sequence

One of the most important relationships when designing a page is *sequence* — the order in which users will encounter design objects as they skim or scan the page. Of course, as we noted in Chapter 1, users will look at whatever they choose, and in whatever order they choose. But

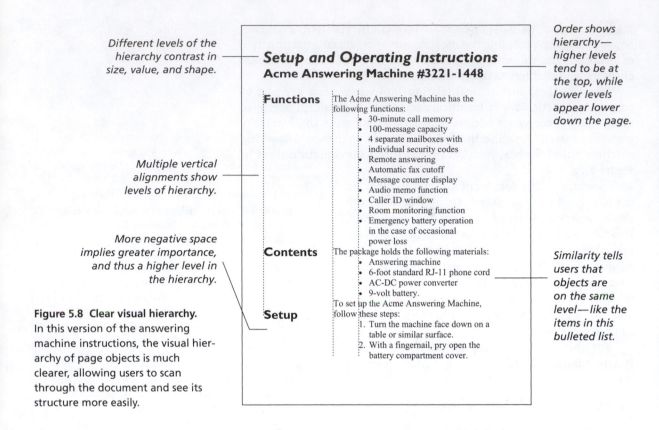

Different levels of the hierarchy contrast in size, value, and shape.

Multiple vertical alignments show levels of hierarchy.

More negative space implies greater importance, and thus a higher level in the hierarchy.

Order shows hierarchy— higher levels tend to be at the top, while lower levels appear lower down the page.

Similarity tells users that objects are on the same level—like the items in this bulleted list.

Figure 5.8 Clear visual hierarchy.
In this version of the answering machine instructions, the visual hierarchy of page objects is much clearer, allowing users to scan through the document and see its structure more easily.

good page designs provide a clear and natural *flow* for users' eyes to follow from design object to design object.

A good flow gives users a clear entry point to the page—a clear sense of where to look first—and then visually implies a clear path through the rest of the objects on the page. The design principle that most comes into play in creating flow is *order*, but *proximity*, *alignment*, *contrast*, and *similarity* also help users pick out where to look first and where to look next.

From practice and convention, users employ two common strategies to guide them through the sequence of objects on the page: *patterning* and *focusing*. As designers we can use these strategies to inform our page designs.

PATTERNING

Most users look at a page in a series of glances that form more-or-less consistent patterns we apply to most new pages we see. We develop

Showing Hierarchy

Use these techniques to show hierarchy in your designs:

- **Deepen the hierarchy**—but not *too* deep. In most documents, a page hierarchy with three to five levels works best. A common design mistake is to create a page that's all on one hierarchical level. More hierarchical levels can help users scan and skim documents successfully. However, too many levels can also confuse users, so don't take this idea too far.

- **Break text into smaller "chunks."** Shorter sentences and paragraphs can be arranged more easily into a deeper hierarchy. Also, users can scan and skim shorter chunks of text more quickly and efficiently.

- **Use similarity to form consistency** in the visual design of each level. Each design object on the third level of the hierarchy should look similar to all the other design objects on the third level; everything on the second level should look similar to everything else on the second level, and so on.

- **Use contrast to show clear distinctions among levels of hierarchy.** Without enough contrast among the levels, users might find the structure of the document confusing. Of course, the more levels, the more difficult it will be to show adequate contrast between them without making the highest level too large or the lowest too small.

- **Use order and alignment to show different levels** of the hierarchy. Users typically expect that the content aligned farthest to the left is the most important and that aligned farthest to the right is least important. By the same token, what's at the top tends to be seen as higher in the hierarchy than whatever's lower down on the page.

these reading patterns by reading many thousands of pages over our lifetime, which builds a strong habit in terms of where we look first at a new page and how our eyes flow through the page from that point. If your designs follow these patterns, users can usually read, skim, and scan more successfully.

Perhaps the strongest pattern in documents written in English and most other European languages is known as the *Z pattern* (Figure 5.9). This pattern applies particularly to documents that are designed to be read, rather than scanned or skimmed.

Text in English is usually represented on pages in successive lines that readers look at from left to right and top to bottom. Because they must move from line to line down the page, readers' eyes actually travel in a zig-zag pattern. We can use this pattern to predict what zones of the page are more likely to receive a reader's attention. Three tendencies are particularly useful for designers:

- Readers tend to look first at the upper left corner when they encounter a page or text field.

- Readers then tend to look across the top of the page or text field on their first pass through the Z. They do so in quick eye

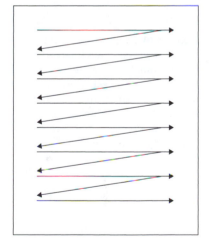

Figure 5.9 The Z pattern. A reader's gaze tends to skip to the right across a line of text in a series of saccades about seven to nine characters long. At the end of the line, gaze returns quickly to the left margin to find the next line.

movements called *saccades*, followed by short *fixations* on partic- ular points of the page. At the end of the line, their eyes leap quickly from the right side of the page back to the left margin to begin the next line, a movement known as the ***return sweep*** (Findlay and Gilchrist 84).

- Readers' eyes hit the left margin repeatedly as they zig-zag across the text field.

Figure 5.10 Power zones. Objects placed in power zones (marked here with shading) receive greater emphasis than objects placed lower down or further to the right. The strongest point of emphasis is at the top left of the page, where readers look first on most pages.

As a result, we can identify ***power zones*** on the page (Figure 5.10). Any design objects placed in the power zones will likely get readers' atten- tion before anything placed outside of these zones. And the more quickly readers are browsing or scanning the document, the more likely they will pay attention *only* to the power zones, looking for something that will capture their attention.

Recent research has shown that users even apply the Z pattern to web pages, which aren't usually intended to be read through (Outing and Ruel). These patterns apply as well to multiple-column layouts, which add a second level of Z patterns to the user's eye movements. In addition to scanning the entire page, readers use the Z pattern to scan individual columns from left to right. They also use the Z pattern to determine which column to read next.

Therein, however, lies a problem: a page design can present am- biguous flows that make a user unsure of where to look next. One com- mon mistake arises when columns of text are wrapped around images, as in Figure 5.11. Columns inherently create a break in proximity between one line of text (the bottom of the first column) and the next line (the top of the second column). Ideally, users can adapt quickly to find out where to read next after finishing one column; the conven- tional Z pattern prompts them to look for the next block of text at the top of the page. But setting an image in the middle of the page gives users ambiguous cues about where to go next. Do they skip up to the top of the next column *above* the image or to the top of the next col- umn *below* the image? Shifting the image to either the top or the bot- tom of the page eliminates this problem.

Giving users a clear path through the document will help them avoid any confusion. And if you keep in mind the well-practiced pat- terns that users bring to documents they read, you will have a better sense of where to position important design features so readers can find them easily.

Keep in mind, however, that the Z pattern applies *only* to docu- ments in English or similar left-to-right languages. For example, read- ers of right-to-left languages, such as Arabic and Hebrew, naturally have different conventional patterns and strategies for reading pages. If you're designing a document for another culture, study the conventions

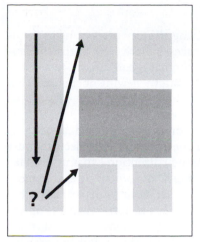

Ambiguous reading order

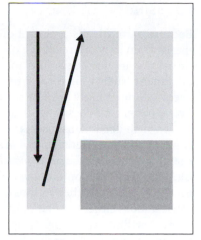

Clear reading order

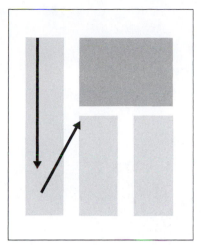

Clear reading order

Figure 5.11 Flow and reading order. Be sure to give users clear cues about where to look next as they work through a page.

and habits of users in that culture and create designs that reflect those users' expectations. You can find out a lot about other cultures' reading habits by talking to and observing users in that culture. Analyzing successful documents from the target culture will also help you create responsive documents that cross the cultural divide successfully.

DESIGN TIP

Using Power Zones

Here are some things to keep in mind when using power zones:

- Put the page entry point inside the power zones. Doing so will help users start their page journey on the right foot.

- Put design objects that are high in the page hierarchy inside the power zones. These objects include navigational cues such as titles and headings.

- Put mission-critical design objects inside power zones, where they'll get the most attention. Mission-critical objects might include cautions and warnings.

- By corollary, avoid putting relatively unimportant information inside power zones. If you place objects that shouldn't receive a lot of attention inside the power zones, they'll get in the way of users skimming or scanning the document for important information. For example, it's usually best to avoid centering headings, which places these important visual cues outside of the power zones.

FOCUSING

Because patterning is a general ordering strategy users bring to documents from previous reading experiences, it works best in the conventional documents users find most familiar — particularly text-heavy documents such as books and reports. But in viewing documents that users will more likely skim or scan, such as posters, signs, catalogs, or flyers, patterning doesn't work quite as well.

In such documents, users rely less on established reading patterns than on the characteristics and arrangement of design objects to order their path through the page, *focusing* their attention dynamically. Like hunters, they latch onto the visual "scent" of something that appeals to them — because they're looking for something in particular, because it looks either familiar or unusual, because it has elements or features they find intriguing, or because it's the biggest, brightest, most striking object on the page. Once that first design object has grabbed their attention, users look for objects connected to it.

The key for designers, then, is to capture the user's attention, focusing it on a particular design object as a starting point, then leading the user's eye to related objects connected by the principles of design. Designers facilitate this process through page design by giving the user a clear starting point and making the flow from that point visually clear. Then they use principles such as *order*, *similarity*, *contrast*, *alignment*, and *proximity* to create a sense of flow.

Consider the flyer for a photography exhibition in Figure 5.12. It uses visual cues to capture attention and guide users through the essential information on the page. The user's eyes might focus first on the compelling image of a man running down an aircraft runway, then move down and right through the title and subtitle to another image. With this arrangement, it's difficult for users to see the images without casting their eyes across the title — an essential piece of information. Now that the flyer has the user's attention, other essential information, such as the date, time, and location of the exhibition, can appear in smaller fonts to the left of the image. Finally, the user's eyes flow down to the sponsor of the exhibition (the University of Virginia Art Museum) at the bottom of the page.

The *alignment* of design objects also encourages this reading pattern. The title "Reverie and Reality" aligns with the left edge of the runway stripe on which the man is running. The photographer's name aligns with the second image. The subtitle aligns with the word "Reality" in the title, as well as with the vertical rule between "University of Virginia" and "Art Museum." And the time, date, and location information right-aligns along an axis slightly displaced from that between "Reality" and the museum title block at the bottom of the page.

Even if the users only glance at the sheet without taking in every detail, the design's use of *contrasts* in color, value, and size in its typography

Figure 5.12 How page layout guides the user's eye.
The design objects on this flyer are arranged to lead the user's eye down and across the page in a predictable and logical order.

University of Virginia Art Museum, "Reverie and Reality: Photographs by Rodney Smith."

helps emphasize the most important information. The contrast between the background color and the text causes text blocks in white to pop out more vibrantly than the text in black, which draws attention to the most essential information: the exhibit title, the date and time, and the location (the Art Museum). Finally, the use of white text and black text is appropriate for a flyer that is advertising a photographer's black-and-white photos.

Of course, users can look wherever they want, but the techniques in this page design draw users' eyes through the information in a logical and carefully orchestrated order, giving them the visual cues they need to hunt down information, first by emphasizing the most essential information (what, when, and where), then by filling in subsidiary information.

Balance

The fourth relationship among design objects is *balance*, which provides a sense of unity and coherence to a page. Ideally, design elements should be placed on a page so that they balance both horizontally and vertically. Designers determine balance by assessing the relative *visual weight* of different objects in the design. Visual weight depends on the subjective vibrancy or dynamism of individual objects in the design. Visual variables such as these can affect the weight of a design object:

- *Size:* Larger objects have greater weight than smaller objects.
- *Shape:* Unusual shapes have greater weight than conventional shapes.
- *Color:* A splash of any color typically has greater weight than a surrounding page of black and white or grays; a dramatically different or highly contrasting color has greater weight than a less-contrasting color.
- *Value:* The more visually dense the object in comparison to its surroundings, the greater its weight. Black on a white field (or white on a black field) carries the greatest visual weight because of the high contrast of value between white and black.
- *Position:* Objects in power zones have more weight than those not in power zones; objects clustered together can form a greater weight, as can objects set within large areas of negative space.

The design objects with a lot of visual weight tend to use several of these factors simultaneously. For example, a visually weighty object might be large, surprisingly shaped, brightly colored, and highly contrastive in value.

Keep in mind two caveats about balance:

- *Balance is relative.* As you might have guessed from the previous list, no object *really* has any particular visual weight, except in comparison to other objects that seem lighter or heavier, less or more emphatic or attractive or surprising.
- *Balance comes from users as much as from the design objects or page design.* Users just skimming or browsing through a document might be attracted by a dynamic but merely decorative photo, giving this element a lot of weight. But users looking for specific information will ignore that same photo in favor of an information-filled heading that might lead them to their goal.

In other words, balance is not always a dependable indicator of good design. Sometimes *unbalanced* designs can seem more dynamic and interesting, and this can be used to good rhetorical effect. However, balance can create an overall coherence and unity between design objects, making it clear that they work and belong together.

The simplest kind of balance is **symmetry**. **Symmetrical layouts** center everything on a single vertical (or, less often, horizontal) axis.

Symmetry often implies a certain formality or traditionalism, so it is often used for conventional genres like invitations or designs that invoke history or nostalgia (Figure 5.13).

Asymmetrical layouts can also have balance, as we can see in Figures 5.14 and 5.15 (page 132). These examples still use a primary axis (either horizontal or vertical), but the axis is off-center. In asymmetrical layouts, the more dynamic or weighty objects are often balanced by larger areas of less dramatic objects, such as paragraphs.

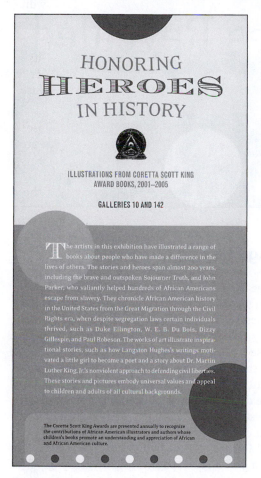

◄ **Figure 5.13 Symmetrical layout.**   The symmetrical layout and the nineteenth-century typefaces mesh with the historical theme of this leaflet.

The Art Institute of Chicago, "Honoring Heroes in History: Illustrations from Coretta Scott King Award Books, 2001–2005."

Figure 5.14 Asymmetrical layouts can also show balance. ►
The asymmetrical layout of this membership brochure uses a broader right-hand area and large, high-value type to balance the dynamic image on the left.

The Art Institute of Chicago, "Join Us."

Figure 5.15 Horizontal asymmetrical balance. The dark shading and images along the bottom of this cover exert a strong downward visual emphasis. But the negative space at the top, which incorporates the title ("Citiscapes Revealed"), half-rosette, and the museum's name, creates an equally strong weight to lift the balance back toward the top. The result is horizontal asymmetrical balance.

National Building Museum, "Cityscapes Revealed: Highlights from the Collection."

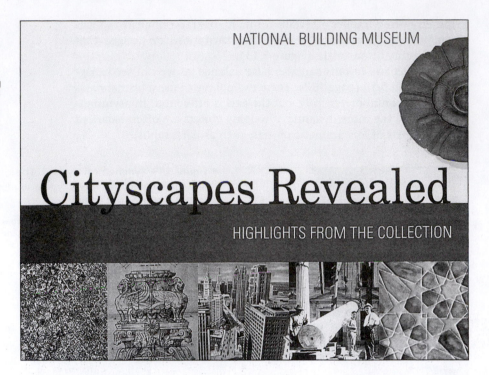

Using Grids for Page Design

So far, we've discussed page design primarily in terms of isolated pages or spreads, such as one might see in a single web page, flyer, or information sheet. Each of these documents might have a unique page design — and they probably should. But most documents have several or even many pages. These longer documents need a structured and consistent page layout system that extends across the entire document, or at least significant parts of it. Users rely on that consistency to guide them through the document. And as users grow familiar with a consistent page design system, they read, scan, or skim each individual page more quickly and efficiently.

One effective method for designing a consistent page design system is to create a consistent *grid* on each page. A grid divides pages into a series of rectangular areas that can organize content — whether text or graphics — that can be dropped into these boxes.

Take a look at Figure 5.16, a two-page spread from a visitors' guide to a tour of public art in downtown Denver, Colorado. This spread was clearly designed to accommodate lots of small pictures and captions — just what you'd expect in a brochure guiding users in seeing many pieces of art. The grid separates photographs and captions into nine

Figure 5.16 Using a design grid.   Notice how this brochure follows a consistent design grid so users can recognize the relationship between illustrations and their captions.

Denver Office of Cultural Affairs, "Public Art Guide to Downtown Denver."

rows and six columns. Some of the photographs are a consistently small size; others are sized precisely to equal several of the smaller photographs. For example, the banner area over the top of the spread extends across six of the pictures below, unifying and connecting them. Two headings also fall into this pattern: the running title "Public Art Downtown" in the rectangle at the top left, and the heading "Platte Valley," which aligns with the second column of photos.

The grid in this spread isn't explicit; you cannot actually see the lines arranging the content. But implicitly, the grid manages the page layout. The diagram in Figure 5.17 (page 134) shows the implicit features of the grid used in Figure 5.16.

Figure 5.17 The design grid for the page spread shown in Figure 5.16. The gripper edge will be trimmed away in line with the trim marks after printing, leaving the printed area of the document extending to the edge of the finished sheet.

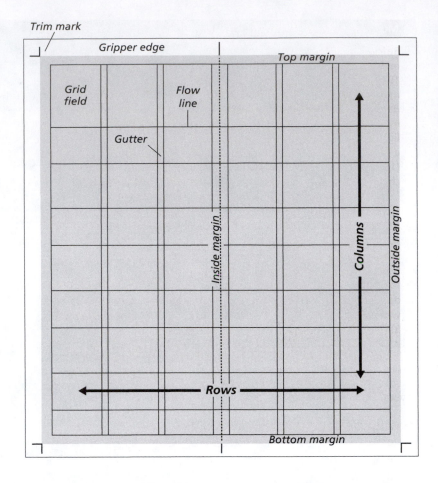

The positive areas of a grid, where content can be inserted, are formed into consistent rectangular areas arranged in rows and columns. Each of the rectangular areas in the grid is called a *grid field*. Collectively, the area covered by the grid fields is known as the *live area* of the page. Content can be made to fit within individual grid fields or to extend across multiple grid fields. Vertically, the grid fields are arranged into *columns*, and *flow lines* divide columns horizontally into *rows*.

Negative areas play a key role in defining the positive areas. The negative spaces between grid fields are called *gutters*. The negative space between the grid and the edge of the page or screen is called a *margin*. For one-sheet formats, the margins are referred to as *top*, *bottom*, *left*, and *right*. For a spread formed by two pages, the margins are referred to as top, bottom, *inside* (next to the binding or fold), and *outside* (away from the binding or fold). These negative spaces play a central role in defining the positive areas of the page.

MORE ABOUT . . . THE BAUHAUS AND ASYMMETRICAL LAYOUTS

Before the early twentieth century, nearly all page layout was symmetrical, regardless of the purpose of the document. But in the 1920s, a group of German designers began to challenge the symmetrical approach. This group was founded at *Das Staatliches Bauhaus*, a design school active from 1919 to 1924 in Weimar, Germany, and from 1924 to 1933 in Dessau, Germany. The leading lights of the Bauhaus movement were Walter Gropius (1883–1969), a founding member of the school; Laszlo Moholy-Nagy (1895–1946), a talented photographer and designer; and Jan Tschichold (1902–1974), an innovative and outspoken typographer.

In his book *Die Neue Typographie* (*The New Typography*, 1928), Tschichold promoted the vitality of asymmetrical layouts as better fitted to a modern industrial age than symmetrical layouts. Asymmetrical layouts provide many options for displaying different kinds of content. These layouts allow designers to show useful relationships between pieces of information, without expecting users to read linearly through an entire document. Tschichold's ideas deeply influenced designers, and we can still see his impact today, when most designs are asymmetrical. For more information on the Bauhaus, see Phillip Meggs's book *A History of Graphic Design*.

A grid such as the one in Figures 5.16 and 5.17 takes advantage of several principles of design at once:

- *Alignment:* Because page grids are clearly rectilinear, they encourage good alignment of design objects, both horizontally and vertically. In this case, the many rows and columns of the grid helped the designers align the small photographs and captions. Not only are these photographs a primary feature of the brochure, but they also serve a primary function: to show users what to look for among the many pieces of public art in downtown Denver.

- *Enclosure:* By nature, a page grid encloses design objects, setting them apart from their surroundings. This enclosure might be positive, with elements such as lines, rules, borders, or shading distinguishing one grid field from the next, or it might be negative space that implies separation. In this example, the consistent horizontal and vertical gaps between different design objects provide a strong sense of enclosure.

- *Similarity:* In this example, the page grid keeps all of the tour images the same size. This similarity of size helps users recognize that other images, such as the sculptures across the top or at the bottom right of the page, aren't necessarily stops on the tour.

Using such a consistent page design grid can help us create page layouts with the same arrangement of design objects on each page.

- *Contrast:* The page grid emphasizes contrasts between design objects. The images (in full color) contrast well with the buff-colored background, which in turn provides good contrast for the text in the captions, and the green banners at the top and bottom contrast with the mostly blues and browns of the content between them. A consistent grid also gives us the opportunity to *break* consistency sometimes. For example, the circled numbers on the tour notes at the bottom of the spread straddle the grid boundary, suggesting to users that these are footnotes, not additional entries.

- *Proximity:* The page grid creates a system of proximities that show the relationship of design objects. As we noted in Chapter 1, the proximity of two objects doesn't mean much except in relation to their proximity with other objects; it's not a matter of absolute distance but of relative distance. Grids help us manage these relationships consistently. For example, the captions are made to "hang" from the bottoms of the photographs, which encourages users to connect the correct caption with the correct photograph.

- *Order:* Page grids can encourage a particular order for users to navigate a page or spread. In this example, three factors encourage users to read in order across the rows rather than down the columns: the strong horizontality of the row of images, the visual separation created by the intervening rows of captions, and the proximity of the captions to the images.

The grid is a powerful convention, and most users will follow it — whether the designer wants them to or not. For example, in this case the grid suggests an order the designers probably didn't intend. The grid might lead users to scan an entire row of photographs all the way *across* the spread. But the numbers on the images suggest that the designer wanted users to read the left page first and then go back up to the top to read the right page. It's important to match the grid design with the users' expectations and needs, as well as with the content and your intentions as a designer. Despite this small flaw, however, this example shows how designers use grids to design a consistent, yet flexible reading system.

In the sections that follow, we'll discuss more fully the advantages and features of grids, what we can place in the grid system, and how we can design grids that meet users' needs while complementing the document's format and content.

Designing Grid Systems

So how do we design grid systems that work? We need to balance two factors that complement each other to meet users' needs. *Content* applies pressure from *inside* the grid, determining the number and width of columns and rows. *Format* applies pressure from *outside* the grid, determining how big the grid can be. We must balance these pressures so that the design objects, the grid, and the format all combine to meet user needs.

Take a look at Figure 5.18, a page spread from a product catalog for kitchen cabinets and accessories. Most users looking at catalogs either *skim* while browsing for something interesting or *scan* for a particular item. This grid design accommodates content within the format to help users accomplish those tasks. It is designed to match the design objects, and the objects are sized to fit the grid. The grid divides each page into four columns, the inner two holding the product images and the outer two holding the product descriptions. This arrangement helps users scan or skim down the central columns. In other words, the grid works from the inside out, arranging content so that the most important design objects and user activities are the focus of the design.

Figure 5.18 Content, format, and user needs determine grid designs. Notice how the design grid in this spread accommodates the content and the format to help users skim for something interesting or scan for a particular product.

The Home Depot, "Home Organization Design Guide" (8½" × 11" pages, 17" × 11" spread).

Ample headspace allows for section headings.

Generous margins and gutters give an open, luxurious, and ordered look to the page and its products.

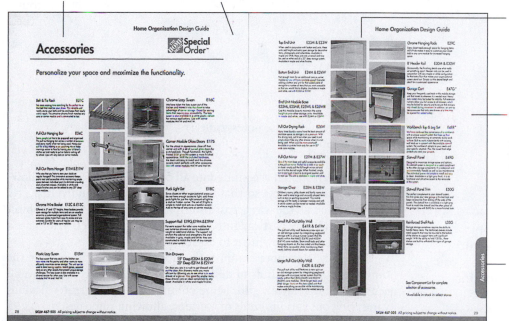

Inside columns reserved for product photos encourage users to browse products visually.

Outside columns allow for arrangement of different-length product descriptions; consistent grid promotes easy skimming or scanning.

Bleed index allows users to thumb through document to find the section they need.

At the same time, the relatively large format (17" × 11" spread) supplies plenty of room for multiple images, allowing users to see many items at once and compare them. The format offers room for generous margins, and gutters provide an ample negative space, framing and supporting the content while bringing the focus to the images from the outside. The margins also provide an area for important metatextual page elements, such as headers, footers, and a bleed index.

Designing Grids for Content

Design the grid system for a document to accommodate every kind of content you need to place in it, *without exceptions*. When planning a grid, you must plan for all of the different design objects in the project and particularly the line length of the basal text.

ASSESSING CONTENT

An effective grid fits all of the different kinds of design objects the project calls for, as well as a wide range of sizes. A document might contain the following objects:

- Headings (levels 1–4)
- Basal text
- Images
- Captions
- Headers/footers
- Tables
- Footnotes
- Special text objects: notes, cautions, warnings, sidebars, pull-quotes

The grid design should accommodate all of these design objects, allowing you to place objects so that they either fit within individual grid fields or extend all the way across multiple grid fields. No design object should extend only partway into another grid field unless you have a specific reason for allowing it to do so.

No design object should extend only partway into another grid field unless you have a specific reason for allowing it to do so.

Generally, the more complex the document and the greater the number of different kinds of design objects, the more columns you'll need in the basic layout grid. More columns give you greater flexibility in laying out various kinds of content, allowing some design objects

DESIGN TIP

Creating Grids in Page Layout Programs

All page layout programs (including InDesign and Quark) include tools to set up page design grids. For example, with InDesign you can set up a grid either on each page individually or on a master page that governs the layout for the entire document.

Doing so requires setting up **guides** (Adobe's term for gridlines) in the Layout : Create Guides dialog. This dialog lets you specify how many rows and columns you want, whether they should fit within the margins or the edge of the page, and how wide the gutter should be. After setting these specifications, you'll see the guides as pale blue or pink lines on the page or spread. These lines won't print, but they will help you align objects to the grid you've created. By default, InDesign will even automatically "snap" objects to these guides, ensuring accurate alignment.

Creating grids in word processing software is more difficult, but it can be done for small-scale jobs. Microsoft Word allows you to set type into columns, or you can use linked text boxes to arrange design objects into something like a gridded design of boxes with text flowing between them. If you use the latter technique, set the text box borders to "none," and select the "Snap objects to grid" option in the Draw : Grid dialog to help you align the text boxes.

to extend across multiple grid fields and others to stay within one. For example, you can create a grid with multiple narrow columns to accommodate small graphics and then allow the text to extend over several columns to create a readable line length.

TEXT SIZE AND LINE LENGTH

The single most important factor determining the width and number of columns is the relationship between *text size* and *line length*. A century of researchers have tried to determine the absolutely most efficient line length for reading, with mixed results. But generally, most designers rely on the rule of thumb that users typically prefer to read lines of text about 7 to 12 words long. Users can read longer or shorter lines with little or no loss of efficiency, but they report that this average line length is most comfortable to read.

Of course, this rule of thumb doesn't lead us to an *actual* width for our columns in terms of inches, picas, or centimeters, because the length of 7–12 words depends on the typeface and font.

Users typically prefer to read lines of text about 7 to 12 words long.

Text set in a small typeface might have a relatively short line length in absolute terms. This text in Tahoma 7-point generates 10-word lines with a line length of about 2³/₄".

However, text set in a larger typeface must have a relatively longer line length. This text in Tahoma 16-point generates lines of about 10 words with a line length of about 6".

And text set in a condensed typeface must have a shorter line length than one set in a broad typeface. This text, set in Arial Narrow 16-point, generates lines of about 10 words with a line length of about 4³/₄".

As a result, much of the question of the width and number of columns is determined by the typeface and font size of the text you intend to use in the document. In the booklet in Figure 5.19, for example, notice that the text on the right-hand page of the spread is relatively small and divided between two columns. On the left-hand page, however, the text runs across both columns, and so must be set in an accordingly larger font size to yield about 7 to 12 words per line. (Also notice, as we suggested in the previous section, that the text on the left-hand page runs all the way across both columns—not just partway—thus respecting the design grid.) This relationship between line length and font size can give you a good sense of the number and width of columns you'll need in your design.

There are some practical limits to line length, however. It's best not to create lines that are too wide or too narrow. Long lines of text can make users lose their place when their eyes move from the end of one line to the beginning of the next. Most users also feel comfortable with columns of text they can read without having to move their head from side to side. Given most people's field of view, this means that lines of text in a typical handheld business or technical document shouldn't be more than 5 or 6 inches (30–36 picas). Of course, the greater the distance between the document and the user's eyes, the longer the line length can be without forcing readers to move their heads. That's why large signs often use much wider lines than smaller documents do.

Narrow lines (fewer than 7 words per line) can also decrease reading efficiency. In reading narrower lines, readers have a greater tendency to *regress*—that is, they flick their eyes back to go over text they've already read. They also tend to fixate for longer periods of time on individual words. Both of these tendencies cut down on reading efficiency.

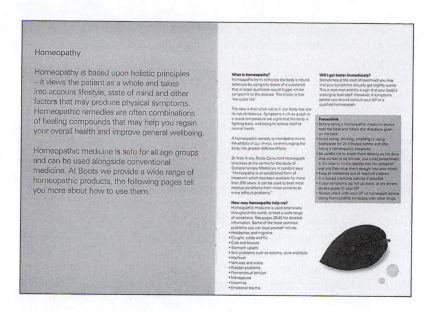

Figure 5.19 Font size, line length, and grids. The text on the left-hand page of this spread extends across both columns of the grid, so the designers used a larger font size to get 7 to 12 words per line. On the right-hand page, the text stays within the individual columns, so the font size must be smaller.

Boots the Chemists, "Complementary Medicine: Your Guide to Choosing and Using Alternative Remedies."

NEGATIVE SPACE: MARGINS AND GUTTERS

We've discussed the positive elements in page designs — the objects we put in grids — but we also need to address the negative elements in page design. By *negative space*, we don't mean *empty space*, which doesn't have a particular function. On the contrary, negative space has specific functions, especially in regulating the proximity of design objects. Negative space can also help draw attention to important design objects, such as graphics, headings (which mark the beginning of a section), paragraph breaks (which mark the beginning of a new topic), bullets (which mark each item in a list), and navigation elements (such as headers and footers). In particular, you'll need to plan carefully for two kinds of negative spaces in every grid layout: *margins*, which separate the grid from the edges of the page or spread, and *gutters*, which separate the grid fields from each other.

When designing margins, take into account both usability and rhetorical effect. Margins are important usability features in documents. Users need margins to focus on the document as something separate from its background; margins enclose the document, giving it a clear frame and boundaries. Margins also give users somewhere to hold the document without covering the content with their fingers. The inside margins can also clearly distinguish between the two pages of a spread. Even on a screen document such as a web page, margins provide valuable space for the user interface (scroll bars and toolbars) and metatextual elements such as navigation bars.

But margins can also have a rhetorical effect. In general, document designers use wider margins to imply openness and luxury. As a result, wide margins are most likely to be employed in high-level designs that deserve the extra expense of paper. In Figure 5.20, a glossy catalog from a university press, the designers have used ample margins to focus users' attention on the photographs. This design builds an ethos of importance for the press and the authors' works, making the products seem valuable and attractive. The result is also very usable, with plenty of open space for users to hold the catalog or write notes.

Narrow margins can imply a business-like air of efficiency and practicality, though at the expense of usability. Figure 5.21 replicates a mutual fund prospectus that uses narrow margins and a low level of design (it's printed on relatively cheap paper with a perfect binding). This page design suggests that the people in charge of the fund will not waste investors' money on fancy documents with lots of artistic negative space, but will provide them with important, unadorned facts. What the designers saved on paper, however, they lost on usability. The inside margins of the prospectus are so tight that users must force the binding open to read it comfortably, and the narrow outside margins give users little space to hold the document.

One common error in designing margins is forgetting that each page or panel needs consistent margins around *all* of its grid areas. For example, consider the inside spreads of two three-panel leaflets. The leaflet in Figure 5.22 is divided into three equal grid fields, and the text is aligned with the edge of each grid field. As a result, in an otherwise adequately designed leaflet, the text margins lie uncomfortably close to the folds.

Figure 5.20 Broad margins imply an ethos of importance.   This brochure has luxurious margins, giving each design object plenty of room to shine. However, it is generally more expensive to print a document with broad margins.

Texas Tech University Press, "America's 100th Meridian," 16" × 8" spread.

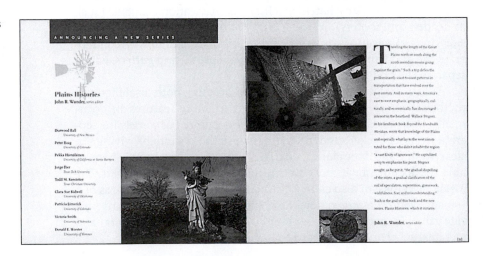

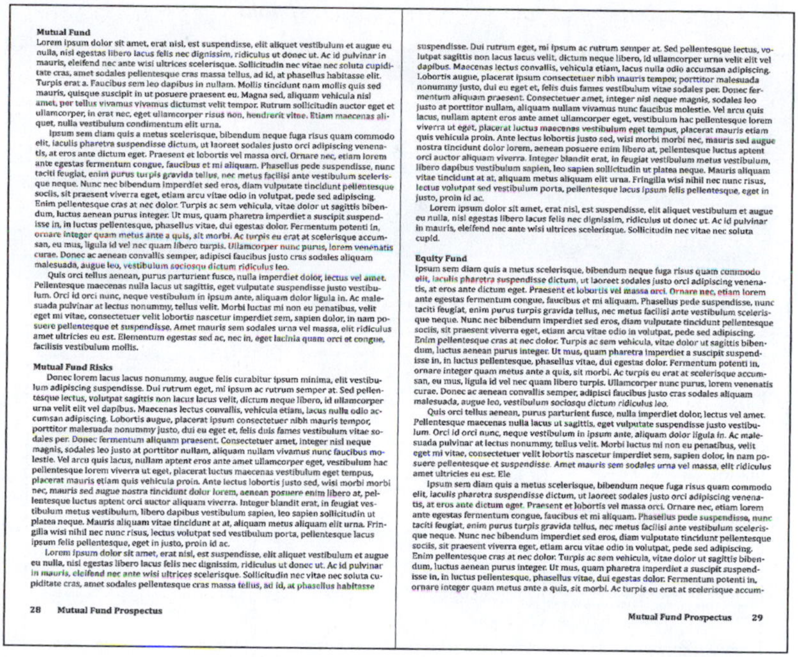

Figure 5.21 Narrow margins imply business-like efficiency. This prospectus for a mutual fund wastes no space on margins. This leads to a sense of utility and economy—just what users would want from someone watching over their investments. However, the narrow margins make the document harder to handle.

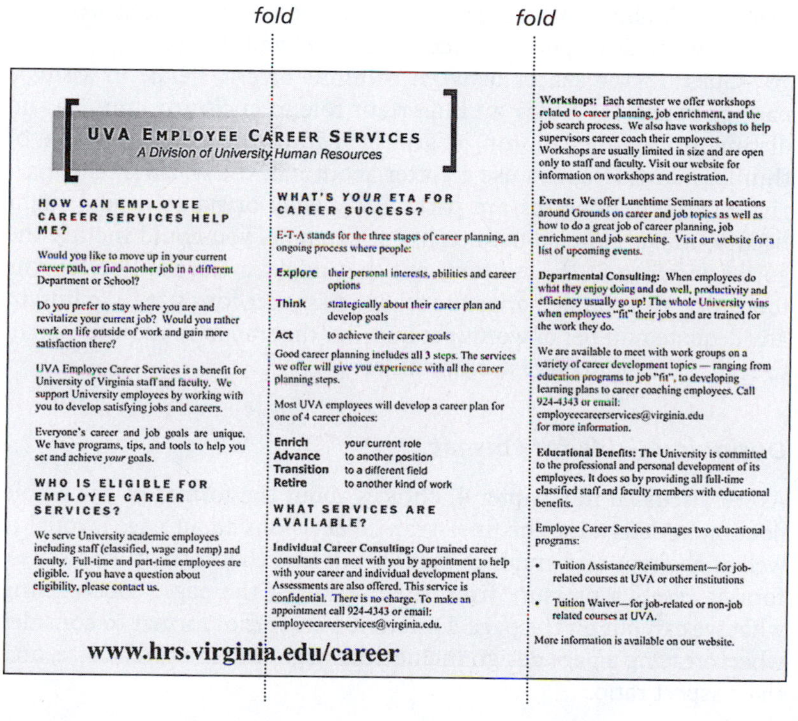

fold   *fold*

Figure 5.22 Using adequate negative space. In this leaflet, adding more negative space to the inside margins between the three columns of the grid would keep the text out of the creases between the panels.

University of Virginia Career Center, "UVA Employee Career Services," 11" × 8½" inside spread.

Figure 5.23 Creating effective inside margins.   Inside margins must be big enough to accommodate the fold without obscuring or cramping content. This leaflet has inside margins twice as big as the outside margins, creating adequate negative space surrounding each text field.

UPS, "International Shipping," 11" × 8½" inside spread of three-panel brochure.

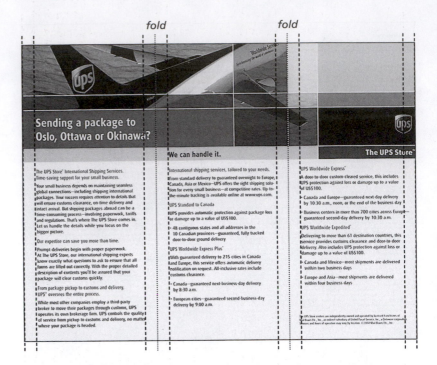

Figure 5.23 uses a consistent margin around each panel, in effect placing a double width at each fold. This preserves the negative space users need to distinguish between one panel and the next.

Gutters—the spaces between columns or grid fields on a single page or panel—also play an important role in enclosing content and distinguishing one column or grid field from the next. As a rule of thumb, many designers use a gutter about half the width of the margin. But if the margins are particularly wide or narrow, you might need to make some adjustments. For example, you could modify the gutter width to fit the content, but that might make the line lengths too short. You could change the text to a smaller font size to maintain an adequate number of words per line, but that might make it too small to read. (Design requires compromise!)

Designing Grids for Format

As we discussed in Chapter 4, choices about the format of the whole document determine the finer-grained decisions about page layout, as well as the type and graphics that we put into that format. In a sense, format exerts a pressure from the outside of the page, constraining what we can put on the page. Different elements of format to consider when creating a page design include the page size, the spread size, and their aspect ratio.

The page or spread size plays a significant role in the page design decisions you'll make. Smaller documents constrain us to simpler grid systems with fewer columns and rows, and with accordingly fewer options for arranging content within the grid. Larger documents, however, encourage more complex grid systems with more options for arrangement.

Size presents a particularly difficult issue in screen documents because you often do not know how big the user's computer screen might be or what its resolution might be. Screen documents must be designed to work equally well on multiple sizes of computer screens and at various resolutions. In practical terms, however, most designers aim at the most common screen sizes and resolutions, hoping that the majority of users will have a positive experience with the design.

More specifically, the width of the page plays a significant role in how we lay out the grid. As we just said, most designers aim for a line length of about 7 to 12 words per line of text. But the wider the page, the more words will fit onto it in a given font size. To maintain 7 to 12 words per line, you must either increase the size of the text or reduce the width of the column. So typically, the wider the paper, the more likely you'll need multiple columns of text or very large margins.

Finally, the aspect ratio of the format makes a big difference in page layout decisions because it changes the way we can arrange content on a page. A taller-than-wide format encourages a vertical arrangement of design objects — for example, vertical columns of text. But a wider-than-tall format, like typical computer screens and common two-page spreads, encourages a more horizontal arrangement of design objects as we try to encourage users to scan across as well as down the visual field. In addition, for bound or folded print documents, we need to create a grid that works both on each page individually and on spreads of two pages or multiple panels simultaneously.

One of the biggest distinctions between printed and screen documents is the aspect ratio of their formats: most printed documents are taller than wide, whereas most screens are wider than tall (Figure 5.24). A typical XVGA computer screen, for example, has an aspect ratio of 4:3 (width:height), while a letter-sized sheet has an aspect ratio of 17:22. But printed documents can also be arranged in formats that fold out to show spreads of two pages at a time. A spread built on a

Computer screen 4:3 ratio	Letter-sized page 17:22 ratio	Two-page spread 17:11 ratio

Figure 5.24 Common aspect ratios on page and screen.   Aspect ratio has a significant effect on page grid decisions. Screen documents are typically designed for a wider aspect ratio than print documents.

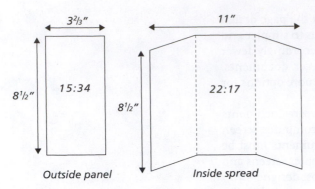

Figure 5.25 **Aspect ratios in a three-panel leaflet.**   In this format, we must design both for the narrow panels and for the wide spread that's visible when users open the sheet fully.

tabloid-size sheet (11" × 17") shows two letter-sized pages but a whole spread with an aspect ratio of 17:11. This capability of pages complicates how we design grid systems because it changes the aspect ratio of the visual field, making it wider than tall when we consider the entire spread.

On the other hand, some formats can also make us accommodate both tall and narrow and short and wide visual fields at the same time. A common three-panel leaflet built on a letter-sized sheet (Figure 5.25) means that we must design both for the single narrow panel users see first (3⅔" × 8½", or an aspect ratio of about 15:34) and for the entire spread of three panels users see when they open the leaflet (11" × 8½", or 22:17).

DIMENSIONS AND MEASUREMENTS

Even after we assess content and format, we still need to specify the width of columns, rows, gutters, and margins with precision and consistency. Fortunately, designers have developed a variety of ways to measure these layout elements.

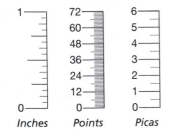

Figure 5.26 **Inches, points, and picas.**   Six picas make an inch; 12 points make a pica.

Some designers (particularly in Europe) prefer to use measurements in centimeters and millimeters. But the most common measurement system in print page design uses English units of measurement based on the inch but with two units particular to document design: *picas* and *points* (see Figure 5.26). As we discussed in Chapter 1, 1 inch = 6 picas = 72 points. In other words,

- 1 pica = 12 points = ⅙" = 0.167"
- 1 point = ¹⁄₁₂ pica = ¹⁄₇₂" = 0.0139"

The notation system for these units represents picas and points in this format:

[number of picas]p[number of points]

For example, 12p6 describes a measurement of 12 picas plus 6 points (or 12 and one-half picas). This measurement would also be equal to about 2.08". The text area of this book's page layout is set at 37p6 wide (37 picas plus 6 points = 37 and one-half picas = 6.25"). Most page layout programs will allow you to specify dimensions of columns and graphics with this notation system.

As you might expect, this notation system is also used extensively in typography to determine font size, which is usually specified by

DESIGN TIP

Creating Grids for Web Pages

Creating grids in web pages is somewhat more difficult than in print design. Most designers use HTML tables with invisible borders to organize and align content into a grid. Alternately, you can use cascading style sheets (CSS) with absolute positioning to specify the grid fields in which to place content.

The biggest difficulty involves specifying widths of grids and columns as **absolute width** or **dynamic width**. Each approach has advantages and disadvantages. With absolute widths, you control the precise width of the grid and columns, usually measured in pixels. This approach will keep the width of the grid and columns the same regardless of how wide the user's monitor might be, and whatever you put in the grid will be arranged pretty much the way you intended it. You will probably be safe if you design for the lowest common denominator of screen resolutions: 800 × 600 pixels. But a user with a lower screen resolution won't be able to see the whole grid without scrolling left and right, and a user with a higher screen resolution will see the grid as a relatively small block that covers only part of the screen.

With dynamic widths, you assign a certain percentage of screen width to the grid and of the grid width to each column. The advantage is that the grid will shrink or stretch to the available size of the monitor. Users with visual disabilities usually appreciate this feature, which works best with the software they use to increase text on web pages to a size they can read. The disadvantage is that the contents of the grid might shift unexpectedly, causing awkward text wrapping and misplaced images. And if you use CSS positioning (a common layout technique for web pages), there's also a possibility that the grid fields you specified might actually overlap on some monitors.

points. It's also used in dimensioning design objects (such as columns of text and the dimensions of graphics).

For pages on screens, designers typically use measurements based in pixels rather than in inches or centimeters. This choice makes sense because it allows the size of the layout and design objects to match the output technology (a computer monitor) very precisely. Keep in mind, however, that pixels differ in size from monitor to monitor. On one monitor, 100 pixels might be about an inch; on a monitor of higher resolution with smaller pixels, 100 pixels might be more like 1¼ inch. When designing documents for the screen, take into account this potential difference in size of pixels.

Breaking the Grid

After you've established a strong grid system, you can choose to *break* that system for emphasis or effect. For example, the magazine page in Figure 5.27 (page 148) uses the common technique of breaking the grid with a *pull-quote*—a quotation from the story

DESIGN TIP

Choose a Dimensioning System and Stick with It

Whatever dimensioning system you choose, use it consistently throughout the entire document design, including the layout and all design objects. Inconsistencies will inevitably creep in if you measure some aspects of the design in centimeters, others in picas, and still others in pixels.

Figure 5.27 Breaking the grid with a pull-quote.   This page layout uses a strong, two-column grid and then breaks it with a pull-quote that straddles the two columns.

Donna Seaman, "The People of the Book: Riding the Third Wave," *American Libraries*, May 2005 (8½" × 11").

COLLECTIONS   53

The People of the Book: Riding the Third Wave

Two new library-based programs examine the immigrant experience that permeates Jewish-American literature   by Donna Seaman

I entered the world of book reviewing, criticism, and literary journalism during the height of the multicultural movement, when academics, critics, and librarians were belatedly recognizing the significance of works by writers from groups left out of the official canon of American literature. During this awakening, books by African Americans, Latinos, Native Americans, and Asian Americans, as well as gay and lesbian writers, were read with fresh eyes, accorded serious critical attention, and embraced by the public. This enrichment of American letters has had lasting and profound effects, and librarians were in the vanguard of this movement, not only by making books available to readers, but also by sponsoring book groups and participating in book discussion events, including the American Library Association's latest "Let's Talk About It" (LTAI) program, "Jewish Literature: Identity and Imagination" (AL, Mar., p. 7–8).

I've given a great deal of thought to the relationship between ethnicity and literature, and as a Jew I've contemplated my heritage. Yet I did not expect to see Jewish literature recognized as a subset of American letters because Jewish writers have long been in the mainstream. Think Saul Bellow, Philip Roth, E. L. Doctorow, and Cynthia Ozick. But a confluence of events has convinced me that there is such a thing as Jewish literature that is recognized as unique and avidly read by Jewish and non-Jewish readers alike.

The gestalt of exile
I was inspired to reconsider the state of Jewish literature after I realized that I was coming across a surprising number of provocative works of fiction about what it means to be Jewish in the 21st century. I was quite taken with Julie Orringer's fiercely beautiful short story collection, *How to Breathe Underwater* (Knopf, 2003), in which she deftly portrays an array of young Jews, includ-

> I thought about all that has changed (and all that has not) since my Russian-Jewish grandfather arrived in New York City.

ing Hasidic teens. As I read Russian-Jewish immigrant Lara Vapnyar's *There Are Jews in My House* (Pantheon, 2003), a stunning short story collection set in Moscow and Brooklyn, I found myself thinking about all that has changed (and all that has remained the same) since my Russian-Jewish grandfather arrived in New York City as a child. Another debut author, David Bezmozgis, who also writes about the Russian-Jewish immigrant experience in *Natasha and Other Stories* (Farrar, 2004), caused me to consider how, from the Exodus forward, exile has been at the core of Jewish existence, and how the Diaspora caused Jews to become known as the people of the book. As Jonathan Rosen, author most recently of a novel featuring a woman rabbi, *Joy Comes in the Morning* (Farrar, 2004), writes so succinctly in his brilliant interpretative treatise, *The Talmud and the Internet: A Journey between Worlds* (Farrar, 2000), the Talmud, the great gathering of Jewish tradition and thought, "offered a virtual home for an uprooted culture, and grew out of the Jewish need to pack civilization into words and wander out into the world."

When ALA's Public Programs Office asked me to help evaluate the materials for its new LTAI program, I had the opportunity to further clarify my perception of Jewish literature. A 22-year-old reading and book discussion series conducted at libraries nationwide, LTAI programs are led by local scholars and supported by exceptionally thoughtful and enlightening materials. Themes have included family and work, books for children, women's autobiography, Latino literature, Native-American writing, the African-American migration, and Japanese literature.

DONNA SEAMAN *is an associate editor for* Booklist, *editor of the anthology* In Our Nature: Stories about Wildness *(Univ. of Georgia, 2002), and host of the Chicago radio station WLUW program "Open Books." Her latest book is* Writers on the Air: Conversations about Books *(forthcoming from Paul Dry Books).*

Let's Talk About It in Chicago
There will be an informational meeting about the LTAI "Jewish Literature" program at ALA Annual Conference on Sunday, June 26 at 10:30 a.m. Libraries interested in being one of the hosts of the second round of programs may apply for a $1,500 grant by September 30. Details about this and other ALA Public Programs Office opportunities for libraries can be found at www.ala.org/publicprograms, or contact publicprograms@ala.org.

set off and enlarged to attract interest. Here, the pull-quote is presented in reverse text on a green field that is centered between two columns of the grid. It differs from elements like the basal text, which stays within individual grid fields, or the subtitle, which extends across both grid fields.

A more vibrant example is Figure 5.28, a layout from a glossy university library newsletter. The design has a strongly established grid with three columns per page (six per spread). The four inside columns on each spread are used for a story on songwriters; the two outside columns on each spread are used for sidebars, photographs, or other ancillary information, most of which stays strictly within the grid.

Figure 5.28 Breaking the grid boldly.   Images of a rare volume of Shakespeare and of a guitar break across the grid in this design. The text wraps around the objects, making the objects seem more three-dimensional and realistic.

Notice, though, how two striking elements break out of the grid: photographs of a rare volume of Shakespeare and of a guitar. These design objects are placed so they extend across the grid borders. The Gestalt law of continuation makes the grid border seem to extend beneath these objects, making them appear to pop out in a third dimension, as if they were laid *on top* of the grid. The Shakespeare volume pokes a corner out of the gold-colored field enclosing the sidebar. The guitar extends across the spine gutter and bleeds completely off the page while itself enclosing a text object: the lyrics to a song. The normally rectangular columns of text are wrapped around the irregularly shaped guitar, allowing a bit of negative space between text and image. The effect is to make the design objects vibrant and interesting — but it depends on the fact that they break the convention of a well-established grid.

Breaking the grid should always be a strategic choice, used sparingly for the most interesting or important information on the page. The drama of breaking the grid depends on the strength of the grid itself. If you break the grid too frequently, you'll undercut that strength, making the effect less emphatic. You might risk looking like the writer who ends all his sentences with exclamation points: after a while, the reader becomes oblivious to them. By the same token, if lots of elements break the grid, none of them will get any particular emphasis.

Breaking the grid should always be a strategic choice, used sparingly for the most interesting or important information on the page.

Exercises

1. Collect three documents that follow the conventional page designs discussed under "Using Grids for Page Design" on page 132. Then look for documents that seem to flout these conventions. In class, form small groups and share your documents with each other. Discuss these questions:

   - What are the purposes of the conventions you see in these page designs?

   - What seem to be the motivations behind breaking page design conventions?

   - What perceptual, cultural, and rhetoric effects does following or breaking conventions seem to involve?

   - How do we decide where to strike a balance between following and breaking conventions?

2. Sometimes looking at another person's page design can give you a better idea of the kinds of details you must consider when you design your own pages. For this exercise, choose a document you explored in exercise 1 that uses a clearly defined grid. Draw out a schematic of the grid — much like the diagrams in this chapter — noting the dimensions of margins, grid fields, columns, rows, and gutters in inches, centimeters, or picas. (For the last one, you'll need a printer's rule.) Be as specific and accurate as possible.

   What do you think were the purposes behind setting up the grid as the designer did? How consistent was the designer in using the grid he or she established? What were the designer's motivations for breaking the grid?

3. Take the worst, most inconsistent page design from those you just explored and sketch out a grid system that will tame its inconsistencies. Then follow these steps:

   a. Analyze what you think are the most serious problems of the page design.

   b. Create several paper sketches to try out several options for new designs.

   c. Choose your best design and recreate a page in page layout software. Use placeholder text ("lorem ipsum") for the text objects, and place frames or basic geometric shapes for the images.

   d. Discuss in what ways you feel your design improves the original document.

Works Cited

Arnheim, Rudolf. *Visual Thinking*. Berkeley: University of California Press, 1997 [1969].

Disraeli, Benjamin. *The Young Duke*. Ed. Miles A. Kimball. London: Pickering & Chatto, 2003.

Findlay, John M., and Iain D. Gilchrist. *Active Vision: The Psychology of Looking and Seeing*. Oxford: Oxford University Press, 2003.

Meggs, Phillip. *A History of Graphic Design*. 2nd ed. New York: Van Nostrand Reinhold, 1992.

Outing, Steve, and Laura Ruel. "The Best of Eyetrack III: What We Saw When We Looked through Their Eyes." The Poynter Institute. Online: <http://poynterextra.org/eyetrack2004/>.

Tschichold, Jan. *The New Typography*. Trans. Ruari McLean. Berkeley: University of California Press, 1995.

Further Reading

Elam, Kimberly. *Grid Systems*. New York: Princeton Architectural Press, 2003.

Müller-Brockmann, Josef. *Grid Systems in Graphic Design: A Visual Communication Manual for Graphic Designers, Typographers, and Three Dimensional Designers*. New York: Hastings House, 1981.

Samara, Timothy. *Making and Breaking the Grid: A Graphic Design Layout Workshop*. Gloucester, MA: Rockport, 2002.

CHAPTER 6

Type

Most people don't pay much attention to typography when they create documents. They simply open a word processor and type, accepting whatever defaults the program gives them. Sometimes that approach works for designers, too. You wouldn't want to spend an hour agonizing over what typeface to use for an e-mail to a coworker.

But for more complex or important documents, paying attention to typography is an absolute must. Good typographic design doesn't just make documents look good — it gives users important clues about the structure of the document, the purpose of design objects, and the ethos of the organization that created the document.

Consider the three-panel leaflet in Figure 6.1, which has a variety of text design objects, including a product logo (ABREVE), a corporate logo (ArchiText), several designs of headings, a pull-quote, captions, and two kinds of basal text. By our count, it uses six typefaces in twelve sizes and modifications (such as bold, italic, reverse text, and different

Figure 6.1 Typographic design in a leaflet. Careful typographic design creates a clear structure, distinguishes between different kinds of text design objects, and implies a positive ethos.

ABREVE, ArchiText.

Outside

Inside

colors) on the outside of the leaflet and one typeface in six sizes and modifications on the inside.

Despite its typographic complexity, the leaflet looks simple and clear. Users can easily understand the role of each text design object because they are easy to distinguish from one another. On the inside panels, the type used in the quotation is different from the caption that identifies the speaker; we can also tell the difference between the headings, basal text, and bulleted lists. On the outside middle panel, we can easily distinguish between the continents, cities, and street addresses.

These visual clues of typeface, color, and size help us *see* a logical structure, with ABREVE at the top of the hierarchy in the largest and boldest type, and office addresses at the bottom in the smallest and lightest type. Finally, the clarity of the typographic design contributes to an ethos of clarity for the client organization—a company that specializes in translating technical documents. Obviously, the designers spent a lot of time thinking about the typography of this document.

Creating typographically successful documents requires a similar attention to detail. To understand how to use type, you'll need to learn minute distinctions—some that may seem too insignificant to worry about. But learning the finer characteristics of type will help you create more successful and usable documents.

In this chapter, we begin by considering how typography relates to the three perspectives discussed in Chapter 2: perception, culture, and rhetoric. We'll help you build a vocabulary that will help you recognize and analyze type more accurately and precisely. Then we'll discuss some of the common distinctions between different kinds of typefaces, as well as some practical advice about how to use type in print and on-screen.

MORE ABOUT . . . TYPOGRAPHIC TERMS

These basic typographic terms will help you throughout this chapter:

- **Type:** letter shapes used for printing or on-screen display.
- **Typeface** (or just **face**): one consistent design of type. Times New Roman is one typeface; Arial is another.
- **Font:** one size of a typeface, including all of the lowercase letters, uppercase letters, numerals, and punctuation. Times New Roman 12-point is one font. Times New Roman 14-point is a different font. (*Font* is also a term used to indicate the digital file for a typeface, so it's increasingly used synonymously with *typeface*.)
- **Font family** or **type family:** a collection of all of the fonts in a typeface, including specialized fonts such as light, medium, demi (between medium and bold), **bold**, *italic*, SMALL CAPS, condensed, and expanded.
- **Typography:** the practice of designing type—or more broadly, the practice of designing documents with type.

Three Perspectives on Type

Perception

Although people often think of reading text as an intellectual activity, it's actually a *visual* activity—a process of scanning shapes that we decipher as signifying something. In most written languages, these shapes (called **letters**, **characters**, or **glyphs**) signify phonetic sounds that combine into words and have their own distinctive shapes, known as **boumas** (pronounced bŏw-muhs). In other written languages, such as Chinese, individual shapes (**ideograms** and **pictograms**) can signify or represent entire concepts.

But if reading is a visual process, how does it happen? Researchers are still trying to find answers to this question, but some theories are generally accepted.

You first learned these shapes by rote, probably as your ABCs, laboriously practicing how to recognize and draw them. Later, you became so good at deciphering letters that you could recognize whole words merely by their shapes. Eventually, as you grew more practiced at reading and writing, you stopped thinking consciously about the shapes and skipped straight to their meanings.

However, the shapes themselves remain important to our ease of reading, which requires text to be created with clearly defined, consistent, and familiar type. From our long experience as both readers and writers, each of us holds archetypal models of what's acceptable for each letter of the alphabet. Of course, people's archetypal models might differ, depending on how and where they learned the alphabet.

But as type design diverges from our archetype, it grows more and more difficult to read. Consider Figure 6.2, which shows glyphs of the same letter represented in different typefaces. They're all *V*s. But you can probably clearly recognize the letters on the left as such, while the letters further to the right probably seem less and less familiar. The *V* in Gigi might look to some people like a lowercase *r*, and in Blackadder ITC, the *V* could even masquerade as a *P* or a *T*. In Abduction, the *V* almost loses its identity entirely. In other words, the letters on the left better exemplify "V-ness": two diverging diagonal lines joined at a bottom vertex. The farther away we get from this archetypal shape, the more difficult it is to connect the shapes and their corresponding significations.

Figure 6.2 How letter shapes affect reading. All of these shapes represent the letter *V*, but the less *V*-like the shape, the harder it is to recognize.

V	V	V	V	V	V	V
Times New Roman	*Franklin Gothic Book*	*Papyrus*	*Bodoni MT Black*	*Gigi*	*Blackadder ITC*	*Abduction*

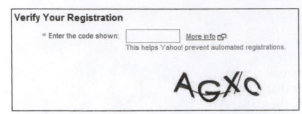

Figure 6.3 Users can recognize remarkably distorted type.   Here, Yahoo! uses distorted letters to defeat programs that create spurious accounts for sending spam and viruses. People can read this type to authorize the new account, but computers can't.

Yahoo.com. Reproduced with permission of Yahoo! Inc. © 2007 by Yahoo! Inc. YAHOO! and the YAHOO! logo are trademarks of Yahoo! Inc.

> You can dream, create, design, and build
> the most wonderful place in the world, but
> it requires people to make the dream a reality.
> —Walt Disney

Figure 6.4 Reading blurred type.   Blurred type is still readable because of boumas, even though individual words might be hard to make out.

> Yuo cna deram, craete, disegn, nad biuld
> the msot wdrnufeol plcae in teh wlord, but it
> riqueers poplee to mkae the darem a reliaty.
> —Wlat Dsneiy

Figure 6.5 Reading transposed letters.   Although some letters in this quotation are transposed, we can still make out the words because of their general shape.

Despite this tendency, users can still recognize remarkably distorted type. Our perceptions allow for a considerable amount of difference in letter forms. Free e-mail services like Yahoo!, for example, commonly ask users to confirm their request for a new account by deciphering distorted type, which keeps automated registration software from opening new accounts (Figure 6.3). And we can often make out sloppy handwritten notes—sometimes even our own! But in general, the further away a letter shape is from our archetypal sense of the letter form, the more effort it requires for recognition; reading slows and comprehension drops as a result.

The significance of individual letters builds up to that of the general word shapes. Most practiced readers do not read one letter at a time, but they do use the combined shapes of letters to perceive words. As we mentioned in Chapter 5, readers' eyes move across a page of text in small, rapid jumps, called saccades. Between saccades, they fixate on a group of three to four letters, and then jump on to another group—although not necessarily the closest or the next group. Readers often skip ahead and back as they read. They also don't typically fixate on all of the letters in a line of text. Instead, they read by deciphering the hazy boumas that surround each fixation. You can see how this works by looking at the sentence in Figure 6.4. Although some letters are hard to make out individually, you should be able to make out the words successfully, if not easily.

Another indication that boumas are important to reading is that readers can still decipher a word when some of the letters are transposed (Figure 6.5). These transpositions clearly slow down reading, but because the general *shapes* of the words are not altered, most people can still read the passage accurately. In Gestalt terms, readers create "closure," making the best meaning they can out of incomplete visual cues.

In Gestalt terms, boumas derive their good figure not just from their shape but from contrast with the surrounding ground and separation from other boumas. You may have noticed that the text on some websites or documents with colored or patterned backgrounds is hard to read. Strong bouma figures require good contrast with the ground, which is why text is often black on a white ground—the highest contrast possible. Boumas also need to be surrounded by consistent negative space—above, below, before, and after each word—so readers can perceive good figures that simultaneously distinguish individual words and connect them into a sentence.

Wordsprintedwithoutspacescanbeveryhardtoread.

So   can   words   printed with   inconsistent   spaces.

Culture

Type has an important role in culture, primarily because of the reciprocal development of printing technologies and cultures. As new printing technologies were developed, printed documents became increasingly common and cheap, deeply affecting culture. At the same time, cultures affected the growth of printing technologies as styles and ideologies changed.

In previous centuries, type design was an expensive, highly skilled, and labor-intensive process. Movable type, developed in China in the eleventh century CE, first took the form of carved wooden blocks, one for each symbol to be printed. But these blocks wore out quickly, and a single letter or symbol might vary considerably (think about how many *e*'s are in an average page of type and how hard it would be to carve dozens of identical *e*'s). So, beginning with Johannes Gutenberg (1398–1468), considered the originator of European letter-press printing, European type designers devised a solution to this problem. They carved each letter of a font onto the end of steel punches and then used these punches to strike each letter into a brass matrix. The matrix was placed in a mold, and molten type metal — an alloy of lead, antimony, and tin — was poured into the mold to form each piece of type. Each matrix could thereby mold many identical pieces of type.

Each size of a typeface, however, required an entire set of punches and matrices. The collected type for each size became known as a font, which included multiple pieces of type for all letters, numerals, capitals, and punctuation in that size. Because type was heavy, awkward to store, and expensive, most letter-press print shops had only a few fonts of three or four typefaces. As a result, most early documents used relatively simple and restrained (although sometimes carefully crafted) typographic designs. European type design went through several stages related to the cultural values of the times. Early typefaces, known as *old style* faces, echoed common handwriting practices from the fifteenth through seventeenth centuries (Figure 6.6). This made sense in that printing was a newer and cheaper technology than handwriting, and printers needed to convince audiences of the value of this new way of duplicating texts. Old style typefaces are typically known by their graceful curves and a moderate contrast between thick and thin strokes.

With the rise of the Enlightenment in the eighteenth century, type designers such as Giambattista Bodoni (1740–1813) and Firmin Didot (1764–1836) designed typefaces that incorporated regular curves and lines. In doing so, they sought to separate typography from

Garamond

Figure 6.6 Old style typefaces. Garamond, an old style typeface, echoes Renaissance handwriting.

Bodoni

Figure 6.7 Modern typefaces.
Bodoni, a modern typeface, was
developed in the eighteenth century
to emphasize ideal geometry rather
than the common handwriting practices reflected by old style faces.

Old English

Figure 6.8 Blackletter typefaces.
Blackletter typefaces like Old English
echo northern European forms of
handwriting. Many blackletter faces
were drawn during the Gothic
Revival of the nineteenth century.

Times New Roman

Johnston Sans Serif

**Figure 6.9 Changes to type in the
early twentieth century.**   Stanley
Morison's Times New Roman and
Edward Johnston's Johnston Sans
Serif were developed in the early
part of the twentieth century to
meet new needs and to work with
new technologies.

handwriting and relate it to the universal, rational principles of abstract
geometry. These faces are still called *modern*—and they *were* modern, for their time (Figure 6.7). Modern typefaces are recognizable
by their geometric consistency and high contrast between thick and
thin strokes.

In the nineteenth century, designers extended Bodoni and Didot's
separation of type from handwriting but left behind their notions of
ideal type geometry. This produced typefaces that were decorative,
brash, and visually interesting—but not always easy to read. This development matched the growth of commercial advertising and the rise
of printed material as a commodity that needed to attract attention as
well as convey information. As a result, many typefaces developed
during this period echoed current styles and fads. For example, a fad
for all things medieval, the Gothic Revival, led to the redrawing of
blackletter typefaces. The Chicago *Sun-Times*, headquartered in a well-
known Gothic Revival–style building in downtown Chicago, still uses
a blackletter face for its newspaper title (Figure 6.8).

The end of the nineteenth century and the beginning of the twentieth century saw a return to old style typefaces. These were often redrawn for Linotype and Monotype, new printing technologies that
used large machines to cast type on the fly; the type was melted down
at the end of each print job and reused. These machines required the
development of new matrices, which gave designers the opportunity
to design new typefaces. For example, during this period Stanley Morison designed Times New Roman for *The Times* of London, and Edward
Johnston designed Johnston Sans Serif for the London Underground
signs (Figure 6.9). At the same time, the eighteenth-century desire for
a rational, geometric type arose again with modernism, with its interest in minimalism, abstraction, and universalism. For example, designers associated with the German Bauhaus movement boiled down
letter forms to their minimal characteristics, designing abstract faces
intended to be effective in all settings.

Later in the twentieth century, two technological developments
changed typography dramatically, increasing its flexibility in the hands
of document designers. First, in the 1950s, printing began to be performed by photography and offset presses (see Chapter 11). Photography allowed much greater flexibility in typesetting than hot metal.

Second, in the 1980s designers began to create documents with
computers, using word processing and page layout programs. The digital type used in these programs led to a renaissance in type design.
Nearly anyone with an interest in typography could become a type
designer using a desktop computer and relatively inexpensive software.
Echoing the development of postmodernism and the Web, graphic
designers in particular used digital typography to experiment with layered, off-kilter layouts and difficult-to-read typefaces, attempting to

draw readers' attention to the physical text as well as to whatever its words were trying to convey. Borrowing a term from popular music, this style was often called *grunge* or *postmodern* typography.

Postmodern type designs tended to grab attention but at the cost of usability. So in recent years, information design has brought the emphasis back to focus on the user's experience of type, favoring designs that users find attractive, useful, and easy to read. As our society grows increasingly complex, this focus on the user's needs will likely continue as a guiding force in document design.

Rhetoric

The perceptual and cultural perspectives lay the groundwork for the visual rhetoric of typography — that is, the use of typography to influence, affect, or guide readers toward their own goals or the goals of the client sponsoring the document.

This assertion is still in some ways controversial, primarily because of the continued popularity of the "crystal goblet" theory of typography. According to this theory, first propounded by typographer Beatrice Warde, typography should be transparent, holding content like a crystal goblet holds a fine wine. When designed and set well, in other words, type shouldn't even be noticed by users, who could focus instead on the content the type held.

However, this theory underestimates the rhetorical significance of visual forms, assuming that there can be content separate from form. Typography can have important effects on users, particularly in terms of conveying structural and rhetorical meta-information about the document. For example, type reinforces the commonly hierarchical structure of documents, showing users how the different parts of a document fit together. Document designers use type to break down a document into sections and subsections, designing headings of different sizes to show the logical hierarchy of a document. In this book, for example, we have used Frutiger in several sizes to differentiate the levels of headings visually (Figure 6.10). This range of sizes and weights of

Heading Level 1: Frutiger 65 Bold, 13 pt

Heading Level 2: Frutiger 66 Bold Italic, 10.5 pt

HEADING LEVEL 3: FRUTIGER 55 ROMAN BOOK, 8 PT

Heading Level 4: Frutiger 56 Italic, 9.5 pt

Basal text: Mendoza Roman Book, 9.5 pt

Figure 6.10 The typography of this book.   The design of this book uses different fonts and typefaces to reinforce the book's logical structure. The heading faces are from the Frutiger family, while the basal text is Mendoza Roman Book.

type helps readers understand that a subsection with a level 2 heading is one that "belongs to" a previous section with a level 1 heading. This book also uses Mendoza Roman Book 9.5-point for the basal text face; notice how it contrasts with the headings.

Applied consistently, these typographic contrasts guide readers through a document. In fact, headings serve as an integral index readers can skim visually, looking for whatever information they need most. Headings and paragraph breaks also make the text looks less like a dense gray field. Many readers are filled with a dogged despair at the prospect of working through long, undistinguished paragraphs; a more open typographic design with multiple paragraphs and section headings encourages readers to continue by giving them many resting places along the way. More open typographic designs also give readers multiple places to enter and exit the text — especially important if the document provides reference or procedural information, such as a manual.

More broadly, typefaces can suggest a specific tone or ethos to readers; typography creates what Katie Salen has called a "voice-over" that influences how people see the document. Some typefaces are very conservative. Times New Roman, for example, until 2007 the default face of Microsoft Word and the most common typeface used in the business world, suggests a tone and ethos of business. Other common typefaces are more informal:

> Comic Sans, for example, looks as if it were written with a felt-tip marker.

> Curlz looks playful and childish.

DESIGN TIP

Using a Rhetorically Appropriate Typeface

Match the visual tone of the document you are designing with the rhetorical situation for which it's intended. You probably wouldn't write an important business memo to your supervisor in Comic Sans because you want to be taken seriously as a professional. By the same token, you probably wouldn't write a love letter in Times New Roman, lest your friend think he or she is being dumped (or worse yet, sued).

But context is everything. If you work at a day care facility or your relationship is very formal, the reverse might be more rhetorically appropriate.

Users recognize the visual tone of type and use it as a clue to the nature and purpose of the document, as well as to the character of the document's author.

Typography has an undeniable effect on how readers respond to documents. As a visual rhetorician, you'll want to take that effect into account and even use it to the advantage of your clients and users.

Looking at Type

You've been using type since you first began to read and write. But if you're like most people, you might not have thought very carefully or precisely about type. Before you can manipulate type with confidence, you'll need to sharpen your senses to recognize the many small but significant differences between typefaces.

Knowing the details of letter forms is a key part of recognizing different typefaces, so we'll start there. Then we'll discuss the various categories of typefaces to help you make good typographic decisions in your own document designs. With your typographic senses sharpened, you will also be able to identify and classify typefaces more accurately.

Letter Forms

Typographers design typefaces so all the letters have consistent features. To do so, they need a comprehensive terminology that describes the shapes and parts of letters. This terminology can be complex, but knowing a little of it can help you recognize differences between typefaces and make good choices for your typographic designs. In general, glyphs in English employ the characteristics shown in Figure 6.11.

Figure 6.11 Characteristics of letter forms. Knowing this terminology will help you identify and distinguish different typefaces.

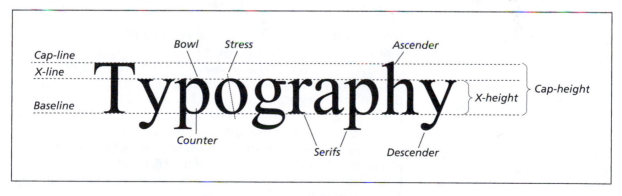

STROKES

Type designers use a basic vocabulary of *strokes* to make most of the letters in a typeface, giving the characters visual consistency with each other as well as a distinction from other typefaces.

Strokes derive their name and their shapes from the fact that most typefaces are based on the stroke marks of a broad-nibbed calligraphic pen. Marks made by the pen are typically broader on vertical strokes and narrower on horizontal strokes. They also transition smoothly from broad to narrow as the pen forms a curve, such as in the letter O. These variations in stroke width survive even in many digital typefaces used today, and they can be used to identify typefaces. Some faces have significant contrast between the thick and thin areas of the strokes; others have a minimal contrast. Many typefaces also break with this tradition entirely, using geometric, irregular, or purposefully inconsistent strokes.

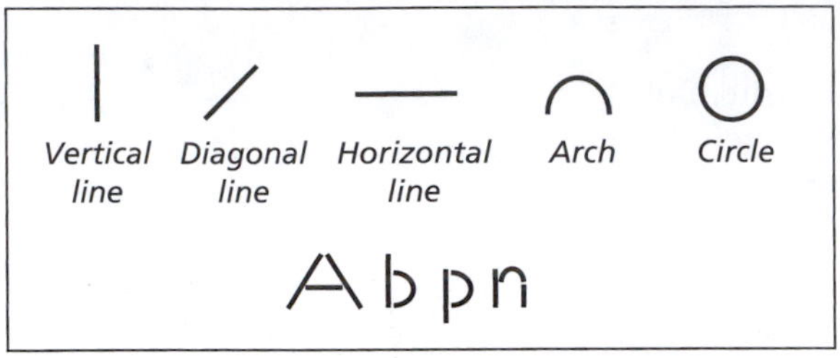

Regardless of their specific shape, strokes are the basic building blocks of most letters in the English alphabet. Figure 6.12 shows the basic strokes that combine to make English characters. For example, the uppercase letter *A* is made by two diagonal lines and one horizontal line, the lowercase letters *b* and *p* are made by a vertical line and an arch, and the lowercase letter *n* is made by two vertical lines and an arch.

Figure 6.12 Strokes from which all English characters are made.   Strokes are the basic building blocks of letter shapes.

SERIFS

Serifs are another tradition derived from the strokes of a calligraphic pen. The pen often leaves a slight horizontal mark at the beginning or ending of each vertical stroke; in time, medieval scribes emphasized such marks as deliberate decorations. These marks survive today as *serifs*—the small "feet" at the beginning or more commonly the end of vertical strokes. Typefaces with serifs are known as *serif typefaces*; typefaces without serifs are known as *sans serif* typefaces, because *sans* means "without" in French (Figure 6.13).

Type designers continue to use serifs not just because of tradition or convention but because serifs increase the readability of text. When the serifs on many letters in a line of type are arranged consistently on the baseline, they imply a subtle horizontal line themselves—almost like a dashed line that leads the user's eye across the page.

As Figure 6.14 shows, serifs can also come in many different shapes, adding visual distinction to the typeface. (For advice on choosing between serif and sans serif typefaces, see "Serif versus Sans Serif Typefaces" on page 163.)

bdfhiklmnpqrx

Serif typeface:
Garamond

bdfhiklmnpqrx

Sans serif typeface:
Century Gothic

Figure 6.13 Serif and sans serif typefaces.   Serifs are the little horizontal marks on the bottoms of vertical strokes. Sans serif ("without serif") typefaces lack these marks.

Figure 6.14 Differently shaped serifs.   From left to right: Times New Roman, Bernard MT Condensed, Bodoni MT, Rockwell, Bookman Old Style, and Calisto MT.

UPPERCASE AND LOWERCASE

Historically, when books were printed with individual pieces of movable type, printers kept the capital letters in one drawer or *case*—the "upper case"—and small letters in another case—the "lower case." We still use this terminology to describe capital (uppercase) and lowercase letters. Most typefaces include a full set of upper- and lowercase letters, but some are formed entirely of uppercase letters. These typefaces are most often designed for titles or signs, where capital letters can sometimes stand out more emphatically than lowercase letters. However, it's important to avoid overusing capitals, as they cut down on readability (see "All Caps and Small Caps" on page 186).

COUNTERS AND STRESS

An enclosed or mostly enclosed space in a letter form is known as a *counter*; the stroke that encloses a counter is called a *bowl*. Because of the shape of the counter itself and the varying width of the bowl stroke, counters can give a very distinct look to a typeface. This distinction applies particularly with the lowercase letters *a* and *g* because both letters can be designed as one-counter or two-counter forms (Figure 6.15).

The shape of the bowl and counter can also make the letters appear to have a vertical alignment, known as *stress*. Stress is usually determined by drawing an imaginary line between the narrowest parts of the bowl that form a lowercase letter *o*. Most typefaces usually have a stress either **vertical** or **oblique** (slanted to the left; see Figure 6.16).

Old style faces usually have an oblique stress, while modern faces use a vertical stress. Sans serif typefaces almost always use strokes that vary little in width, so they may have little or no stress.

One-counter letters   Two-counter letters

Figure 6.15 One-counter and two-counter letters. These distinctive letters are often a good way to distinguish between typefaces.

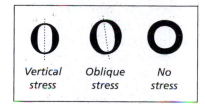

Vertical stress   Oblique stress   No stress

Figure 6.16 Stress in letter forms. Stress is determined by drawing an imaginary line across the two narrowest points of the bowl stroke that forms the letter *o*.

BASELINE, X-LINE, AND CAP-LINE

Although we need visual distinctions between letter forms to read efficiently, we also need consistency. To help create this consistency, typographers in Western languages use three horizontal lines (see Figure 6.11 on page 159):

- The *baseline*, the line on which all letters sit
- The *x-line*, the line at the tops of a lowercase letter *x*
- The *cap-line*, the line at the tops of uppercase (capital) letters

You may already be familiar with these lines because you practiced writing letters in copybooks that provided them as guides, and notebook paper still has baselines on which to write. For most documents, however, these lines are merely *implied* by the typeface, formed by the mostly consistent heights and alignment of the letters on a line of type. Serif faces make these implied lines somewhat stronger by including serifs at the baseline.

Typographers use these lines to make each letter approximately the same height, known as the *x-height* for lowercase letters and the ***cap-height*** for uppercase letters, measured from the baseline to the x-line or to the cap-line, respectively. Some letters break this pattern, giving them greater visual distinction. In many typefaces a number of letters, such as *n*, *r*, and *h*, might rise slightly above the x-line. The letters *i* and *j* include diacritical marks — the dots — that sit above the x-line. And most dramatically, letters with *descenders* (*g*, *j*, *p*, *q*, *y*) dip below the baseline, and letters with *ascenders* (*b*, *d*, *f*, *h*, *k*, *l*, *t*) rise above the x-line. But these letters still include a relationship to the x-line; for example, the lowercase *f* has a horizontal line at or near the x-line.

MEASURING FONTS

Baselines also serve as a convenient way to measure fonts. The size of a font is measured in points from the baseline of one line of type to the baseline of the next line of type, set with no extra space between lines (see "Vertical Spacing" on page 173). As we discussed in Chapter 5, a point is $\frac{1}{72}$ of an inch (or $\frac{1}{12}$ of a pica).

However, some typefaces are designed to "sit" differently within this vertical distance. Typefaces can have a wide variability of actual sizes even within the same point size — for example, 12-point Antique Olive is actually a much bigger font than 12-point Centaur. When mixing typefaces in a design, compare fonts carefully by eye as well as by point size.

Fonts can also be specified in pixels for on-screen designs, but the size of pixels differs from monitor to monitor: some monitors have higher resolution and smaller pixels; others have lower resolution and larger pixels. So measuring font sizes by pixels is pretty imprecise. With designs meant to be used exclusively on-screen, however, dimensioning fonts with pixels can lead to greater legibility across a variety of monitors (see "Type on Screen," page 193).

Typeface Categories

Now that you have a better sense of the characteristics of letter forms, we can discuss typefaces in more detail. Many thousands of typefaces have been designed over the past six centuries — most of them since the development of digital type design in the 1980s. Some come standard with computer systems, and others can be purchased from type design bureaus like Linotype or Adobe or from individual type designers for a relatively small fee.

When mixing typefaces in a design, compare fonts carefully by eye as well as by point size.

It's a luxury to have so many typefaces to choose from, but choices can also lead to confusion. In this section, we'll discuss four overlapping ways to distinguish between typefaces:

- Serif versus sans serif typefaces
- Roman versus italic typefaces
- Text versus display typefaces
- Monospace versus proportional typefaces

These distinctions will help you make good choices about what typeface to use in different situations. Keep in mind, however, that these are overlapping categories — for example, some typefaces are simultaneously sans serif, italic, *and* display faces. Also remember that many typefaces purposefully blur the boundaries between categories; type designers love to get creative and break the mold!

SERIF VERSUS SANS SERIF TYPEFACES

Serifs are one of the most common distinctions between typefaces: some typefaces have them, some don't. For the most part, use *serif typefaces* for paragraphs that are meant to be read through, such as those in a report or a book.

Because they don't have serifs, **sans serif typefaces** typically look more vertical than serif faces do. So use sans serifs where you want to direct the reader's eye down rather than across a line of type — for example, in lists and tables. Although some designers have used sans serifs for paragraph text, most designers reserve them for shorter text objects like headings, captions, and titles.

Sans serif faces are sometimes called *gothic* typefaces because they typically lack the amount of ornamentation of serif faces. This simplicity also makes sans serifs work well for signs and other large-scale work because their shapes are easily legible from a distance.

ROMAN VERSUS ITALIC TYPEFACES

When printing first became common in the sixteenth and seventeenth centuries, two styles of type became common: **roman** and **italic** (neither is usually capitalized). Most people think of roman typefaces as regular, plain, upright, "normal" text. Most text meant to be read in sentences and paragraphs — such as the text of this book — is set in roman typefaces. Italic typefaces slant to the right, echoing the slant of Renaissance handwriting. As a result, italics use thinner strokes and thus have a less dense value than roman text (see Figure 6.17).

---

romans: more dense
italics: less dense

Figure 6.17 Comparing roman and italic typefaces. Roman type tends to be more dense than italic type in the same point size.

You've probably used word processors to make roman text into italic (just press Ctrl-i, right?). But strictly speaking, the romans and italics you would be using are different fonts within the same type family. Earlier in the development of digital type, word processors made roman type into italic by artificially leaning it over at an angle, which often created awkward-looking italics. If you wanted a truly well-designed italic, you had to specify an entirely different font, which was tedious if you just wanted to italicize a word here or there. But newer digital type technologies can include specifically designed italic and roman fonts within the same font file, so when you use a word processor's italic command, you're actually invoking a specially designed italic font.

Most of the time, use roman typefaces in your designs; they're easier to read, clearer, and usually denser than italics, creating a better figure-ground contrast. When you do use italics, however, avoid using them for long stretches of text, which can fatigue readers quickly. (For information on using bold or italic for emphasis, see "Modifying Type for Emphasis" on page 184).

TEXT VERSUS DISPLAY TYPEFACES

Some typefaces are designed to be set in text; they are intended to help readers make their way through many lines of prose in sentences and paragraphs. Common text faces are Times New Roman, Book Antiqua, and Bookman Old Style, but there are many others. As we mentioned before, the basal text in this book is set in Mendoza Roman Book.

Display faces, on the other hand, are designed to make a bold visual statement. They work best in small doses — for example, in titles or headings. The headings in this book are set in Frutiger.

The table on page 165 lists six common kinds of display faces. As you can see, display faces are best used in moderation because they require readers to slow down and pay attention to each letter. Sometimes that's the desired rhetorical effect, but readers may also lose patience and skip over something that looks too hard to read. So for most situations, use text typefaces for text and display typefaces for display.

> For most situations, use text typefaces for text and display typefaces for display.

MONOSPACE VERSUS PROPORTIONAL TYPEFACES

One of the great tragedies of type design started as a technological compromise. The letters in most typefaces naturally have different widths — for example, an *i* is narrower than a *w*. These typefaces are called **proportional** because each letter gets only its fair share of horizontal space.

But when mechanical typewriters were first introduced in the late nineteenth century, they required that each letter be as wide as the next,

Display Typefaces

Kind of Typeface	Description	Samples	
Script	Echoing handwriting or calligraphy	*Mistral* Comic Sans	*AaBbCcDdEeFf12345* AaBbCcDdEeFf12345
Blackletter	Echoing fraktur or early modern script	Old English Goudy Text	AaBbCcDdEeFf12345 AaBbCcDdEeFf12345
Inscribed	Echoing stone inscriptions	Imprint MT CASTELLAR	AaBbCcDdEeFf12345 ABCDEF12345
Engraved	Echoing texts engraved on metal	*Edwardian Script* *Kunstler Script*	*AaBbCcDdEeFf12345* *AaBbCcDdEeFf12345*
Grunge	Drawing attention to themselves as art	Chiller Jokerman	AaBbCcDdEeFf12345 AaBbCcDdEeFf12345
Dingbats	Providing glyphs as images	Wingdings Webdings	

since the typewriter platen or print head shifted over a consistent space with every key pressed. To solve this problem, typewriter companies designed *monospace* typefaces such as `Courier`, which made each letter the same width. They arbitrarily narrowed the wide letters and widened the narrow letters — i became about the same width as w, mostly by awkwardly extending the serifs. With the success of the manual typewriter, monospace faces became a familiar fixture on typed business reports and school essays.

Although we rarely use manual typewriters anymore, monospace faces still show up in documents to this day. In general, avoid monospace typefaces; use proportional typefaces instead.

However, a few justifiable uses do remain for monospace faces. They're sometimes used in tables that require a precise vertical alignment of numbers and letters. They're also often used to show computer code in a document such as a manual (such as on pages 189–90).

> Avoid monospace typefaces; use proportional typefaces instead.

Designing Documents with Type

Now that you have a better sense of how to categorize typefaces, you still need to make smart choices about what typefaces to use in your designs. In this section, we'll discuss some guidelines for choosing and combining typefaces.

Choosing Type for Legibility, Readability, and Usability

When choosing a typeface, pay attention to three complementary features of type — legibility, readability, and usability:

- *Legibility* refers to the extent to which readers can make out the individual letters of a typeface easily and efficiently.
- Good legibility leads to good *readability*, a general measurement of the ease of reading, scanning, or skimming a document.
- Both legibility and readability lead to *usability*, a measure of how well readers can use a document to complete a task.

Usability is the ultimate goal; we want to create document designs that allow users to do useful things in their lives. But the usability of type depends on legibility and readability, which rely on three important factors: typeface design, font, and x-height to cap-height ratio.

TYPEFACE DESIGN

It may sound simple, but users find some typefaces easier to read than others. The problem is that not everyone agrees on *which* typefaces are easier to read. As we discussed earlier in this chapter, users have both a conventional sense of what makes letters look normal to them and an ability to recognize remarkably distorted type. But users can lose interest when they have to read type that is very different from what they consider "normal."

For the most part, the most legible and readable typefaces are those with relatively simple, unadorned designs — those closest to the archetypal forms most people carry in their heads. That would suggest that for many purposes, a sans serif face would be the most legible. And, in fact, that's exactly what you see most often on large-scale work, such as signs or posters.

The only ornamentation that some users seem to prefer, especially when reading paragraphs of text, is the serif. But this preference depends on each user's experience, training, and culture. If a user is used to reading sans serif faces, he or she will prefer reading sans serif faces. So rather than declare a simple rule about whether to use typefaces of one category or another, it's best simply to ask users what they prefer or to observe what typefaces seem to work best with the users — for example, by comparing documents designed for a similar purpose and audience.

FONT

Legibility and readability also depend on the size of type. Obviously, too small a font can be difficult to see (which is why legal documents put

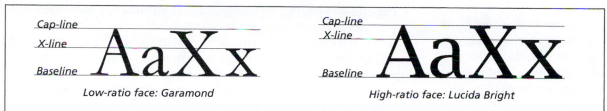

Low-ratio face: Garamond   High-ratio face: Lucida Bright

Figure 6.18 X-height:cap-height ratios in different typefaces.   High-ratio typefaces, with their relatively tall x-height, tend to be more legible in smaller font sizes than low-ratio typefaces.

the details in the "fine print," where they're hard to make out). By the same token, using too large a font in a typical print or screen document can make it hard for the eye to take in enough of the shape to discern meaning — much like looking at a billboard from a few feet away. (Of course, if you really are designing a billboard, you should use as large a font as possible!)

X-HEIGHT TO CAP-HEIGHT RATIO

You'll recall from earlier in the chapter that the distance between the baseline and the x-line is the *x-height*, while the distance between the baseline and the cap-line is the *cap-height*. But some typefaces place the x-line closer to the cap-line than others, creating different ratios between the x-height and the cap-height. Typefaces with a relatively tall x-height are known as **high-ratio typefaces**; those with a relatively short x-height are known as **low-ratio typefaces** (Figure 6.18).

High-ratio typefaces, such as Times New Roman, Lucida Bright, and Georgia, have an x-height relatively nearer the cap-height than low-ratio typefaces, like Centaur, Perpetua, or Garamond, which have an x-height closer to halfway between the cap-line and the baseline. A high-ratio typeface is often more legible than a low-ratio typeface in the same general size. So you can often use a high-ratio typeface in a smaller size to conserve space while retaining legibility.

You can often use a high-ratio typeface in a smaller size to conserve space while retaining legibility.

Matching Type to Visual Rhetoric

In addition to usability, typography can play a role in the rhetorical impact of a document. Even in the blandest of documents, some element of rhetorical persuasion is at work — if nothing else, the need to persuade users that the document holds useful information pertinent to their lives. Other documents, such as annual reports, brochures, and flyers, are more obviously and highly persuasive.

As we discussed earlier in this chapter, typography creates a voice-over for the content; it gives a tone to whatever the document is conveying. So type should mesh with the client's rhetorical purposes and users' expectations. As we learned from examining typography's

Choose typefaces and fonts according to their rhetorical purpose—particularly, according to what tone or sense of ethos you want to convey to users.

cultural background, typefaces also have cultural and ideological connections that still influence readers today. Bauhaus faces—with their uniform strokes rooted in modernism—still imply clarity, universality, and minimalism. Many grunge faces imply a validation of difference, otherness, and novelty. Choose typefaces and fonts according to their rhetorical purpose—particularly, according to what tone or sense of ethos you want to convey to users.

Creating a Typographic System

Ideally, a document's typographic design should work as a system that shows users how to use the document. For example, typography should accomplish all of these tasks as a coherent system:

- Show users the document's structure
- Help users find where to look first on a page
- Tell them what's most important on the page
- Indicate how each textual element relates to other elements on the page, in terms of the document hierarchy

So when choosing typefaces for a document, it's essential to think holistically about all of the different kinds of text your document will include, as well as how all of those kinds of text are related to each other in the document hierarchy. As we discussed in Chapter 5, the most common way to show a document hierarchy is by thinking about the various kinds of textual design objects and their relationships (see Chapter 5, "Hierarchy," on page 122). For example, documents might include different kinds of text, like those listed in Figure 6.19.

Figure 6.19 Kinds of text in a typical technical document and a typical website.   It's important to assess what different kinds of text will be included in your document design so you can create a system of typography that distinguishes between content types visually.

Technical document	Website
Document title	Site title
Heading level one	Page title
Heading level two	Footer
Heading level three	Heading level one
Heading level four	Heading level two
Header and footer	Heading level three
Basal text (paragraphs)	Basal text (paragraphs)
Numbered lists	Numbered lists
Bulleted lists	Bulleted lists
Tables	Tables
Captions	Hyperlinks within paragraph text
Callouts	Hyperlinks in the navigation bar

Choose type so that each of these different kinds of text is visually distinct from the others as design objects. But also make sure that each kind of text has a clear visual relationship in a hierarchy with other kinds of text. In other words, balance the design principles of *similarity* and *contrast* to create a unified, systematic design.

Most designers approach this problem for technical documents by choosing one or two type families for each document. Often, they'll use one type family for the basal text (for sentences and paragraphs) and another for the many metatextual design objects users need to navigate the document, such as the title, headings, headers, and footers in a paper document or site titles, page titles, footers, and navigational links in a screen document. This technique creates a good sense of unity and consistency, while retaining an important distinction between basal text and navigational/structural text.

Within this relatively small palette of typefaces, we can use *type variations* to make hierarchical distinctions between different kinds of text, visually creating the different levels of the document's hierarchy. Readers must be able to recognize a first-level heading, and they should be able to recognize which second-level headings belong under that first-level heading. The key is to match the typeface or font to its logical importance in the document hierarchy and use adequate contrast so users can tell the difference between one level and the next.

Don't be afraid to use contrast when choosing typefaces for textual and metatextual elements. This contrast can apply within a single typeface, using a variety of fonts and styles, or it can work by combining different typefaces with contrasting appearances. Figure 6.20 on page 170, for example, uses typographic contrast to create a hierarchy with the same kinds of textual elements as in Figure 6.19. This hierarchy tells users how to distinguish visually between the levels of the hierarchy; it also helps them distinguish between the metatextual elements (all in a sans serif typeface) and the textual elements (all in a serif typeface).

We can use the visual variables of design objects we discussed in Chapter 2 to make sure our designs have adequate typographic contrast. In particular, four kinds of contrast are particularly useful in providing typographic distinction between design elements and levels of the hierarchy: contrasts of size, shape, value, and color.

> Don't be afraid to use contrast when choosing typefaces for textual and metatextual elements.

CONTRASTS OF SIZE

Perhaps the easiest way to create contrast in a document is by using a range of *sizes* of type for design objects at different levels of the document hierarchy. Readers usually assume that large fonts imply more importance than smaller fonts.

Title (Lucida Sans 28pt)

Heading level one (Lucida Sans 22pt)

Heading level two (Lucida Sans 18pt)

Heading level three (Lucida Sans Italic 16pt)

Heading level four (Lucida Sans Italic 14pt, indented)

Header and footer (Lucida Sans 9pt)

Paragraph text (Lucida Bright 10pt)
1. Numbered lists (Lucida Bright 10pt)
- Bulleted lists (Lucida Bright 10pt)

Tables (Lucida Sans 9pt)
Captions (Lucida Sans 9pt)
Callouts (Lucida Sans 8pt)

Figure 6.20 Typographic contrast.
Creating a typographic hierarchy requires using a system of contrasts in typefaces and fonts.

For example, Figure 6.21 shows three versions of a flyer for a speaker at a Society for Technical Communication meeting. Although Version A gets the basic ideas across—who's speaking, what the topic will be, and when and where to show up—it gives equal weight to all the pieces of information. The only visual cue that tells the reader how to read the flyer is the design principle of order: the convention of starting at the top and going to the bottom.

This isn't necessarily a problem, but adding size contrast would improve the flyer's visual impact and help readers understand the relative importance of the information being presented. Version B prints the title in a different font, giving greater prominence to the speaker's topic. Of course, if the speaker is a big celebrity—someone a lot of people would want to see—then the speaker's name might be more important than the topic. Version C places the name of the speaker at the top of the typographic hierarchy. Each of these versions gives users a remarkably different sense of the information being presented, but the only difference is in the size of the various text design objects.

To set up a reasonable typographic hierarchy in a document, start with the size you want to use for basal text, and then size the various

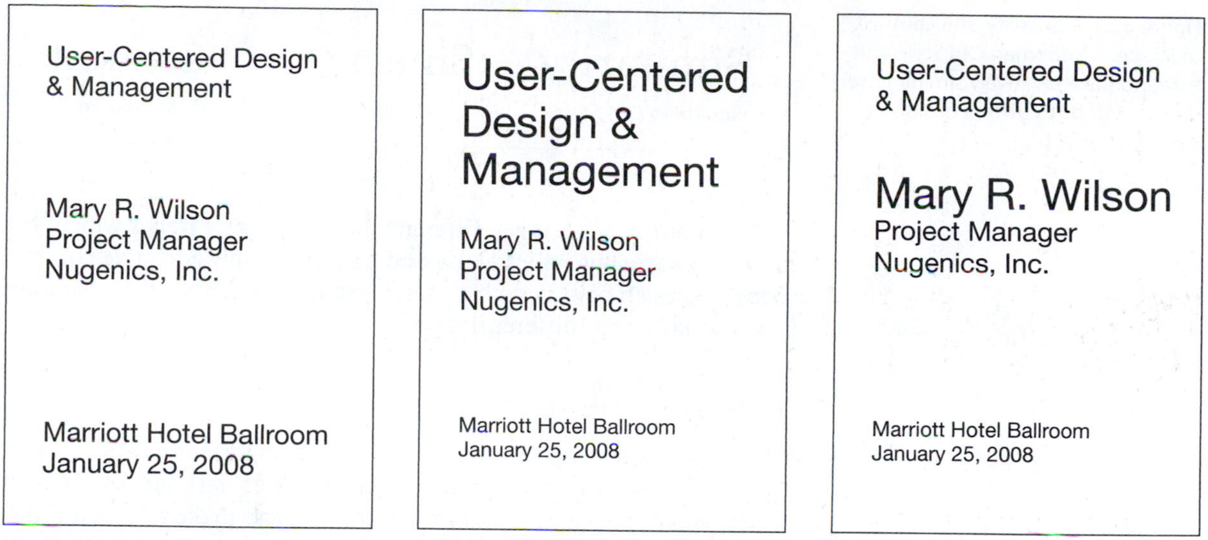

User-Centered Design & Management Mary R. Wilson Project Manager Nugenics, Inc. Marriott Hotel Ballroom January 25, 2008	User-Centered Design & Management Mary R. Wilson Project Manager Nugenics, Inc. Marriott Hotel Ballroom January 25, 2008	User-Centered Design & Management Mary R. Wilson Project Manager Nugenics, Inc. Marriott Hotel Ballroom January 25, 2008
Version A	*Version B*	*Version C*

Figure 6.21 Using contrasts of size to create hierarchy.   Contrasts of size can help create typographic hierarchy. Version A offers no visual distinction between the different kinds of textual content. Version B uses font size to make the title appear most prominent, and Version C emphasizes the speaker's name.

hierarchical levels up or down from this standard. For typical business and technical documents, start with something between 9 points and 11 points for text. Then step up to larger sizes (up to around 36 or even 48 points) for headings and titles and down to smaller sizes (sometimes down to 6- or 7-point fonts) for captions and callouts.

A 9-point font for text might seem small to you, particularly if you work primarily in Microsoft Word, which uses 12-point type as a default. But if you look at a wide variety of business and technical documents, you'll notice that most use fonts smaller than 12-point for basal text. Again, be sure to check font sizes visually, as well as by point number; 9 points in some typefaces is smaller than in others.

Of course, there are exceptions. If the document itself is large or intended to be viewed from a distance, start with a larger size of basal text—in fact, as large as possible. Nobody will read a banner, sign, or flyer in 9-point type. Also, use a slightly larger font for screen documents so they can be read easily on low-resolution screens (see "Type on Screen" on page 193).

For typical business and technical documents, start with something between 9 points and 11 points for text. Then step up to larger sizes for headings and titles and down to smaller sizes for captions and callouts.

CONTRASTS OF SHAPE

Typefaces come in a variety of contrasting shapes. Typically, the more contrast in the *shape*, the easier it will be for users to tell the difference between one level of the typographic hierarchy and another. Figure 6.22 (page 172) shows how shape can make a big difference in the amount of contrast between two typefaces.

Figure 6.22 Similarity and contrast of shape. Bookman Old Style and Palatino have relatively similar letter shapes, but both differ considerably from Myriad Pro.

Similarity	Similarity	Contrast
Bookman Old Style	*Palatino*	*Myriad Pro*

Of course, we can get different shapes by using italics within the same typeface, but italics alone don't always supply adequate contrast between design objects such as basal text and headings, where we want an especially clear differentiation.

CONTRASTS OF VALUE

We can also use contrasts of value to show typographic contrast. *Value* refers to the contrast between the brightness or darkness of a design object and its background. Contrasts of value can make a very clear distinction between levels of the hierarchy. The more dense or high-value-contrast the type, the more likely the user's eyes will be drawn to that type—particularly when the surrounding type has a lighter or lower-value contrast. Value increases with size, simply because there's more ink on the page (or pixels on the screen) devoted to the type:

as fonts get larger, they look more dense

than smaller fonts in the same typeface.

But some faces are designed to look denser than others, even at the same font size (Figure 6.23).

Many type families also come in a variety of values, also known as *weights* (Figure 6.24). You can use these weights to great effect, keeping a general typographic coherence within your design while taking advantage of their natural value contrasts.

Figure 6.23 Density of typefaces. Some typefaces are designed to look more dense than others.

Low-value typefaces	High-value typefaces
Trebuchet MS 11pt	**Myriad Pro Black 11pt**
Palatino Linotype 11pt	*Magneto 11pt*
Futura 11pt	**Impact 11pt**
Century Schoolbook 11pt	**Haettenschweiler 11pt**

CONTRASTS OF COLOR

Finally, you can use contrasts of *color* to distinguish different textual elements from each other. Many document designs take a step up from one-color to two-color design by using colored headings. Doing so can definitely attract a user's eye to the structure of the document. And for on-screen designs, colored type is no more expensive than black and white.

However, one disadvantage of colored type is that any color contrast other than black on white (or vice versa) will decrease the value contrast. In other words, type of any color other than black usually looks less dense than black type on a white background. So make sure you choose relatively dark colors for type on a white background or relatively light colors for type on a dark background. Avoid low-value-contrast color combinations, such as bright yellow type on a white background or dark gray type on a black background.

Eras Light ITC

Eras Medium ITC

Eras Demi ITC

Eras Bold ITC

Figure 6.24 Using a variety of weights in the same type family. Weights of fonts in the same type family allow designers to use a consistent type design but vary the value for different purposes within the document.

Setting Type

Setting type successfully requires paying careful attention to the spaces between, above, below, and beside pieces and groups of type. Word processors and page layout programs give considerable control over spacing, both horizontally and vertically.

VERTICAL SPACING (LEADING)

In the age of letter-press printing with movable type, the distance between each line of type was set by placing strips of lead between the lines. Accordingly, the distance between lines of type is still known as *leading* (rhymes with "heading"). Most typefaces are already designed to provide a little extra space between one line and the next, even when they are set with no leading (that is, single-spaced). For example, a 10-point font will likely be designed so there are about 12 points from baseline to baseline, and a 9-point font will be set on an 11-point *body* (the more traditional way of saying the same thing). This practice keeps descenders and ascenders from running into each other from one line to the next. Leading is specified with a notation such as 10/12 or "10 on 12," which means a 10-point font leaded with baselines 12 points apart.

With digital type we can specify more or less leading with great precision. Most word processing and page layout programs also allow you to adjust leading decimally or by percentages, usually with 1.0 or 100 percent representing the "normal" leading (such as 10/12), 1.1 or 110 percent as a little more than normal (10/13) and 0.9 or 90 percent as

Avoid low-value-contrast color combinations, such as bright yellow type on a white background or dark gray type on a black background.

a little less (10/11). Most designers set the leading initially by eye and then note the exact leading so they can set other paragraphs the same way.

The vertical space created by leading is essential for readers to recognize each horizontal line of type. In Gestalt terms, the individual letters — though not actually connected to each other in most faces — must line up in such a way as to invoke visual continuation. One way to do so is to make sure that the height of the *vertical* space between lines exceeds the width of a typical *horizontal* space between pieces of type or words. Otherwise, readers may have trouble recognizing the line of type as a strong figure (see Chapter 2, "Proximity," on page 31, as well as Figure 2.13).

For example, Figure 6.25 shows paragraphs set with different leadings. The 10/8 leading makes the text look like columns of letters rather than rows of type. The ascenders and descenders overlap, causing awkward interferences. On the other hand, as you can see from the 10/25 paragraph, if the lines of type are set too far apart, readers might have a hard time making the visual leap from one line to the next.

10/12 leading
(single-spaced)

The quick brown fox jumps over the lazy dog. The quick brown fox jumps over the lazy dog. The quick brown fox jumps over the lazy dog. The quick brown fox jumps over the lazy dog.

10/8 leading

The quick brown fox jumps over the lazy dog. The quick brown fox jumps over the lazy dog. The quick brown fox jumps over the lazy dog. The quick brown fox jumps over the lazy dog.

10/25 leading

The quick brown fox jumps over the lazy dog. The quick brown fox

jumps over the lazy dog. The quick brown fox jumps over the lazy

dog. The quick brown fox jumps over the lazy dog.

Figure 6.25 Paragraphs with different leadings.   Lines leaded too closely together can make ascenders and descenders run into each other, creating problems with continuation. Lines leaded too far apart can impede readers from making the return sweep to the next line of text successfully.

Leading for paragraphs.   You can specify the leading both *within* and *between* paragraphs of text. Within paragraphs, you can often rely on the default leading (such as 10/12) built into the computer font, especially for low-level designs such as letters, memos, and internal reports that must be completed quickly and cheaply and don't justify much of a design effort. For higher-level designs, however, consider adding a bit more leading than the default — 10/13 or 10/14, for example. This amount of leading is significantly less than double-spacing, but more than single-spacing, and makes reading easier.

In addition, set paragraphs with long lines for the particular font to greater leading than paragraphs with shorter lines for the font. For example, if you have a long line with small type, you'll need to increase the leading slightly to help users keep their place as they read from one line to the next.

Set paragraphs in sans serif with slightly greater leading than those with serif faces (Figure 6.26). Sans serif typefaces lack the horizontal cues of serifs, so users need a bit more separation between lines to make each line of text a strong figure.

Between paragraphs, you can specify a certain amount of space before or after each paragraph, usually in points or decimal inches (for example, "6 points before and 3 points after" each paragraph). This technique streamlines setting type for single-spaced paragraphs in business documents; rather than double-spacing after each paragraph, you can just set each paragraph to include a certain amount of space "after." Typically, set the leading between single-spaced paragraphs larger than the leading between lines within paragraphs so readers can recognize each paragraph as a strong figure, as well. Above

Figure 6.26 Leading for serif and sans serif typefaces.   Set sans serif typefaces with a slightly larger leading than serif typefaces. Sans serifs need the extra space to make up for the lack of the horizontal cues provided by serifs.

Lorem ipsum dolor sit amet, consectetuer adipiscing elit. Fusce leo. Aliquam condimentum elit vitae urna. Nunc tincidunt feugiat pede. Integer enim nulla, vulputate ut, mattis a, cursus sit amet, massa. Aliquam lacinia tortor sit amet lacus. Fusce gravida. Mauris quis lorem nec arcu ultrices dictum. Vivamus magna. Ut luctus, ante eu posuere consectetuer, nisi nisl dictum urna, eget luctus metus enim at.

New Century Schoolbook 10/12

Lorem ipsum dolor sit amet, consectetuer adipiscing elit. Fusce leo. Aliquam condimentum elit vitae urna. Nunc tincidunt feugiat pede. Integer enim nulla, vulputate ut, mattis a, cursus sit amet, massa. Aliquam lacinia tortor sit amet lacus. Fusce gravida. Mauris quis lorem nec arcu ultrices dictum. Vivamus magna. Ut luctus, ante eu posuere consectetuer, nisi nisl dictum urna, eget luctus metus enim at.

Tahoma 10/14

Avoid double-spacing, which slows down reading by providing too much space between lines of type.

all, avoid double-spacing, which slows down reading by providing too much space between lines of type. Teachers and editors request double-spacing because it gives them space to write comments and mark changes between the lines of type on a manuscript or school report. Most users don't need double-spacing.

Leading for headings.   The ability to set leading between paragraphs is particularly useful for headings, which in word processing and page layout programs are essentially specially formatted paragraphs. Headings should usually rest a little closer to the text they introduce than to the text they follow. Look at the headings in this chapter. You can see that they're leaded to give more space before than after each heading. As we discussed in Chapters 2 and 3, this practice implements the Gestalt principle of proximity to help readers associate the heading with the section it belongs to rather than with the section that precedes it.

HORIZONTAL SPACING

In this section, we'll discuss the various aspects of the horizontal dimension of type, including the space between letters and words, line length, paragraph justification, and indentation.

Line length.   As we discussed in Chapter 5, one of the biggest factors in setting easily readable type is the length of each line of type. Although users can read text in many line lengths, most feel comfortable with a line length that corresponds to about 7 to 12 words. Although this is basically a typographic issue, it's also a page layout issue because line length is established by the page layout grid within which the type is set. This grid determines how type can be arranged, forming a frame to constrain the length of lines. (See Chapter 5, "Using Grids for Page Design," on page 132.)

Kerning, letter spacing, and ligatures.   Adjusting the spacing between *individual* letter pairs is generally called **kerning**; adjusting the spacing between *all* letters in a word, line, sentence, or paragraph is called **letter spacing**. There's some variation in terminology here, however: letter spacing is also known in some word processing and page layout programs as **character spacing**, **tracking**, or (even more confusingly) **track-kerning**. Let's just say that you have a lot of control over the horizontal space between letters.

Strictly defined, kerning shifts a letter horizontally so it extends into the negative space of a neighboring letter (Figure 6.27). For example, in the word "for," you might want to move the *o* slightly under the ascender of the *f* to avoid a too-large negative space between the

for   for

Georgia   *Comic Sans*

Figure 6.27 Automatic kerning. Georgia automatically kerns the *o* under the curl of the *f*, but Comic Sans does not.

letters. In some digital fonts, such as Georgia, the *f* is designed to do this automatically. Other digital fonts, such as Comic Sans, require manual kerning. However, the automatic adjustment to the *f* in Georgia causes problems in other combinations: in the letter pair *fl*, the ascenders overlap each other, looking especially awkward in large fonts. In this case, you may need to add extra space between the letters or, better yet, use a ligature.

Ligatures are special combined letters such as *fi* and *fl*; they echo the natural connections that people make between letters in handwriting (Figure 6.28). Ligatures tend to look formal and elegant, but currently ligatures must be inserted manually into the text. So reserve ligatures primarily for high-level design projects and large font sizes, such as those used in titles and signage.

For text intended to be read (rather than scanned or skimmed), it's usually best to trust the digital typeface itself for appropriate space between letters. In a well-designed typeface, the type designer will have built in a much better sensitivity to kerning than you're likely to have time to tinker with. As fonts get larger, however, the spaces between different letter combinations might create awkward negative spaces. In particular, you may need to adjust kerning between individual letters in large-format work. The higher the level of design, the more attention you'll want to dedicate to kerning.

Letter spacing is a rougher technique than kerning; it's typically used to make text fit in the space the layout provides—a technique also known as *copyfitting*. In most programs, you can specify letter spacing with great flexibility. You can set the type to a looser (expanded) letter-spacing, or to a tighter (condensed) letter spacing. The resulting inconsistency can make the text more difficult to read, so avoid using letter spacing for paragraph text except as a last resort. Again, the exception is large-format work. It's common to set the letter spacing tighter the larger the font, as otherwise, many typefaces begin to look too spaced out.

Word spacing, justification, and hyphenation.   Spaces between words are what readers use to distinguish one bouma from the next, and, as such, these humble bits of negative space are often underestimated in importance. For easy readability, use consistent spaces between words.

One of the most common ways designers mess up consistent word spacing is by using fully justified text. Typically, paragraphs can be aligned in three ways:

Left-aligned: all lines of text lined up to the left-hand edge of the column. Use left-aligned text for most designs. It helps readers get through the text quickly because it gives them a consistent vertical line to return to as their eyes seek the next

Georgia letter pairs   *Georgia ligatures*

Figure 6.28 Ligatures. Because Georgia uses automatic kerning, the *f* runs into the *l* and comes too close to the dot of the *i*. Ligatures solve the problem by connecting letter pairs into one glyph.

For easy readability, use consistent spaces between words.

Use left-aligned text for most designs.

line of text on the left side of the paragraph. This alignment is often called *ragged right* because the variety of line lengths leaves a ragged edge on the right-hand side of the column.

> *Right-aligned:* all lines of text lined up to the right-hand edge of the column. Use this alignment for some callouts, labels, and columns of tables.

> *Fully justified* (or just *justified*): lines of text stretched out to meet both the left and right edges of the column.

Designers have debated extensively about the merits and problems of left-aligned and justified text. Research suggests that most readers find either alignment readable, but justified text can slow down reading slightly.

Fully justified paragraphs often look good from the designer's perspective — everything lined up squarely and neatly. But from the reader's perspective, full justification often creates awkward word spacing, particularly in narrow columns. If the word processing or layout program does not have enough space to fit in another word in the line, it often stretches the spaces between words to make the line meet the right edge. The resulting inconsistent word-spacing can make reading very difficult.

The resulting wide spaces between words can also lead to *rivers* and *lakes*: bodies of empty space that distract the reader's eyes from the text.

A careful designer can mitigate or avoid this inconsistent word spacing with careful layout and typography, but doing so requires extra time and work. In particular, designers often use **hyphenation** to break up words at the end of a line, making smaller chunks that are easier to align to both sides.

But this practice causes its own problems. Hyphenation breaks up the natural shapes of words and makes readers complete the return sweep to the next line before reading the whole word. Multiple consecutive lines ending in hyphens can also create a distraction, since the hyphens will line up vertically at the right side of the column. Most word processing and page layout programs allow you either to disallow hyphenation entirely or to limit how many hyphenated lines can appear in a series. In general, don't allow more than two or three consecutive hyphenated lines.

In general, don't allow more than two or three consecutive hyphenated lines.

Indentation and centering.   Indentation usually refers to extra horizontal space added at the beginning or end of lines of type, measured from the margin or column edge. Three kinds of paragraph indentations are commonly used in document design: first line, hanging, and whole paragraph.

First-line indentation, which you can see in this paragraph, is a traditional way to show the beginning of a paragraph. Typically, designers indent the first line of a paragraph by somewhere between 0.25" (0p3) and 0.5" (0p6), depending on the typeface and font of the paragraph (for more about inches, picas, and points, see Chapter 5, page 146). Another common practice is to forgo first-line indents on the first paragraph after a heading but to use them in subsequent paragraphs. This helps readers move from the heading to the first paragraph more easily.

> Hanging indentation, exemplified by this paragraph, makes the first line of the paragraph start at the left margin or column edge but indents all subsequent lines.

Hanging indentation is also the technique of choice for bulleted or numbered lists, since the bullets or numbers stick out and mark each new item:

- This is the first item in the list of three bullets. The second line of text in this item will wrap to line up with the text of the first line, not with the bullet.
- Second item
- Third item

You can also use hanging indents for alphabetized lists, like indexes or bibliographies, since it makes the alphabetized word stick out from the rest of the paragraph, increasing the reader's ease of scanning.

> To emphasize a single paragraph, you can indent the whole paragraph on one or both sides. This practice creates additional negative space around the text, drawing attention to it and making it a stronger figure. It's also a common way to indicate a long quotation, usually of three or more lines.

Paragraph indentations are usually specified in picas or inches in the United States, in centimeters in Europe, or in pixels for screen design. Some designers might also use older dimensional units such as *quads* (four spaces, also known as an *em*) or *half-quads* (two spaces, or an *en*), but with digital typesetting, these are becoming less common because they aren't consistent or universally standardized.

Centering paragraphs is rarely a good idea, primarily because it creates an inconsistent boundary on the left side of the paragraph — as you can see here. This inconsistency makes readers' return sweep very difficult as their eyes saccade across the paragraph from right to left, looking for the next line. The next line never begins at a consistent place, so it's hard to find. Centered paragraphs do have some traditional uses, such as in formal invitations, but in most situations, centering paragraphs causes too many problems.

PUNCTUATION AND SPECIAL FEATURES

One of the most overlooked features of typography is punctuation. We can't hear a period or a dash, but these and other signs are essential to the meaning of texts. In this section, we'll discuss some of the details about using these quiet heroes of typography.

In word processing and page layout programs, you can access some of the specialized punctuation marks discussed here by using key combinations (system, program, or Unicode) or the Insert : Symbol dialog box. Check your software documentation for instructions on how to do so.

We'll concentrate on the punctuation marks themselves and the common typographical practices for using them in English. Punctuation as a grammatical practice differs from culture to culture, language to language, and writer to writer, so refer to grammar handbooks to find out how to use punctuation marks correctly.

MORE ABOUT . . . SPACING AND PUNCTUATION

The legacy of the typewriter has caused a particularly bad habit: double-spacing after periods and colons. On a typewriter that uses a monospace typeface, one space after a period or colon does not create enough visual separation between one sentence and the next, so adding an extra space increases legibility.

But periods and colons in proportional typefaces are already designed with appropriate surrounding negative space. *Accordingly, use only one space after a period or colon in a proportional typeface.*

If you can't break the habit of double-tapping the space bar after every period, then make a new habit. After entering text in a document, do a global search, replacing every instance of two spaces with one. Most programs will let you do this with a quick and painless "replace all" command. And if you receive text from other authors to include in your design, this step will ensure consistent single-spacing after all punctuation marks.

Periods, commas, semicolons, and colons.   Readers use these common punctuation marks and the space after them to see the beginnings and endings of syntactical units such as phrases, clauses, and sentences. To see a sentence as a visual figure, readers need a certain amount of negative space between one sentence and the next. That space has to be more than the typical space between words in the sentence, or readers won't recognize the space as meaning "a new sentence begins here," rather than just "a new word begins here." The period contributes to that space because it's usually set at or near the baseline, leaving plenty of negative space above it. That negative space is almost as important as the period itself in visually distinguishing one sentence from the next.

Hyphens and dashes.   Hyphens and dashes look similar, but this class of marks includes three completely separate punctuation marks, each with its own specific purposes.

Mark	Name	Description	Use
-	Hyphen	These short, relatively thick, horizontal marks indicate a tight connection between what comes before and what comes after. In some faces (such as Californian FB or Goudy Old Style), hyphens are diagonal (⁻ , -).	Use hyphens to join some compound words (such as "forget-me-not") or to break a single word at the end of a line between syllables.
–	En dash	An en dash gets its name from being about as wide as a capital letter *N*. It's longer and usually thinner than a hyphen in the same font.	Use en dashes between numbers: • 25–35 books • 8:00–9:00 a.m. • 1996–2009 Some designers (particularly in Europe) use an en dash for parenthetical or appositive expressions, adding a thin (¼ em) space before and after the dash – as you see in this sentence.
—	Em dash	Em dashes are about as wide as a capital *M*.	Use em dashes to set off parenthetical or appositive expressions in sentences — like this.

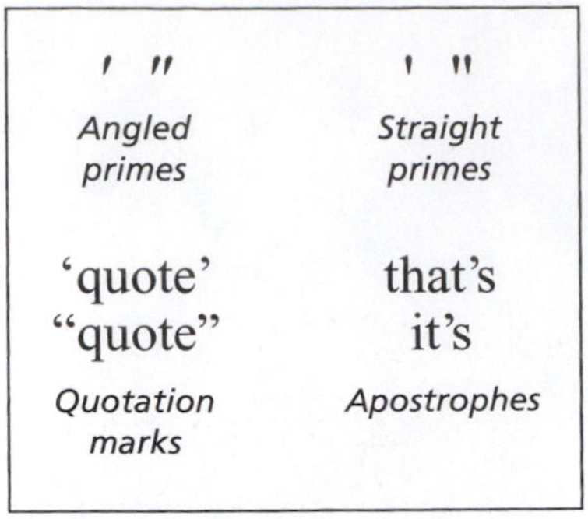

Angled primes | *Straight primes*

'quote'
"quote"

that's
it's

Quotation marks | *Apostrophes*

Figure 6.29 Quotation marks, apostrophes, and primes. Primes are upright or slightly angled, and they usually taper from top to bottom. Quotation marks curve around the quotation with the "tail" pointing up on the beginning mark and down on the ending mark. Apostrophes look like a single ending quotation mark, with the tail pointing down.

Quotation marks, apostrophes, and primes.   Quotation marks, apostrophes, and primes also look alike, but they have significantly different purposes and meanings (Figure 6.29).

Primes, also sometimes known as hash marks or tick marks, are used mostly for showing dimensions in feet and inches (5' 11") or degrees and minutes of an arc (270' 30"). Most typefaces include vertical primes, but you may need to use the Symbol font (available on almost all computer systems) for the more sophisticated-looking angled ones. Quotation marks and apostrophes, however, are almost always curved or slanted.

Ellipsis marks.   Most digital typefaces include a special glyph to indicate ellipsis—not just three periods but a single, combined *ellipsis mark* (...). Use this glyph if it's available in the digital font you're using, as it's usually spaced somewhat tighter than three periods would be. Most word processing programs now automatically insert an ellipsis mark when you type three periods in a row. If the ellipsis occurs at the end of a sentence, don't forget to include the period as well. . . . The result may look like four dots, but it's really a period and an ellipsis mark, followed by a space before the beginning of the next sentence.

SPECIAL TECHNIQUES

In this section, we'll discuss some guidelines for setting diacritical marks, numerals, fractions, drop caps, lists, and reverse type.

Diacritical marks.   Diacritical marks—small dots, curls, or lines added to the tops or bottoms of letter forms, such as á, ç, ñ, đ, ü—are important elements of many written languages. For example, some languages include only consonants, relying on the diacriticals to indicate the intervening vowel sounds. If you are designing a document for read-

---

DESIGN TIP

Converting Primes to Quotation Marks and Apostrophes

Many word processing programs automatically change primes to quotation marks and apostrophes as you type (the "smartquotes" setting in Microsoft Word), but page layout programs don't.

If you place copy from a *.txt file into a word processing or page layout program, you'll run into another problem. Basic text files include only primes, so you'll need to replace the primes with quotation marks. Just use your program's replace function to make this replacement. (You can do it at the same time you replace the double spaces after periods with single spaces!)

ers in a language that uses diacriticals, take particular care to use them correctly. Many digital typefaces can now create a full range of diacritical marks. Most can be accessed by Unicode key combinations (see "Digital Type" on page 190).

Arabic numerals. Typefaces typically include either **inline** Arabic numerals, which are a little shorter than a capital letter in the font, or ***oldstyle*** Arabic numerals, which have a basic shape closer to the size of a lowercase letter and dip above or below the baseline and x-line, depending on the numeral (Figure 6.30). Oldstyle numerals provide more distinction between the forms of the glyphs, increasing legibility when they're used in a line of text. However, the inconsistency of oldstyle numerals can cause problems in other settings where alignment is especially important. Tables and forms, for example, should use inline numerals.

Inline: AaBbCc1234567890
Oldstyle: AaBbCc1234567890

Figure 6.30 Using inline and oldstyle Arabic numerals. Use inline Arabic numerals in tables and forms. Use oldstyle Arabics for numbers within paragraphs.

Fractions. In many computer fonts, common fractions are designed as one combined glyph, ½, as opposed to the inline 1/2, which is formed of three glyphs (1, /, 2). In the one-glyph fraction, the numerator is slightly raised (superscripted), the denominator is slightly lowered (subscripted), and both are kerned tightly to the slash and reduced in size.

Setting the common fractions (⅛, ¼, ⅜, ½, ⅝, ¾, ⅞) is easier now than it used to be, since most word processing programs automatically replace typed fractions with one-glyph fractions. You can set less common fractions manually or just allow them to stay as inline glyphs.

Drop caps. For greater distinction at the beginning of a chapter or section, designers sometimes use a drop cap. This technique increases the font of the initial letter of the text, making it as large as two, three, or even four lines of the text font.

Some drop caps are set into the column, with the text wrapping around them (like this paragraph).

Other drop caps are set into the margin beside the paragraph (like this paragraph).

Using a drop cap can be a good technique to tell readers where to start reading; the density of the large initial letter naturally draws the reader's eyes to that point. For example, you might consider using drop caps to begin chapters or to begin the text on a single-page design such as a flyer. However, it's easy to overuse this technique, so employ it with caution.

Reverse type.   Thus far we've focused primarily on black text on a white field, but designers often use white or light-colored text in a colored field for greater emphasis. This technique is known as *reverse type*. It's not a good idea to use reverse type for long passages of text; we've all struggled through web pages with black backgrounds and white text. But reverse type is useful for emphasizing the column heads in a table or creating a strong visual band across the page for a major heading. It can also mark a header or footer emphatically.

When using reverse type, keep two things in mind. First, the visual density of the colored field can overpower the lighter-colored type. You'll need to increase the value or density of the typeface slightly so the text will show up adequately against its background (Figure 6.31). To increase the visual density of the white area enclosed by the text, use a larger font or a demibold or bold font in the same typeface. Doing so will make the type slightly broader and more visually dense.

Second, make sure that the field gives the type adequate breathing room, particularly above and below the type. Leave plenty of space between the baseline and the bottom of the field especially, to accommodate descenders (see "Vertical Alignment" in Chapter 9, page 289).

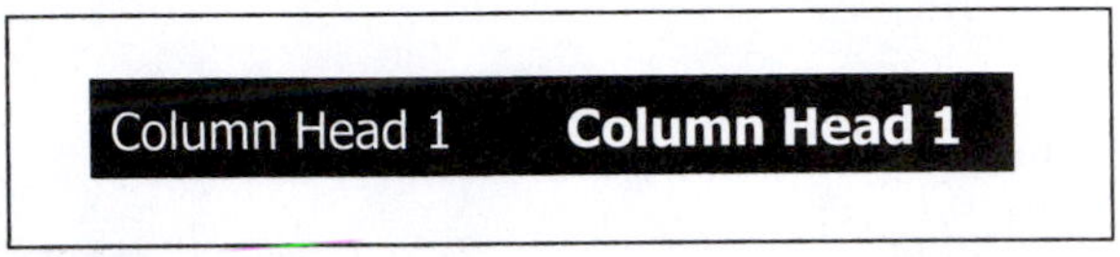

Column Head 1	**Column Head 1**

Figure 6.31 Visual density and reverse type.   Because the visual density of the dark background can overpower the lighter-colored type, it's a good idea to bold the reverse text.

MODIFYING TYPE FOR EMPHASIS

With the development of digital type technologies used on word processors, it's now possible to apply type modifications such as bold, italic, underlining, caps, small caps, outline, shadow, and WordArt. Designers often use these modifications as a quick way to add emphasis to typography, and each has its own advantages and disadvantages.

In all situations, however, it's best to use these modifications sparingly. If you bold everything, the bold text loses its meaning. If you bold only one word in a paragraph, however, that word is sure to stand out due to the contrast with its surroundings.

Bold and italic.   In most situations, use bold rather than italic for emphasis. Bold increases the value (density) of type, while italic decreases value. Increasing the value makes a lot more sense if you really want a bit of text to pop.

As we mentioned previously, bold and italic type modifications are not the same as bold or italic fonts, although the border between the two has grown increasingly hazy. Word processors often make bold and italic modifications by applying algorithms to type, stretching (for italic) or widening (for bold) the strokes, usually with some distortion. Boldface and italic fonts, however, are separate fonts in a typeface, supplied in a variety of sizes and designed individually to work well both internally and within their font family. For quick, low-design level work, it's usually fine to use the bold and italic commands for bold and italic. But for high-design level work, use the specialized bold and italic fonts when they are available.

However, faces designed to the OpenType standard include the roman, bold, and italic fonts within the same digital file (see "Digital Type" on page 190). With these faces, it's not necessary to use a separate bold or italic font; just apply bold or italic in the word processor or page layout program, and the appropriate font will be used automatically.

Underlining.   Avoid using underlining—unless you're working on a typewriter. Like double-spacing after a period, using underlining for emphasis came from the typewriter age. Since most typewriters can print in only one font and typeface, the only option for typists who wanted to emphasize a word was to type the word, move the platen back, and then underline the word. So underlining was a compromise—the quickest (but not the best) way to emphasize text within a typewritten document.

Avoid using underlining—unless you're working on a typewriter.

Underlining has some significant typographic disadvantages. It cuts across descenders, changing the letter forms people need to read efficiently. Note how underlining cuts across the descenders in this phrase: ugly typography. Underlining also obscures the essential space *between* words, which readers need in order to distinguish one bouma from the next. And underlining distracts readers when it's used on more than one consecutive line of text (Figure 6.32).

You can dream, create, design, and build the most wonderful place in the world, but it requires people to make the dream a reality.
—Walt Disney

Figure 6.32 Underlining text.   Underlining obscures descenders and the spaces between words.

DESIGN TIP

Removing Underlined Links in Microsoft Word

Microsoft Word autoformats anything that looks like a web or e-mail address as an underlined, colored hyperlink. These hyperlinks look terrible in print—the sure sign of an amateur designer.

If you're creating a document meant to be printed, remove the underlining and color from web and e-mail addresses. If you're typing the document yourself, just choose the *undo* command (Ctrl-z) immediately after Word changes the address to a hyperlink—the hyperlink will be removed, and you can continue typing. If the copy text was delivered to you from another author with the hyperlinks already in place, you can right-click on each address and choose "Remove hyperlink" from the contextual menu.

About the only justifiable use of underlining today is on websites, where links are underlined by default. This practice is still unfortunate for the perceptual difficulties just noted, but people have gotten used to being able to click on underlined text. That means it's especially important to use underlining on websites *only* for links and not for emphasis. Few things are more annoying than discovering that an underlined word or phrase can't be clicked!

All caps and small caps.   Writers often use text in all caps for emphasis, but doing so often doesn't work well. As we said earlier in this chapter, users tend to read by whole word shapes rather than letter by letter. This suggests that readers find words with distinctive shapes easier to read than those with fewer differences. ALL CAPS TEND TO MAKE EACH WORD LOOK PRETTY MUCH THE SAME: A VAGUELY RECTANGULAR SHAPE. Words in lowercase, however, have all sorts of distinctive bumps and ridges, particularly along the tops of the words. These distinctions make them easier to read than words in all caps.

WARNING: USING THIS PRODUCT IN WET CONDITIONS CAN LEAD TO ELECTROCUTION. WATER CAN CAUSE A SHORT BETWEEN THE SWITCH AND THE OPERATOR'S HANDS. DO NOT OPERATE WHILE STANDING IN WATER.

Figure 6.33 Using all caps.   Setting warnings in all caps can make them more difficult to read.

This problem becomes more significant when more than one line is set in all caps. Ironically, some designers use all caps for caution and warning statements, which defeats the point: making sure people read them (Figure 6.33).

One compromise designers often use for headings is SMALL CAPS. Small caps retain some of the shape of lowercase words, while giving some extra emphasis. But like all caps, small caps are still mostly rectangular. Use them in moderation.

Using Typographic Styles

As you can see, typography requires managing many small details—so many that it's hard to keep to a consistent typographic system within each document. You want every paragraph to be set in the same type with the same leading, justification, before- and after-spacing, and so on. You want every second-level heading to look like all of the other second-level headings and every callout to use the same typographic design. Maintaining this kind of consistency manually can be a nightmare.

An even bigger problem is if your client decides that Gill Sans wasn't really the look he or she wanted for the headings in this document and asks you to change them all to Eras Demi on the Friday before the document goes to press. If you set the type for each of the head-

---

DESIGN TIP

Outline, Shadow, and WordArt

If you get the urge to use outline, shadow, or WordArt—*stop*, put down the mouse, and step away from the computer. Outline is a product of the same kind of computer algorithms that fake italic and bold type. It removes visual density from the text, giving it inadequate figure-ground contrast. Avoid using outline for almost any purpose.

Shadow is almost as bad as outline, creating a gray step in density between figure and ground and thus decreasing contrast. However, on colored backgrounds, shadows can increase figure-ground contrast and create the illusion of the type popping out in three dimensions. Shadow is often used on large signs for that reason. Even so, use shadow cautiously.

Microsoft Word's WordArt is tempting, colorful, and fun to play with—but it can easily lead to ill-considered and clichéd designs. Most of its templates use awkward color combinations and distortion to draw attention to the type, which unfortunately decreases legibility. And because everyone using Microsoft Word has access to the same templates, most people recognize WordArt as a cheap design shortcut.

---

ings as Gill Sans manually, you'll have to change each one of them to Eras Demi manually, as well. There goes *your* weekend.

But with a little foresight and some computer skills, you can change each of these headings in a matter of seconds with one simple command. This technique is known as using *styles*. A style is simply a set of characteristics you can apply with one click to a paragraph or a string of characters. You can use this technique when creating documents for paper or for electronic media.

> A style is simply a set of characteristics you can apply with one click to a paragraph or a string of characters.

Styles on Paper

Most word processors and all page layout programs allow you to create two kinds of styles. A style designed for a whole paragraph is called a *paragraph style*; a style designed for a string of words or letters within a paragraph is known as a *character style*.

PARAGRAPH STYLES

Imagine that you've decided to make your first-level headings Gill Sans Bold 18-point, leaded with 12 points before and 3 points after. Setting each heading this way manually would be a pain. But if you design a style that carries all of these characteristics, all you have to do is apply the style to each heading—a one-click operation.

Even more conveniently, if you decide you want to change all the first-level headings to Eras Demi, you don't have to change every level-one heading; you just change the style. The software then applies the new characteristics to all of the paragraphs you've identified as using that style.

Typically, page layout and word processing software lets you set up styles three ways:

- *Modify a default style.* Most programs include a variety of ready-made styles for paragraphs, such as several levels of headings, captions, and footnotes. You can apply these ready-made styles or modify them to suit your design.

- *Format a sample first, then define the style from the sample.* In this method, you format one paragraph to have the design you want, and then create a new style from that paragraph.

- *Define the style from scratch.* Most programs have a dialog box for defining a new style from scratch by specifying the name of the style and all of the characteristics one at a time. You can then apply this style to as many paragraphs as you like.

Most programs include a menu or dialog that lists all of the available styles for you to choose from. Most programs also let you export styles from one document to another, so you can create many documents with the same formatting—for example, if you need to follow an organization-wide style sheet.

A final advantage of using paragraph styles is that most programs can auto-generate a table of contents from headings styles. The procedure usually goes something like this:

1. Set up the document so that each heading is styled consistently as a "Heading 1," a "Heading 2," and so on.

2. When you're finished writing the document, place the cursor on the page where you want the table of contents to appear and choose the command to create a table of contents.

Upon receiving this command, the software goes through the document looking for paragraphs styled as "Heading 1" or "Heading 2" (or whatever styles you have specified for the table of contents to include). It then copies the text from those paragraphs and assembles them in order, along with the page numbers on which the headings appear. *Voilà*—a table of contents!

The best part of this technique is that if you need to change the order, contents, or headings in the document, all you have to do is regenerate or update the table of contents to create an accurate navigational guide for users.

CHARACTER STYLES

One limitation of paragraph styles is that the entire paragraph must use the same style. That's where *character styles* come in. Character styles work very similarly to paragraph styles, but they're applied to a string of characters instead of to an entire paragraph. They're also a bit simpler because they don't include settings for paragraph-level features such as leading.

Character styles are very useful for applying special formatting to words or phrases that might appear in a paragraph, such as glossary terms, proper names, or trade names. You can apply a paragraph style to the entire paragraph and then apply one or more character styles to individual words or phrases within the paragraph. The program will apply the character style first, so even if you change the paragraph style, the words to which you applied the character style will stay the same.

Styles on Websites: CSS

In web development you can also apply a similar technique, known as *cascading style sheets (CSS)*. CSS is a powerful tool, allowing the same kind of style functionalities of page layout and word processing programs, plus many other features like layering and positioning design objects.

Unlike styles in word processing and page layout programs, cascading style sheets are either made part of the HTML code of a web page or kept in a separate CSS file, where they can be referenced by many web pages. This CSS file (with the extension *.css) is just a text file that holds specifications for the typographic details of any HTML tagset you want to format. By changing an external CSS style sheet, you can alter the look of an entire website in an instant, since the changes will "cascade" to every page in the site that invokes that style sheet.

While a full discussion of CSS is beyond the scope of this book, here is a brief summary of how it works for typographic design. For example, the HTML tagset for typical body paragraphs (<p>...</p>) could be set up in the CSS file as follows:

```
p { font-size: 10pt; font-family: Tahoma; margin-left: 20 }
```

This style specifies that every paragraph using the <p>...</p> tagset should be in 10-point Tahoma and indented 20 pixels from the left margin. Text for any of the other standard HTML tagsets can be specified the same way, including that for headings (`</h1>`…`</h1>`, `<h2>`…`</h2>`, `<h3>`…`</h3>`), table cells (`<td>`…`</td>`), and list items (`<li>`…`</li>`).

You can also apply a cascading style to structures smaller or larger than the contents of a single HTML tagset. Doing so requires creating a *class* that contains the characteristics you want to apply. A class might look something like this:

```
.update { font-size: 9pt; font-family: Tahoma; background-color:
       #330000 ; color: #FFFFFF; font-weight:bold }
```

This class specifies Tahoma Bold 9-point, in white (FFFFFF) text on a dark red background (330000). You can invoke this class style in an HTML page by putting it within paragraph tags (`<p>`…`</p>`) for individual paragraphs, division tags (`<div>`…`</div>`) for multiple paragraphs, or span tags (`<span>`…`</span>`) for a few words—like this:

```
<span class="update">Content goes here.</span>
```

Any text content you put between these tags will appear formatted as you specified in the `.update` class style.

For more information on CSS, see the World Wide Web Consortium's website on the subject at <www.w3.org>.

Digital Type

Typography on a computer can be complex, but fortunately, computers do most of the work for us. Digital type technologies use mathematics to describe the curves and shapes of each letter so it can be resized and still look good. These technologies also must make letters display correctly on low-resolution computer screens (about 100 pixels per inch, or ppi), as well as on high-resolution printouts (above 300 dots per inch, or dpi). Type technologies must also work with a variety of computers, operating systems, and software programs.

Software makers have worked hard over the past two decades to make using digital type a relatively straightforward task. Still, knowing something about digital type technologies can help you choose a typeface that will work well with the particular document you are designing, as well as with your production method. It will also help you understand more about the possibilities and flexibilities of using type in word processors and page layout programs.

This is one area where type terminology can get hazy. Many people in desktop publishing and commercial printing refer to typefaces simply as "fonts," using that term to cover everything from the typeface design to the computer files used to hold the typeface design. We'll use the term *font file* to describe computer files and stick with the traditional definitions of typeface and font described at the beginning of this chapter.

PostScript and TrueType

Type technologies involve complex standards that require investment from a variety of stakeholders, including software companies and operating system companies — most prominently Apple, Microsoft, and Adobe. As a result, the desktop publishing period has seen several competing standards come and go.

PostScript, a standard created by Adobe in the 1980s, was particularly good at describing type for output to printers, but it didn't work as well on screens. So Apple (later in partnership with Microsoft) developed TrueType, which was designed to work well both on screen and in print. Today, TrueType fonts are much more common than PostScript, especially for basic business and technical documents. But PostScript is still preferred by some designers and commercial printers.

TrueType was further developed as OpenType (also known as TrueType Open), which can accommodate both PostScript and True-Type glyph descriptions. It also provides good support for high-end features such as ligatures and swashes (decorative strokes added onto certain characters); specialized fonts such as italic, boldface, and small caps; and optics (specially drawn fonts for very small or very large sizes). Because it also incorporates Unicode (see the next section), OpenType also works well with other writing systems, including right-to-left languages such as Hebrew and Arabic.

OpenType has yet to develop the following of TrueType or PostScript, but all of these type technologies are likely to change as digital display technologies change, so it's worthwhile to keep up on new developments.

Unicode

TrueType and PostScript work fine for Western languages, which use a relatively limited alphabet. But what about all of the other languages and their writing systems?

Unicode is an international standard addressing this problem. Strictly speaking, Unicode is not a type standard because it describes *characters* — abstract signs with linguistic meanings — as opposed to *glyphs* — the many possible visual representations of characters. But it's

---

MORE ABOUT . . . FONT STANDARDS

For most document design jobs, TrueType (and OpenType) typefaces work just fine. With support from Apple and Windows, they're common, convenient, flexible, and available on both of the major computer operating systems. TrueType works equally well on screen and in print. And TrueType typefaces are encapsulated in a single font file, making them easy to send along to a commercial printer with your print job.

For high-level work, however, some designers and commercial printers still prefer PostScript. Many commercial printers have invested heavily in PostScript, so they're likely to have whatever typeface you specify. If not, you can typically send along the font files with your print job.

Keep in mind that PostScript Type 1 typefaces include two files: one for the screen typeface and one for the printer typeface. Be sure to send both files to the printer. Also check the font file licensing agreement; some designers don't allow their font files to be transferred from one computer to another, or they might have other limitations you'll need to follow.

---

still a dramatically broader way of describing writing systems than earlier type technologies. TrueType and PostScript limited a digital font file to 256 characters, or 8-bit encoding. Unicode's 16-bit encoding, however, allows it to hold 64,000 characters — enough space to provide a unique code for every character in most of the world's written languages, including those that use ideographs, pictographs, or lots of diacritical marks.

OpenType takes advantage of Unicode to apply glyphs to the many different characters available in different writing systems. On most systems, you can access Unicode characters with key combinations on the numeric keypad of your keyboard. The key combination for the Cyrillic letter Э, for example, is 042D, Alt+x. These key combinations aren't always easy to remember, but fortunately many programs provide a dialog box from which to insert the appropriate character or find its key combination.

ASCII, RTF, and XML

Page layout programs don't make very good word processors, and not everyone knows how to use them. So the text for most documents is written and edited in word processors first (sometimes by several different authors) and then dropped or *placed* in a page layout program for design.

This process can lead to some complications, primarily because of the hidden coding in many word processing files. So you should know something about the three most common file formats in which text will likely arrive in your inbox: Microsoft Word files, Rich Text Format files, and American Standard Code for Information Interchange (ASCII) files. You can recognize these file types by their filename extensions:

- Microsoft Word: *.doc
- Rich Text Format: *.rtf
- ASCII: *.txt

Microsoft Word files are based on **XML** (eXtensible Markup Language), a behind-the-scenes coding language that describes the structure and appearance of screens and pages. Unfortunately, Microsoft's implementation of XML is idiosyncratic, so it's often best to translate DOC files into a simpler format like RTF or ASCII before placing them in a page layout program. In most programs, you can do so by choosing "Save as" from the File menu, specifying the desired format, and saving the file. This strips out all the hidden XML code.

Often called just "text" or "plain text," **ASCII** (*.txt) boils text down to the basic numbers, punctuation, and letters used in English, leaving behind no hidden markup that might affect later formatting applied in a page layout program. That means, however, that any text settings such as bold or italic will be stripped out of the file. You'll have to reinsert those settings manually in the page layout program.

RTF is a compromise between ASCII and DOC/XML files. It incorporates all of the basic ASCII characters but retains basic formatting elements such as typefaces, fonts, bold, and italic.

Type on Screen

With the advent of the World Wide Web, PowerPoint presentations, and electronic documents in formats such as Adobe Acrobat, typography designed to be read on computer monitors or projected onto a screen through a projector has become more important.

The easy implementation of color and the flexibility of on-screen type can make design for the screen simpler in some ways than design for print, increasing our options for typographic design. But type on screen also has some significant limitations. In this section, we'll discuss those limitations and some strategies for addressing them.

Resolution

Screen resolution refers to the size of pixels computers can turn on or off to show images on a computer screen. The higher the resolution, the smaller the dots and the smoother and clearer the type and other images are likely to look to a viewer. The lower the resolution, the larger the dots, making it harder for readers to make out intricate shapes like type.

As we discussed in Chapter 4, computer screens have a much lower resolution than most printers do. The pixels on most computer screens are relatively large—about 100 pixels per inch (ppi), although this can vary considerably from system to system and screen to screen. This compares poorly to the resolution of even cheap computer printers, which can usually print at least 300 dots per inch (dpi). Higher-quality laser printers can print at 600 or even 1,200 dpi, and the printers and typesetters used in production printing are typically 2,400 dpi or higher.

The low resolution of computer screens is a particular problem with the curved or diagonal portions of letter forms. Because the rectangular pixels lie in a grid, horizontal and vertical lines render clearly, with good contrast and smooth edges. But curved and diagonal lines don't line up with the rectangles of the pixel grid, so they end up looking jagged.

Two primary technical innovations have helped improve this situation: antialiasing and screen typefaces.

ANTIALIASING

As the number of grays and colors that could be used on screens increased, digital type standards began to use *antialiasing* to smooth out these rough edges. Antialiasing creates a halo of gradually lightening gray pixels around the black pixels of the type. TrueType offered the further refinement of *font smoothing*, which antialiases only the curved and angled portions of letter forms, leaving vertical and horizontal strokes untouched because they already align with the pixel grid. However, both of these techniques can leave the edges of letter forms looking somewhat fuzzy and indistinct, decreasing legibility and readability.

More recently, OpenType has incorporated a subpixel-level smoothing technique called ClearType. Previously, pixels could be turned only on or off. But color screen pixels are actually created with three subpixels: one red, one green, and one blue. (See Chapter 8 for more information on how screens make color.) ClearType can turn on two subpixels—for example, the red subpixel of one pixel and the blue subpixel of a neighboring pixel—to draw letter forms that extend *across* the rectangular grid of pixels. In effect, this creates antialiasing on a scale one-third the natural resolution of the screen. This technique reduces but cannot entirely eliminate the haziness of antialiasing.

SCREEN TYPEFACES

One of the biggest challenges of type technology is making what we see on the screen similar to what we see when we print out a document. In the early days of desktop publishing, designers had to use entirely different typefaces for on-screen and on-paper designs, often called *screen fonts* and *printer fonts*. PostScript still includes separate font files for screen and printers. Later, TrueType allowed designers to create typefaces in single files that work well on screen and in print. Unfortunately, sometimes a single typeface doesn't work ideally in either medium—and often it's the screen version that suffers most. This became a significant problem as we began to design more and more screen documents, such as web pages.

In response to this dilemma, some typefaces, known as *screen typefaces*, are specifically designed to be used on screen rather than in print. Common screen typefaces include the following:

- Georgia: abcdefghijklmnopqrstuvwxyz1234567890
- Arial: abcdefghijklmnopqrstuvwxyz1234567890
- Tahoma: abcdefghijklmnopqrstuvwxyz1234567890
- Verdana: abcdefghijklmnopqrstuvwxyz1234567890
- Trebuchet MS: abcdefghijklmnopqrstuvwxyz1234567890

These typefaces render well at a variety of screen resolutions with minimal jaggedness. You'll notice that most of them are sans serif typefaces, which have less ornamentation and therefore greater clarity on screen.

Font Availability

In addition to the disadvantages just discussed, other problems can arise when a font file isn't available on the computer on which a digital document is viewed. Say you design a website using a typeface from a font file on your computer. It looks great on your screen. But if other users don't have the same font file on their computers, they won't see the design you intended. Three common workarounds try to solve this problem: font substitution, font embedding, and font images.

FONT SUBSTITUTION

If a computer doesn't have a font file the design calls for, the computer will have to replace it with either a default typeface (usually Times New Roman or Arial) or the best available matching typeface. This technique, known as *font substitution*, can often mess up a screen document's design.

To avoid this problem, most web designers stick primarily with common typefaces, including Times New Roman, Arial, Tahoma, and Verdana. But not all of these typefaces are available to Apple computers, which typically substitute Times for Times New Roman and Helvetica for Arial, Tahoma, and Verdana.

FONT EMBEDDING

Another solution to the limitation of font file availability is *font embedding*. This technique actually includes the original font file specifications in the electronic document file itself, making the document work as designed regardless of whatever font files the user's computer might have.

However, font embedding isn't available for all electronic document types. Adobe Acrobat can embed most kinds of fonts in PDFs, and Microsoft Word can embed TrueType fonts in DOC files. But web pages rely entirely on the user's computer and cannot accommodate embedded fonts. Another disadvantage to this workaround is that font embedding can significantly increase the size of the digital file, which now has to include the information for the embedded font files as well as the text, images, and layout information it would normally include.

A final but very important disadvantage to font embedding is that not all type designers allow their font files to be embedded. Although type *designs* cannot be copyrighted, a computer *font file* is a piece of software protected by a copyright. Embedding a font in a document (or worse, distributing the font file directly to users) can be a copyright violation, since it publishes a new copy of the font over which the copyright owner has no control. Be sure to read and follow the terms of use of any font before you decide to embed it in a document.

FONT IMAGES

Finally, you can work entirely around the font file availability problem by creating image files on your computer that use exactly the typeface you want and then save them typically as GIF image files (or less commonly as JPGs or Flash files). You can then insert the image files into your on-screen design. The type in the image will look pretty much the same on your screen and on the user's. Designers often use this technique for the navigation buttons on websites.

This approach has a couple of disadvantages, though. First, it increases bandwidth requirements; images are entirely separate files that must be loaded into a web page, while type can be part of the HTML coding itself. Second, it can cause accessibility problems for users with limited vision. HTML-coded text can easily be read by the text-to-

---

DESIGN TIP

Strategies for Using Type on Screens

Here are some tips to help you manage type on screens. But the most important strategies are to plan for some variability from system to system and to test your designs on a variety of systems.

To address resolution issues:

- Set type for on-screen viewing in a slightly larger font than type to be viewed on paper. Larger fonts minimize the sense of haziness caused by antialiasing.

- Use simple, relatively unadorned typefaces, such as sans serifs. Ornate details often don't display well at screen resolutions.

To address line width issues:

- Use tables, frames, or columns to reduce the line length to about 7 to 12 words per line.

- Increase fonts to allow about 7 to 12 words per line.

To address font file availability issues:

- On websites, limit the typefaces used to those most common on all computers: Times New Roman, Arial, Helvetica, and Verdana.

- Specify alternate typefaces in HTML code in case the primary font isn't available on the viewer's computer. (See a good HTML reference for instructions on how to do so.)

- Embed the fonts used in your document into the computer file. This option is available in Acrobat, PowerPoint, and Word.

- For websites, use images (JPG or GIF) or Flash for text that must be in a special font. Keep in mind, however, that doing so can increase the file sizes of your website and slow down performance. It also makes it difficult for people with visual disabilities to access websites using text reading software.

---

speech software that many visually impaired users rely on to read web pages to them. A font image, however, doesn't really have any text in it; the file includes only visual information, not textual information. One solution to this difficulty is to describe each font image within an HTML alt (alternative text) attribute, like this:

```
<img src="home_button.gif" alt="Link to Home Page">.
```

Overall, however, use font images sparingly, when the on-screen visual design really needs to look the same on your computer and on those of your users.

Exercises

1. Take an old copy of your favorite magazine and snip out a sample of each different typeface you find. Tape or glue these samples onto a sheet (or several sheets) of paper and bring them to class. Compare your samples with those of your classmates and discuss the following questions:

   - Which typefaces do you think would work particularly well for reading text, headings, or display?

   - What rhetorical "voice-over" do you think these typefaces convey? Are they businesslike, fun, dramatic, playful, stern?

   - Which typefaces do you find most interesting to look at? Using the vocabulary you've developed from reading this chapter, what exactly do you like, in particular, about these typefaces?

2. Explore the typefaces available at one of the following digital type foundries or design bureaus:

   - <www.fonts.com>

   - <www.myfonts.com>

   - <www.linotype.com>

3. Type this phrase in a word processing program in 24-point type, copy it, and paste it three extra times: *The quick brown fox jumps over the lazy dog*. Then change each of the four versions to four different typefaces—two that look very similar and two that look very different. What specific differences do you see in the letter forms? Look in particular at the serifs (or lack of serifs), unusual letters like *a*, *g*, and *q*, stroke width, x-height:cap-height ratio, stress, counter shape, and other features covered in this chapter.

4. Analyze the typographic hierarchy of a document. How did the designers use typographic characteristics such as size, shape, value, and color to create this hierarchy? Do you see any potential problems in the design of the typographic hierarchy in terms of how well it reinforces the structure of the document?

5. Analyze the typographic design of a print or electronic document for its legibility, readability, and usability. How well does the document's typography match its purpose and the users' needs and expectations? What changes or improvements would you make if you were to redesign the document?

6. Redesign a page of the document you just analyzed, changing the typographic design to better fit the document's mission and intended use. Be ready to explain and justify your design choices.

7. Explore the typographic identity guidelines of an organization. To find a suitable organization, search for "identity guidelines" (in quotation marks) in a search engine such as Google. What aspects of typography does the organization specify that its employees must use? How do the typographic guidelines differ for screen and paper documents? Why do you think the organization is making such a big effort for typographic consistency in its documents? What explanations does the organization give for its efforts in creating a stable typographic identity?

Further Reading

Arah, Tom. *Web Type Expert: All That You Need to Create Fantastic Web Type*. New York: Friedman/Fairfax, 2003.

Heller, Steven, and Philip B. Meggs, eds. *Texts on Type: Critical Writings on Typography*. New York: Allworth, 2001.

Lupton, Ellen. *Thinking with Type: A Critical Guide for Designers, Writers, Editors, & Students*. New York: Princeton Architectural Press, 2004.

McLean, Ruari. *The Thames & Hudson Manual of Typography*. London: Thames & Hudson, 1980.

Papazian, Hrant. "Improving the Tool." *Graphic Design & Reading: Explorations of an Uneasy Relationship*, ed. Gunnar Swanson. New York: Allworth, 2000. 111–31.

Salen, Katie. "Surrogate Multiplicities: In Search of the Visual Voice-over." *Graphic Design & Reading*, ed. Gunnar Swanson. New York: Allworth, 2000. 77–90.

Warde, Beatrice. "The Crystal Goblet, or Printing Should Be Invisible." *Looking Closer 3: Classic Writings on Graphic Design*, ed. Steven Heller and Rick Poynor. New York: Allworth, 1999. 56–59.

World Wide Web Consortium (W3C). Cascading Style Sheets. Online: <http://www.w3.org/Style/CSS/>.

CHAPTER 7

Graphics

Graphics are a powerful way to convey information and ideas, and thus an essential part of any document designer's toolkit. Graphics are also easier to create today than ever before, leading to a somewhat different approach to incorporating them in documents. Years ago, designers composed the text of a document and *then* decided what graphics they needed. Today, most designers first consider what must be conveyed visually and then write the text to support those images — if text is necessary at all. In other words, designers now work in what Robert E. Horn called "visual language": using graphics either without prose or as a full partner with prose.

Graphics have two main functions in document designs: conveying information and influencing users through visual rhetoric. Some graphics lean more toward one function than the other, but most graphics play both roles in some way. Consider the graphic in Figure 7.1, which appeared on the packaging for a microbrewed beer. This graphic's primary purpose is to convey useful information. If this beer were a mass-market variety, consumers might know what to expect from it. But consumers will likely want to know how this unusual, small-batch beer tastes before they buy it. The graphic, therefore, characterizes the taste of the beer on two scales: light versus dark and malty versus hoppy (sweet versus bitter). Although the graphic uses some text, it delivers this essential information primarily through visual communication, providing Xs to show where this beer falls on the two scales. The light/dark scale even reinforces this information by using a bar that gradually shifts from light to dark along its length. As flavors, "malty" and "hoppy" are pretty difficult to describe, but the kind of people who'd buy such an esoteric beer might already know what these terms mean and can imagine the taste that this graphic shows visually.

The information the graphic conveys is important, but the graphic also uses visual rhetoric to convince people to buy the beer by giving it

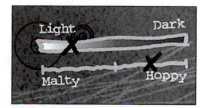

Figure 7.1 Conceptual graphics on microbrewed beer packaging. Notice how the graphic conveys information about the taste of the beer on two scales: from light to dark and from malty to hoppy. Also notice the visual style of the graphic. Like an informal sketch, the graphic fits both the product image and the user's expectations.

Flying Dog Brewery, "Flying Dog IPA."

a brand identity. Even though the scales in this graphic resemble statistical graphics, they seem casually and roughly hand-drawn. The graphic has a funky, grungy look, making the beer look appealing to people looking for an alternative taste. This visual style makes it clear that the information provided through the graphic should help you enjoy the beer, rather than read statistics about it. The graphic doesn't tell us precisely *how* hoppy or *how* light the beer is—just that it generally tends toward lightness and hoppiness. Brewers might need precise measurements for color and bitterness, but most beer drinkers don't care about that level of precision. Overall, the visual rhetoric of the graphic reinforces a casual, yet stylish approach to discriminating beer drinking.

In this chapter, we discuss a variety of techniques for creating and using graphics in document designs, in terms of both conveying information and presenting effective visual rhetoric. We'll use the term *graphics* generally to describe design objects intended to *show* ideas or information rather than to *tell*, which is the primary function of prose. However, keep in mind that graphics can also include text to help users understand what a graphic means.

Graphics are often intimidating to new document designers, who might be more familiar with working with prose. But most of us are already experienced consumers of graphics, even if we haven't created very many yet. This chapter will build on your own experiences to give you a basic introduction to the most common forms of graphics, while discussing the rationale for using graphics in your document designs and the ethics and practicalities of doing so.

Three Perspectives on Graphics

As users and consumers of graphics, we tend to take them for granted. A picture *is* sometimes worth a thousand words, but sometimes it takes more than a thousand words to explain why a picture works as it does. Scholars have approached this challenge through the perspectives of visual perception, visual culture, and visual rhetoric.

Perception

Scholars interested in the perceptual aspect of how we respond to graphics tend to work on the assumption that images are made up of universally recognizable visual elements that require active perception but no particular training to understand.

For example, scholars suggest that we interact with visual images cognitively by assembling their basic features into complex shapes, recognizing graphics first by their component parts—Irving Biederman's concept of the *geon*. Geon theory suggests that we perceive all objects as made up of abstract, three-dimensional objects. Geons are mostly geometrical, such as cylinders, cones, blocks, and wedges. We assemble these basic shapes to recognize more complex shapes — a tree being a collection of branching cylinders or long, narrow cones, for example. Once we recognize the basic building blocks and their relationship to each other in a complex object, we can recognize the object from many viewpoints — below, above, beside, near, or distant.

According to geon theory and other theories based on cognitive psychology, the ability to turn basic visual perceptions into the recognition of an image is more or less inherent in the human visual system, supported by both our physiology and psychology. In the case of geons, we don't need to learn anything to recognize these primitive objects or see how they assemble into complex objects; we can do it from birth. Our mind simply assembles complex objects from the bottom up, starting with the basic building blocks of perception.

Culture

Approaches from this bottom-up perspective, however, tend to underestimate the power of training and culture on what we see. This is true particularly in the consideration of graphic images because graphics are by definition *created* by people for other people to see. Although these created images might use our inherent perceptual abilities, they are tied just as strongly to social and cultural factors — particularly in terms of how we ascribe meaning to images. We learn how to read images through experience and association, not just through raw perception.

Consider the cover of a leaflet guiding visitors to the Helen & Peter Bing Children's Garden at the Huntington Library, Art Collections, and Botanical Gardens in San Marino, California (Figure 7.2). The title of this leaflet uses two images: a fern and a hummingbird. If we consider these images only perceptually, they show us nothing other than a plant and a bird. But our training, education, and experience help us recognize them in this context as a stylized C and apostrophe.

Undeniably, cultural values and expectations play a role in our interpretations of what we see. Without visual culture, users would have a difficult time creating meaning from images.

Rhetoric

This relationship between perception and culture suggests that we should think about both factors in our designs, taking into account our inherent ability to see images and the cultural values users might apply to those images.

Consider another example from the Huntington, a general "Information Guide" leaflet distributed to visitors (see Figure 7.3 on page 202).

Figure 7.2 Culture and experience influence how we see graphics. Most users will recognize the graphics of a fern leaf and a hummingbird in the title of this leaflet not only as representative images, but also as a stylized letter C and apostrophe.

The Huntington Library, Art Collections, and Botanical Gardens, "The Helen & Peter Bing Children's Garden at The Huntington."

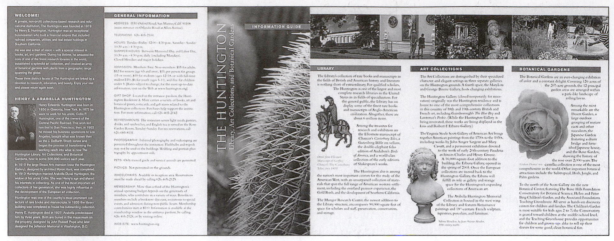

Side A

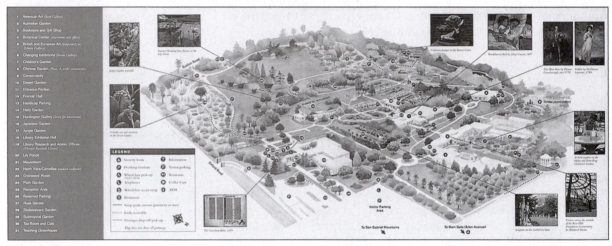

Side B

Detail: Legend with pictograms

Detail: Pictograms on panoramic map

Detail: Visual callouts with captions

Figure 7.3 Graphics help form a visual rhetoric for documents. This leaflet uses a broad variety of graphics to present information to visitors, including photos, maps, visual and textual callouts, pictograms, and a legend. These graphics also give users a positive impression of the site, allowing them to build an attractive mental picture as they begin their visit.

The Huntington Library, Art Collections, and Botanical Gardens, "Information Guide."

The leaflet presents a lot of information about the Huntington, but it does so using a consistent visual rhetoric that encourages users to look forward to their perambulations through the grounds and galleries. The leaflet uses several graphic forms both to convey information and to present a visually coherent view of the multifaceted institution:

- *Decorative photographs* of many attractive aspects of the collections and gardens, including photographs of the founder, paintings, sculptures, galleries, buildings, flowers, cacti, people walking in gardens, and children playing in fountains.

- A *panoramic map* of the grounds, showing the various facilities, paths, roads, and parking within the landscape.

- *Visual and textual callouts* from the panoramic map, showing visitors what they can expect to find and see in different locations.

- *Pictograms* marking useful facilities on the panoramic map, such as information kiosks, telephones, water fountains, restrooms, and access for the disabled.

- A *legend* identifying what the pictograms mean.

These graphics provide essential information to users about the Huntington. The leaflet's visual images also present a consistent visual rhetoric that encourages people to think that this is a nice place for individuals or families to visit, with many things to see, all arranged for easy access and enjoyment.

Because the Huntington is a private institution, it relies on visitors' fees and donations to remain open and to support the work of many researchers who use its extensive library. That means this leaflet carries a persuasive burden as well. It must convince visitors that they're welcome at the Huntington and that it's a friendly, comfortable, and beautiful place to visit — well worth their financial support. So the graphics — and in turn, the whole document — must be presented in a very high-level design: beautiful, clear, and useful. Without graphics, this leaflet could scarcely do as good a job of both informing and persuading.

Graphics and Principles of Design

One of the most challenging aspects of communicating through graphics is to present a clear and accurate idea of the information or ideas. But what exactly is clarity, and how do we design graphics with this quality?

As always, the first consideration is the user and his or her situation, needs, and limitations. The better you know your user, the more likely you will create graphics that meet his or her needs successfully. Ideally, the decision to use graphics at all should arise from your analysis of users and their needs (see Chapter 9 for more information on researching users).

But once you've decided a graphic is necessary, your best guide is the principles of design we've outlined in this book:

- Similarity
- Contrast
- Alignment
- Proximity
- Order
- Enclosure

As you'll recall, document design is object-oriented; a good designer pays attention to the qualities of various visual objects on the page and then uses principles of design to show clear relationships between those objects.

The simple bar chart in Figure 7.4 uses all of these principles to tell an important story about Dickinson College's endowment. The story

Figure 7.4 How a bar chart uses the principles of design.   This bar chart uses the principles of design to imply relationships between various design objects.

The Chronicle of Higher Education, "Dickinson College's Endowment."

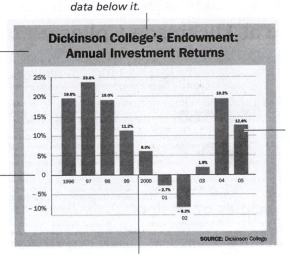

Contrast. *Typographic density emphasizes the title over the data below it.*

Enclosure. *A shaded border encloses the graphic and sets it off from the surrounding text.*

Alignment. *All bars are aligned to the 0 line of the horizontal axis.*

Similarity. *The similarly shaped and shaded bars encourage comparison.*

Proximity and Order. *All bars are in equal proximity to each other, suggesting their parallel meaning—each representing one year in chronological order.*

is that over the past 10 years (1996–2005), the rate of return on the college's endowment fell, reaching its lowest point in 2002 before coming back again in 2003–2004. But all is not rosy: The figure is down again for the most recent year. The story even has suspense: Will 2005 be the start of a new downward trend, or is it merely a dip on a mostly upward trend?

But notice how this graphic tells the story visually using the principles of design. The graphic is *enclosed* in a border to set it off from the rest of the article, which discusses trends in college endowments across the country. It also uses *alignment* within the framework of an *x-y* coordinate grid: the *x*-axis shows different years, and the *y*-axis shows the endowment's performance. The bars are arranged in *order* of years. *Proximity* helps users associate labels with the appropriate design objects within the graphic.

In all of your work designing graphics, try to keep in mind how principles of design can help you tell a story, reveal a truth, or show a good way to do something. Graphics are a powerful tool for communicating complex information and ideas.

Graphics and Ethics

It's often said that people believe what they can *see*. But as a result, they're also sometimes less skeptical about what they see than about what they hear. That tendency makes it particularly easy to mislead users with graphics, whether intentionally or unintentionally. As a designer, you'll need to be cautious about and aware of the ethical implications of what you show users through graphics. Three important ethical aspects of using graphics involve distortion, viewpoint, and copyright.

Distortion

Mark Twain was said once to comment that there are three kinds of lies: "lies, damned lies, and statistics." Statistics themselves are easy to manipulate to fit many arguments and ideas. When expressed graphically, statistics are even more prone to distortion. Consider what is perhaps the most commonly distorted statistical graphic: the line graph. The graph in Figure 7.5 (page 206) accompanied a story about a survey of British opinions of the new European Union currency, the euro.

In 2002, Great Britain was involved in considerable debate about whether to join the European Union in its new unified currency. The line graph on the left shows the exchange rate between the euro (€) and the British pound (£). It suggests that the value of the euro had

Figure 7.5 A distorted line graph. This newspaper graphic visualized British opinions during the controversy over whether the United Kingdom should take part in the European Union's new currency, the euro. What distortions do you see in this graphic?

The Times, "Anti-Euro Mood Hardens among Britons," July 31, 2002.

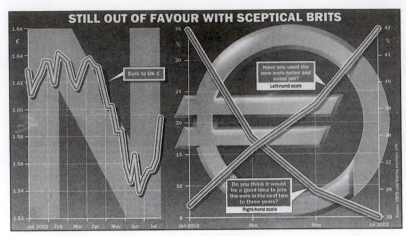

Original graphic, showing euro-GBP exchange rate on the left and responses to survey questions on the right ("Have you used the new euro notes and coins yet?" and "Do you think it would be a good idea to join the euro . . . ?").

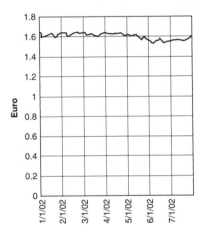

Revised graphic of euro-GBP exchange rate using a normal zero point. Notice that the dips in the exchange rate appear much less drastic now.

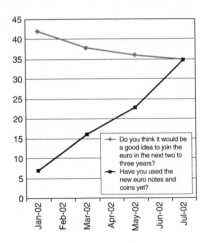

Revised graphic of survey responses using the same zero point for both graphs. Notice that the graph no longer forms the "X" of the original graph, which helped support the idea that the euro was being received negatively in Britain.

dropped dramatically compared to the pound. The combined line graphs on the right show the results of the survey questions "Have you used the new euro notes and coins yet?" and "Do you think it would be a good idea to join the euro in the next two to three years?" Taking advantage of the shape of the line on the left-hand graph, the designers placed an N behind the left-hand graph and a euro symbol (€)

behind the right-hand graph. "N€" seems to form the word "NO" behind the combined graphic; the open ends of the euro symbol are even joined to make it look even more like an O. The lines of the right-hand graph also form an *X* over the euro symbol. Together, these visual cues emphasize the idea that Britons are strongly rejecting the currency.

But notice that on the left-hand graph, the scale for the vertical axis starts at 1.52 rather than at 0. Compare this to what a version of the graphic would look like if the vertical axis started at 0, as in the first redrawn graph in Figure 7.5. What's going on here? In the original graph, the line seems to show a significant drop in the value of the euro, but in the redrawn version, the drop seems much less drastic, the value of the euro holding more or less steady at around £1.60. This distortion is called an *elevated zero point*. By starting the vertical axis above zero, the graph exaggerates the changes in currency exchange rates.

The right-hand graph in Figure 7.5 also uses an elevated zero point. The two lines of the graph are marked against different vertical scales — one on the left, one on the right — neither of which starts at zero. The second redrawn graph in Figure 7.5 shows what the graph would look like if the lines shared a common scale starting at zero. This redrawn version seems to suggest that although there has been a drop in support for joining the euro, there's been a dramatic increase in the number of people who have actually used the new currency. This story differs significantly from the story told by the original graphic, which suggests that people are strongly rejecting the euro.

These distortions are remarkably easy to make, particularly with the statistical graphics tools commonly available in office software. Often, the distortions are unintentional; the designer has made a misleading graphic out of ignorance or inattention. Just as often, however, the distortions arise from a desire to make data say something it really doesn't. Figure 7.5 tells a dramatic story of Britons rejecting the euro, but it does so only by manipulating the visual display until the line graphs form "NO" and "X" over this issue.

Another common distortion derives from an innocent desire to make data look fancy. Microsoft Office products allow you to apply a three-dimensional (3D) look to information graphics, even if the data doesn't really need that many dimensions. In Figure 7.6 on page 208, a pie chart has been made 3D, even though the third dimension doesn't add any information to the graphic. This technique has the potential to distort users' perceptions of the data because the pie wedges nearest the viewer might seem unduly large, while those farthest away might seem smaller than they really are.

Nor do we find distortion only in abstract images; distortion can appear just as easily in representational images. Through the wonders of Photoshop and similar image editors, it's very easy now to alter photographs to make something appear to have happened that never did. For example, on the cover of the University of Wisconsin's 2001–2002

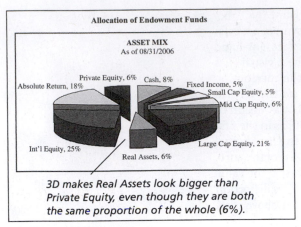

3D makes Real Assets look bigger than Private Equity, even though they are both the same proportion of the whole (6%).

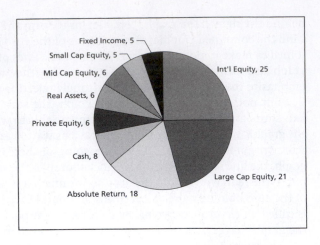

Figure 7.6 A pie chart in 3D and 2D.   Meaningless 3D effects in graphics can distort user perceptions. In the original graphic, the pie slices closest to the viewer (Large Cap Equity, Real Assets, and Int'l Equity) appear larger than those farther away. Even portions that are actually the same, such as Private Equity (6%) and Real Assets (6%), look remarkably different in the 3D version of a pie chart.

Texas Tech Foundation, Inc.

Design graphics that portray the truth as accurately as possible, without bias.

---

undergraduate application folder, the university pasted in the face of an African-American student in a crowd of Caucasian students to make the school look more diverse than it really was.

Scholars such as Edward R. Tufte (1983), Stephen M. Kosslyn (1994), and Nigel Holmes (1984) have catalogued many of the most common distortions, particularly of information graphics. But the most significant point is to design graphics that portray the truth as accurately as possible, without bias.

Viewpoint

Graphics inevitably show the world from a particular viewpoint or perspective. Unfortunately, this means that they can conceal as much as they reveal, through either abstraction or outright exclusion. For example, Sam Dragga and Dan Voss have criticized the tendency of graphics in federal accident reports to exclude figures of human beings. Diagrams and statistical graphics in these reports use abstraction to exclude any reference to humans, using geometric lines and shapes to describe the accidents or to measure human pain and loss. Similarly, photographs tend to focus on vehicles, facilities, roads, and equipment, leaving human beings outside of the frame. This practice might be intended to avoid alarming images, but it has the effect of making the accidents seem less significant than they are.

It's particularly easy to use the viewpoint of photography to conceal important information. A photograph asks users to look at whatever is pictured from a particular perspective. That perspective might easily hide aspects of the scene that are unattractive or counter to the client's agendas. One photographic technique particularly sensitive to concealment is *cropping*. Cropping a photograph to exclude important information and mislead users can be unethical (Figure 7.7).

Figure 7.7 Cropping an image to conceal information.   Cropping can leave out the whole truth. The cropped version of this image might make a very appealing picture of an old-fashioned home on a real estate website. But the uncropped version shows large construction cranes and semitrailers behind the house. Would you buy the house if you saw the untouched photograph?

Of course, viewpoint can also be a great guide to users, showing them how to look at information from a useful perspective. But make sure that the viewpoint you use in your graphics is factual and honest, not concealing or excluding important information.

Copyright

A common first impulse when using graphics in documents is to borrow someone else's graphics, rather than to create your own. These existing graphics are often called *clip art*. Today, most word processors and page layout programs come with at least a small collection of clip art, such as cartoons, drawings, and photographs. Designers are also sometimes tempted to use graphics copied from websites or scanned from previously printed documents.

Using borrowed graphics isn't necessarily wrong. Modifying or combining existing graphics can be a good way to start using graphics in your document designs — and it can save a lot of time. But like all created works, graphics are protected under *copyright*. Copyright is a legal status in which the creator or owner of the graphic has the right to say whether and how the graphic can be reproduced by others. This system makes sense from the creator's viewpoint: if you created a graphic, you wouldn't want someone else to use it without your permission.

Copyright is granted by U.S. law as soon as a graphic is created. It's not necessary to register the graphic to gain copyright. Under current U.S. law, simply creating the graphic (or text, for that matter) gives you the copyright for your lifetime (and your heirs for decades after that). Copyright does expire, typically a century or more after the creation date, but it can be renewed.

So how do we use borrowed material within the boundaries of copyright? It's possible to use a portion of a created work under a principle called *fair use*. However, this concept works better for text rather than graphics. The idea is that if you quote only a small part of a text—for example, to comment on what the author said—you are not preventing the author from profiting from his or her text as a whole. Usually, it's appropriate to quote 5 percent or so of a whole work under fair use, so long as you give full credit to the author.

But unlike text, *every single graphic* is counted as a whole work, even if the document or website that it comes from contains many graphics. And graphics are difficult to use any way except as a whole—5 percent of a graphic isn't often very useful. Accordingly, you can assume that any graphic you scan from someone else's document or copy from the Internet probably requires the copyright holder's permission before you use it in your own designs. Using copyrighted graphics without permission can hold serious legal consequences; don't do it.

Fortunately, getting the copyright holder's **permission** to use the graphic isn't usually very difficult. It simply involves contacting the copyright holder, asking if you can use the graphic in your document, and explaining how you intend to use the graphic. If at all possible, get the permission in writing. Some copyright holders will give you permission for free, but others will ask for a fee. The more famous the graphic or artist, the higher the price; don't expect to get a photo of da Vinci's *Mona Lisa* or Monet's *Water Lilies* cheaply. You can also purchase more generic pieces or collections of clip art from businesses called *design bureaus*.

Permission usually comes with a few strings attached. For example, copyright holders might restrict the number of times you can use the graphic, or they might restrict its use to nonprofit purposes. These restrictions are often expressed in a legal document called the **terms of use** or **conditions of use**; follow the requirements of these documents explicitly.

Even if it's not explicitly required in the conditions of use, *always* give credit to the copyright holders for their work. There are many ways to do so, depending on the document's context. In corporate documents, it's common to provide source information in a **source line**—a caption directly below the image. For published documents, you might also need to create a **credits page** that lists the copyright owners of all the images you used, along with the page on which each image appeared in your document. For academic documents, including student projects, provide a full **citation** and **bibliographic entry**.

Copyright law can be ambiguous, so err on the side of caution. If you have any doubts about the legality of using a borrowed graphic, look for a firmer alternative.

Using copyrighted graphics without permission can hold serious legal consequences; don't do it.

DESIGN TIP

Copyright Checklist

- Find out who owns the copyright to the graphic you want to borrow.
- Obtain the copyright owner's *written* permission to use the graphic.
- Read and follow the terms or conditions of use.
- Give appropriate credit through citations (footnotes, endnotes, image credits, source lines).

Why Use Graphics?

Graphics can both provide information and encourage people to act or think in particular ways. Most graphics, however, fall toward one or the other end of the spectrum between *information* and *persuasion*. Robert L. Harris suggests that **information graphics** are those "whose primary function is to consolidate and display information graphically in an organized way so a viewer can readily retrieve the information and make specific and/or overall observations from it" (198). He distinguishes between these graphics and those "whose primary functions are artistic or for purposes of entertainment, promotion, identification, etc." — what we'll call **promotion graphics** (198).

Information graphics, such as charts, diagrams, maps, and illustrations, were developed primarily to help users see meaning in a mass of data. William Playfair (1759–1823), the inventor of the pie chart, once commented that

> Figures [numbers] . . . may express with accuracy, but they can never *represent* either number or space. A map of the river Thames, or of a large town, expressed in figures, would give but a very imperfect notion of either, though they might be perfectly exact in every dimension; most men prefer *representations*, though very indifferent ones, to such a mode of painting. (*Commercial and Political Atlas*, 3)

As Playfair suggests, information graphics can help users recognize both quantitative information ("figures") and nonquantitative information (geography, spatial relationships, and concepts) at a single glance — often much more quickly than we could with text or numbers.

Promotion graphics, such as logos and decorative graphics, are used primarily to convince users of the ethos of a document. Logos, for example, are carefully designed to give users a particular idea of the company or organization they indicate. They are intended as a graphic shorthand for everything the company or organization represents — an approach often called **branding**. Corporations and organizations take branding very seriously, spending millions of dollars creating and protecting their logos and their corporate "look." Other promotion graphics can create a visual tone for a document. For example, opening each chapter of a manual with a repeated decorative element can make the document look sophisticated or casual, serious or playful, professional or trendy, as the rhetorical situation demands. Although promotion graphics might not convey as much information as information graphics, they help create a visual tone for the document, which can influence how users respond to it.

This difference between information and promotion graphics isn't exclusive. The *primary* purpose of information graphics is to convey

Figure 7.8 A logo with promotional and informational purposes. The logo of the United States Department of Agriculture (USDA) appears on the labels of certified organic foods. This logo has both promotional and informational purposes. It promotes the USDA and organic foods, while conveying important information about organic standards to consumers.

United States Department of Agriculture, <www.usda.gov>.

information, but information graphics can also play a role in visual rhetoric. For example, information graphics can convince audiences by simplifying complex information—something that is harder to do with prose. Likewise, promotion graphics can convey useful, although generally limited information; a logo can help users quickly recognize what organization a document speaks for and where it comes from. For example, consider the logo of the United States Department of Agriculture (USDA), used on the labels of certified organic foods (Figure 7.8). This logo both represents the USDA and conveys important information to consumers.

The following table lists some of the most common purposes and genres (types) of information and promotion graphics.

Purpose	*Common Genres*
INFORMATION	
• To show how something looks	Representational illustrations, such as photographs and line art
• To show how things are related in space	Maps
• To show how actions or occurrences are related in time	Process diagrams, such as Gantt charts, flowcharts, and PERT charts
• To show ideas and relationships visually	Concept diagrams, such as Venn diagrams, network diagrams, and organizational charts
• To show quantitative relationships	Statistical graphs, such as bar/column graphs, line graphs, pie graphs, and scatter graphs
• To provide a simple mark for an idea	Pictograms
PROMOTION	
• To mark identity	Logos
• To establish a visual tone	Decorative graphics

Naturally, we can't cover all the myriad kinds of graphics commonly used in document designs. (Robert L. Harris's *Information Graphics: A Comprehensive Illustrated Reference* is a particularly useful encyclopedia of the many different options for information graphic design.) But the next sections discuss each of the categories in the table, with examples and explanations of the dynamics of the most common genres.

Information Graphics

Illustrations: Showing How Something Looks

Often, users simply need to know what something *looks* like. Illustrations help us to show users how objects such as buildings, tools, interfaces, or product features *appear*, as if the user were looking at the objects themselves. This feature of illustrations is known as **representation**, because the graphic temporarily stands in for the real object. Three kinds of illustration are particularly common in technical documents: photographs, line art, and screenshots.

> ### MORE ABOUT . . . GRAPHIC TERMINOLOGY
>
> The terms applied to even common types of graphics vary from field to field. For example, some designers call pie charts *pie graphs* or even *circular area graphs*. More broadly, even the terms *chart* and *graph* are difficult to pin down. They're often used interchangeably, and *chart* is also a common term for sea navigation maps.
>
> We'll try to be consistent with our terminology in this chapter, but don't be surprised if you encounter some of these other terms in reading other books.

PHOTOGRAPHS

One of the most common ways to illustrate how something looks is to photograph it—either chemically on film or digitally with a digital camera or scanner. For quick illustrations, photographs are very convenient. With little skill or forethought, you can take a digital photo and insert it into a document in just a few minutes. Photographs are one of the first graphics that beginning designers consider adding to their document designs.

However, photographs are more complex than they might seem. To print well, photographs require careful color management and a full awareness of how production methods will affect how a photo will appear in a document. Photographs used on screen also present technical challenges. Due to the low resolution of most screens, it's difficult to get good detail in a photograph in electronic documents such as web pages or PowerPoint presentations. If the resolution is high enough, digital photographs can take up too much computer memory and network bandwidth, or they may simply be too large to show on the fixed resolution of a computer monitor.

In addition, sometimes photographs convey *too much* data to be understandable. The level of detail in photographs can distract users from their immediate task. For example, think about navigating on a road trip: would you rather have a road map or a satellite photograph to help you get to your destination? Most people would prefer the road map because it strips out the extraneous information that doesn't help them understand how to get where they're going. Ironically, *less data* can mean *more usable information*.

Finally, photographs can represent only what the camera captures. It's difficult to use a photograph to show how something looks from different perspectives—inside, outside, top, or bottom. Getting a camera into those positions to take a picture can be difficult or impossible — but sometimes these perspectives are exactly what users need to see (for more information on using photographs, see "Digital Photography" on page 230).

LINE ART: DIAGRAMS AND DRAWINGS

Diagrams and *drawings*, together called *line art*, can sometimes do what photography cannot. As the term suggests, line art usually employs lines or other abstract shapes to show something. It presents an abstracted version of what someone might see, stripping away all the extraneous details and concentrating the user's attention on the important details.

Line art also allows us to show users things that a camera can't access — such as the inside of an object. *Cross-sectional drawings*, for example, take an imaginary slice off of an object to show us the interior. Similarly, *cutaway drawings* peel a section of the "skin" from an object to let us see the inside. And *exploded drawings* show how the individual parts of an object fit together by separating them a short distance from each other. None of these things are easy to show with a photograph (Figure 7.9).

Figure 7.9 Examples of common line art. Line art (drawings and diagrams) can come in many forms. Three common genres are cross sections, cutaways, and exploded diagrams.

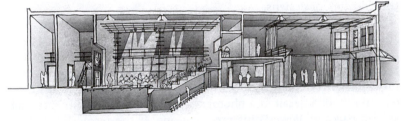

A cross section of a theater building.

Commonweal Theatre Company.

An exploded diagram of the space shuttle.

National Aeronautics and Space Administration.

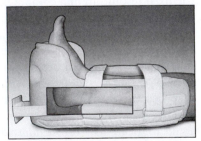

A cutaway diagram of an orthopedic device.

DM Systems, Inc.

Line art can also have disadvantages—the most significant being that drawings require more skill and time to create than photographs do. For this reason, designers often save line art for the most important points in a document and reuse or modify existing drawings as much as possible. Another common technique is to use photographs as the basis for line art. Using a drawing program, it's easy to place a photograph on one layer and then trace the important parts of the photograph onto another layer. When the photograph layer is deleted, only the line art remains.

SCREENSHOTS

Because so many technical documents show users how to use software, screenshots have become very popular. Screenshots are a snapshot of the image a computer screen is showing when the screenshot was made. They are particularly useful for showing software interfaces and dialog boxes in manuals.

Screenshots are so easy to produce that they're sometimes overused. Remember, every graphic must have a purpose. Do you really need a screenshot for every single step of a procedure or only for the most important or potentially confusing steps? (For more information on creating and working with screenshots, see "Screenshots" on page 234.)

Maps: Showing How Things Are Related in Space

Mapmaking is one of the earliest developments of graphic communication, and an amazing one at that. Remember that for most of human history, people had never seen Earth from an aerial view. Whoever discovered that a sheet of paper, parchment, or bark could represent an abstract version of Earth's surface must have been a genius indeed.

Now, maps are an essential tool of modern life, as well as a common part of documents. Maps are usually two-dimensional representations of three-dimensional spaces. In documents, maps are commonly used for three significant roles: to convey geographic information, to show us how to get from one place to another, and to show the geographic distribution of statistical information.

Geographic maps are perhaps the most common, showing the two-dimensional spatial relationship between objects and places from an overhead view. Literally meaning "world writing," geographic maps can represent any portion of the world, from the layout of a single building to the entire globe. In this regard, geographic maps are particularly useful for showing *where* something or someplace is in relation to other things or places with which the user is already familiar.

Closely related to geographic maps are *wayfinding maps*, which are specifically designed to help users navigate through geography.

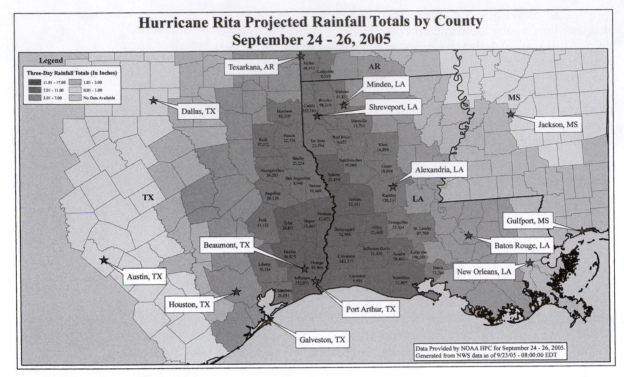

Hurricane Rita Projected Rainfall Totals by County
September 24 - 26, 2005

Legend

Three-Day Rainfall Totals (In Inches)

11.01 - 17.00   1.01 - 3.00
7.01 - 11.00   0.01 - 1.00
3.01 - 7.00   No Data Available

Data Provided by NOAA HPC for September 24 - 26, 2005.
Generated from NWS data as of 9/23/05 - 08:00:00 EDT

Figure 7.10 A choropleth thematic map. This choropleth thematic map shows the projected rainfall by county during Hurricane Rita. The darker the color, the more intense the effect being recorded—in this case, the more rain.

Federal Emergency Management Agency, "Hurricane Rita Projected Rainfall Totals by County September 24–26, 2005."

Wayfinding maps include road maps and facilities maps, which help us find important information such as the path out of a building in an emergency or the path to the nearest restroom. Facility wayfinding maps can be incorporated into other kinds of documents, or they can be posted in a useful position in a facility—for example, in a kiosk near the entrance or next to the elevator on each floor of the building. (Figure 7.3 on page 202 shows a wayfinding map.)

Thematic maps show the geographic distribution of statistical information. There are hundreds of kinds of thematic maps, but one common kind is the *choropleth map*, which uses shading to indicate the statistical density of phenomena in a geographic region (Figure 7.10).

Process Diagrams: Showing How Actions Are Related in Time

Process diagrams focus on showing how actions or steps are related in time. They're most often useful in documents that explain how something works, such as process descriptions and procedures, or in those that show how something is *planned* to work, such as proposals and project planning documents.

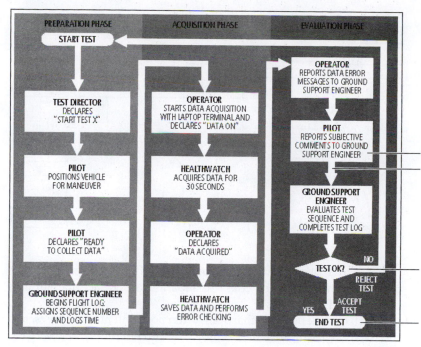

Figure 7.11 A flowchart. This flowchart uses shapes and arrows to show the steps in testing radio transmissions from helicopters. The designers also used enclosure to group phases of the process.

NASA Ames Research Center.

— *Rectangles mark steps in the process.*
— *Arrows connect steps.*

— *Diamonds mark decision points.*

— *Rounded rectangles show the beginning or end of a process.*

The most common kind of process diagram is probably the *flowchart*. Flowcharts use a small, relatively standardized geometric vocabulary to indicate the starting and ending points of a process, as well as the steps and decision points along the way (see Figure 7.11). Steps are connected by lines, often with arrows to show the direction of time. Flowcharts are useful for showing complex procedures graphically, and they're easy to create with the drawing tools in most office software.

Gantt charts and *PERT charts* were developed in the twentieth century as graphic means for planning and tracking progress on large projects. Gantt charts were first developed by Henry Laurence Gantt (1861–1919). They present each activity in a project as a separate horizontal line, measured on a horizontal scale of time and marked by beginning and ending points. These charts make it easy to see relationships between simultaneous activities.

PERT (Program Evaluation and Review Technique) charts (Figure 7.12, page 218) are also organized chronologically, but they do not use a consistent time scale. PERT charts are formed by simple lines joining labeled shapes. The shapes represent milestones—important points in the project timeline. Although Gantt charts are great for planning simultaneous actions, PERT charts work best for identifying the relationships between actions. They're most often used to analyze *critical paths*—essential activities that must be completed before others can

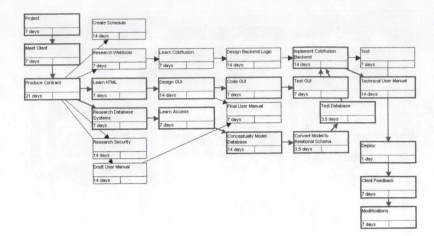

Figure 7.12 A PERT chart.   Teams use PERT charts to organize their work on complex projects. This PERT chart shows the tasks involved in creating a piece of software called TikTok, an online time clock. The critical path of absolutely essential tasks is represented with thicker borders around the boxes (printed in red in the original).

David Stotts, University of North Carolina.

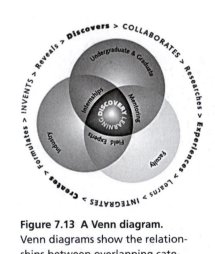

Figure 7.13 A Venn diagram. Venn diagrams show the relationships between overlapping categories. In this example, the University of Colorado's Discovery Learning Center shows how it serves the common needs of students, faculty, and industrial partners.

University of Colorado.

commence. Critical paths are sometimes difficult to see in Gantt charts, which separate activities into separate lines rather than joining them, as do PERT charts.

Both Gantt and PERT charts are often posted in project offices, but they're also typically included in project documentation and proposals. Because project plans sometimes change dynamically, a variety of software programs have been developed to help implement and automate Gantt and PERT charts.

Concept Diagrams: Showing Ideas and Relationships Visually

Concept diagrams are perhaps the most abstract of diagrams because they focus on showing otherwise intangible ideas in graphic form. One common type of concept diagram is the Venn diagram, named after the Cambridge University logician John Venn (1834–1915), who first proposed them in 1880. Venn diagrams are particularly effective for conveying how overlapping groups of concepts or objects are related to each other (Figure 7.13).

Network diagrams are frequently used in planning computer networks to show the logical relationships between the different computers, databases, routers, and nodes used in network design. Network diagrams use simplified icons to represent these different parts of the network and lines to show how they connect to each other. A similar conceptual diagram, the *site map*, is used to plan websites, showing how the various web pages link to one another. As websites grow increasingly dynamic, using information from databases to make web pages on the fly, site maps and network diagrams have begun to look more alike.

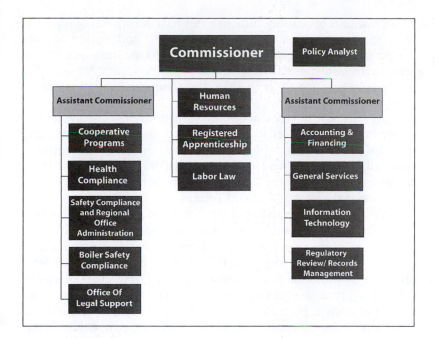

Figure 7.14 An organizational chart. This organizational chart shows the management structure of the Virginia Department of Labor & Industry. Organizational charts and others like them are known as tree-root diagrams because they show entities in a branching hierarchy.

Virginia Department of Labor & Industry.

Organizational charts and other *tree-root diagrams* (Figure 7.14) show hierarchical relationships. An organizational chart usually starts with the highest and broadest position of responsibility at the top and divides into lower and narrower areas of responsibility. Organizational charts are useful for showing how different positions are related to one another in terms of supervision and responsibilities.

Statistical Charts: Showing Quantitative Relationships

In this book, we can only scratch the surface of statistical charts, perhaps the most varied and complex information graphics used in communication. Statistical charts are the product of a field of statistics once known as *graphic statistics*, which uses geometric forms to show the relationships between different kinds of statistical information. Common statistical charts include forms such as bar/column graphs, line graphs, and pie charts, most of which you probably already know well. (If not, consult a basic technical communication or statistics textbook such as Markel or Freedman, Pisani, and Purvis.)

Many information graphics use a two-dimensional coordinate grid arranged on a *horizontal axis* (also known as the **x-**axis, or *abscissa*) and a *vertical axis* (also known as the **y-**axis, or *ordinate*). Often, the horizontal axis shows consistent divisions of time, and the vertical axis shows divisions of quantity, although this relationship can be reversed. Data points are plotted on this coordinate grid and marked or connected with lines or rectangles. Other chart forms show quantity by area, angle, or distance from a central point. Pie charts, for example, use the angle of pie slices to show the comparative relationship of parts to a whole.

Over the past 20 years, many new ways to visually display statistical information have been invented. With advances in computer technologies, the basic forms of statistical charts are often combined or modified, and entirely new forms have been developed to show more complex data relationships. To examine some of these innovations, see in particular the books of Edward Tufte.

When designing anything other than basic statistical charts, you will probably need to work closely with content experts, statisticians, and even software programmers (for dynamic charts). But you will be the one to decide how to present the statistical data. Content experts disagree on which kind of chart would work best or whether charts are the best way to show statistics. But because *you* are the ambassador between the content providers and the users, you must explore ways to help users *see* the complex relationships between different kinds of data.

Pictograms: Showing a Common Idea with a Simple Mark

Pictograms (sometimes called **pictographs**) are simplified, abstract marks used to express common ideas such as *restroom*, *fire hose*, *stairway*, *home page*, and so on. Pictograms are especially useful for wayfinding and signposting, as they don't rely on language to convey an idea. But they can also be used effectively to mark repeated elements in technical documents, such as helpful tips, cautions, and warning statements. In computer interfaces, they're often used to mark buttons on software toolbars or navigation buttons on websites (Figure 7.15).

In computer interfaces, such pictograms are often called *icons*, but don't confuse this with Charles Saunders Peirce's concept of icons, as discussed in Chapter 3. Speaking in Peircean terms, pictograms are closer to indexical marks than to icons, since they indicate something but don't always represent (look like) what they point to. And some are even closer to symbols: the international pictogram for recycling, for example, has an entirely abstract relationship to this complex concept.

The biggest limitation of pictograms is that they are easy to misunderstand or misrecognize. Pictograms are meant to be self-explanatory, but frequently users must be trained (or train themselves) to recognize what a pictogram means. For example, the pictograms in Figure 7.16

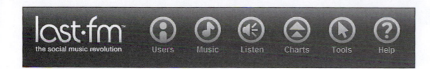

Figure 7.15 Pictograms as navigational tools.   Pictograms are used in signposting, technical manuals, and software interfaces. Here, pictograms show the main links in an Internet radio website.

Last.fm, <www.last.fm>.

Figure 7.16 Pictograms can be confusing.   It might be difficult for users to recognize the function of these toolbar buttons in Microsoft Word: one checks spelling, and the other checks the validity of e-mail addresses. However, pop-up labels that appear when the user mouses over a button can help remind users what the button does and resolve any confusion.

mark two common buttons in Microsoft Word. Without some prior knowledge, it's difficult to recognize or remember that one means "check address" and one means "check spelling." (This is one reason that well-developed software now typically includes labels that pop up when the user cursors over a graphic icon.)

Promotion Graphics

Although graphics used for promotional purposes might seem less important than information graphics, they still have an important role to play in marketing and conveying information about ideas, products, and organizations.

Logos: Marking Identity

Logos are similar to pictograms in that they serve as indexes to more complex ideas, such as corporate identity and product quality. Unlike pictograms, however, logos can and often do include text or initials. As we discussed earlier, corporations spend many millions of dollars to establish a consistent and meaningful graphic identity, in which logos play a significant part. Corporations pay large fees just to own the copyright to a well-known, easily recognized logo. For example, the Italian firm Bugatti, renowned before World War II as a maker of luxury automobiles, was entirely defunct for decades; its only remaining property was its distinctive logo, a backward *E* against a *B* (for Ettorio Bugatti, the company's founder). Volkswagen purchased the rights to the logo in 1998 before they had even developed a car to put it on. VW paid this high price not only to own the logo itself, but also to own the cultural ideas the logo represents: luxury, exclusivity, and high performance. Logos are so important that legal disputes about them can drag on for years. For example, Apple Computer and Apple Corps (the music production company started by the Beatles) contested the use of their similar-looking apple logos for more than a decade.

The challenge of designing logos lies in creating a relatively simple graphic that will fit the organization, its identity, and its products, while making a distinctive statement that users can recognize instantly. Logos often take the form of the stylized name or initials of the organization, as we can see in the logos for corporations such as GTE, Verizon, Coca-Cola, and Ford. They can also be a graphical play on words, such as Apple Computer's stylized apple with a bite taken out of the side. Or they can be entirely abstract, such as Chevrolet's "bowtie" or Nike's "swoosh" trademark, which have nothing to do with cars or athletic shoes except for the associations created by successful marketing.

And in fact, a good part of logo recognition *must* come from marketing — training users to associate the logo with a desired organizational identity or ethos. To build brand identity, designers use logos wherever they can, including on products, product labeling, documentation, and advertisements. The more the public sees the logo associated with the identity the organization wants to promote, the more likely the logo will grow in meaning and value.

You may not be professionally involved in designing logos, but if you design documents in a corporate environment, you should at least expect to display your corporation's logo prominently and repeatedly. For example, title pages, headers, and footers of printed documents are common display spaces for logos, since those positions indicate to users what organization the document speaks for. Navigation bars or headers of websites commonly include logos as well.

Consistent use of logos is one key to successful branding, so be sure to check if your organization has stated requirements for using its logo. Organizations often include information in an organization-wide style guide about how logos should be used in documents from business cards to websites.

Decorative Graphics: Establishing a Visual Tone

The least information intensive of promotion graphics serve a primarily decorative function. **Decorative graphics** can include graphics in any form, including photographs, drawings, and cartoons. They are typically distinguished by their purpose: to give a visual style or tone to a document and to capture the user's attention. Designers typically use decorative graphics to create an appealing thematic connection with the subject or purpose of the document (Figure 7.17). The style or tone of a decorative graphic can influence how users react to a document and create a sense of ethos for the organization that created it. Decorative photographs can also model a desired response to the document.

Given this definition, decorative graphics are more likely to be used in documents with a primarily promotional focus, such as flyers and advertisements. But they can also appear in more information-driven documents such as reports, proposals, and manuals, especially if those documents are intended to persuade the user or evoke a par-

Figure 7.17 Decorative graphics.
Decorative graphics often carry a
thematic connection to the purpose
or subject of the document, but they
don't usually contain much direct
information.

*▲ This guide to an art museum uses an image of a horse statue to emphasize
the theme of the document: The horse seems to invite us to "Explore."
Because the statue is also in the museum's collection, this image could also
be considered an illustration that shows visitors what kind of art to expect at
the Center. But its primary function here is to attract attention and interest.*

Luce Foundation Center for American Art, "Explore."

*This leaflet uses toy blocks to create a visual link to the document's
subject by spelling out "asthma." The blocks create a sympathetic
tone, but they don't tell us much about childhood asthma.* ▶

American Academy of Allergy Asthma & Immunology, "Childhood Asthma."

ticular tone in keeping with corporate branding. And any document
that needs to capture a user's attention is a good candidate for decorative graphics.

Decorative graphics have legitimate functions, but using them
successfully requires good taste and an artistic eye. It can also be difficult to anticipate consistently how users will react to decorations, and
decorations can overwhelm or contradict the message or essential
information of the document. Images are inherently ambiguous, and
decorative graphics are especially so because they hold little informational weight. So for the most part, use decorative graphics sparingly
and strategically.

Use decorative graphics
sparingly and strategically.

Figure 7.18 Clip art. Clip art might be well executed, but it's often an obvious mark of amateur design. If you use clip art, think about how you might modify it to match the purpose of your design (if the terms of use allow doing so, of course).

Bitmaps describe graphics pixel by pixel, while vectors describe graphics with mathematics.

Creating and Modifying Graphics

Even if used within the bounds of copyright, clip art and other borrowed or reused graphics have certain disadvantages. Borrowed graphics are so easy to use that people don't always think carefully about incorporating them into a document design. All borrowed graphics were designed for a particular context (or in the case of clip art, for no particular context), so they can often look strange, conspicuous, or awkward in a different design. Users also can usually recognize clip art when they see it (Figure 7.18), which can give the impression of a cheap shortcut rather than a thoughtful, integral component of the design.

Fortunately, we have alternatives: you can learn to create your own graphics or at least to modify existing graphics in creative and rhetorically effective ways. All it takes is time and a willingness to experiment with software that might be new to you.

Bitmap Graphics versus Vector Graphics

Before we go on, you'll need to understand one central distinction: the difference between *bitmap graphics* and *vector graphics*. These represent the two main approaches for creating digital graphics, and whether you're designing for screen or print, your graphics will at least *start* digitally. Each approach has its own advantages and disadvantages, abilities and limitations. In short, bitmaps describe graphics pixel by pixel, while vectors describe graphics with mathematics.

BITMAPS

Most digital photographs and scans are originally created as bitmaps (also known as *rasters*, the German term for a grid). A bitmap graphic file describes each individual pixel of information in the graphic.

Bitmaps allow minute control of each pixel so you can specify its color and brightness precisely. Bitmaps work particularly well for photographs and scans because these graphics use a wide variety of colors with smooth blends between them. Most photo retouching software packages focus on manipulating bitmap images (although some of these programs can also make limited vector graphics). These programs also allow us to "paint" smooth, flowing forms by altering a swath of pixels with simulated tools such as a paintbrush or pencil with a mouse or graphics tablet.

Because all graphics (vector and bitmap) are eventually displayed on screen or printed as bitmaps, nearly all software capable of displaying graphics can display bitmaps. Bitmap file formats include Windows Bitmap (BMP), Tagged Image File Format (TIFF or TIF), Joint Photographic Experts Group (JPEG or JPG), and Graphics Interchange For-

MORE ABOUT . . . GRAPHICS PROGRAMS

Most graphics programs specialize in bitmaps or in vector graphics, but increasingly, they include some support for both approaches. These are a few of the most popular choices, but new software is being produced all the time.

Bitmap Graphics Programs

- **Adobe Photoshop.** Focuses on bitmap graphics but can do limited vectors. Powerful, complex, and expensive—but the industry leader. Good integration with other Adobe software, such as Illustrator and Imageready.

- **JASC PaintShop Pro.** Mostly bitmaps but good support for basic vectors. Almost as powerful as Photoshop but more affordable.

- **Graphic Image Processor (GIMP).** An open-source bitmap graphics program. Idiosyncratic, but the price is right—it's entirely free. Constantly updated by a group of volunteers.

Vector Graphics Programs

- **Adobe Illustrator.** The vector graphics companion to Adobe Photoshop. Good integration with other Adobe software.

- **Macromedia Freehand.** Good alternative to Illustrator, with good support for web graphics.

- **Corel Draw.** Often less expensive than the industry-leading Adobe Illustrator. Also handles imported bitmaps.

- **Adobe Imageready.** Focuses on the development of web graphics. Good though limited sets of vector and bitmap tools; great control of output to GIF and JPG graphics (the formats used on most websites), including automated scripting for mouseover effects. Works exclusively in screen resolution (72 ppi).

mat (GIF). Bitmap graphics saved in these standard file formats can be read in many kinds of software on most computer platforms, making bitmaps a very common format for exchanging graphics.

The biggest limitations of bitmaps are their size, shape, and links to resolution. Size is the most obvious problem: saving an image as a bitmap typically makes for a large computer file. It just takes a lot of data to describe every pixel, even in a small image. The higher the resolution, the more data the file must contain to describe in an image of a given size. And the greater the color depth—the number of colors possible for each pixel to display—the more data is necessary to describe each pixel. In response, computer scientists have developed a number of compression algorithms, such as JPEG, that allow computers to describe some pixels and "guess" at the remainder. However, such compression typically degrades image quality.

A second limitation is that all bitmaps are essentially rectangular. This shape results from the rectangular grid of rectangular pixels that makes up a computer display. Even if the object pictured by a bitmap is some other shape—a circle, for example—the file itself remains rectangular, and the remaining pixels in the corners must be filled with some color. The exception is with TIF and GIF files, which can incorporate transparent pixels, effectively allowing us to "see through" the corners

MORE ABOUT . . . COMMON BITMAP FILE FORMATS

This table lists the bitmap file formats you'll encounter and use most often. You can always recognize graphics file formats by their filename extensions.

Extension	Name	Description	Common Uses
BMP	Windows Bitmap	The basic file format for bitmaps. Easily read by most Windows and Apple programs, but very large file sizes.	Any bitmap graphic editing; transferring uncompressed images
TIF (TIFF)	Tagged Image File Format	A basic uncompressed file format that can be read by most graphics programs. Less common than BMP overall, but more common in publishing and document design.	Incorporating images into page layout programs
JPG (JPEG)	Joint Photographic Experts Group	A compressed format for bitmap images. JPG uses lossy compression, meaning that some information is discarded in the process. Most bitmap graphics programs allow you to specify the amount of compression (and thus the resulting image quality) on a sliding scale from 10 (little compression = large file, great quality) to 0 (maximum compression = small file, poor quality).	Creating photographic images for websites; archiving photographic images
GIF	Graphics Interchange Format	Another compressed format. GIF files can include a maximum of 256 colors, so they're best for images with consistent areas of color (as opposed to color gradients). GIFs compress images by recording every color used in the image, and then recording in a table which pixel gets which color. Because there are so few colors possible in a GIF, this method can describe every pixel in a very small file. GIFs can also include transparent pixels, allowing nonrectangular graphics.	Creating line art such as logos, pictograms, and diagrams for websites
PNG	Portable Network Graphics	A compressed format designed as an alternative to GIF. PNG files can incorporate up to 48-bit color, far beyond the 256 colors allowed by GIF files. PNGs can be used successfully for both line art and photographs, but they are much less common than GIFs or JPGs.	Line art and photographs for websites
RAW	Raw	Various proprietary image file types designed for use on digital cameras. Many digital cameras save images as RAW and then translate them into BMP, TIF, or JPG for transfer to a computer. Increasingly, bitmap graphics programs allow direct editing of RAW files. The lack of standards makes using RAW files more complicated; not all programs can read all types of RAW files.	Capturing images on digital cameras; image editing in some programs

of a nonrectangular graphic. GIFs, however, are limited to 256 colors, making them more suitable for line art, logos, and pictograms than photographic images (see "More about Common Bitmap File Formats" on opposite page).

Because bitmaps describe the individual pixels of a digital image, they're also closely tied to *resolution*, a measurement of the density of pixels in the image. Resolution is usually measured as *pixels per inch* (ppi). Graphics that are intended for computer monitors have a relatively low resolution, usually less than 100 ppi. Graphics intended for print typically have a higher resolution, as determined by the production method. Most laser printers print at between 300 and 600 dots per inch (dpi), while most commercial imagesetters work around 2,400 lines per inch (lpi). The higher the resolution, the smoother and more lifelike the graphic looks, but the larger and more computer-intensive the graphic file must be (for more information about resolution, see Chapter 4).

Because bitmaps are inherently tied to resolution, they limit modification. Resizing (also known as *scaling*) is a particular problem. If you make a bitmap larger, each original pixel is actually spread to many pixels, leading to a distorted, jagged look known as *pixellation* (see Figure 7.19). If you make a bitmap smaller, you force the software to *downsample* the image, or pack the average data from many original pixels into a smaller number of pixels—with inevitably poor results. Similar problems arise from other manipulations, such as skewing or rotating the image.

Original

Scaled 450%

Figure 7.19 Pixellation in a bitmap graphic. Here is a bitmap graphic in original size, then scaled up 450 percent. In the scaled-up version, you can clearly see fuzziness and pixellation around the diagonal edges of the signs.

Finally, it's difficult to modify individual parts of a bitmap graphic, such as a particular object in a photograph. You can select and modify an area of pixels, but for a bitmap, "object" doesn't really mean anything because bitmaps record information only in terms of individual pixels. Even if those pixels *appear* to form an object when we look at the photograph, it's difficult to change the size or shape of the object by manipulating individual pixels.

VECTORS

Fortunately, changing size and shape is the strength of vector graphics. While bitmaps describe every pixel in the graphic, vectors use mathematics to describe the lines, shapes, patterns, and colors of drawing objects. Vectors work best for drawing images with sharp edges and consistent areas of color, such as line art, diagrams, maps, and statistical graphics.

Look at the rectangle filled with a color in Figure 7.20. A bitmap would record every pixel covered by the rectangle; in a sense, it doesn't record "rectangle" at all, but just the characteristics of each pixel in the graphic. A vector version of this object, however, would describe it simply as having a certain width, height, position, line width, and fill color. This vector information is much more efficient than describing every pixel, making for significantly smaller file sizes. The same goes for any object, whether it's a triangle, circle, oval, octagon, curve, line, or complex polygon.

Because vector objects are described by their basic characteristics, you can change those characteristics easily. This control allows you to manipulate the objects in vector graphics with great precision and flexibility. You can change the size, position, and color of an object as much as you like; you can rotate or skew it at will; and you can change

Figure 7.20 A rectangle drawn with a vector graphics program. The vector shape is described by its essential characteristics (width, height, position, fill color, border width) rather than by recording every pixel. Because the vector shape is described this way, it can easily be resized and reshaped.

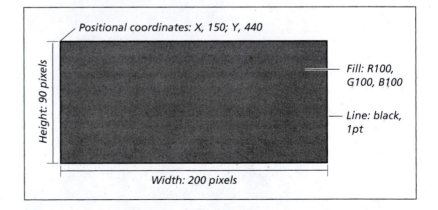

the width of the line and apply patterns or textures to its surface. In short, vectors let you treat each design object *as* an object.

Vectors are also resolution-independent, meaning they scale up or down very smoothly without jaggedness. What's more, while bitmap graphics must be manipulated as one big piece, vector graphics can include many individual design objects, each of which can be manipulated separately. We can combine (*group*) vector design objects to build up more complex graphics, and we can *align* objects precisely and *distribute* objects evenly across a given area.

Vectors do have some disadvantages. They don't manage smooth gradations of color very well — one of the strengths of bitmaps. The files for vector graphics are also often proprietary to the software used to make the graphics, such as Macromedia Freehand (extension *.FH), Corel Draw (*.CD), or Adobe Illustrator (*.AI). These proprietary file formats mean that for the most part those graphics will be editable as vectors only within the program used to create them. There are a few standardized file types for vector images, such as Windows MetaFile (*.WMF) and Enhanced MetaFile (*.EMF). In addition, one very common proprietary format is used primarily for exchanging vector graphics from one program or platform to another: Adobe's PostScript (*.PS), which is also the page description language used by Adobe Acrobat and many computer printers. However, although PostScript saves graphics as vector data, it doesn't let you modify the graphic as easily as if you'd stayed with the native file format of the program with which you created the graphic.

Keep in mind that although vectors are great for *creating* graphics, they will eventually need to be *output* as bitmaps. Printers and computer monitors both require bitmap images for image display. Once you've exported a vector graphic to a bitmap format, you will no longer be able to modify the new bitmap file as a vector. Instead, you'll need to go back

---

MORE ABOUT . . . BITMAPS AND VECTORS

Bitmaps

- Describe graphics pixel by pixel
- Best for photography and scans
- Always rectangular
- Minute control over individual pixels
- Mostly standardized file types (BMP, TIF, JPG, GIF, PNG), with a few proprietary ones (PSD, PSP)

Vectors

- Describe object characteristics with mathematics
- Best for diagrams, maps, and statistical graphics
- Any shape
- Flexible control over individual and grouped objects
- Mostly proprietary file types (AI, CDR, FH, PS), with a few standardized ones (EMF, WMF)

to the original vector file, make your changes, and export the file to bitmap format again.

Working with Photographs and Other Bitmap Graphics

ACQUIRING BITMAP GRAPHICS

Before you can modify bitmap graphics or incorporate them in documents, you'll first need to acquire raw versions of the graphics. The methods you'll find most useful are digital photography, scanning, and making screenshots. All of these approaches use hardware to digitize visual data one pixel at a time.

Digital photography.   Digital photography is so common and inexpensive now that it needs little explanation, but one issue is particularly important for document designers: the relationship between camera resolution, measured in megapixels, and image resolution, measured in ppi. Digital camera resolution is usually measured in megapixels, a raw counting of the number of pixels in the digital image created by the camera. A megapixel is one million pixels, so a one-megapixel camera would make a theoretical image resolution of 1,000 by 1,000 pixels (1,000 × 1,000 = 1,000,000). (In practice, of

---

MORE ABOUT . . . BITMAPS AND RESOLUTION

Keep in mind that the most important issue in creating bitmaps is the relationship between **native resolution**, the resolution at which the image was captured, and **output resolution**, the resolution at which it will be printed on screen or on paper. (*Resolution* refers to the size of pixels and their density in the display area, usually measured in ppi.) So as you create bitmaps, remember the following two general principles.

Resolution affects not only the detail level of the image but its output size as well. The actual size of the output device's pixels (for monitors) or dots (for printers) determines how big a bitmap image will be produced in physical dimensions. For example, an image with a native resolution of 300 ppi displayed on a 100 ppi screen will appear three inches wide, while the same image printed on a 600 dpi laser printer will appear one-half inch wide. That's a big difference!

You can decrease resolution, but you can't increase resolution. If you create an image at a particular resolution, you can always **downsample** to a lower resolution. But you can't go the other way and "upsample" to a higher resolution. Doing so would require using more data than the image contains. The only way to obtain that data would be to reacquire the image at a higher native resolution.

Downsampling has some advantages, especially because very high-resolution images take up a lot of computer memory—and certainly, there's not much point in using higher-resolution images than you intend to output. You'll discard some of the bitmap image information through downsampling, but you can manage exactly how far to go without losing important details.

DESIGN TIP

Bitmaps and Compression

Once you count all the linked and embedded graphics a document can contain, it's very easy to create a document with a combined file size of a gigabyte or more. These files can take considerable time to render or save, and they're awkward to transport. In these situations compression can be a great bonus—but it also reduces the quality of your images, making it seem more like a necessary evil. Here are some tips for handling compression:

- In most cases, use JPG for compressing photographic images and GIF for compressing line art. The exceptions are small, low-resolution thumbnails of photographs, which are often more efficient to save as GIFs.

- Make all editing changes to bitmaps at native resolution in a noncompressed format, such as BMP, TIF, or RAW. Compress your graphics to JPG or some other compression format only at the last moment—just before incorporating them into your design.

- Learn how to manipulate the level of JPG compression. Most bitmap graphics programs allow at least 10 levels of JPG compression, and some divide the scale into 100 levels. The higher the number you choose, the less compression applied and the higher the resulting quality.

- For GIFs, try reducing the number of colors recorded in the image file. GIFs can include up to 256 colors, but they don't have to include that many. If the graphic you're working on is black and white, a GIF holding it would need only two colors. Most bitmap and vector drawing programs allow you to specify how many colors are included, from 2 (black and white) to 256. You can also specify whether you want a restricted palette of colors (such as the common browser-safe palette or the Windows or Apple standard 256-color palette) or a palette indexed as closely as possible to the RGB values in the original image.

- Choose the highest compression settings that look acceptable *for your particular project.* Sometimes, saving digital file space is more important than including beautiful but space-intensive graphics.

If possible, check how your graphics will look using your final output method. If you intend to laser print and photocopy the output, for example, you can easily and cheaply experiment with finding a compression level that works best for that production method. Of course, it's a little harder to do so with offset lithography, but get as close as you can to the final output.

---

course, most digital cameras take rectangular rather than square photographs.)

The good news is that the resolution of digital cameras has increased remarkably over the years, from the early, one-megapixel cameras of the 1990s to cameras of 5, 10, or even 20 megapixels today. At the same time, the cost for high-resolution images has plummeted, as has the cost of digital media storage for those images. If your means and equipment permit, always take the highest possible resolution digital photographs. You can always downsample them later, but you can't create a higher-resolution image from a lower-resolution one.

Inexpensive, low-resolution digital cameras (between one and two megapixels) are still widely available. Although the photographs taken with such low-resolution cameras are often fine for screen documents such as websites, they don't usually work as well for the higher resolutions required by print documents.

Scanning.   Scanners are the most common hardware for digitizing existing paper images into bitmaps. Most scanners are easy to use and increasingly inexpensive to buy. But as a rule, cheap scanners make it hard to acquire high-quality images. If you're going to be working with scanned images frequently, invest in a high-quality scanner. When choosing a scanner, also pay attention to the scanning software. Some scanning software usually comes free with the scanner, but there are special third-party programs that give greater control over the image capture. Even if you use the "acquire" function in your bitmap graphics program to import scanned images, you will still be relying on the scanner software to run the scanner itself.

But even with the free scanning software that comes with a scanner, you get a considerable amount of control. You can set the resolution easily, usually with a slider or drop-down menu to choose whatever ppi level is appropriate to the job. You can scale the image to a particular output size, or you can adjust the orientation of the image. You can also set the color depth—the number of colors each pixel is capable of showing—anywhere from black and white (1-bit) to grayscale (usually 8-bit) to millions of colors (24-bit or even 32-bit). The greater the color depth, the more data that will be captured, so the higher the image file size and the longer the scan will take to complete.

That leads us to a significant disadvantage of scanning: time. Scanners take considerably more time to capture images than the typical digital camera, and high resolution or high-color depth will exponentially increase the amount of time needed. With a digital camera, taking a five-megapixel photo takes the same amount of time as a one-megapixel image. Click, you're done. But scanners rely on the computer they're attached to for most of their computer power, so they can work only as fast as the computer and the cable that connects the two devices. For some hardware setups, the speed for high-resolution scans can best be described as glacial.

As a result, it's usually best to scan images at a resolution around 1.5 times the desired output resolution. Any higher resolution will waste your time, since the extra data will have to be discarded in downsampling the image to the output resolution.

Getting a good scan involves some significant challenges. If you're going to be scanning halftone images, you'll probably run into problems with *moiré* (see Figure 7.21). Halftones are usually used to create photo-graphic images in offset printing. If you're scanning an image from a newspaper, magazine, or other offset document, you'll probably be scanning a halftone. Moiré refers to the interference pattern that can build up between the grid of pixels the scanner creates in making a bitmap and the pattern of dots that make up the halftone image. These two patterns can interfere with each other and create distract-

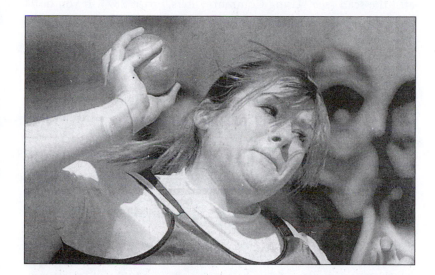

This image was scanned from a newspaper halftone at 96 dpi.

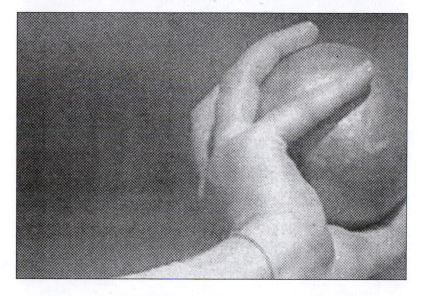

A closeup of the upper left-hand corner of the original shows moiré interference.

Figure 7.21 An example of moiré. Moiré can occur when you scan a halftone image on a digital scanner. The raster (grid of pixels) created by the scanner interferes with the halftone screen of the original, cre-ating odd patterns in the resulting digital image.

Independence *Examiner*, March 27, 2006, p. 3B.

ing patterns and artifacts in the final image scan. The problem is more common with the lower-lpi halftones used in newspaper graphics, but it can also occur when scanning high-resolution, glossy documents such as magazines.

The most common cure for moiré is applying a digital filter (often called a *descreen* filter) to blur the input somewhat. Most scanning software includes such a filter and can apply it as the image is scanned (which, of course, takes more time). You can also apply descreen or blur filters in bitmap graphics programs such as Photoshop after having created the scan (see "Using Common Filters," page 237). If you don't have access to such filters, you can use a low-tech solution: turn the original on the scanner glass so it sits at a slight angle. You can straighten the image again in a bitmap graphics program. With a little experimentation, this can decrease moiré considerably, but, again, with the loss of time trying to find the right angle.

Scanners are also prone to hardware problems such as *barring*, *speckling*, and *artifacting*. Barring happens because the scanner head must take multiple passes over the original to build up the digitized bitmap. It physically moves back and forth across the image on a carriage mechanism. If the mechanism is worn or sloppy, these passes can lead to visible bars across the bitmap, particularly in dark areas of the image. Speckling and artifacting usually occur because of dust, smudges, or scratches on the scanner glass or on the original itself. These imperfections refract and reflect the light the scanner shines on the original, leading to some odd effects. Most of these problems can be overcome with judicious use of blur and unsharp mask filters in a bitmap graphics program (see "Using Common Filters," page 237).

Screenshots.   Screenshots are a common part of software documentation, but creating them brings up some of the same challenges as making digital photographs with low-resolution cameras. Screenshots are very simple to make. The operating system software for both Microsoft Windows and Apple computers can take basic screenshots of windows or dialog boxes:

- *In Windows*, press Ctrl-Print Scrn to take a screenshot of the whole screen and Alt-Ctrl-Print Scrn to take a screenshot of the active window or dialog box. After you take the screenshot, it is copied to your computer's clipboard; you can then paste it directly into bitmap editing software or a word processing file.

- *In Apple OS X*, press Command-Shift-3 to take a screenshot of the entire screen as a PNG file saved on your desktop; press Command-Shift-4 to take a screenshot of the active window.

Specialized software can help you create more complex screenshots, such as allowing a time delay before the shot is taken, capturing cursors on the screen, and taking an image of a web page that's larger than your actual screen.

Screenshots are limited to taking an image of the screen at its current viewing resolution. With some computer screens, resolution can be set as low as 72 ppi—far too low for print production and pretty low even for screen production, since most screens are now at higher native resolutions. Screenshots often look blurry and indistinct as a result, defeating the purpose of showing a screenshot in the first place.

Another problem arises in the images that screenshots capture: computer screens, windows, dialog boxes, and text. These images are not only resolution-dependent, but they also use lots of straight lines and large areas of single colors. Type is a particular challenge because of antialiasing, which blurs the edges of screen type slightly to make it look better against its background (see Chapter 6 for more information about antialiasing). This blurring might look good on a computer screen, but it can make screenshots difficult to read.

These issues make resizing screenshots particularly challenging. Resized screenshots often end up fuzzy and difficult to read. Both of these problems are exaggerated when a screenshot is printed as a halftone on paper, since the halftone grid pattern can interfere with the bitmap grid and create moiré (see "Scanning," page 232).

The best strategy for dealing with these problems is to assess your output methods before taking the screenshots. If you intend to output to screen, match your screenshot resolution with the expected or most common output screen resolution. If you intend to output to paper, take screenshots on a system using the highest possible native screen resolution, and then resize carefully in a bitmap graphics program.

In moving from screenshot to output, also keep in mind that the raw size of pixels is not a constant from monitor to monitor. System software measures monitor resolution in terms of the number of pixels in width and height, but we're more interested in the pixel *density*: the number of pixels per actual square inch of screen. Although monitors can typically be set at a variety of resolutions, each monitor has a native resolution; at that resolution, some monitors have bigger or smaller pixels than others. So a very large monitor, even set at its highest monitor resolution settings, can still have relatively large pixels, resulting in a fuzzy screenshot image.

DESIGN TIP

Screenshots

- For screen output, match screenshot resolution to expected output resolution.

- For print output, capture the highest possible native screen resolution.

- Experiment with turning off or modifying screen font smoothing options before taking the screenshot, especially if you expect users to read the text in dialog boxes.

- If you take a screenshot using the Print Scrn button in Windows, it will look like nothing happened. But in fact, the image was copied to your clipboard; just paste it into the program you'll be using.

- For complex screenshots, consider purchasing specialized screenshot software.

EDITING BITMAP GRAPHICS

We can only begin to discuss the many techniques available for editing bitmap graphics, but the following are some of the most common ones you'll need to work with photographs, scans, and other bitmaps. Because bitmap graphics programs work differently and change constantly, we'll stick with general concepts. You'll also need to check out the help files for the program you own for specific instructions. But don't be afraid to experiment with some of the many tools, settings, and filters these programs offer. Sometimes the best effects are the results of serendipity, and experimentation is a great way to learn a new program.

Saving the original file.   Before you do anything else to a newly acquired bitmap, use "Save as" to create a new version of the file. Archive the original in a safe place. If you make changes to the original and save it, you're stuck with the changes you've made, even if they were mistakes. But if you make mistakes on a copy, you can always just go back to the original.

Setting the output mode: CMYK or RGB.   Your next step should always be to set the output mode as either *CMYK for print output or RGB for screen output.* (You can read more about these terms in Chapter 8.) Most programs will even prompt you for this information in a dialog box when you open a new document. Do nothing else to the file until you've completed this step. If you make changes to the file in the wrong mode, you'll find the image doesn't come out as you expected when translated to the correct output mode. In most programs, you can also choose to change a graphic to grayscale if you're going to be printing in black and white.

Adjusting image quality.   Almost every bitmap graphics program will allow you to adjust at least the brightness and contrast of your bitmap images. But some provide more complex and flexible tools:

- *Levels:* This tool allows you to adjust the highlights, midtones, and shadows of the image to appropriate levels. It also allows you to set the black point (the darkest pixel) and the white point (the brightest pixel) of the image, which helps you use the entire available range of tones.

- *Curves:* This tool provides even more flexibility, allowing you to adjust many levels of brightness. It also allows you to adjust the red, green, and blue channels separately.

Many programs also include automated, one-step commands for adjusting levels, contrast, and color to the best generic settings. In Photo-

> Remember: CMYK for print output; RGB for screen output.

shop, these are Auto Levels, Auto Contrast, and Auto Color. They might not give you the best results, but they're often a good place to start.

Using common filters.   Once you've adjusted the image quality, you can tackle other problems, such as moiré, speckling, striping, and blurriness. Most programs include *filters* that will fix these problems for you, such as *descreen, despeckle, unstripe,* and *sharpen.* One particularly useful general-purpose filter for modifying photographs is the **unsharp mask filter**. Unsharp mask sharpens the edges of color areas, creating greater distinctness and density in the image.

For the wide variety of other filters available, you'll find the best results simply by experimenting. But keep in mind a cautionary note: bitmap graphics programs can come with some pretty wild and crazy filters. They're fun to play with, but make sure that whatever graphic you create is rhetorically appropriate for the document you're designing, its users, and your client.

Cropping.   One of the most powerful tools available to you is the ability to crop images. Cropping, as it might sound, involves cutting off unwanted parts of an image. But this definition makes it sound less important than it really is. With cropping, you have the opportunity to guide the user's eye to what's most important in an image.

Consider the first photograph in Figure 7.22, a garden scene. Cropping the image slightly brings the focus to the foliage and the bust. Now, rather than thinking "garden," viewers might think "leaves" or "statuary." Crop the image even further, and the focus changes to the bust and its subject: John Henry Newman. In this way, cropping can allow you to adjust the rhetorical focus of an image.

As we said before, you should always be ethically sensitive about what you crop out of a picture. You have an obligation to show users the truth (see "Viewpoint," page 208).

Figure 7.22 Cropping a photograph. Cropping a photograph can help you adjust an image to focus on whatever you think is most rhetorically important. The first image seems to be a garden scene. The second image highlights the foliage. The third image focuses on the bust.

Creating Drawings, Diagrams, and Maps with Vector Graphics

The tools for creating vector graphics differ remarkably from those for bitmaps, but there's always some overlap. For example, vector programs can typically import bitmap graphics to be used as part of a vector design, and they typically use similar approaches for color, layers, and filters. You may already have experimented with the limited vector drawing tools available in the Draw toolbar of Microsoft Word. Dedicated vector graphics programs are not so very different, but they are more flexible and precise.

Again, this section isn't intended to replace software documentation, but to give you a sense of some useful techniques common to most programs. Most of the functions of vector graphics programs start with a collection of tools. The techniques outlined in the following sections use one or more of these tools, so it's a good idea to experiment with them.

DRAWING COMMON SHAPES

Vector graphics programs excel at creating regular and irregular geometric shapes. Most will include tools that draw rectangles, triangles, ellipses, and polygons of any shape or size. Just click on a tool and start drawing. You can change the shape of what you've drawn by using a selection tool and grabbing one of the "handles" that will appear on the shape.

Odd shapes or curves are a bit more complex. Most programs allow you to use a pencil tool to draw freely, simply by clicking and dragging the cursor wherever you want the line to go. For more precise shapes, another common tool is the pen tool, which works by clicking where you want the line to begin, and then clicking again where you want the next connection point to be. If you click and drag on the second connection point, the line between the two will become a curve that you can adjust to your liking (also known as a *bezier curve*). Finally, you can apply colors, gradients, patterns, or even bitmap images to the different surfaces of the objects you've created.

GROUPING OBJECTS

All of these shapes can become hard to keep track of, so you can also combine objects by *grouping* them together into larger assemblies. To do so, you typically select all the objects to be grouped by pressing down the shift key on the keyboard and clicking on each object you want to select. After all the objects are selected, choose the group command to group the objects into a single composite object.

Grouping allows you to solidify one part of the drawing while you work on the rest. It also allows you to move and manipulate several related objects as one piece. If you need to make further adjustments to individual objects in a group, you can always ungroup the objects and regroup them when you're finished making changes.

ARRANGING OBJECTS

One of the most powerful advantages of vector graphics programs is the ability to arrange and rearrange objects to your liking. Three important tools are ordering, distributing, and aligning objects. These tools give you tremendous control over the design relationships between your design objects — especially in terms of proximity and (naturally) alignment.

- *Ordering* refers to how the objects are "stacked," much as you can stack playing cards on top of one another. Most programs allow you to change this order, to bring one object in front of or behind another.

- *Distributing* objects allows you to spread out several objects equally. It usually works by selecting all the objects to be distributed (remember, shift-click to select multiple objects) and then selecting a command to distribute the objects in equal spacing vertically or horizontally. The objects will be equally spread out between the far left and right objects (for distributing horizontally) or the far top and bottom objects (for distributing vertically).

- *Aligning*, as the term might suggest, lines up a series of objects. You can choose whether to align objects horizontally or vertically. For horizontal alignment, you can also choose to line them up along their tops, bottoms, or middles; for vertical alignment, you can choose to line them up on their left sides, right sides, or centers.

With these techniques, you can manage the relationships between individual design objects easily and consistently.

USING PATHS AND TYPE

Most vector graphics programs create type within text boxes. You can change the width or height of the text box just as if it were any other drawing object. You can also modify the type in many of the ways you would in a page layout or word processing program, controlling typeface, font, leading, kerning, tracking, and so on. Most programs allow

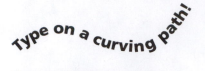

Figure 7.23 Typing on a path.
Most drawing programs let you draw a path with the pen or pencil tool and then apply type to the path. If you need to adjust the path afterward, the type will conform to the new path. This technique gives you a lot of flexibility, especially for titles and other kinds of display text.

you to draw a path (using the pen or pencil tool) and then apply text to it (see Figure 7.23).

LAYERING, MASKING, AND TRACING

Both vector and bitmap graphics programs let you create multiple layers in an image. You can imagine layers as sheets of cellophane laid on top of each other to create a composite image, and you can rearrange the sheets, just as you do with individual drawing objects. You can apply individual effects to one sheet that will affect the sheets above or below it by masking part of the image. Layers are particularly useful for tracing (see "Design Tip: Tracing Layers" on page 243).

Creating Statistical Graphics

Statistical graphics are particularly challenging to prepare, primarily because they must both work well visually and represent statistical data faithfully. Four approaches are most common: using office software, drawing graphics manually with vector drawing software, using diagramming programs, and using specialized data visualization software.

USING OFFICE SOFTWARE

The most common approach for very common genres such as pie charts, bar/column charts, line charts, and scatter plots is simply to rely on the statistical graphics tools in office software, such as Microsoft Word or Excel. The biggest advantage of preparing statistical graphics with office software such as Microsoft Word is that nearly everyone has access to this software; sometimes in team-based document development, that access is the key to a successful project. Even if you're working alone, creating graphics for business documents that don't require unusual graphic forms is easy and convenient with office software.

In most office software the chart design tools allow you to follow a wizard to help import or input the chart data, choose a chart type from a limited series of common genres, and modify design features such as labeling, legends, titles, borders, and shading. The software then places the resulting graphic as a design object in the office program you're using. The graphic will be resizable and editable, and you can quickly change or correct the base data to automatically redraw the chart.

However, office software typically constrains you to the most common graphic forms, and it encourages some graphic practices that should be deprecated, such as meaningless 3D effect (see Figure 7.6 on page 208). In addition, the default settings on colors and shading are often ineffective. Graphics prepared in office software also have the disadvantage of being usable *only* within office software documents. In other words, you won't be able to import a graphic made in Microsoft Word into InDesign or Quark for print production. You can take a screenshot of an office software–derived graphic, but it will be at a low, monitor-level resolution. That approach might be acceptable for a website, but it probably won't work for print.

USING VECTOR GRAPHICS SOFTWARE

Vector graphics software avoids some of the limitations of word processing software, but it has its own limitations. Naturally, vector graphics software is very flexible, allowing you to draw pretty much whatever you need. You can create graphics with a much higher level of polish with vectors than with office software. You also have considerably more output options to import files into other programs, such as a page layout program.

However, drawing statistical graphics with vectors takes a lot of time and introduces some statistical inaccuracy — particularly if the graphic is complex. Rather than letting the software determine data plots automatically from a spreadsheet, you will probably be approximating data points manually. Vector software allows you to size and position objects with great accuracy, so this isn't an impossible task — just one you must manage yourself.

For example, if you're drawing a bar chart, you'll have to figure out exactly how long the bar from the 0 point to the data point would be. To do so, you'd need to divide the total height of the vertical scale by the total increments in the scale and then multiply the result by the data point. If your scale will run from 0 to 50 and it's going to be four inches long, that means each step on the scale will be 0.08" apart ($4 \div 50 = 0.08$). A bar at a data point of 38 would then be

$$0.08" \times 38 = 3.04"$$

Fortunately, some vector graphics programs, such as Adobe Illustrator, provide a graph tool with functionality similar to that of the automatic graphic generation of office software. But these tools can be just as inflexible as those in office software, besides being rather fiddly to work with.

USING DIAGRAMMING PROGRAMS

If your project calls for creating a lot of conceptual diagrams, such as flowcharts or network diagrams, consider using a specialized diagramming program. Programs such as Microsoft Visio (<office.microsoft .com/visio>) use a standard library of ideograms and shapes that you can assemble into useful diagrams quickly. Most of these programs allow diagrams to be exported to a variety of graphics formats and to a variety of other kinds of software.

USING SPECIALIZED DATA VISUALIZATION SOFTWARE

For more complex data visualization, you can also use a specialized software package. Some of these packages come tied to statistical programs, such as Mathcad (<www.mathsoft.com>) and SAS/GRAPH (<www.sas.com>). Others are dedicated plotting programs, such as Gnuplot (<www.gnuplot.info>) and Grace (<plasma-gate.weizmann .ac.il/Grace>). These programs offer very flexible and powerful graphing tools, but they take considerable expertise to use.

In addition, while the output of this kind of software is very accurate, it's not always designed well visually. So you might want to consider creating a draft of a graphic in the specialized software, then tracing it in a vector graphics program (see "Design Tip: Tracing Layers").

Incorporating Graphics into Documents

Once you've created your graphic, how do you incorporate it into your document in a way that makes clear the relationship between the graphic and the rest of the document? The key is to use both explicit labeling and the implicit design principle of proximity to forge a clear relationship between graphics and text — or other graphics, for that matter.

Using Proximity

The simplest way to show a relationship between a graphic and its surroundings is with proximity — just putting it close to what it's related to. Try to design your page layouts so the graphics are as close as possible to the text that discusses them.

Make every effort to place graphics on the same page or at least in the same spread as the text that refers to the graphic. There's nothing more annoying to users than having to flip back and forth through a printed document or scroll around through a web page to see the graphic being discussed.

Consider using *text wrapping* options to embed the graphic in the text. Most page layout programs give you considerable control over exactly how text will wrap around the object. You can set the object's *wrap points* to give a lot of space or just a little. Use the principle of proximity to good effect by editing your wrap points carefully.

DESIGN TIP

Tracing Layers

You can start to create stylistic graphics with office software or specialized data visualization software and then use the layering capabilities of vector graphics software to create the finished graphic.
In general, here's how to do it:

1. Create your graphic with office software or specialized data visualization software.

2. Make a screenshot.

3. Paste the screenshot into a new layer in your vector graphics program.

4. Create a second layer above the layer with the screenshot.

5. Use the vector drawing tools to trace a new graphic over the top of the screenshot version.

6. Delete the screenshot layer and save and export the final graphic.

This approach works equally well for other kinds of graphics. For maps, you can import a screenshot from online mapping software or a scanned paper map. For line art illustrations, you can import a photo and trace line art over it. In all cases, make every effort to be as accurate as possible in your tracing so that unwanted distortions don't creep in to your graphics.

Using Alignment and Enclosure

Just as you did with proximity, you can use alignment and enclosure to show the relationship between text and graphic. Many product manuals align diagrams or screenshots beside each step, giving users direct visual instruction or feedback. Or you can actually use a box or a shaded area to show that a portion of text is related to an accompanying graphic.

Using Explicit References

You can also incorporate explicit references between the text and the graphic. First, you have a couple of traditional options for labeling the graphic so you *can* refer to it from the text:

- *Titles:* Strong and descriptive titles on your graphics give you a good marker to refer to and help readers recognize what your graphic is about.

- *Numbers:* In formal documents with lots of graphics, it's common to use figure and table numbers as a reference system. Traditionally, figures (anything that's *not* a table) are numbered separately from tables. You can also create a separate **list of illustrations** or **list of figures** to help users access your graphics more immediately. Such lists are usually included after the table of contents or at the end of a document.

Of course, after giving your graphics a handle, you'll need to grab onto it by providing clear references from the text to the appropriate graphic. You can do so parenthetically "(see Figure A)," or work the reference into the text itself, "as you can see in Figure B."

Making Graphics Self-Supporting

Although you might refer from the text to the graphics, graphics should also be self-supporting. Users will often skim through a document and just look at the pictures. Your graphics should be able to stand on their own, while also being well integrated into the text.

To make your graphics work independently of text, consider these techniques:

- *Callouts:* Incorporate plenty of callouts in your graphics to explain important points or point out significant information.
- *Captions:* Include a caption with each graphic to explain what it is and what it means.

These techniques won't undercut the connection between the graphics and the text — they'll simply give users more points of entry into the document, letting them decide how they want to read the document.

Exercises

1. Go through the design portfolio you started in Chapter 1 and find a document with lots of graphics. What kind of graphics do you see, according to the categories discussed in this chapter?

   - Information graphics (illustrations, maps, process diagrams, concept diagrams, statistical charts, pictograms)
   - Promotion graphics (logos, decorative graphics)

2. Imagine that you're designing a document to be printed, and you want to use a graphic from one of the following websites:

   - <www.cnn.com>
   - <www.si.org>
   - A personal blog at <www.blogger.com>

   What ethical, legal, and technical issues would you have to deal with before using the graphic in your own document? How would you resolve these issues?

3. Create an information graphic of the required coursework in your degree program for the use of prospective students. The graphic can use text as well as graphics, but it should focus on showing how the curriculum works visually.

4. Import a digital photo into a bitmap editing program such as Adobe Photoshop and perform the following actions:

   - Adjust the color, levels, and contrast—first by using the automatic commands (in Photoshop, Auto Color, Auto Levels, and Auto Contrast) and then by hand.
   - Crop the photo. To do so, choose the Marquee tool (usually the first tool in the toolbar palette), then click and drag to form a rectangle around what you want to keep. Then choose the crop command to complete the cropping.
   - Apply one or more filters from the Filter menu to change the look of your photo. If you don't like what a filter does, you can always choose File : Undo (for one step back), or in Photoshop, choose File : Step backward for multiple steps back.
   - Change the image mode to CMYK. In Photoshop, choose Image : Mode : CMYK Color.
   - Save the file as a TIF. To do so, choose File : Save as, and change the file type to .tif.

5. Draw a map of your hometown or campus to use for directions to your home for visitors:

   - Go to a mapping website, such as Google Maps (<maps.google.com>), Mapquest (<www.mapquest.com>), or Yahoo Maps (<maps.yahoo.com>), and search for a map to the appropriate area of town.
   - Create a screenshot (Windows: Alt-Print Scrn; Apple OS: Command-Shift 3).
   - Open a new drawing in a vector drawing program such as Adobe Illustrator, and paste the screenshot into the drawing. (If you made your screenshot from Apple OS, open the resulting PNG from your desktop in the drawing program.)
   - Create a new layer above the map layer.
   - Use the drawing tools to trace a new map, focusing on only the important details. Be sure to label streets and landmarks!
   - Delete the bottom layer (the one with the map screenshot on it), and save the file as a GIF.

Works Cited

Biederman, Irving. "Recognition-By-Components: A Theory of Human Image Understanding." *Psychological Review* 94 (1987): 115–47.

Dragga, Sam, and Dan Voss. "Cruel Pies: The Inhumanity of Technical Illustrations." *Technical Communication* 48.3 (2001): 265–74.

Harris, Robert L. *Information Graphics: A Comprehensive Illustrated Reference*. Oxford and New York: Oxford University Press, 2000.

Holmes, Nigel. *Designer's Guide to Creating Charts and Graphs*. New York: Watson-Guptill, 1984.

Kosslyn, Stephen M. *Elements of Graph Design*. New York: W. H. Freeman, 1994.

Tufte, Edward. *The Visual Display of Quantitative Information*. Cheshire, CT: Graphics Press, 1983.

Further Reading

Freedman, David, Robert Pisani, and Roger Purvis. *Statistics*. 3rd ed. New York: Norton, 1997.

Horn, Robert. *Visual Language: Global Communication for the 21st Century*. Bainbridge Island, WA: Macrovu, 1999.

Markel, Mike. *Technical Communication*. 8th ed. New York: Bedford/St. Martin's, 2007.

McCloud, Scott. *Understanding Comics: The Invisible Art*. New York: Harper, 1994.

Venn, John. "On the Diagrammatic and Mechanical Representations of Propositions and Reasonings." *Philosophical Magazine and Journal of Science*, July 1880.

Wainer, Howard. *Visual Revelations: Graphical Tales of Fate and Deception from Napoleon Bonaparte to Ross Perot*. Mahwah, NJ: Lawrence Erlbaum, 2000.

CHAPTER 8

Color

Designers have worked on how to use color effectively for many centuries. Paleolithic hunters recorded their hunts on cave walls in pigments of ochre, sienna, and carbon. Mayan cartographers painted their linear maps in color, laying out the paths between cities. European document designers, beginning with the medieval period, used red ink, or rubrication, to mark the beginnings of sections of text. After the development of printing, printers learned how to use color in their documents more consistently, and they developed new technologies such as process printing to expand the range and uses of colors in document design. Color in a document became a mark of the importance and value of its contents.

With the digital age, color has become steadily more accessible and cheaper to print. In screen documents, using color involves no added expense, opening up new opportunities for design. But despite these changes in the cost of color, users still find color attractive and impressive—making color a good way to promote a strong ethos.

Color Figure 1 shows a website for the Ethanol Promotion and Information Council (please see the color insert for color images associated with this chapter). The designers used a consistent, vibrant color scheme of bright blue and green, which has several advantages. It creates a coherent visual impression for the entire site, implying that EPIC speaks with one voice. The colors match the organization's logo, a stylized letter "e" with a blue bowl and a wavy green crosspiece. These colors also have cultural significance, the blue implying clean air and water, and the green representing the fields where

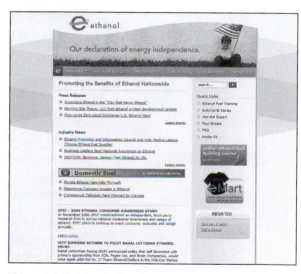

Figure 8.1 A color design shown in grayscale. Take a moment to compare the web page shown here in grayscale to the color version in Color Figure 1 (see color insert). What rhetorical effects would be lost if a user chose to print this page in black and white?

Ethanol Promotion and Information Council (EPIC), <www.drivingethanol.org>.

247

farmers grow the corn used to make ethanol. But the blue and green color scheme also allows for some distinctive contrasts. Some of the text—such as the "click here" for the online ethanol fuel training course—is yellow, and the American flag held by the small boy integrates dark blue with red, which pops out remarkably against the lighter blue and green shades. This emphasis makes rhetorical sense, implying that it's patriotic to use ethanol, a homegrown product. This careful attention to color helps the site express the organization's values and agenda with a coherent rhetorical voice.

Using color successfully sometimes seems mysterious, a matter more of taste than of principle. But the principles and concepts discussed in this chapter will help you make good choices about color in your design, helping you to

- Understand color perceptually, culturally, and rhetorically
- Use common color systems for print and screen
- Use color contrast for emphasis and focus
- Create effective color schemes

Although this chapter covers basic technical issues about color, the focus of the chapter is on designing *with* color. (For more information on managing color through the printing process, see Chapter 10.)

Three Perspectives on Color

Perception

To use color effectively in design, you must understand how people perceive color both physiologically and cognitively. This will help you lay the groundwork for much of the management of color in printing and computer applications.

As we experience it, color is not a quality of objects or light but a complex of physical, neural, and mental processes that respond to light. Typically, humans can perceive light in a small range of wavelengths between 700 and 400 nanometers (nm)—what is called the *visible spectrum* (Color Figure 2).

What we perceive as color, however, relies on more than just a mechanical response to different wavelengths of light, which make up only part of our perceptions. Specifically, we can perceive three interacting qualities of light in the visible spectrum: *hue*, *saturation*, and *brightness* (HSB).

HUE

Hue refers to a human perception of wavelengths of light. What we experience as hue is actually a response to reflected or transmitted light as it hits light-sensitive cells at the back of our eyes, called *cones*. The typical human eye has about 6 million cone cells. To make the wavelengths of light into what we experience as colors, the eye uses three kinds of cones:

- *Red-sensitive cones*, which react to wavelengths from about 700 to 450 nm, peaking at about 575 nm. About two-thirds of all the cones are red-sensitive.

- *Green-sensitive cones*, which react to wavelengths from about 680 to 400 nm, peaking at about 535 nm. About one-third of all the cones are green-sensitive.

- *Blue-sensitive cones*, which react to wavelengths from about 550 to 400 nm, peaking at about 445 nm. Only a small number of cones are blue-sensitive.

The wavelengths that can be seen by the three types of cones overlap considerably — for example, green cones (680–450 nm) are sensitive to light through most of the wavelengths we perceive as blue (550–400 nm). So what we perceive as a color is often some *mixture* of perceptions of the three different kinds of cones and cannot be directly mapped to the neat layout of the visible spectrum. The combination of these three perceptions is also known as **tristimulus**.

These three kinds of cones feed their inputs into a series of nerves called **ganglion cells** (or just **ganglia**), which make a further discrimination in color:

- Some ganglia distinguish between red and green. They can sense either red or green but not both at the same time.

- Other ganglia distinguish between blue and yellow. They can sense either blue or yellow but not both at the same time.

This discrimination between red/green and blue/yellow is why most people would never describe a color as "bluish yellow" or "reddish green." That would be asking a ganglion to do two things at once: sensing blue and yellow at the same time or red and green at the same time. However, red-green ganglia sensations can mix with blue-yellow ganglia sensations, creating colors we might describe as greenish yellow (lime), bluish green (turquoise), or yellowish red (orange). And red-green sensations can overlap in the cone stage of the process; combined red and green cone responses lead to yellow ganglion sensations.

Graphically, the hues are often represented on a circle or wheel (Color Figure 3). The traditional color circle represents the three basic hues or *additive primary colors* (red, green, and blue) 120 degrees apart from each other. The combination of two primary colors is known as a *secondary color* — for example, red and green mix to create yellow, and green and blue mix to create cyan. Two colors directly opposite from each other (180 degrees apart) are known as *complementary* colors. Colors close together on the same side of the wheel are known as *analogous* colors.

SATURATION

The basic responses of cones to red, green, and blue also lead to our perceptions of color *saturation* (also known as *chroma*), which is our perception of the relative *purity* of color. The more fully saturated a color, the less we perceive mixtures of other colors. We see fully saturated colors as strong and pure perceptions of a single hue, but the addition of other colors reduces the saturation. For example, if we start with red and add in equal portions of blue and green, we see pink — a relatively unsaturated color. Unsaturated colors often look muted, whereas saturated colors look vibrant.

On a hue-saturation color circle (Color Figure 3), colors placed closer to the edges are more saturated than colors closer to the middle. At the very center, all colors combine equally to make grays.

BRIGHTNESS

The third component of color perception is *brightness*, sometimes referred to as *luminance* or *value*. Brightness describes the viewer's perception of the intensity of light that is transmitted or reflected from a surface. For projected light, such as light beaming from a computer monitor, we perceive brightness directly — the higher the intensity of the light, the greater the brightness we perceive. But the perceived luminance of an object such as a document printed on paper depends on the intensity of the light shining on the object, the object's own reflectivity, and the reflection angles from the light to the surface and on to the viewer. Highly reflective objects reflect more light than less reflective objects and thus appear more luminous. But even a highly reflective object also looks different in stronger light than it does in less intense light.

Whereas hue and saturation are perceived by the cones in the eye, brightness is perceived by another type of cell called a *rod*. We have considerably more rods than cones — about 120 million per eye, on average — making our eyes much more sensitive to the presence of light than to color. But the sensations from rods can affect the sensations of our cones, and thus our perception of color. You may have noticed this at dusk, when objects take on different colors than they did in the bright light of noon. If you're like most people, you notice that as the sun sets, everything gradually turns gray. That's because as the light fades, our perceptions of hue and saturation become less distinct, whereas our perception of brightness remains active. As a result, *brightness* can best be described as a range from white (full brightness and equal mixture of colors) through a range of grays (less brightness but still equal mixture of colors), and finally to black (the absence of light).

Brightness is also linked to hue because some hues are simply brighter than others, regardless of saturation. Red and yellow, for example, have a naturally higher brightness than blue and green at the same level of saturation. For this reason, reds and yellows are often called "warm" colors, and blues and greens are called "cool" colors. Some people perceive warm colors as advancing toward them and cool colors as receding away from them — but this perception isn't universal.

OTHER GRAPHICAL COLOR MODELS

The traditional hue-saturation color circle does a good job representing hues as degrees around the circle (0 degrees–360 degrees) and saturation as the distance from the center, but it doesn't do as good a job of describing brightness. More complex graphical models have tried to supply this information by describing color as a three-dimensional space, in keeping with the three sensations of color (HSB).

One common way to represent this three-dimensional relationship graphically is based on the work of Albert H. Munsell, an influential color theorist. In essence, Munsell-based color models represent brightness by adding a third axis that projects at right angles from the disc of the color circle — like a spindle piercing the center of a spinning top (Color Figure 4). This third dimension arranges the amount of brightness from no brightness (black) at one end of this axis to full brightness (white) at the other end of the axis.

What many accept as the most accurate graphical model of color perceptions is the CIE L*a*b model (Color Figure 5), sponsored by the Commission Internationale de l'Éclairage (the International Commission on Illumination, or CIE). CIE L*a*b also measures color on three dimensions, but it takes into account the secondary distinction that we make between red/green and blue/yellow (see page 249). The three dimensions are as follows:

- *L*, or **luminance**, which corresponds to perceptions of brightness
- *a*, the range of sensations from red to green
- *b*, the range of sensations from blue to yellow

Graphically, this three-dimensional space has the same disadvantage as the Munsell space: it buries most of the colors inside the color solid. So it's often represented in two dimensions as a curved line with blue and red at the ends and green in the middle. The area inside the curve holds all the colors that viewers report as being perceptible, ranging from full saturation at the edge to white in the middle.

SIMULTANEOUS CONTRAST

People rarely see a color isolated from all other colors, so another factor comes into play in color perception: simultaneous contrast. Simultaneous contrast refers to the fact that multiple colors in the viewer's field of vision can interfere with each other and alter our perceptions of the individual colors (Color Figure 6). For example, a yellow square on a blue background takes on a subtly green cast when compared to a yellow square on a white background. A circle of blue on a background of red will look slightly more purple than it would by itself. Accordingly, it's important to consider colors in their context.

COLOR VISION DEFICIENCY

For some people, differences in color perception rise to the level of a limitation called *color vision deficiency* (commonly known as *color blindness*). About 5 to 10 percent of men and about 0.5 percent of women experience color vision deficiency because of a genetic difference from the majority of human beings.

Color vision deficiency is rarely a complete inability to see colors; almost always, it's a limitation in the ability to perceive one or two hues. By far the two most common conditions are *protanomaly*, a limitation of the ability to perceive red, and *deuteranomaly*, a limitation of the ability to perceive green. In both of these conditions, the perception of color is shifted away from the hue that's hard to detect and toward hues that are easier to detect. So for someone with protanomaly (red weakness), purple (red + blue) will just look like a kind of blue, and most pure reds will look green.

Obviously, color vision deficiency can present significant problems for designers using color in communication. In general, desaturated colors are more difficult for color-deficient people to perceive than fully saturated colors. Colors that are close to each other are more difficult to distinguish than highly contrastive colors. And due to

---

DESIGN TIP

Designing for Color Vision Deficiencies

To accommodate users' possible limitations in color perception, consider these tips in your designs:

- Use highly saturated colors rather than desaturated colors.
- Use colors with a high contrast in hue and brightness.
- Avoid presenting important information in ways that make users distinguish between red and green. For example, if you want to use red for cautions and green for tips in a document, be sure to include another clue to the nature of the information, such as a small pictogram.

the common occurrence of protanomaly and deuteranomaly, colors in the red or green parts of the spectrum are particularly problematic.

Culture

Despite the general accuracy of the models of color perception discussed above, they remain attempts to universalize color perception. CIE L*a*b, for example, is based on the idea of a "standard observer"—a generalized, average human being. However, color perception varies considerably from person to person. What looks blue to you may look purple to someone else; their orange may be your red. Different cultures ascribe different values and significances to colors. So determining what a particular color means to a particular person in a particular culture is a difficult issue.

However, people *do* commonly assume that colors have meaning, or at least general values. You can probably name some of these assumed general color meanings off the top of your head: red associates with blood, black with a dark negativity, yellow with a sunny positivity, green with nature, gray with ambiguity. But even within the same culture, colors can have multiple connotations, depending on context. The association of red with blood can be good or bad, depending on whether we're in love or bleeding. Black can mean sleek instead of evil, if it's on a cocktail dress or tuxedo. Yellow can imply cowardice, green can imply illness or envy, and gray can imply sophistication.

Our cultural background also deeply influences how we apply meaning to color. For example, in Western cultures white is often associated with purity or innocence; this association is reinforced every time we see a bride's white wedding dress. But in other cultures, this association can be remarkably different: in Japan, white is commonly worn at funerals.

Colors can be linked to changing and competing ideologies, but these connections are often tenuous, and context is everything. Red can mean communism, when considered in terms of mid-twentieth-century propaganda. But red can mean democratic patriotism when on a piece of red, white, and blue bunting in a Fourth of July parade.

Moreover, cultures change. Avocado green and harvest gold were popular colors for kitchen appliances in the 1970s, but if you see those colors at all today, they're probably considered retro or nostalgic. Because the meanings or values associated with colors differ so much between and within cultures, it makes sense to pay attention to user preferences before making color specifications for a document. In particular, focus groups can help us to assess users' attitudes toward different colors and color schemes. Industrial designers commonly use focus groups to gauge customer responses to color schemes for products from automobiles to household appliances.

It's also a good idea to find out more about the client context of your document. For example, corporations, universities, and agencies frequently make a universal decision about what color scheme their products and documents will use. Sometimes, these color schemes stretch across all aspects of the corporate identity, from packaging to advertising to internal communication. Coca-Cola's use of a consistent scheme of red and white is one example. Corporations make these specifications to encourage users to associate these colors with a corporate identity — a technique known as *branding*. So users may actually expect to see a document published by a company to share its corporate color scheme, and they might be confused if it doesn't.

Rhetoric

Despite the ambiguities of color associations, there are at least three tendencies we can generally rely on for rhetorical purposes.

COLOR CAN CONVEY MEANING

Users will often accept colors as meaning something in a document if we *explicitly indicate* what they mean. For example, if a road map legend indicates that red marks interstate highways, users usually allow that meaning to override any broader cultural meaning of red, such as its common association with caution or danger.

But we can't always expect a specified color association (such as a map legend color) to work without being explicitly connected (indexed) to its meaning, and we can't assume the color association to extend beyond that document. In some cases, a broader cultural meaning can overpower a local indexed meaning, no matter how much we indicate otherwise. In Western cultures, for example, documents rarely index male with pink and female with blue, so powerful are the associations of blue with masculinity and pink with femininity. On the other hand, if you are designing a brochure for a conference on gender equity, switching these color associations might be an appropriate reminder of cultural values of gender. And indexing pink or blue to mean something *not* connected to gender wouldn't necessarily activate the cultural association.

COLOR CAN IMPLY VALUE

The very presence of color suggests expensiveness and therefore a certain cultural status. Purple, for example, was for centuries the most expensive pigment in the world (the color, *purple*, is named after it), and anything colored with purple was considered rare and precious. Accordingly, royal robes were dyed with purple, and even the paint used for royal portraits used purple as the pigment. Even today, with color inkjet printers as common as they are, color printing costs significantly more than black and white. Users often accordingly assume that a document printed in color is more important than one in black and white and give it more initial attention, if only because its producers thought it was important enough to spend money printing it.

Of course, color is free on screens, so a rhetoric that links color to value might not work as well there. But even on screen, users recognize color as an extra step in the design and value it accordingly. A lack of color can imply that the information being conveyed is boring, dull, ephemeral, or highly technical.

Which colors say "money" to people depends on broad cultural values and conditions. In the eighteenth century, rich people in Europe and America painted rooms in brilliant and expensive blues, yellows, and greens because these colors advertised wealth; less affluent families painted their rooms with milder, earthier colors like white and buff (if they could afford paint at all). In the mid-nineteenth century, however, the development of new dye technologies made bright colors more widely available and affordable, so by the end of the century, the poor (trying to keep up with earlier standards of taste) painted rooms in bright, garish colors. In the meantime, the rich had moved on to the muted, earthy shades of the Arts and Crafts movement, and later to the whites and pastels of modernism.

Given these evolutions in color and tastes, many companies today actually pay color consultants to predict what colors will be popular or even cool, hoping to use the information to confer an added perception of value to the user experience.

COLOR CAN ATTRACT ATTENTION

While the specific meaning of a color is nearly impossible to pin down, designers can use contrasts of color to great rhetorical effect. Within a uniformly gray, black, or white field, a small amount of nearly *any* color can make users at least look. For example, imagine a typical black-and-white document that begins with a large dropped cap in bright red. Wouldn't you be drawn to that spot and start reading there?

Of course, this use of color depends on our physical perceptions of figure-ground separation. If the color you use to bring attention to a design object is too close to the background color in hue, saturation, or brightness, it might fade into the background. A dropped cap in bright yellow won't contrast well with a white background because both yellow and white have a high brightness. So when determining color contrast, be sure to take into account all dimensions of color: hue, saturation, and brightness.

> **DESIGN TIP**
>
> ## Color Rhetoric
>
> - Use color to convey meaning.
> - Use color to imply value.
> - Use color to attract attention.

Creating Color on Screens and Paper

Given our perceptual and cultural responses to color, it's clear that color can be a useful technique in visual rhetoric. But reproducing color in documents involves some technological hurdles, both in print and on the screen. The technological approaches to reproducing color in these two media are complementary but significantly different enough to require separate explanations.

In this section, we'll examine two ways to reproduce color:

- *Additive color (RGB)*, which reproduces color on screens
- *Subtractive color (CMYK)*, which reproduces color on reflective surfaces, such as paper

We'll start with additive color because it's the more basic of the two systems — in fact, subtractive color is based on additive color.

Color on Screens: Additive Color (RGB)

As we said earlier, the three basic hues that our eyes respond to are red, green, and blue. These colors are known as the *additive primary colors*, commonly abbreviated *RGB*. Our perceptions of light in these three colors combine to create all of the other colors we perceive — hence the term *additive*.

MAKING RGB COLORS

Computer monitors reproduce color by transmitting light in the three additive primary colors. They do so by regulating the light that glows from many small, digitally controlled, glowing *pixels*. Each pixel in turn is formed of three *subpixels*: one red, one green, and one blue. Computers can turn these subpixels off or on individually. They can also digitally modulate the brightness of subpixels, mixing RGB to create a perception of hundreds, thousands, or even millions of different colors.

To understand how this works, imagine a single pixel as a tiny cluster of three lightbulbs in red, blue, and green. If we turn off all three of the lightbulbs, we get black, the absence of light. Conversely, if we turn on all three bulbs at full strength, the colors mix to produce white (Color Figure 7).

```
  0% Red +     0% Green +     0% Blue = Black (no light)
100% Red +   100% Green +   100% Blue = White (all light)
```

If we turn on one of the bulbs at full strength and leave the other two off, we get the additive primary colors, RGB:

$$100\% \text{ Red } + \quad 0\% \text{ Green } + \quad 0\% \text{ Blue } = \text{ Red}$$
$$0\% \text{ Red } + 100\% \text{ Green } + \quad 0\% \text{ Blue } = \text{ Green}$$
$$0\% \text{ Red } + \quad 0\% \text{ Green } + 100\% \text{ Blue } = \text{ Blue}$$

If we turn on two of the lightbulbs at full strength and leave the third off, we get the *additive secondary colors*, cyan, magenta, and yellow:

$$0\% \text{ Red } + 100\% \text{ Green } + 100\% \text{ Blue } = \text{ Cyan}$$
$$100\% \text{ Red } + \quad 0\% \text{ Green } + 100\% \text{ Blue } = \text{ Magenta}$$
$$100\% \text{ Red } + 100\% \text{ Green } + \quad 0\% \text{ Blue } = \text{ Yellow}$$

If we turn on the lightbulbs at different strengths, we can create all the combinations of colors that the monitor can show, such as these:

$$90\% \text{ Red } + \quad 40\% \text{ Green } + 60\% \text{ Blue } = \text{ Rose}$$
$$0\% \text{ Red } + 100\% \text{ Green } + 60\% \text{ Blue } = \text{ Sea green}$$
$$30\% \text{ Red } + \quad 50\% \text{ Green } + 20\% \text{ Blue } = \text{ Olive green}$$

Likewise, if we turn on all of the bulbs at equal strengths below 100 percent, we get different shades of gray:

$$30\% \text{ Red } + 30\% \text{ Green } + 30\% \text{ Blue } = \text{ Dark gray}$$
$$90\% \text{ Red } + 90\% \text{ Green } + 90\% \text{ Blue } = \text{ Light gray}$$

Notice that with low strengths, we get darker grays because there's less light being emitted. Conversely, the greater the brightness of the sub-pixels, the lighter the gray (that is, the closer to white).

Computer programs that allow you to design in color for screen documents will allow you to specify RGB values for the colors you want. Most do so through a *color picker* (see "Using Color Pickers," page 268).

SPECIFYING RGB FOR WEBSITES

RGB is also the primary way to describe colors for websites, so lots of web design programs also have color pickers. But HyperText Markup Language (HTML) uses a numbering system known as **hexadecimal**, or just **hex**, to specify colors on web pages. Understanding hex will allow you to specify web colors more precisely and consistently.

You're probably more familiar with decimal (base-10) numbering, using the digits 0123456789. As decimal numbers rise above 9, we add a digit to represent the next decimal unit:

```
 0  1  2  3  4  5  6  7  8  9
10 11 12 13 14 15 16 17 18 19
20 21 22 23 24 25 26 27 28 29

...

90 91 92 93 94 95 96 97 98 99
```

Hexadecimal numbering works much the same way, but with 16 digits — 0123456789ABCDEF — with 0 as the lowest digit and F as the highest.

Above the first 16 digits, we can continue numbering with two-digit hex numbers, like this:

```
00 01 02 03 04 05 06 07 08 09 0A 0B 0C 0D 0E 0F
10 11 12 13 14 15 16 17 18 19 1A 1B 1C 1D 1E 1F
20 21 22 23 24 25 26 27 28 29 2A 2B 2C 2D 2E 2F
30 31 32 33 34 35 36 37 38 39 3A 3B 3C 3D 3E 3F
40 41 42 43 44 45 46 47 48 49 4A 4B 4C 4D 4E 4F
50 51 52 53 54 55 56 57 58 59 5A 5B 5C 5D 5E 5F
60 61 62 63 64 65 66 67 68 69 6A 6B 6C 6D 6E 6F
70 71 72 73 74 75 76 77 78 79 7A 7B 7C 7D 7E 7F
80 81 82 83 84 85 86 87 88 89 8A 8B 8C 8D 8E 8F
90 91 92 93 94 95 96 97 98 99 9A 9B 9C 9D 9E 9F
A0 A1 A2 A3 A4 A5 A6 A7 A8 A9 AA AB AC AD AE AF
B0 B1 B2 B3 B4 B5 B6 B7 B8 B9 BA BB BC BD BE BF
C0 C1 C2 C3 C4 C5 C6 C7 C8 C9 CA CB CC CD CE CF
D0 D1 D2 D3 D4 D5 D6 D7 D8 D9 DA DB DC DD DE DF
E0 E1 E2 E3 E4 E5 E6 E7 E8 E9 EA EB EC ED EE EF
F0 F1 F2 F3 F4 F5 F6 F7 F8 F9 FA FB FC FD FE FF
```

Computers use hexadecimal numbering because it corresponds more closely than decimal numbering to the 8-bit, 16-bit, or 32-bit color systems used on most computer monitors, mostly because 16 is evenly divisible by 8 and is half of 32. This also matches nicely to the basic mathematics of computer memory, in which each **bit** of memory consists of 8 **bytes**. Using hexadecimals allows computers to specify values in a very consistent set of regulated steps. The preceding hexadecimal grid entirely from 00 to FF includes 256 numbers — 16 columns times 16 rows. This allows us to turn on each RGB subpixel of a computer in 256 regulated steps of brightness.

As a result, HTML specifies RGB values with three 2-digit hexadecimal numbers. The first number controls red, the middle number controls green, and the last number controls blue:

RR, GG, BB

These three numbers are run together into one long string: RRGGBB. The higher the hexadecimal number we put in each of these slots, the brighter the light shining out through the corresponding subpixel. So to specify black, we turn *off* all three subpixels, and to specify white, we turn *on* all three subpixels at full strength:

> Black = 000000 (red off, green off, blue off — no light)
> White = FFFFFF (full red, full green, full blue — white light)

Making fully saturated red, green, or blue requires turning on the appropriate pixel at full strength (FF) and turning off the other two (00):

> Red = FF0000 (full red, green off, blue off)
> Green = 00FF00 (red off, full green, blue off)
> Blue = 0000FF (green off, red off, full blue)

And if we turn on the pixels at different strengths, we get different combinations of colors:

> Cyan = 00FFFF (red off, full green, full blue)
> Orange = FF6600 (full red, some green, blue off)
> Dark purple = 660066 (some red, green off, some blue)
> Gray = 999999 (some red, some green, some blue in equal proportions)

Because we can specify 256 strengths for each color with this system, we have access to more than 16 million colors for websites ($256 \times 256 \times 256 = 16,777,216$).

You can use these hexadecimal numbers in HTML to specify the precise color you want to display. For example, 036A9E gives a nice sky blue (a tiny bit of red, a little more green, about two-thirds strength blue). But remember that every computer monitor is different. That beautiful 036A9E won't look exactly the same on your monitor as it does on the user's monitor.

Because of the differences among monitors and operating systems, many early web designers followed the practice of relying on 256 basic *web-safe colors* — a subset of the 16 million allowed by hexadecimals. Sticking with 256 colors also ensured that colors would reproduce on basic 256-color monitors, which were still common in the early 1990s. The web-safe colors were determined by equally spaced values in the hexadecimal grid:

00 33 66 99 AA CC FF

DESIGN TIP

Website Colors

Test your website design on a broad range of monitors before making a final decision about colors.

Any combination of these values in the RGB notation (RRGGBB) results in a web-safe color that will look relatively consistent on most monitors. For example, 9900FF creates a web-safe medium purple, and 99FF00 creates a web-safe lime green. As 256-color monitors have become obsolete, it's much less common now to restrict web designs to the web-safe colors, however.

Color on Paper: Subtractive Color (CMYK)

Considering red, green, and blue as primary colors might sound odd to you—especially if you remember the primaries from your child-hood paint set as red, blue, and *yellow*. But when we mix watercolors, paints, or inks, we aren't really mixing *colors*—we're mixing **pigments** or **dyes**. These materials *reflect* light in some wavelengths and *absorb* light in others. The reflected wavelengths are what we perceive as tri-stimulus values, or RGB.

Imagine looking at a piece of red-colored paper in a sunlit room. Because sunlight is an even mixture of all visible wavelengths of light, the light isn't making the paper seem red by itself. Instead, the paper con-tributes by reflecting light in wavelengths that we recognize as red, while absorbing light in the wavelengths that we recognize as blue or green. The paper isn't inherently "colored"—it merely reflects light in some wave-lengths and absorbs others. Likewise, blue paper would reflect blue light and absorb red and green light, and green paper would reflect green light while absorbing red and blue light. This process works for combinations of RGB colors as well. For example, paper that absorbs red and reflects blue and green will give us a perception of cyan; paper that absorbs blue and reflects red and yellow will appear yellow; and paper that absorbs green and reflects red and blue will appear magenta.

This process is called **subtractive color** because some wavelengths of light are absorbed or filtered out, leaving only the remaining wave-lengths to be reflected (Color Figure 8). When all of the wavelengths of light are reflected, as on white paper, they combine to create a sen-sation of white. But when all of the wavelengths of light are absorbed, we perceive black—the absence of light.

Subtractive color might seem completely different from additive color. But in fact, the two systems are closely related in that the pro-cess of absorption and reflection that leads to subtractive color still cre-ates reflected light in the additive system, as a mixture of RGB. In other words, subtractive color is based on additive color.

PROCESS COLOR

Then why should we even bother with subtractive color? Because it cre-ates a mechanism for producing color in print. The print medium relies on external light reflecting off the inked surface of the paper to create our perceptions of RGB colors. In other words, we can print in color by using colored inks that absorb light in some wavelengths and reflect light in others. We could simply use lots of different colors of ink to get full-color printing. But except for some special situations (see spot color in the following section), using many inks isn't very practical in production. The trick is combining a small number of inks to create all of the colors in a full-color image.

This technique is known as *process color* because it creates a full-color image through a process of overprinting the same sheet four times with four different inks. In this process, the red, blue, and yellow we traditionally think of as the subtractive primaries in painting are actually not quite the right pigments. Instead, process color printing typically uses translucent inks in cyan, magenta, and yellow, or **CMY**.

These subtractive primaries are directly related to the three additive primaries (RGB) that we can perceive: the subtractive (CMY) primary colors are the additive (RGB) secondary colors, and vice versa. This relationship is tied to how inks reflect or absorb wavelengths of light. Each of the process inks absorbs light in the wavelength of one of the additive primaries (RGB) and reflects and combines light of the other two:

Ink Absorbs	Ink Reflects	Ink Appears
Red	Green + Blue	Cyan
Green	Red + Blue	Magenta
Blue	Green + Red	Yellow

Conversely, we can combine the subtractive primaries CMY to produce red, green, and blue:

Ink Absorbs	Ink Reflects	Ink Appears
Yellow	Cyan + Magenta	Blue
Cyan	Magenta + Yellow	Red
Magenta	Yellow + Cyan	Green

By mixing CMY in different strengths, we can produce the appearance of many other colors.

In full-color (process) printing, we print dots of the translucent CMY inks at various strengths by using *screens* and *filters* to create *halftone separations* — one to print each color of ink. When combined, these color separations make up a full-color image.

This process happens mostly digitally now, but it's easier to imagine by going back to older photographic methods. Traditionally, printers made separations by photographing an image through a red, green, or blue filter and a sheet of glass that contained a tiny wire grid, like a tight window screen. Taking a picture through the red filter and screen would result in a field of small cyan dots (remember, filtering red allows green and blue light to continue, creating cyan). The dots would be bigger where there was more light in the unfiltered colors and smaller where there was less. Repeating this process with the green and blue filters would result in three separations, one for each of the three subtractive primaries, CMY (Color Figure 9). These film separations were then used to make plates for a printing press. Printing every sheet three times — once with the cyan plate, once with the magenta plate, and once with the yellow plate — recreates the entire "full-color" image. (See Chapter 10 for more information on color printing.)

Or perhaps not the *entire* image — we still need black to make it work. As you'll recall, subtractive color creates black by filtering out or absorbing all of the wavelengths of light, leaving nothing to reflect. You might think that doing so would require mixing together the subtractive primaries (CMY) at full strength; together, they'd absorb all of the RGB light, leaving black. But in fact, doing so creates a dark, muddy, brownish gray — like the color you got when you mixed together all your watercolors when you were a child. So if we print using only the C, M, and Y plates, the shadows tend to be faint and the colors less saturated than we might like.

Adding a black plate to the mix solves these problems. A black screen can be printed in a truly black ink, which absorbs light much better than any mixture of translucent CMY inks. This black plate is where the *K* in CMYK comes in: K stands for **key** because black is usually the first color printed and the other three are aligned or "keyed" to it. The key plate also typically includes the text, which is usually printed in black ink as well. This plate produces a good, strong black for all of the text, plus a full range of colors and shadows for images.

SPOT COLOR

Process color is a great way to produce many colors, especially for graphics with lots of color variation or gradients, such as photographs. But process color doesn't work nearly as well for creating areas of a single color, such as a solid-colored background, a logo, or colored text. In those situations, process color tends to come out looking weak and inconsistent. This weakness occurs primarily because process color creates color sensations by printing overlapping dots of CMYK inks, all of which, except black, are translucent.

So designers typically specify areas of one color with a **spot color**, which is printed in a particular color of ink, different from CMYK. Spot color gives clear, strong, even color across a whole area. It's not unusual for a high-design document to be designed with six-color printing:

CMYK, plus two spot colors. Each additional spot ink, however, increases the complexity and the cost of the print job.

Spot colors come in a wide variety — every color, tint, and shade you can think of, including metallic and high-visibility inks. You will need to coordinate with your print shop personnel when you specify spot colors because they may need to order the particular colors of ink your document calls for. Usually, printers ask that you specify spot colors with a commercial system such as the Pantone Matching System (PMS), which provides standard codes for the different colored inks.

Color Gamut

Why is it so important to understand the difference between these two systems? Because the range of colors we can produce with RGB differs significantly from the colors we can produce with CMYK (see Color Figure 5). The range of available colors in a color space is called a *gamut*. A color that cannot be reproduced in the current color space is called *out of gamut*.

Most page layout, drawing, and image editing programs require that you choose whether to work in the RGB or CMYK color space, and they will warn you if you choose a color that's out of gamut according to the color space you have specified. In Adobe color pickers, for example, an out-of-gamut color will be marked by a triangular warning icon in the color picker. Clicking on the warning icon shifts the color

---

DESIGN TIP

Use RGB for Screens and CMYK for Print

All computer monitors use additive color mixing (RGB). If you use CMYK to specify colors on a website, computer monitors may not be able to replicate the color you specified. In other words, the color might be out of gamut. The same applies if you use RGB to specify something that will be printed with process (CMYK) printing: the technology may not be able to replicate the color you specified.

If you choose an out-of-gamut color, what you'll get is the closest color the computer can estimate within the appropriate gamut — and sometimes computers make really poor estimates.

One common mistake when designing for print is to be fooled by a vibrant color on your computer monitor, only to find out that the color prints quite differently in process color. Remember that computer monitors use RGB — even when you're designing in CMYK. So what you see on the computer screen is already the computer's best RGB estimate of the CMYK value you specified. To remedy this problem, see "Matching Colors" and "Calibrating Your Monitor" on page 270.

you've chosen to the nearest in-gamut color (see "Using Color Pickers," page 268).

Designing with Color

Now that you have a solid foundation for working with color, let's examine some ways to create color schemes for your designs. At some point early in the design process, it's usually best to specify several colors that work well together rhetorically and aesthetically. Rhetorically, try to choose colors that users will subjectively associate with the tone you wish to set. Aesthetically, try to choose colors that fit with the users' cultural sense of beauty, utility, or professionalism, depending on the purpose of the document.

Because of the many ambiguities of color communication, choices about color schemes can never be entirely dependable or predictable. For subjective or cultural reasons, some readers will inevitably respond differently to the color scheme than you intended. But there are some common tendencies designers usually follow, and by repeatedly encountering documents designed with these tendencies, users become trained to expect certain colors to be associated with certain tones.

Color Similarity and Contrast

One of the most common approaches is to use the principles of design of similarity and contrast to create color schemes. Design objects with similar colors — colors that lie close to each other in one or more of the dimensions of color (hue, saturation, and brightness) — imply a similarity of purpose, function, or identity. By corollary, contrasting colors can dissociate a design object from the rest of the design, creating emphasis or establishing a contrast in purpose, topic, or function.

For example, we might choose a series of similar colors as the main colors of the design and then add in a single contrasting color to highlight important features — such as a company logo, a dropped cap, a title, or a heading.

Similarity of color is pretty obvious, but creating effective color contrast is a little more complicated because of the different *ways* colors can contrast. Colors can contrast in four primary ways (see Color Figure 10):

- *Hue:* The farther apart hues are from each other on a color circle or an HSB color picker, the greater the contrast between them. The highest level of contrastive hues takes one color from one side of the circle and its *complementary color* from 180 degrees opposite.

- *Saturation:* Even within one hue, we can create contrasts of saturation. The farther apart the colors lie in terms of their saturation, the higher the contrast.

- *Brightness:* A relatively dark color will contrast strongly with a relatively bright color.

- *Temperature:* We can make a further distinction between *cool colors*, on the blue-green side of the color circle, and *warm colors*, on the red-yellow side. When cool and warm colors are viewed together, the cool colors often seem to recede away from the viewer, and warm colors seem to advance toward the viewer. Matching a cool color with a warm color creates a contrast of temperature.

You can use any of these kinds of contrasts individually or combine them to create strong color contrast between different elements in your design. Keeping colors relatively close in hue, brightness, saturation, and temperature leads to greater similarity—a terrific tool for showing coherence and unity in your design. But you must also consider the interactions of these different contrasts. For example, saturation affects color temperature: a light pink (desaturated red) might not seem to advance over a highly saturated blue, even though pink is from the warm (supposedly advancing) side of the color circle.

Color Schemes

Choosing a consistent color scheme can help create a consistent identity within and between documents. It's particularly important to use a consistent color scheme for websites, which can have a myriad of pages; for documentation sets, which include a variety of related documents; and for organizational style sheets, which can regulate the many documents an organization creates.

Designers often rely on several traditional color schemes: monochromatic, analogous, complementary, split-complementary, triadic, and tetradic. All of these schemes are based on choosing hues according to their positions on a color circle. These color schemes are not rules but simply guidelines for choosing hues that work well together. And even after you've chosen a set of hues, you'll still need to make decisions about an appropriate saturation and brightness for each color. Most designers make these decisions by eye, making careful and sometimes subtle adjustments to get just the right set of colors.

MONOCHROMATIC AND ANALOGOUS

Monochromatic schemes use colors restricted to one hue—that is, one point around the color circle. *Analogous* schemes broaden this approach somewhat, using a narrow range of hues contiguous to a central hue (Color Figure 11).

Monochromatic and analogous schemes often seem very coherent to viewers, and they're particularly well suited to designs restricted by cost or production capability to one color of ink. But because they are concentrated in or around one hue, these schemes offer fewer possibilities for pointing out contrastive elements than other color schemes.

COMPLEMENTARY AND SPLIT-COMPLEMENTARY

Complementary color schemes specify two colors on opposite sides of the color wheel, or close to it. A common design strategy selects one hue from the cool side of the wheel and then a complementary hue from the warm side of the wheel (Color Figure 12).

Split-complementary color schemes work similarly but with a little more flexibility. To form a split-complementary scheme, choose one hue, and then choose two or more hues close to the complementary of the first hue (Color Figure 12).

The downside of complementary and split-complementary color schemes is that they make it easy to create garish designs. If you use one of these schemes, consider using a mostly cool, receding hue for the main color, and then pick out important elements with the complementary or split-complementary hues from the warm side of the circle. (On the other hand, sometimes garishness is just what the rhetorical situation calls for!)

TRIADIC AND TETRADIC

Designers often use hues that are separated at either three (*triadic*) or four (*tetradic*) points around the color circle. A triadic scheme might use red, blue, and green, or cyan, magenta, and yellow. A tetradic scheme might use red, blue, green, and orange, or cyan, magenta, yellow, and purple. The three or four hues are sometimes spaced equally around the circle, but often the designer adjusts the angles between the hues by eye. As with the other schemes we've discussed, designers often focus most of the design on one hue, using the others to highlight important features (Color Figure 13).

Triadic and tetradic color schemes can appear playful and colorful, but they can also look unsophisticated (perhaps because it's common to color children's toys in such widely spaced colors).

Designing with Limited Colors

In print design especially, you might be limited by cost or production factors to designs that can be printed with a limited palette of one or two colors.

The American flag incorporates red, which stands out strongly from the green and blue color scheme.

The "CLICK HERE" link is in yellow, which also contrasts with the green/blue scheme.

Color Figure 1 A consistent and vibrant color scheme. This website uses a consistent blue and green color scheme to create a sense of coherent ethos. It incorporates contrasting colors such as red and yellow to emphasize important information or rhetorical concepts.

Ethanol Promotion and Information Council (EPIC), <www.drivingethanol.org>.

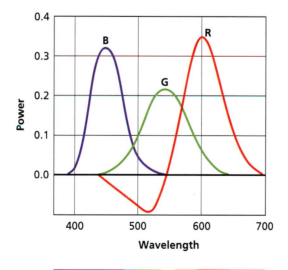

Visible spectrum

Color Figure 2 The visible spectrum and tristimulus values (RGB). Notice that the wavelengths of light we perceive as red, green, and blue (RGB) overlap considerably. As a result, some colors we perceive, such as brown and orange, exist not as a particular wavelength but only as a combination of wavelengths.

Williamson and Cummins, 64.

Color Figure 3 A hue-saturation color circle. This hue-saturation color circle shows the additive primary (RGB) and additive secondary (CMY) hues spaced equally around the perimeter. The most saturated colors are on the edge of the circle, while mixtures (desaturated colors) increase toward the center.

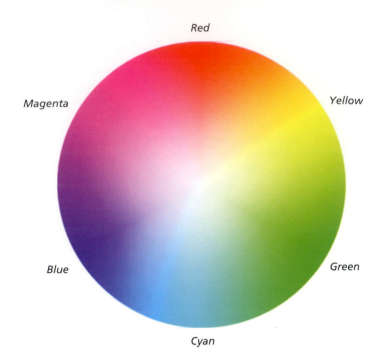

Color Figure 4 A three-dimensional color circle. This three-dimensional color space shows the interactions of hue, saturation, and brightness (HSB). The hue and saturation dimensions are arranged the same as in Color Figure 3 but tilted back. The brightness dimension extends in a range from black (no brightness) through grays (some brightness, equal mixture of hues) to white (full brightness, equal mixture of hues).

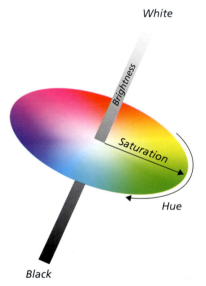

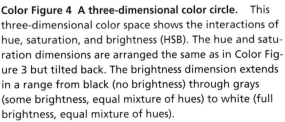

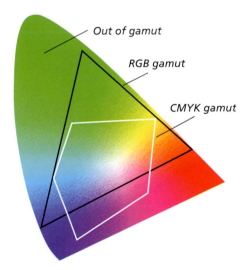

Color Figure 5 CIE L*a*b color space. CIE L*a*b describes the full range of colors perceivable by a typical human being. This color space shows the gamut of possible perceptions of color with additive (RGB) and subtractive (CMYK) gamuts. RGB and CMYK technologies can reproduce only a subset of the perceivable hues.

Williamson and Cummins, 60.

Color Figure 6 Simultaneous contrast. Our perceptions can change when we set colors against other colors. A color surrounded by another color is particularly susceptible to this effect. Here, the small squares are identical in each set, but the surrounding colors make the colors of the small squares look different from set to set.

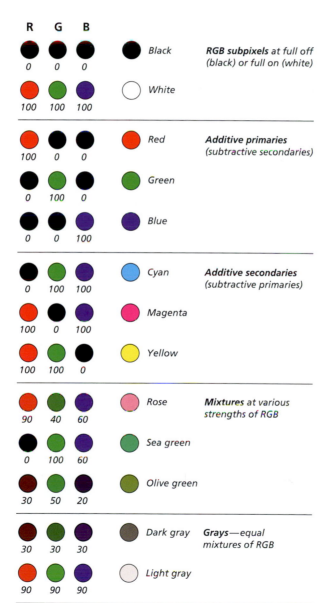

Color Figure 7 Additive color (RGB). Light in wavelengths that we perceive as red, green, or blue mixes to create all the other colors. On a computer monitor, RGB subpixels can be turned on in different strengths (0–100 in this illustration) to create all the colors in the RGB gamut.

R	G	B			
0	0	0	Black	*RGB subpixels* at full off (black) or full on (white)	
100	100	100	White		
100	0	0	Red	*Additive primaries* (subtractive secondaries)	
0	100	0	Green		
0	0	100	Blue		
0	100	100	Cyan	*Additive secondaries* (subtractive primaries)	
100	0	100	Magenta		
100	100	0	Yellow		
90	40	60	Rose	*Mixtures* at various strengths of RGB	
0	100	60	Sea green		
30	50	20	Olive green		
30	30	30	Dark gray	*Grays*—equal mixtures of RGB	
90	90	90	Light gray		

Color Figure 8 Subtractive color (CMYK). Subtractive color works when a surface absorbs light in some wavelengths and reflects light in others. The reflected wavelengths mix together additively to create the mixture of light we perceive as a color. In the first example, the surface absorbs red and reflects green and blue, creating cyan. The second example shows green absorption, reflecting red and blue to make magenta. The third shows blue absorption, resulting in a perception of yellow.

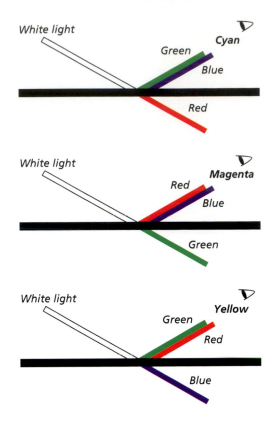

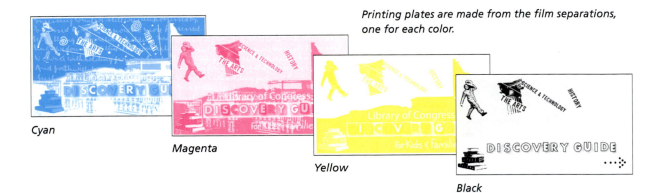

Printing plates are made from the film separations, one for each color.

Cyan

Magenta

Yellow

Black

Color Figure 9 CMYK color separations in process printing. By filtering out combinations of red, green, and blue, printers create lithographic plates to print cyan (filter out red, leave green + blue), magenta (filter out green, leave red + blue), and yellow (filter out blue, leave red + green). The black or "key" plate (K) usually carries all of the text, plus a black screen to help increase the saturation and deepen the shadows in process images.

When printed, the overlapping dots of the colors reproduce the full color image.

Hue contrast

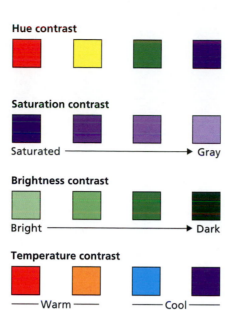

Saturation contrast

Saturated ⟶ Gray

Brightness contrast

Bright ⟶ Dark

Temperature contrast

⟵ Warm ⟶ ⟵ Cool ⟶

Color Figure 10 Color contrasts.
You can form color contrasts by altering hue, saturation, brightness, and temperature.

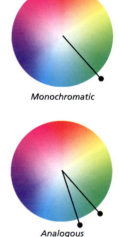

Monochromatic

Analogous

Color Figure 11 Monochromatic and analogous color schemes.
Monochromatic and analogous color schemes use different brightnesses and saturations of one hue or a small range of hues, respectively. This example is monochromatic, focusing on the hue of green.

Shaun Inman Design & Development, Inc., <haveamint.com>.

Color Figure 12 Complementary and split-complementary color schemes. Complementary color schemes choose two hues from opposite sides of the color circle. Split-complementary color schemes choose one hue from one side of the circle and two or more hues slightly displaced from the complementary hue. This example shows a complementary color scheme.

Folger Shakespeare Library, "Shakespeare's Home in America."

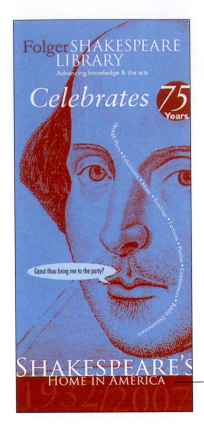

Complementary

Split-complementary

The dark red and cyan of this leaflet are almost exactly opposite each other on the color circle, lending strong contrast to the design.

Color Figure 13 Triadic and tetradic color schemes. Triadic and tetradic color schemes use hues spaced at three or four points around the color circle. These color schemes often look bright and playful. This example shows the front and back cover of a brochure in a triadic color scheme of orange, blue, and green.

Library of Congress, "Discovery Guide for Kids and Families."

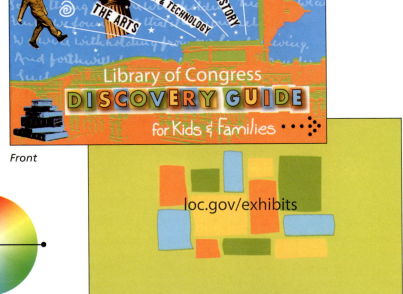

Front

Triadic

Tetradic

Back

Color Figure 14 Designing with two colors. This play program uses purple and black inks not only to build interest but to establish the layout grid. There's enough contrast between the purple spot ink and the black ink that the text stands out clearly from the background.

Shakespeare Theatre Company, "The Beaux' Stratagem."

Color Figure 15 Duotones. This calendar of events for an art gallery uses a duotone image built up of purple and orange spot inks to give a sophisticated look to the design.

Freer-Sackler Gallery, Smithsonian Institution, "Discoveries 2006."

Color Figure 16 Color pickers in Microsoft Word and Adobe Photoshop. Note that each color picker allows you to specify colors either numerically or graphically using multiple color models.

The rectangle controls hue and saturation.

The drop-down menu allows choosing between RGB and HSL color models.

The slider controls brightness.

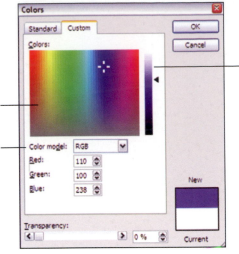

Microsoft Word color picker

This icon warns that the color is out of the chosen gamut.

The slider's function changes according to which color dimension is activated. Here, the Hue dimension is activated, so the slider controls hue.

Since hue is controlled by the slider, the rectangle controls saturation and brightness.

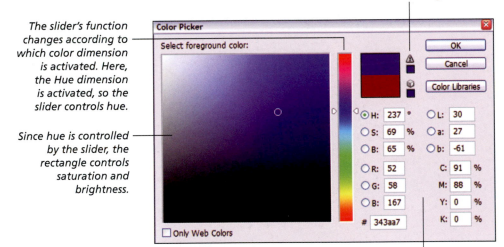

Adobe Photoshop color picker

This color picker allows specifying colors in HSB, L*a*b, RGB, CMYK, or hex.

DESIGNING WITH ONE COLOR

Designers frequently must work with only one color—and that color is often black. For example, if you know that your design must be printed on a laser printer and photocopied, there's little reason to spend time thinking about grandiose color schemes. But even black can come in different "colors"—the range of saturations we call grays. A design that uses several grays and a strong black can be quite striking and effective. This book, for example, relies mostly on grays and black, due to production costs.

Designing with grays usually involves applying a *screen* to areas of black. In other words, the only ink used is black, but it's applied in small dots; as the dots get smaller and farther apart, they give the appearance of lighter grays. Most page layout and graphic programs allow fine control over screens, from 0 percent (white) to 100 percent (full black).

However, screens can sometimes be visible—enough to distract users from the purpose of the document. This problem arises particularly with photographs and other graphics that use smooth tonal gradients. If your printer resolution is relatively high—at least 600 dpi—most viewers won't be able to see the small dots without careful scrutiny. Professional offset printing will yield an even higher printer resolution, leading to smoother-looking grays. But if your job will be printed on a low-resolution printer, such as a standard laser or inkjet printer at 300 dpi, the dots that make up the screen will be large enough for most people to see. (Ironically, photocopying a low-resolution printout can smooth out the screens somewhat, making the dots less obvious.)

If your one-color job will be printed professionally on an offset press, you can specify a color of ink other than black, using screens of that color to create your design. This technique can be a good way to create a distinctive-looking document. But remember that black is the darkest, most dense, and most striking contrast with white paper, and users need strong figure-ground contrast to make out the design—especially the text. Any other color will have less contrast with the paper and therefore make text more difficult to read. Some hues, such as yellow, will have an effective luminance too close to white to be usable in one-color designs on white paper.

DESIGNING WITH TWO COLORS

Typically, two-color designs on white paper use black as one of the colors (for text) plus a strikingly different color for important elements of contrast. For example, a company letterhead design might have the text for the address in black and the logo in a fully saturated spot color. Or a technical document might use black text but have headings and other navigational design objects in a different color.

DESIGN TIP

Get Inspired by Other Designs

Start a collection of documents you think have interesting color schemes or color practices. You can look to your collection for ideas before you begin a design project or for inspiration when you get stuck. Try to find a variety of different kinds of documents:

- Paper and electronic media
- Different formats, sizes, and paper stocks
- Different rhetorical purposes (persuading, reporting, instructing)
- Different genres (reports, brochures, flyers, instructions)
- Four-color, two-color, and one-color
- Some with graphics; some with photos; some with both

The trick is to choose a color that will contrast adequately with the black text while still providing good figure-ground contrast. A dark blue might have good contrast with the background but too little contrast with the black text. For example, in Color Figure 14 the Shakespeare Theatre Company has used a spot ink in purple to establish the layout grid of the page spread, but it contrasts well with black.

It's also possible to use any two contrasting spot inks, such as in the cover of the Freer-Sackler Gallery events calendar in Color Figure 15. Here, color "grayscale" images are printed with purple and orange spot inks, a technique known as duotone printing.

Working with Color on Computers

Whether designing for print or for the screen, you will definitely use computers to create your designs and manipulate colors. In this section, we'll look at three important techniques for working with color on computers: using color pickers, matching colors, and calibrating monitors.

Using Color Pickers

Most software color pickers—the dialog boxes in which you specify colors—use both numbers and a graphical model for color. Typically, different programs have their own designs for color pickers, or you can use the system color pickers that come with Windows or Apple OS. As you can see in Color Figure 16, what these systems share is an ability to specify color using several different models, including RGB, CMYK, hex, CIE L*a*b, and HSB/L (Hue, Saturation, and Brightness/Luminance).

In these color pickers, color specifications are often represented graphically by a two-dimensional space (usually rectangular or circular) and a slider. For example, in basic rectangular HSB/L color pickers, the color picker splits the color circle at the top and flattens it *horizontally* stretching from left (0 degrees) to right (360 degrees). Because red is traditionally represented on the color circle at 0 degrees/360 degrees, it's represented at the far left and far right sides of the rectangle, with the other colors ranged in between in order of the spectrum. Saturation is represented *vertically* in the rectangular color picker, ranging from full saturation at the top to low saturation (grays) at the bottom.

Brightness/luminance is controlled by a vertical slider that ranges from high brightness/luminance at the top to no brightness/luminance at the bottom. You can choose colors in a color picker through three different mechanisms:

> **DESIGN TIP**
>
> ## Color Pickers
>
> Make yourself familiar with the color pickers in the software you use. A little bit of experimentation can give you a lot of confidence in your work with color.

- *Clicking in a rectangular or circular color space:* A target mark (usually a small ring or crosshair) will show what spot you've chosen.

- *Adjusting sliders:* Some HSB/L pickers include a vertical slider for Brightness/Luminance, but many pickers also include sliders that can be dragged to adjust the other dimensions of the color. These sliders are particularly useful for adjusting one dimension while leaving the other settings alone. For example, you can change saturation without altering hue or brightness.

- *Specifying each dimension of the color numerically:* Keeping with the metaphor of the color circle, many color pickers measure hue as 0–360 degrees for both additive and subtractive color. RGB values, because they are intended for use in on-screen designs, are often represented as steps from 0 to 255. CMYK pickers typically use percentage values from 0 to 100 percent.

All of these controls are coupled together. For example, if you change the hue numerically, you'll see the target move in the color space and the appropriate sliders shift to whatever color you've chosen.

Different programs use different designs for color pickers. Adobe Photoshop includes a single rectangular color picker that shows numerical values for RGB, CMYK, HSB, CIE L*a*b, and hexadecimals in one view. Microsoft Word offers only RGB and HSL settings. Many software programs use a color picker that is designed to fit the purpose of the program, so a web graphics program will likely put a hexadecimal or RGB picker in the forefront, while a page layout program will default to CMYK.

Matching Colors

When designing documents, you'll want to use colors consistently from page to page. Doing so requires specifying colors precisely as you use the same color in different parts of your design. Accuracy in color specification is particularly important if you're designing with spot colors. Designers use three techniques to make sure their colors stay consistent: keeping track of numerical color settings, applying styles, and using the eyedropper tool.

As we discussed in the previous section, color pickers specify colors not only in a three-dimensional color space but also by specific numbers for colors in HSB/L, RGB, or CMYK. *Keep track of these numbers as you design.* For example, if you want every caption throughout a document to use the same color of type, take note of the color by copying down the corresponding HSB/L, RGB, or CMYK numbers. That way, when you want to make another caption or use the same color for another purpose, you can specify exactly the same color by entering the same numbers. This technique is particularly important if you decide to create multiple documents in the same color scheme, as corporations often do. In fact, you might use or even be involved in writing an organizational style sheet that specifies what colors are to be used in your organization's documents, usually with RGB for screens, CMYK for process color, and Pantone for spot inks.

A second technique, using styles, applies primarily to colored text. You can use a repeatable paragraph or character style to replicate the color of text, just as you can specify its typeface, font, leading, and indentation. Each time you want to use the same color of text, just apply the style to the appropriate words or paragraph. For more information on using styles, see Chapter 6.

As a faster and less formal alternative, you can use the eyedropper tool and the palette in many page layout and graphics programs. The eyedropper tool allows you to click on a pixel to pick up its color specification. You can then switch to a different tool to draw objects or enter text using that same color. The palette allows you to save colors in a small window to create a list of your favorite or most-used colors.

Calibrating Your Monitor

An additional difficulty arises when we prepare print jobs digitally on a computer: sometimes documents that look great on-screen look significantly different when printed. Why? Because whether you're working in CMYK or RGB, computer monitors display everything in RGB. So the colors you see while designing a brochure or manual in a page layout program are merely RGB approximations of the CMYK colors you've specified. Several steps can help you avoid this problem:

- *Control the computer environment.* Set the background of your computer monitor to a medium gray or a subtle grayscale pattern. Remember, simultaneous contrast can make colors look different; that cheerful photo wallpaper on your desktop can distort your perception of colors in a design.

- *Control the lighting in your workspace.* Light shining on your computer monitor can change perceived color, so indirect workspace lighting is best. Keep the lighting consistent from day to day, and avoid natural light, which can change remarkably throughout the day. Also avoid overhead fluorescent lights, which often lend a blue cast to your perceptions. Use incandescent or halogen lights instead.

- *Color calibrate your monitor regularly.* Most operating systems come with display calibration software, and many sophisticated third-party options for monitor calibration are available. Page layout programs also allow you to specify a particular color set to use, such as Pantone color sets.

These techniques will help you create the greatest possible consistency between what you see on screen and what you get in print. But keep in mind that there will always be some difference between what you see on your computer screen and what users see after the document is reproduced, whether on paper or on their own computer screen. Ideally, it's best to test out color calibrations by proofing color print jobs (see Chapter 11) and by trying out on-screen designs with several different monitors.

Exercises

1. Software designers create predesigned color schemes for user interfaces and document templates. Their color design choices can be interesting:

   a. Explore the color schemes that come with PowerPoint presentation templates. To see the templates in PowerPoint 2003 and newer editions, choose Slide Design from the Format menu; thumbnails of the templates will appear in the Slide Design bar on the right. To see all of the colors for a template design, click on a design in the Slide Design bar to apply it to the main editing screen. Make a couple of slides to see how the design changes from the title slide to the body slides.

   b. Think about and discuss these questions:

      • For what rhetorical purposes would you choose one of these templates? Why?

      • Do the color schemes of the templates follow one of the common schemes described in this chapter?

      • How does the design use color for emphasis?

      • PowerPoint slides are usually projected on a screen or viewed on a computer monitor. What effect do you think the medium had on the designer's color choices?

2. Collect a few documents in a variety of media, formats, and genres, with different color schemes and rhetorical purposes.

   • Paper and electronic media

   • Different formats, sizes, and paper stocks

   • Different rhetorical purposes (persuasion, reporting, instructing)

   • Different genres (reports, brochures, flyers, instructions)

   • Four-color, two-color, and one-color

   Choose two for comparison and analyze their use of color. For each document, think about and discuss the following questions:

   • How would you describe the color scheme? Does it follow one of the common schemes described in this chapter?

   • How does the design use color for emphasis?

   • How does the design use color to create consistent patterns?

   • What rhetorical tone do you think this color scheme was intended to convey? From your viewpoint as a user, is it successful?

3. In PowerPoint, use the Slide Master View to design your own PowerPoint template with a custom color scheme. Choose one of the following tasks to guide your design, or create your own context:

   • A presentation for retirees about a retirement community

   • A presentation for international students about computer services at your university

   • A slide show to accompany an art exhibit.

   Be sure to keep in mind the medium, format, and viewing conditions of PowerPoints as you make your design decisions. To start your design, follow these steps:

   a. Choose Master → Slide Master from the View menu. You'll see the slide master open in the main editing space. A new toolbar will also appear: the Slide Master View toolbar.

   b. Start making your design:

      • To design a new title slide, click on Insert New Title Master on the Slide Master View toolbar. To switch back to the regular slide master, click on the appropriate thumbnail in the navigation pane on the left.

      • To set a background color, right-click in the margin of a slide and choose Background.

      • To draw designs on the background of the slide, use the tools in the Drawing toolbar. (If the Drawing toolbar isn't visible, right-click on any of the toolbars and choose Drawing.)

272

- To change the color, typeface, or font size of standard text such as titles, subtitles, and bullets, choose the appropriate text in the master view and use the Formatting toolbar to make whatever changes you like.

c. When you're finished with your design, click on Close Master View in the Slide Master View toolbar.

d. Choose Save As from the File menu, enter a name for your new template, and choose Design Template (*.pot) as the file type. Now you can use this custom-designed template for your own PowerPoint slideshows.

4. Spend some time exploring what designs might look like to people with color limitations.

a. Go to the Color Schemes Generator at <wellstyled.com/tools/colorscheme2/index-en.html> and create a color scheme. (Alternately, you can recreate a color scheme from a sample document.)

b. Using the drop-down menu at the bottom right-hand corner, change the color scheme to see how it would look to someone with deuteranomaly or protanomaly, the two most common kinds of color blindness.

What differences did you notice between viewing your color scheme with normal vision and with deuteranomaly or protanomaly? How would you change your color scheme to make it more easily perceivable for users with these conditions?

Work Cited

Williamson, Samuel J., and Herman Z. Cummins. *Light and Color in Nature and Art*. New York: John Wiley and Sons, 1983.

Further Reading

Albers, Josef. *Interaction of Color*. Revised ed. New Haven and London: Yale University Press, 1975.

Gage, John. *Color and Culture: Practice and Meaning from Antiquity to Abstraction*. Boston: Little, Brown, 1993.

Gage, John. *Colour and Meaning: Art, Science, and Symbolism*. London: Thames & Hudson, 1999.

Itten, Johannes. *The Elements of Color*. New York: Van Nostrand Reinhold, 1970.

Peterson, L. K., and Cheryl Dangel Cullen. *Global Graphics: Color, a Guide to Design with Color for an International Market*. Gloucester, MA: Rockport, 2000.

Zollinger, Heinrich. *Color: A Multidisciplinary Approach*. Weinheim and Zürich: Wiley-VCH, 1999.

CHAPTER 9

Lists, Tables, and Forms

Imagine that you work for a property management company and you're reviewing applicants' resumes for a property manager position. Which of the versions of an entry from a resume in Figure 9.1 would you consider most impressive? Both resumes present pretty much the same information, but if you're like most managers, you'd probably prefer to read the version with the bulleted list of job duties. Why? Because it's easier to scan down a list to see what the applicant has to offer than it is to read through a long description. As a paragraph, the job duty items lose visual impact. For example, the item "keeping the books" might be impressive data, but the phrase is lost in the middle of the paragraph. As a bulleted list, however, each item has its own space, helping you concentrate on each item individually.

Like many technical documents, resumes contain many individual pieces of data—names, numbers, addresses, places, and facts. Absorbing all that information can be a challenge—especially if you have piles of resumes to wade through. The bulleted version in Figure 9.1 reduces the reader's workload by visually emphasizing the individual pieces of data. And making the reader's job easier gives a better impression of the applicant.

Some of the most difficult tasks a document designer will face are the display and collection of data. By *data*, we mean the myriad small pieces of information—numerical, factual, or visual—that technical documents are often designed to convey or, in some cases, to gather. Users need a clear way to understand the sometimes complex relationships between pieces of data so they can make decisions and take action.

Property Manager
Detroit Properties, Inc.
As property manager, I managed a 25-unit apartment complex. My duties included collecting rent and keeping the books. I also hired and managed repair and renovation subcontractors, and I contributed to advertising campaigns.

Property Manager
Detroit Properties, Inc.
- Managed 25-unit apartment complex
- Collected rent
- Kept books
- Hired and managed repair and renovation subcontractors
- Contributed to advertising campaigns

Figure 9.1 Two versions of a resume entry. One of the resumes uses a paragraph to describe job duties, and the other uses a bulleted list. If you were an employer, which version would you prefer to read?

Over the centuries, designers have come up with two highly conventional modes of conveying data to users—the list and the table—and one powerful mode for collecting data from users—the form. These modes are common in technical documents but are not often discussed thoroughly from a document design perspective. So this chapter focuses on these three modes of handling data in technical document designs.

Lists, tables, and forms allow users to scan information quickly and to compare different pieces of information easily, visually representing the relationships between pieces of data. These tasks are important whether the user is scanning to find information, such as in a list or table, or providing information, such as in a form.

We discuss all three modes in one chapter because they all involve the organization of data and because they have many design strategies in common:

- *They all use both the horizontal and vertical dimensions of the page.* Paragraphs take advantage primarily of the horizontal dimension, as word follows word in lines of text. But lists, tables, and forms also make a conscious use of the vertical dimension to convey or gather data.

- *They all use alignment to show relationships between data.* Lists use a vertical alignment, tables use both horizontal and vertical alignments, and forms can use either or both. These alignments give designers an opportunity to show different relationships between pieces of data.

- *They all use enclosure to group data and draw attention to it.* Enclosure (either through positive borders or negative space) groups data into a logical structure so users can more easily compare data.

This chapter provides ideas and guidelines for designing effective lists, tables, and forms. It concentrates on visual design, but it includes suggestions about logical designs for all these modes.

Three Perspectives on Lists, Tables, and Forms

Perception

Well-designed lists, tables, and forms depend on our perceptions of visual relationships to express the logical relationship between items of data, each of which stands as a design object in relation to surrounding design objects. More specifically, we can use the principles of design (similarity, contrast, alignment, proximity, order, and enclosure) to show how data points are grouped and connected.

Similarity and contrast can help create a sense of grouping between design objects in lists, tables, and forms. For example, the bullets in a bulleted list imply that the items in the list are logically connected to each other in a relationship of parallelism. Users will typically assume that all of the items in the list have some factor in common. Each entry in the bulleted list in Figure 9.1, for instance, is a duty performed at that particular job. On the other hand, we can use contrast to show different levels of data in a hierarchical relationship — for example, by boldfacing the column headings or row headings in a table to separate them visually from the data.

Good uses of alignment and proximity are essential in lists, tables, and forms. Users typically assume that design objects aligned with each other belong with each other, or at least have some sort of parallel relationship with each other. For example, lists are usually aligned to a consistent left-hand margin. Tables rely even further on alignment, since they're aligned both horizontally and vertically. And each column of a table can have its own internal alignment scheme, such as left-aligned, centered, or in some cases (such as for currency figures), right-aligned. Forms also rely on alignment: a form with clearly aligned design objects for the instructions, questions, and form fields is easy to fill out and easy to gather accurate data from.

Because lists, tables, and forms can gather many individual pieces of data, we can also use proximity to show how these design objects relate to one another. Proximity pairs with alignment to help users recognize how the individual design objects in a table create a sense of rows and columns. It also helps users associate questions with their answers in a form.

We can also create larger groupings of individual objects through enclosure. Explicit lines or background shading can separate and group data elements, but we can also group data elements implicitly, using negative space. In a table, for example, borders can delineate rows, columns, and cells, though negative space often works just as well.

Finally, lists, tables, and forms emphasize relationships of order between design objects. Lists can be either ordered or unordered, depending on the nature of the data they convey. Tables can be sorted by the contents of particular rows or columns. And forms often start with identification data (such as names, Social Security numbers, addresses, and so on) and end with an authorization — a signature. These orderings help users understand the relationships between pieces of data. Without clear visual cues, users may not be able to access information successfully, or in the case of forms, they may not be able to provide all of the requested information accurately and completely.

Culture

Lists, tables, and forms have been used in manuscripts for millennia, and in print culture for centuries. Lists are found in very early manuscripts, but they became more common as paper and printing became cheaper. Some of the earliest uses of printed tables were in the astronomical and astrological books of the Renaissance, which recorded the positions and appearances of stars, planets, and comets.

The earliest printed forms were developed for indulgences, documents that were sold by the medieval and Renaissance churches to certify the forgiveness of a sin. We usually think of the first document created with movable type as Johannes Gutenberg's 42-line Bible. But before printing the Bible, Gutenberg tried out his technological innovation by printing indulgence forms, with blanks for a priest to enter the name of the person seeking forgiveness. Governments soon realized the efficiencies of forms for gathering information and for personalizing repetitive documentation. Before printing, repetitive documents such as leases and warrants had to be individually written by hand, but printing could turn out hundreds of copies quickly and cheaply.

These developments in conveying and gathering data were closely linked to changes in cultures and societies. Our culture is drowning in data, making lists and tables essential tools for managing and understanding data. And forms have become an essential device for governments, corporations, organizations, and even individuals to gather data.

Rhetoric

Because lists, tables, and forms typically contain what we might think of as raw data, it might be hard to imagine that they employ a visual rhetoric. But in fact, even these everyday modes for representing data do have a rhetorical power in that they visually imply relationships between pieces of data.

When data is supplied in a list form, it implies that the items are parallel and equal in kind, and potentially related in order. This can have a considerable rhetorical effect, especially because it shows users that the information being represented is organized and clear. Users often complain about the density of information that is expressed in sentences and paragraphs, but they feel much more comfortable about the same information arranged in a list. Lists let users pay attention to one item at a time — for example, completing one step in a procedure before going on to the next.

Tables express two-dimensional relationships in data by arranging data in columns and rows. This layout can have a significant effect on the way people view the data by organizing data in a way that seems logical and reasonable. The same data explained in a paragraph might not be nearly as convincing as in a table. However, tables sometimes over-simplify data by making it look like *only* two-dimensional relationships apply, when in fact most data have relationships in multiple dimensions.

Forms are a special case rhetorically because they often have two sets of users: the people who fill out the form and the people who read and use the data from the forms. Users filling out forms are definitely affected by the visual rhetoric of the form, which represents the ethos of the organization that is requesting the information. People often don't like to provide information on forms, especially if it's personal information. If the visual rhetoric of the form doesn't assure users that the information will be kept carefully and used appropriately, they may refuse to provide any information at all.

To build a positive ethos with these primary users, forms must have a clear organization of data and an open, friendly visual style. Well-designed forms also group questions into logical chunks to help users understand exactly *what* is being asked. The most common relationship in forms is the one between questions and answers.

After these primary users fill out the form, a secondary set of users reads the data from the forms and incorporates it into some larger information architecture. In the most basic situation, a secondary user might need to enter data from the form into a database. In more automated systems such as web forms, the form must be designed so that the data will enter a database automatically, where it can then be accessed and combined for other purposes. We need to design forms so that these secondary users can gather and use data successfully.

Lists

Designers often use lists to break up paragraphs of text in a document, such as a report or a set of instructions. But sometimes lists are the main feature of a document. Telephone books, for example, are typically one or several long lists with only a small amount of basal text to introduce them. As familiar as lists may seem, however, designing good lists requires some careful thought.

What *is* a list? Strictly speaking, it's simply a series of logically parallel elements in a sequence. Lists *can* be formatted horizontally as text—for example, *apples, pears, mangos, bananas*—but one of the most common visual techniques is to orient lists vertically:

- apples
- pears
- mangos
- bananas

Doing so allows readers to scan the items quickly and efficiently. But this simple list only begins the possibilities that lists offer for designers. In this section, we'll look at some ways we can use the principles of design to make visually useful and appealing lists.

List Entries

Lists always include at least two entries (logically, one entry by itself can't be a list). The entries in a list can be short (words or phrases) or long (sentences or even brief paragraphs). Lists imply that the items in the list are parallel and have something in common, that they relate to some central principle in a logical manner. Lists often include some sort of heading or introductory text that expresses this central principle succinctly (Figure 9.2; see if you can find a small problem in the lists on this example.).

Because lists imply a logically parallel relationship for the items they contain, we typically make the entries both grammatically and visually parallel. In terms of grammar, if one entry in a list is a noun, all of the entries should be nouns; if one entry begins with a verb, they all should begin with a verb. The visual principle of *similarity* emphasizes this logically parallel relationship. Make sure that all entries in the list are formatted in precisely the same way.

Glyphs and Ordering

Lists sometimes have an inherent order, such as the alphabetical order used in telephone directories, but most lists don't have an inherent order.

In some lists, order simply doesn't matter — none of the items necessarily needs to appear before or after any of the others. Such **unordered lists** usually employ a **glyph** to mark the beginning of each entry (see Figure 9.3 on page 280). The most common is the printer's bullet (•), named because it looks like a bullet hole in the page. This glyph also gives us the term **bullet text** — that is, a bulleted, unordered list. Some designs might call for more unusual glyphs, such as arrowheads, squares, or diamonds.

In other situations, the order of list items is important, but the entries don't have any inherent order (such as alphabetical order). For

List headings can express a list's central organizing principle. Like any heading, they should contrast with the list items to show hierarchy and dependence.

Figure 9.2 A well-structured list. Lists and list headings need a consistent design to structure data clearly.

U.S. Postal Service, Publication 614.

Glyphs for ordered lists		Glyphs for unordered lists	
1.	I.	•	➤
2.	II.	•	➤
3. . . .	III.	•	➤
10.	IV.		
a.	i.	■	◆
b.	ii.	■	◆
c.	iii.	■	◆
d.	iv.		

Figure 9.3 Common glyphs for ordered and unordered lists. You can use many different images for glyphs in unordered lists, but it's usually best to stick with glyphs that users are familiar with. Glyphs should mark the list item and draw users' attention to it but not overpower the text. Notice the alignment of numbered glyphs: although the list entries are left-aligned, the glyphs are right-aligned on the period so multiple-digit numbers (like 10, III, and so on) don't mess up the alignment of the entries.

example, the list of steps in a procedure must be completed in a particular order. In these cases, we commonly create an *ordered list* by using glyphs such as numbers or letters to establish and reinforce the order of items. The glyphs used in ordered lists are most often Arabic numerals, but we can also use capital Roman numerals (I, II, III, IV), small Roman numerals (i, ii, iii, iv), uppercase letters, or lowercase letters. Designers rely on the conventional order of these glyphs to indicate and reinforce the logically ordered nature of the items in the list.

The glyphs for both ordered and unordered lists are typically in the same font size as the entries they introduce, although some designs might use a larger size, a different color, or a contrasting typeface to make the glyphs more prominent. Avoid using glyphs that won't stand out enough to mark the beginning of each entry—but also avoid using glyphs that overwhelm the entries.

Lists and Alignment

By convention and function, lists almost always align on the left. Left alignment gives users an implied vertical line formed by the bullets and the beginnings of the entries; this helps them scan down the list and distinguish each item. Centering a list or aligning it to the right makes the beginnings of the lines uneven and thus makes the list harder to scan, while making it easier for readers to skip lines accidentally (Figure 9.4).

Align bulleted and numbered lists with a hanging indent so the glyphs (the bullets or numbers) align vertically on one implied line and

Figure 9.4 Using left alignment for lists. Lists need a consistent left alignment to work successfully. Otherwise, we lose much of the advantage of using lists and increase the chances that users will skip items.

- Managed 25-unit apartment complex
- Collected rent
- Kept books
- Hired and managed repair and renovation subcontractors
- Contributed to advertising campaigns for the property management company

- Managed 25-unit apartment complex
- Collected rent
- Kept books
- Hired and managed repair and renovation subcontractors
- Contributed to advertising campaigns for the property management company

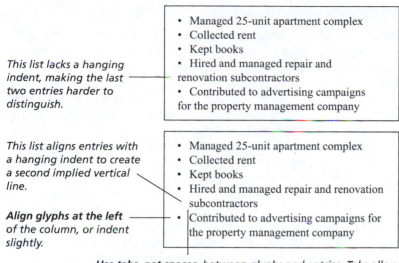

This list lacks a hanging indent, making the last two entries harder to distinguish.

- Managed 25-unit apartment complex
- Collected rent
- Kept books
- Hired and managed repair and renovation subcontractors
- Contributed to advertising campaigns for the property management company

This list aligns entries with a hanging indent to create a second implied vertical line.

- Managed 25-unit apartment complex
- Collected rent
- Kept books
- Hired and managed repair and renovation subcontractors
- Contributed to advertising campaigns for the property management company

Align glyphs at the left *of the column, or indent slightly.*

Use tabs, not spaces, between glyphs and entries. Tabs allow you to align second and subsequent lines with the first line. The space between the glyph and the entry should be large enough to make the entry stand out but small enough for the entry to be linked to the glyph by proximity.

Figure 9.5 Using hanging indents in lists.   Hanging indents clarify the content of the list, allowing users to scan vertically down the list items to find the information they need.

the entries align on a second implied line parallel to the first (Figure 9.5). This makes the glyphs stick out slightly from the items, notifying readers of the beginning of each item. Without a hanging indent, the second or subsequent lines of any item will obscure the negative space around the glyphs, making it harder for readers to see where the next item begins.

Most word processing and page layout programs have a special setting for bulleted and numbered lists that takes care of alignment and indentations automatically. If your software has such a setting, use it rather than making the list manually. This will also give you lots of extra options for modifying the list design.

If you format lists manually, separate the glyphs from the text with a tab rather than by a space or spaces. Tabs stay consistent from line to line, while spaces introduce misalignments. A tab also gives considerable control over the horizontal distance between the glyphs and their entries. This distance should be large enough to make the bullets or numbers stand out, but small enough that each glyph still seems visually connected to its entry.

Typically, each glyph in an ordered list is followed by a period or closing parenthesis before the tab. The glyphs are aligned by this mark rather than by the glyph itself. For example, a list ordered with Roman numerals is vertically aligned by the periods so the increasing widths of the numerals don't change the alignment of the entries (see Figure 9.3).

Managing Long Lists

We often use lists to break up long stretches of paragraphs, since these can cause user fatigue and inattention. But long lists can cause as much fatigue as long stretches of paragraphs, so designers try not to make lists longer than around seven to nine items. This is just a rule of thumb. A collection of simple items might work well in a long list, particularly if the list is inherently ordered; after all, phone books and dictionaries have thousands of items.

If the data you need to present requires a list longer than seven to nine items, you can subdivide it into smaller sublists—in effect, a list of lists. Designers use the design principles of alignment, contrast, similarity, proximity, and order to group items in a sublist and distinguish that list from the larger list. For example, Figure 9.6 shows how a list of items on a menu might be logically and visually divided into appetizers, entrees, sides, and drinks. The sublist items are typographically distinct from the main list items, they're indented further, and they're closer to each other. Designing the list this way might make the list slightly longer, but that increase in length is offset by an increase in usability.

In electronic documents such as websites, you can also manage long lists by creating dynamic lists with headings that expand or collapse when clicked on. Dynamic lists allow users to see the subheadings as a coherent list in themselves and then click on the subheading they want to expand into a more detailed list. Dynamic lists give users

Figure 9.6 Grouping items increases usability.   In paper documents, you can group list items into sublists to create a clearer structure for users. In electronic documents, you can even use computer scripts to make dynamic lists that users can expand or collapse to show or hide subitems.

Long, Undivided List	Subdivided List	Dynamic List
Chips & salsa	**Appetizers**	▶ **Appetizers**
Fried cheese sticks	Chips & salsa	▼ **Entrees**
Hamburger	Fried cheese sticks	
BLT		Hamburger
Chicken-fried steak	**Entrees**	BLT
Grilled chicken breast	Hamburger	Chicken-fried steak
Green beans	BLT	Grilled chicken breast
French fries	Chicken-fried steak	
Side salad	Grilled chicken breast	▶ **Sides**
Sodas		▶ **Drinks**
Coffee	**Sides**	
Tea	Green beans	
	French fries	
	Side salad	
	Drinks	
	Sodas	
	Coffee	
	Tea	

a clear overview of a long list, while still giving them access to individual items.

If your design needs sublists, restrict the design to no more than two or three levels. Make sure the design of each level remains internally consistent, as well as contrasts enough with other levels. For example, to distinguish sublists, you might use a different kind of glyph, a smaller font, or a different color of type.

Tables

In some ways, tables are just supercharged lists that can show data in two dimensions instead of one. This multiplies the possible relationships we can imply between entries, allowing the user to compare data along a row, down a column, or between multiple rows or columns. Although often used for numerical data, tables can also incorporate text or small graphics.

The table's ability to show multiple relationships, however, means that you must be particularly careful to use the principles of design to establish or even emphasize the relationships you want users to recognize most, or that readers most need to recognize. Like any feature of document design, your primary consideration should be how users will want to use the data in the table.

Components of Tables

Tables like the one in Figure 9.7 (page 284) include a number of features that you should know about; some are necessary, and some are optional.

NECESSARY PARTS OF TABLES

- *Columns:* The vertical axis of arranging data in a table
- *Rows:* The horizontal axis of arranging data in a table
- *Cells:* The individual area reserved for each data element in a table

OPTIONAL PARTS OF TABLES

- *Column heads:* Labels entered at the top of each column to identify what that column holds. Simple tables with a clear internal ordering of data might not need column heads, but most tables include them.

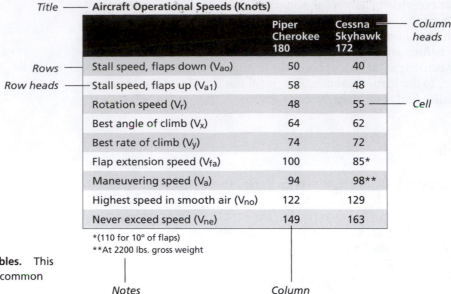

Aircraft Operational Speeds (Knots)

	Piper Cherokee 180	Cessna Skyhawk 172
Stall speed, flaps down (V_{ao})	50	40
Stall speed, flaps up (V_{a1})	58	48
Rotation speed (V_r)	48	55
Best angle of climb (V_x)	64	62
Best rate of climb (V_y)	74	72
Flap extension speed (V_{fa})	100	85*
Maneuvering speed (V_a)	94	98**
Highest speed in smooth air (V_{no})	122	129
Never exceed speed (V_{ne})	149	163

*(110 for 10° of flaps)
**At 2200 lbs. gross weight

Title — *Rows* — *Row heads* — *Column heads* — *Cell* — *Notes* — *Column*

Figure 9.7 Features of tables. This example shows the most common features of tables.

- ***Row heads*** (also known as side heads or stub heads): Labels entered for each row to identify what the row contains. Some tables use the entries in the first cell of each row to serve both as data and as an indicator of what that row contains, such as in Figure 9.7.
- ***Titles:*** Many tables use a title to identify the purpose of the table.
- ***Captions or notes:*** Some tables include captions or notes, to identify the source of the table's data.
- ***Legends:*** Because of the limitations of cell space, some tables use abbreviations or symbols and supply a legend that defines what they mean.

Designing Tables

FIT CONTENT TO TABLES, AND FIT TABLES TO CONTENT

One of the biggest challenges of designing tables is fitting all the content appropriately into cells. Two factors affect how content fits into tables: the space allowed by the page or screen design constrains the space available for the table from the outside, and the contents of the table determine the space needed for the table from the inside.

Theoretically, tables could be designed with unlimited numbers of columns and rows, extending far beyond the field of view. Microsoft Excel, for example, allows users to create spreadsheets of up to 65,536 rows by 256 columns — more than anyone can see at one time. When designing documents, however, we're usually limited to the visual space a single user can see at one time: a single page, a spread of pages, or a screen. And even though we can create large tables on-screen for users to scroll through, they can quickly get lost once the column heads scroll up beyond their view.

So the first consideration of table design involves taking into account the format and layout of the page or screen. Tables should fall within the grid design of the page or screen. For example, in a simple business document, a table should typically not extend beyond the main text area (or in other words, into the margins). This often causes problems because many tables contain lots of horizontal data elements — that is, cell data longer than it is tall.

Given page design space constraints, designers of paper documents sometimes rotate a table 90 degrees so the table can take advantage of the often greater height of the page — for example, on an 8.5" × 11" page, laying out the table so the rows run along the 11" axis. Doing so can allow some additional space, but it can also inconvenience users, who must physically turn the document to read the table and then turn it upright again. If you know a document will include a table that must be rotated this way, it's best to design the entire document around the table rather than inconvenience the user.

Just as the format of the page or screen constrains the design of the table from the outside, the data held in a table determines the table's dimensions from the inside. For example, if we have one cell that must contain more data than others, that cell dictates the width of the columns and the height of the rows. Figure 9.8 on page 286 shows the compromises that are sometimes necessary when accommodating the data in the table to the surrounding format of the document.

CHOOSE APPROPRIATE TYPOGRAPHY FOR TABLES

Tables can hold a large amount of data in a relatively small space. Because this compression can cause legibility problems for users, it's important to choose simple and clear typefaces for tables.

For this reason, many designers use sans serif typefaces (see Chapter 6 for more information on serif and sans serif typefaces). Serif faces work fine for text, where users' eyes move primarily horizontally, but in tables, users must read data both vertically and horizontally. Sans serif typefaces lack the horizontal "feet" of serif faces, so they tend to look more upright and enable vertical scanning. Sans serifs also tend

Equipment and Features		Lancair Columbia 400	Cirrus SR22	Beechcraft Baron G58	Beechcraft Bonanza G36	Mooney Bravo GX	Piper Mirage
Powerplant	Turbocharged Intercooled	●	N/A	N/A	N/A	●	●
	Horsepower	310 HP	310 HP	300 HP	300 HP	270 HP	350 HP
Electrical System	Dual Electrical System	●	●*	●*	●*	●*	●*
Avionics	Primary Flight Display with ADHARS and Flight Director (10.4")	●	○	●	●	●	●
	Multi Function Display (10.4")	●	●	●	●	●	●
	Coupled Autopilot with Altitude Preselect, Autotrim and GPSS	●	○	●	●	●	●
	GPS (Approach/IFR) Nav/Com with Glide Slope	●	●	●	●	●	●
	Second GPS (Approach/IFR) Nav/Com with Glide Slope	●	○	●	●	○	●
Equipment	Inflatable Door Seals	●	N/A	N/A	N/A	N/A	●
	Built In Oxygen	○	N/A	○	○	●	●
	Speed Brakes	○	N/A	N/A	N/A	●	N/A
	Air Conditioning	○	N/A	○	○	○	●
	Automatic Climate Control System	○	N/A	N/A	N/A	N/A	N/A
	Ice Protection	○	○	○	○	○	●
	Heated Prop	○	N/A	○	○	○	●
Certification Standard	Certification Standard	Utility	Normal	Normal	Normal	Normal	Normal
Performance	Max Cruise Speed	235 Kts @ FL250	185 Kts @ 8,000 Ft	203 Kts @ 5,000 Ft	176 Kts @ 6,000 Ft	220 Kts @ FL250**	213 Kts @ FL250
	Stall Speed	59 Kts	59 Kts**	75 Kts	59 Kts	59 Kts	59 Kts
	Range – Economy Cruise	1,301 NM/55% power (205 Kts) @ FL250	939 NM/55% power @ 17,000 Ft**	1,520 NM @ 8,000 Ft, 194 Gal	914 NM @ 6,000 Ft, 74 Gal	960 NM/55% power**	1,345 NM
	Range – Max Cruise	715 NM/ FL250	744 NM/75% @ 10,000 Ft**	1,025 NM @ 5,000 Ft, 194 Gal	697 NM @ 8,000 Ft, 74 Gal	750 NM/75% power**	990 NM**
	Service Ceiling	25,000 Ft	17,500 Ft**	20,688 Ft	18,500 Ft	25,000 Ft	25,000 Ft
	Take off Distance – Hard surface, gross weight, sea level	1,300 Ft	1,058 Ft**	2,300 Ft	1,913 Ft	1,080 Ft	1,090 Ft

Original table

Figure 9.8 Creating a table that fits the format and content.   Table design is constrained from the outside by format and from the inside by content. This table needed to accommodate some long entries, making some columns very wide. The designers responded to this problem by using a wide landscape format for the entire document to give more space to the table. Inside the table, they also used a sans serif typeface in a very small font to maximize available space. But as a result, the type is difficult to read.

Columbia Aircraft, "Columbia 400."

Primary Flight Display with ADHARS and Flight Director (10.4")
Multi Function Display (10.4")
Coupled Autopilot with Altitude Preselect, Autotrim and GPSS
GPS (Approach/IFR) Nav/Com with Glide Slope
Second GPS (Approach/IFR) Nav/Com with Glide Slope
Inflatable Door Seals
Built In Oxygen
Speed Brakes
Air Conditioning

Close-up of second column

Utility
235 Kts @ FL250
59 Kts
1,301 NM/55% power (205 Kts) @ FL250
715 NM/ FL250
25,000 Ft
1,300 Ft

Close-up of third column

to look more open and clear in tight spaces than serif faces do. Finally, many sans serifs are narrower than their serif counterparts, which saves horizontal space in a table.

Consider Figure 9.9, a table of lots for sale in a collectible postage stamp auction. We'll use this data in several examples to show different design techniques, evolving the table design as we go along. Here, notice how the sans serif version of the table reads more clearly than the serif version, particularly in the vertical axis.

If column heads or row heads are important cues to the content of the table, they should present some typographical contrast. Use a larger size, a greater density, or a different typeface to provide a clear

Lot #	Cat #	Condition	Comments	Price
1	137	S	A fine example	1740.00
2	149	XF/S	Clean & sharp	500.00
3	430	XF/S	A rich green, sharp perforations	185.00
4	88	S	A very pretty stamp; no gum skips	440.00
5	371	S	Post Office fresh	460.00
6	138	VF	Vertical pair	360.00
7	383	VF/XF	Small thin lower right corner	225.00
8	292	VG	Ex-Miller Collection	1150.00
9	27	XF	Good example	385.00
10	389	F/VF	Good centering for this issue	150.00

Figure 9.9 Using sans serif typefaces in a table. Sans serif typefaces maximize available space and make it easier to scan vertically down columns.

A table using a serif typeface

Lot #	Cat #	Condition	Comments	Price
1	137	S	A fine example	1740.00
2	149	XF/S	Clean & sharp	500.00
3	430	XF/S	A rich green, sharp perforations	185.00
4	88	S	A very pretty stamp; no gum skips	440.00
5	371	S	Post Office fresh	460.00
6	138	VF	Vertical pair	360.00
7	383	VF/XF	Small thin lower right corner	225.00
8	292	VG	Ex-Miller Collection	1150.00
9	27	XF	Good example	385.00
10	389	F/VF	Good centering for this issue	150.00

A table using a sans serif typeface

Lot #	Cat #	Condition	Comments	Price
1	137	S	A fine example	1740.00
2	149	XF/S	Clean & sharp	500.00
3	430	XF/S	A rich green, sharp perforations	185.00
4	88	S	A very pretty stamp; no gum skips	440.00

Figure 9.10 Emphasizing column heads with boldface type. This version of the table in Figure 9.9 emphasizes the column heads with boldface type.

contrast between the heads and the cell content — but not so different that the heads don't seem to belong to the same table. The example in Figure 9.10 does the job adequately by bolding the column heads.

Avoid the temptation to overuse all caps in tables. Tables are already rigid and square enough — there's little reason to emphasize that rigidity and squareness with all caps. Besides, the additional contrast

Cell data and column heads in all caps

LOT #	CAT #	CONDITION	COMMENTS	PRICE
1	137	S	A FINE EXAMPLE	1740.00
2	149	XF/S	CLEAN & SHARP	500.00
3	430	XF/S	A RICH GREEN, SHARP PERFORATIONS	185.00
4	88	S	A VERY PRETTY STAMP; NO GUM SKIPS	440.00

Cell data and column heads with initial caps

Lot #	Cat #	Condition	Comments	Price
1	137	S	A fine example	1740.00
2	149	XF/S	Clean & sharp	500.00
3	430	XF/S	A rich green, sharp perforations	185.00
4	88	S	A very pretty stamp; no gum skips	440.00

Figure 9.11 Avoid using all caps in tables. Text in all caps makes the cell data harder to distinguish and takes up more space than lowercase type (or lowercase with initial caps, as shown here).

between letter forms in lowercase or with initial caps will make scanning and reading the table easier (Figure 9.11). Lowercase letters also take less space, as you can see from the relative narrowness of the lowercase table.

ORDER TABLES CONSISTENTLY AND LOGICALLY

Because tables organize data both horizontally and vertically, they offer a number of options for ordering data. For example, you can order a table numerically or alphabetically by the contents of any single row or column. You can also switch around the columns to help readers find the information they need in a logical progression. For example, in Figures 9.9 through 9.11, the table is ordered by the lot number column, from Lot 1 to Lot 10. This makes sense if the designers intend users to refer to this table while the auction is under way, using it as a guide to what's coming up next.

But imagine if the table were designed as a price list to go in a catalog. In that case, it would make more sense to order the table's contents by the catalog number so users could read along in the catalog and refer to the table when necessary (Figure 9.12). It would also make sense to change the order of the columns to place the ordering column leftmost.

USE ALIGNMENT TO INCREASE USABILITY

Tables offer many options for horizontal and vertical alignment of cell contents — in other words, where cell data "sits" in the cell.

Cat #	Lot #	Condition	Comments	Price
27	9	XF	Good example	385.00
88	4	S	A very pretty stamp; no gum skips	440.00
137	1	S	A fine example	1740.00
138	6	VF	Vertical pair	360.00
149	2	XF/S	Clean & sharp	500.00
292	8	VG	Ex-Miller Collection	1150.00
371	5	S	Post Office fresh	460.00
383	7	VF/XF	Small thin lower right corner	225.00
389	10	F/VF	Good centering for this issue	150.00
430	3	XF/S	A rich green, sharp perforations	185.00

Figure 9.12 Ordering a table. In this version, the auction table is ordered by catalog number (rather than by lot number as in the previous figures). This ordering would make more sense if the table appeared in a price list to go in a catalog so users could refer from the catalog to the price list easily. Notice that the order of columns has also changed: *Cat #* is leftmost, since it serves as an index to the table data.

Columns with numbers are right-aligned to emphasize numerical order.

Column with condition code is center-aligned.

Column with text is left-aligned.

Figure 9.13 Aligning a table. The stamp catalog table has been revised with a more appropriate pattern of alignment to increase readability.

Lot #	Cat #	Condition	Comments	Price
1	137	S	A fine example	1740.00
2	149	XF/S	Clean & sharp	500.00
3	430	XF/S	A rich green, sharp perforations	185.00
4	88	S	A very pretty stamp; no gum skips	440.00
5	371	S	Post Office fresh	460.00
6	138	VF	Vertical pair	360.00
7	383	VF/XF	Small thin lower right corner	225.00
8	292	VG	Ex-Miller Collection	1150.00
9	27	XF	Good example	385.00
10	389	F/VF	Good centering for this issue	150.00

Column with currency is aligned at decimal point.

Vertical alignment. Vertically, different kinds of cell content call for different alignments, and inappropriate alignments can cause significant reductions in usability. For example, consider the table of stamp auction lots in Figure 9.12. All of the columns are left-justified, but that justification might make reading some of the fields more difficult.

In Figure 9.13, the changes we made to the vertical alignment let users scan the numerical columns more easily, particularly in the *Lot #* column, which creates an order for all the rows. Centering the *Condition* column emphasizes the condition code for each stamp. The

Comments column contains only text, so a left alignment makes sense there, just as it would in a list. And the *Price* column, aligned at the decimal point, allows users to distinguish between expensive and inexpensive stamps very quickly.

Horizontal alignment.   Horizontally, it's usually best for the cell data to sit with about an equal amount of space above and below the data, in relation to the cell boundaries. Some typefaces, however, may require some careful manipulation of cell data alignment to give the data a comfortable space in its cell. You want to provide enough space in the cell to accommodate caps, ascenders, and descenders: you wouldn't want anything to extend beyond the cell boundaries or make one row taller than the rest.

As we already discussed, it's best to set cell contents in lowercase type. When doing so, provide roughly equal space between the baseline and the lower cell boundary as between the x-line and the upper cell boundary (see Figure 9.14).

Whatever horizontal alignment you choose, be consistent. The table in Figure 9.15, for example, would probably slow down and confuse users, especially because it doesn't use borders. Notice that the price data is aligned closer to the bottom of its cells, while the matching content in each row is aligned near the tops of the cells. As users read across the rows, it would be difficult to figure out which price goes with which lot.

USE PROXIMITY TO BUILD RELATIONSHIPS BETWEEN DATA

Designing effective tables requires paying attention to both horizontal and vertical distance between a variety of elements, including the cell

Figure 9.14 Using appropriate spacing within cells.   Make sure to use balanced horizontal spacing between text and cell boundaries, accommodating caps, ascenders, and descenders. In most situations, try to space the x-line and the baseline equally from the top and bottom cell boundaries, respectively.

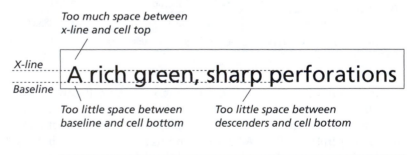

Lot #	Cat #	Condition	Comments	Price
1	137	S	A fine example	1740.00
2	149	XF/S	Clean & sharp	500.00
3	430	XF/S	A rich green, sharp perforations	185.00
4	88	S	A very pretty stamp; no gum skips	440.00
5	371	S	Post Office fresh	460.00
6	138	VF	Vertical pair	360.00
7	383	VF/XF	Small thin lower right corner	225.00
8	292	VG	Ex-Miller Collection	1150.00
9	27	XF	Good example	385.00
10	389	F/VF	Good centering for this issue	150.00

Figure 9.15 Use consistent horizontal alignment in a table. An inconsistent horizontal alignment in cells might confuse users about what row they're reading, particularly if you don't use cell borders.

contents, borders, rows, columns, and column and row heads. Differences in proximity can radically change the way users approach tables because they affect users' perceptions of good figure between the design objects (that is, the cell data) we put in the table.

In Figure 9.16, the distance between the columns and the close proximity of rows give the columns strong figure; the columns appear more prominent than the rows. This encourages users to scan down each column. In Figure 9.17 (page 292), moving the columns closer together and the rows farther apart makes the rows seem the stronger figure, encouraging users to scan across rows.

Either of these approaches might be appropriate. It depends on how you think (or have found out) that users actually want to use the table. Just make sure that you don't put so much space between the rows or columns that users don't recognize the data as a table or have trouble recognizing both rows and columns visually.

Figure 9.16 Creating strong vertical figures. The rows are closer together than the columns here, making the columns a strong figure and encouraging users to scan vertically down the columns.

Lot #	Cat #	Condition	Comments	Price
1	137	S	A fine example	1740.00
2	149	XF/S	Clean & sharp	500.00
3	430	XF/S	A rich green, sharp perforations	185.00
4	88	S	A very pretty stamp; no gum skips	440.00
5	371	S	Post Office fresh	460.00
6	138	VF	Vertical pair	360.00
7	383	VF/XF	Small thin lower right corner	225.00
8	292	VG	Ex-Miller Collection	1150.00
9	27	XF	Good example	385.00
10	389	F/VF	Good centering for this issue	150.00

Figure 9.17 Creating strong horizontal figures.   Closer horizontal proximity and more distance between rows might encourage more horizontal scanning.

Lot #	Cat #	Condition	Comments	Price
1	137	S	A fine example	1740.00
2	149	XF/S	Clean & sharp	500.00
3	430	XF/S	A rich green, sharp perforations	185.00
4	88	S	A very pretty stamp; no gum skips	440.00
5	371	S	Post Office fresh	460.00
6	138	VF	Vertical pair	360.00
7	383	VF/XF	Small thin lower right corner	225.00
8	292	VG	Ex-Miller Collection	1150.00
9	27	XF	Good example	385.00
10	389	F/VF	Good centering for this issue	150.00

USE ENCLOSURE FOR CLARITY AND EMPHASIS

Tables are essentially a grid of rectangles that enclose data, so think carefully about using enclosure to create successful tables.

Borders.   We often default to using borders to emphasize the enclosure of cells, but in many designs, borders can actually obscure the data. After all, a border is an additional positive element that users must decipher. And borders take up extra positive space in the design, requiring additional negative space to keep them from crowding the table's contents.

Sometimes tables work better with limited or selective use of positive borders, relying on the alignment of cell contents and the negative space between cells, rows, and columns to emphasize the visual structure of the grid. Besides, using borders only selectively gives additional opportunities to emphasize data or encourage the users to see the table in a certain way.

Consider the tables in Figures 9.18 and 9.19. Both tables look cleaner and easier to scan than the previous versions of this table that included a full grid of borders. The single horizontal rule in Figure 9.18 gives extra emphasis to the column heads. The single vertical rule in Figure 9.19 emphasizes the *Lot* column, helping users locate the lot that

Lot #	Cat #	Condition	Comments	Price
1	137	S	A fine example	1740.00
2	149	XF/S	Clean & sharp	500.00
3	430	XF/S	A rich green, sharp perforations	185.00
4	88	S	A very pretty stamp; no gum skips	440.00
5	371	S	Post Office fresh	460.00
6	138	VF	Vertical pair	360.00
7	383	VF/XF	Small thin lower right corner	225.00
8	292	VG	Ex-Miller Collection	1150.00
9	27	XF	Good example	385.00
10	389	F/VF	Good centering for this issue	150.00

Figure 9.18 Emphasizing column heads with horizontal rule. The horizontal rule emphasizes the column heads.

Lot #	Cat #	Condition	Comments	Price
1	137	S	A fine example	1740.00
2	149	XF/S	Clean & sharp	500.00
3	430	XF/S	A rich green, sharp perforations	185.00
4	88	S	A very pretty stamp; no gum skips	440.00
5	371	S	Post Office fresh	460.00
6	138	VF	Vertical pair	360.00
7	383	VF/XF	Small thin lower right corner	225.00
8	292	VG	Ex-Miller Collection	1150.00
9	27	XF	Good example	385.00
10	389	F/VF	Good centering for this issue	150.00

Figure 9.19 Using vertical rule to emphasize a column. The vertical rule emphasizes the lot number column.

is being auctioned. Of course, in comparison, this de-emphasizes the other columns and column heads, making them clearly subsidiary to the lot number.

Shading.   Reverse text or shading can also be used for enclosure. In Figure 9.20 (page 294), we shift the balance of emphasis back to the column heads by enclosing the column heads with a dense black field and using reverse text (for more on reverse text, see Chapter 6). This brings the focus back to the columns as strong figures while making the *Lot* column a slightly less strong figure.

Figure 9.20 Using reverse text for emphasis. The reverse text places emphasis on column heads.

Lot #	Cat #	Condition	Comments	Price
1	137	S	A fine example	1740.00
2	149	XF/S	Clean & sharp	500.00
3	430	XF/S	A rich green, sharp perforations	185.00
4	88	S	A very pretty stamp; no gum skips	440.00
5	371	S	Post Office fresh	460.00
6	138	VF	Vertical pair	360.00
7	383	VF/XF	Small thin lower right corner	225.00
8	292	VG	Ex-Miller Collection	1150.00
9	27	XF	Good example	385.00
10	389	F/VF	Good centering for this issue	150.00

Shading alternate rows in a gray screen or in color makes the rows a strong figure, while still not overwhelming the stronger elements of reverse-text column heads and the bordered *Lot* column (Figure 9.21). If you decide that the columns are more important to users than the rows, shade alternate columns instead. You can also use shading as a tool for emphasis.

Enclosure is another method that can be used to inset tables within tables, usually by merging cells. One of the problems with the example we've been using is the awkward *Condition* code for each

---

DESIGN TIP

Shading

Be careful when using shading in tables:

- **Keep the shading very light** (10 to 20 percent gray and light colors). If you use more than 20 percent, the shading will undercut the figure-ground contrast necessary to read the text. Use just enough shading to distinguish the shaded rows or columns from the unshaded rows or columns.

- **Pay attention to production technology.** Shading on computer monitors or on printed documents using spot-color inks typically produces a consistent, smooth color. But with the coarser printing technologies (like laser printing) or process color, shading can create a very noticeable dot pattern that might distract users. Even with spot-color printing, sometimes the printer will use a screen (a fine pattern of dots) of a darker ink to produce a lighter shade. (See Chapter 8 for more information on spot colors and process color.)

Lot #	Cat #	Condition	Comments	Price
1	137	S	A fine example	1740.00
2	149	XF/S	Clean & sharp	500.00
3	430	XF/S	A rich green, sharp perforations	185.00
4	88	S	A very pretty stamp; no gum skips	440.00
5	371	S	Post Office fresh	460.00
6	138	VF	Vertical pair	360.00
7	383	VF/XF	Small thin lower right corner	225.00
8	292	VG	Ex-Miller Collection	1150.00
9	27	XF	Good example	385.00
10	389	F/VF	Good centering for this issue	150.00

Lot #	Cat #	Condition	Comments	Price
1	137	S	A fine example	1740.00
2	149	XF/S	Clean & sharp	500.00
3	430	XF/S	A rich green, sharp perforations	185.00
4	88	S	A very pretty stamp; no gum skips	440.00
5	371	S	Post Office fresh	460.00
6	138	VF	Vertical pair	360.00
7	383	VF/XF	Small thin lower right corner	225.00
8	292	VG	Ex-Miller Collection	1150.00
9	27	XF	Good example	385.00
10	389	F/VF	Good centering for this issue	150.00

Lot #	Cat #	Condition	Comments	Price
1	137	S	A fine example	1740.00
2	149	XF/S	Clean & sharp	500.00
3	430	XF/S	A rich green, sharp perforations	185.00
4	88	S	A very pretty stamp; no gum skips	440.00
5	371	S	Post Office fresh	460.00
6	138	VF	Vertical pair	360.00
7	383	VF/XF	Small thin lower right corner	225.00
8	292	VG	Ex-Miller Collection	1150.00
9	27	XF	Good example	385.00
10	389	F/VF	Good centering for this issue	150.00

Figure 9.21 Using shading for emphasis. Shading can help distinguish between rows or columns. It can also be used for emphasis, drawing users' attention to the most rare and expensive stamps.

Figure 9.22 Combining several table design techniques. Here, the conditions of the stamps are provided in a legend, and an embedded table gives users a quick visual sense of the conditions of the stamps.

Lot #	Cat #	Condition					Comments	Price
		S	XF	VF	F	VG		
1	137	○					A fine example	1740.00
2	149	○	○				Clean & sharp	500.00
3	430	○	○				A rich green, sharp perforations	185.00
4	88	○					A very pretty stamp; no gum skips	440.00
5	371	○					Post Office fresh	460.00
6	138			○			Vertical pair	360.00
7	383	○	○				Small thin lower right corner	225.00
8	292					○	Ex-Miller Collection	1150.00
9	27		○				Good example	385.00
10	389			○	○		Good centering for this issue	150.00

Conditions

S:	Superb
XF:	Extra Fine
VF:	Very Fine
F:	Fine
VG:	Very Good

stamp, which could really use some clear explanation. If we use a legend to accompany the table, we can create a visual guide that might help users diagnose each stamp's condition more readily (see Figure 9.22). This table creates a new row at the top with a single merged cell that contains the *Condition* column head and adds subcolumn heads for the condition labels: S, XF, VF, F, and VG. It also uses a symbol to mark the condition of the stamp, rather than the more complex condition code, which is explained in a legend at the left. It employs vertical, alternating shading to help readers scan down the *Condition* columns if they are looking for stamps of a particular condition. But because these vertical shadings make reading across the rows more difficult, we've added horizontal borders between the rows as well.

Designing Tables for the Screen

Most of the features of tables we've discussed can work equally well on paper or on screens. However, the HyperText Markup Language (HTML) behind websites has some constraints. HTML includes tags to specify the following features of tables:

- *Table:* width, height, alignment, and background color
- *Row:* height and background color
- *Cell:* width, height, alignment, cell spacing (the distance between cells), cell padding (the distance between a cell's content and its boundaries), and background color
- *Cell borders:* width

In addition, in HTML we can merge cells by using the *rowspan* attribute (to merge a cell with one or more below or above it) and the *colspan* attribute (to merge a cell with one or more to its right or left). However, most web designers avoid using standard HTML borders, which include a shadowing effect that most users find quaint (as in "That's so 1995!").

Cascading Style Sheets (CSS) allow much more flexible designs of tables in web pages, including greater control over borders. But their implementation is somewhat more complex than the scope of this book allows. See a good CSS reference, such as the W3C's online CSS description (<www.w3.org/Style/CSS>), for more information on how to use CSS for table layouts.

Finally, dynamic websites (those using a database to hold their contents) can use sortable tables, which are convenient for users in many situations. Usually, users sort the table by clicking on a column head, which then re-sorts the rows according to the contents of that column. These tables are particularly common in online web mail applications, which often use tables to display the messages waiting to be read, with columns for sender, date, subject, and so on. They require computer scripting to work, however, which places them beyond the expertise of some document designers.

Forms

Not many of us get through more than a few days without encountering a form to fill out. In fact, the familiarity of forms sometimes breeds contempt. When a form is badly designed, asks ambiguous questions, or requires repetitive information, we often find it annoying and distracting to complete.

But forms hold an important place in the exchange of data from users to producers of documents. Forms, after all, are the medium through which users communicate important data to producers. Companies rely on forms to gain important information about their customers, whether users wish to order a product, register it, or complain about it. Governments rely on forms to gather information from citizens — anything from Selective Service registration to taxes. Hospitals use forms to gain vital information from patients, such as allergic reactions and medical histories. And most employers use forms to gather information from their employees.

As we said at the beginning of this chapter, the difficulty in designing forms lies in the fact that they have two sets of users: those who fill out the form and those who must gather the data from the filled-out form. This two-way relationship embodied in forms can make them complex to design. For the form to gather data accurately, it must work well from both perspectives.

Users who fill out forms must understand the form well enough to enter accurate and complete data. If the form's design de-emphasizes an important data entry field, for example, users might skip it. If the relationship is unclear between the questions the form asks and the spaces it provides for answers, the users might provide unusable data. The design also must adequately instruct users in how to fill out the form. Bagin and Rose (1991) reported that nearly half of the users they surveyed complained that forms were too complicated and that instructions were unclear. Good design can help minimize both of these complaints.

At the other end of the process, form processors — whether human or computerized — must be able to extract the data quickly and efficiently, usually so it can be entered into a database. For forms that will be read by human eyes, this means creating a design that a person can scan quickly and accurately. For computer-read paper forms, this means creating a design that computer scanners can read effectively and that optical character recognition (OCR) software can translate into editable text with high accuracy. Online forms require that each answer field must have a unique and accurate name by which a computer can identify its contents and populate the correct field in the corresponding database.

Components of Forms

Designing good forms requires knowing a bit about their typical parts and the conventions they use for gathering information in data acquisition fields.

FORM AREAS

Most forms have the following four main parts (see Figure 9.23):

- *Masthead:* The masthead can include the form's title, as well as a logo or the name of the sponsoring organization.
- *Instructions:* Users need to know why and how to fill out the form, as well as what to do with it when they're finished. A section at the beginning of the form typically provides these explanations and directions.
- *Data acquisition area:* This area typically makes up the bulk of the form and includes all the requests for information. It often ends with a request for a signature and date, which asks users to authorize their responses.

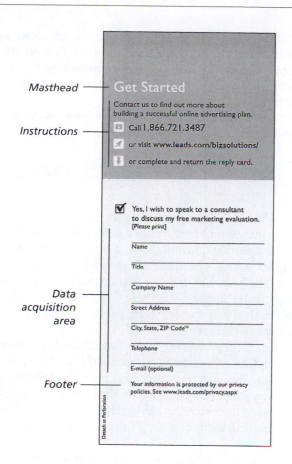

Figure 9.23 Typical parts of a form. Forms typically include four essential parts: a masthead, instructions, a data acquisition area, and a footer.

"Point Customers to Your Business," Leads.com, <www.leads.com/bizsolutions>.

- **Footer:** The footer can include a variety of information. For the user, it might include final instructions about how to submit the form. For the organization, it might include a form number or version control information.

Not all forms require all four parts, and some parts might be abbreviated. For example, a simple magazine subscription card might have a very short masthead ("Subscribe to our magazine today!"), little in the way of introduction or instructions, and no footer. Still, users have seen so many of these forms that they usually have little trouble understanding that all they must do is fill out the data acquisition area and drop the form in the mail.

DATA FIELDS

Forms gather data through a series of data fields in the data acquisition area. Each data field has two parts: a **prompt** and a **response**.

The prompt asks the user for information, and the user responds by supplying the information in a way the organization can process efficiently. Form designers must create prompts that encourage the appropriate response from users, as well as areas that constrain the response to the desired kind of information.

Although forms can look very complicated, only two kinds of data fields are usually sufficient to fulfill these needs:

- Alphanumeric entry fields
- Option fields

Alphanumeric entry fields.   Alphanumeric entry fields prompt users to write a response in text or numbers within a designated space. That space might appear as a simple horizontal line, a box, or even a negative space that implies a box. The space allowed for response constrains the length of the response, but in general, users can enter or write whatever they choose in the field. These fields work best when gathering information that varies widely from person to person, such as address information or comments.

Forms designed for OCR processing might further constrain users with a box or implied box for each letter or number of the user's response so computer software can decipher the letters more easily. And computer forms (such as those on websites) can constrain the contents of alphanumeric fields by allowing users to enter only a certain number of characters in a field or requiring them to enter a valid e-mail address.

Option fields.   While alphanumeric entry fields allow users to enter whatever text or numbers they choose, option fields restrict user responses to one or a few choices among a list of options. These fields allow organizations to gather information quickly on topics that are somewhat consistent from person to person, such as gender (one choice out of two) or state of residence (one choice out of fifty).

Option fields increase the accuracy of response, but they might also exclude potential responses. For example, one doesn't usually see an "other" box under gender for intersexual persons, and a lot of controversy has arisen over the options government forms provide to ask about a user's ethnicity or race.

The most common form of option field is a checkbox. Checkboxes prompt users to enter a check mark, an *x*, or a tick mark in a square beside responses in a list of options. Checkboxes are common when there are several possible answers to one question.

For other questions, you may want to constrain the response to one option. One example is the ubiquitous machine-readable multiple-choice test form, which includes option fields as ovals to be filled in with a pencil. If the user fills in more than one oval, it typically invalidates that question.

For paper forms, you must inform users in the instructions whether they can make multiple responses or are restricted to one. HTML forms, however, can manage these responses automatically. A list of HTML checkboxes will allow users to mark more than one choice. But HTML uses radio button fields to constrain users to one response: if users change their mind and click on a different option than the one they chose initially, the form automatically deselects the first radio button and selects the new one. Online forms can also use drop-down menus, which similarly allow users to choose only one option from a list.

Designing Forms

Designing successful forms involves paying attention to at least these issues:

- Include clearly designed information about the form, including its purpose, procedures, and organizational sponsor.
- Group data fields visually.
- Use alignment to encourage consistent and complete responses.
- Design response spaces that encourage accurate responses.

INCLUDE CLEARLY DESIGNED INFORMATION ABOUT THE FORM

People don't often enjoy filling out forms, so they like to know *why* they have to do so and what they should do with the form after they fill it out. These rhetorical and instructional functions are usually carried at the top of the form. A clear visual design will draw users' attention to this area of the form and encourage them to fill out the form attentively and accurately.

The Avon Walk for Breast Cancer form in Figure 9.24 on page 302, for example, has a difficult rhetorical situation: it must convince users to become members of a voluntary organization and donate money to it. The form employs a distinctive bar of reversed text at the top to attract users' attention. Then it formats the benefits of participating as a series of pictures with captions detailing four good reasons: "Fun, Friendship, Heart and Hope." Only after this rhetorical argument do the data fields of the form begin.

Different forms call for different approaches. The Internal Revenue Service, for example, doesn't spend much time persuading people to fill

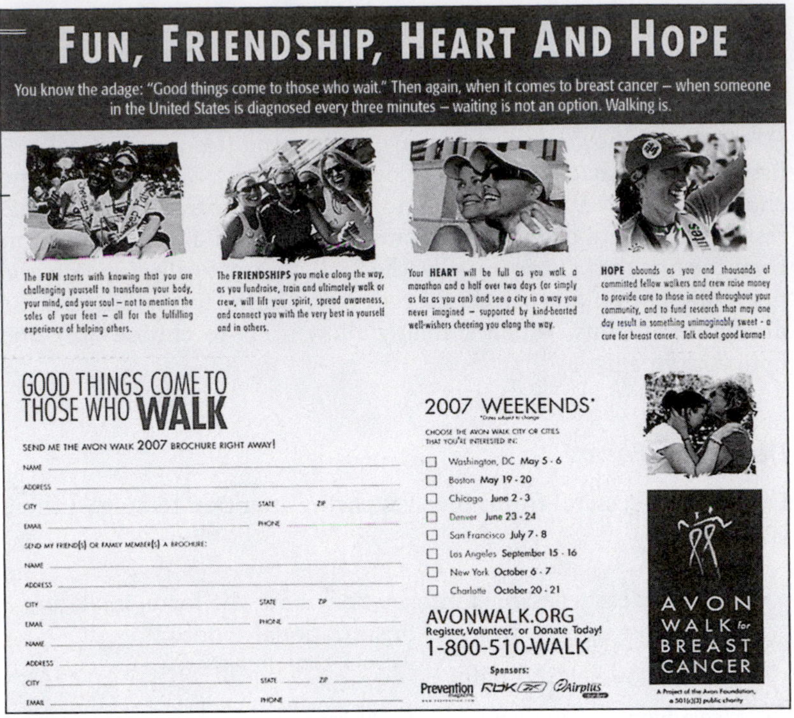

A clear call to action in a vibrant pink field asks people to take part in a walk to support breast cancer research.

Pictures of participants might give users a desire to help out as well.

Figure 9.24 Design and forms.
Visual design can draw attention to the *why* of the form.

Avon Walk for Breast Cancer, "Walk Don't Wait."

out *its* forms because the penalties for not doing so are pretty severe. But IRS forms gather very complex information, so they typically include more explanations and instructions about *how* to fill out the form and *what* to do with it. In fact, IRS forms come with separate instruction booklets that are much longer than the forms themselves.

GROUP DATA FIELDS VISUALLY

When forms ask for many different pieces of information, users may get tired and frustrated. And the more tired they get, the sloppier their answers to questions can be. Good form designs provide resting places for users by visually and logically grouping the information requested. For example, the United States Postal Service change of address form (Figure 9.25) groups three different kinds of information:

- Personal information (including fields for last name, first name, and business name)
- Information about the user's old address (including fields for the street address, apartment number, city, state, and zip)
- Information about the user's new address (including fields for the street address, apartment number, city, state, and zip)

Personal information

Old address information

New address information

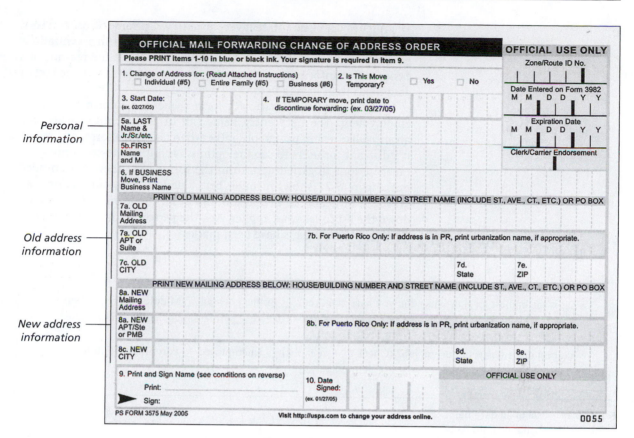

Figure 9.25 Logically grouped fields. This form groups together different kinds of information in a logical way.

U.S. Postal Service, "Official Mail Forwarding Change of Address Order."

This structure makes sense: to change your address, the USPS needs to know who you are, where you used to live, and where you're living now. But the form also emphasizes this structure visually by including a broader-than-usual border and a heading before the old mailing address section and the new mailing address section.

We can use a variety of techniques to visually emphasize the logical structure of the data. Simple descriptive or numbered headings, much as you might include in a straightforward business report, can do wonders. Alternately, we can use heavy rules (lines) between sections or enclose sections with borders, shading, or negative space.

USE ALIGNMENT TO ENCOURAGE CONSISTENT AND COMPLETE RESPONSES

One of the biggest challenges users face when filling out forms is simply seeing all the data fields and recognizing what they still have to fill out. Users often unintentionally skip areas because the fields are misaligned or scattered across the page or screen.

Aligned data fields make it very obvious when some fields have been filled out and others haven't. Aligned data fields also help organizations gather information efficiently from forms, for the same reasons: it's easier to find information by running your eyes down an aligned set of data fields than having to look all over the place.

Figure 9.26 shows part of a form requesting information about employment. The data entry fields (all of them option fields) are arranged like text in paragraphs rather than fields on a form. As a result, it's difficult for users to see the options, and it's time-consuming for organizations to gather data from the forms after they've been filled out. Figure 9.27 shows a much better design. Now the options are arranged vertically, so the person filling out the form can easily look down the list to see what applies. And the person reading the form can quickly see what items have been marked.

What is the highest level of education you have achieved? __Primary school __Middle school __High school __Trade school __Associate's degree __Bachelor's degree __Professional degree __Doctorate

What best describes your current job? (Check all that apply.) __Unemployed __Part time __Full time __Hourly wages __Contract __Salary __Self-employed

Figure 9.26 Misaligned data fields.
A form with misaligned data fields makes it difficult for users to see all of the options.

What is the highest level of education you have achieved?
❏ Primary school
❏ Middle school
❏ High school
❏ Trade school
❏ Associate's degree
❏ Bachelor's degree
❏ Professional degree
❏ Doctorate

What best describes your current job? (Check all that apply.)
❏ Part time
❏ Full time
❏ Hourly wages
❏ Contract
❏ Self-employed
❏ Salary
❏ Unemployed

Figure 9.27 A revision of the form in Figure 9.26, with aligned data fields.
Aligning the data fields makes the form easier to use. The users filling out the form can more easily see what options are available, and the users processing the form can quickly record what options have been marked.

DESIGN RESPONSE SPACES TO ENCOURAGE ACCURATE RESPONSES

Users need a space in which to respond to prompts appropriately and conveniently. Some of the biggest hassles when filling out forms involve recognizing which response fields match with which prompts and having an adequate amount of space in which to respond fully. Use proximity and enclosure to create a relationship between the prompt and the response field and to create a usable space in which to respond. Figure 9.28 provides options for linking prompts to responses in alphanumeric forms. Any of these designs can work successfully, and each has its own advantages and disadvantages:

- *Placing the prompt on a response line* uses proximity to create a strong visual relationship between prompt and response. But it takes up a lot of room on the line.

- *Placing the prompt below the line* also creates a strong relationship between prompt and response, without taking up unnecessary room. But this design runs the risk that users won't understand which prompt goes with which enclosed space: the user might enter a response in the space below the prompt rather than on the line above it.

- *"Hanging" the prompt from the top of a box* keeps it out of the way, and the box's borders enclose the prompt/response pair so

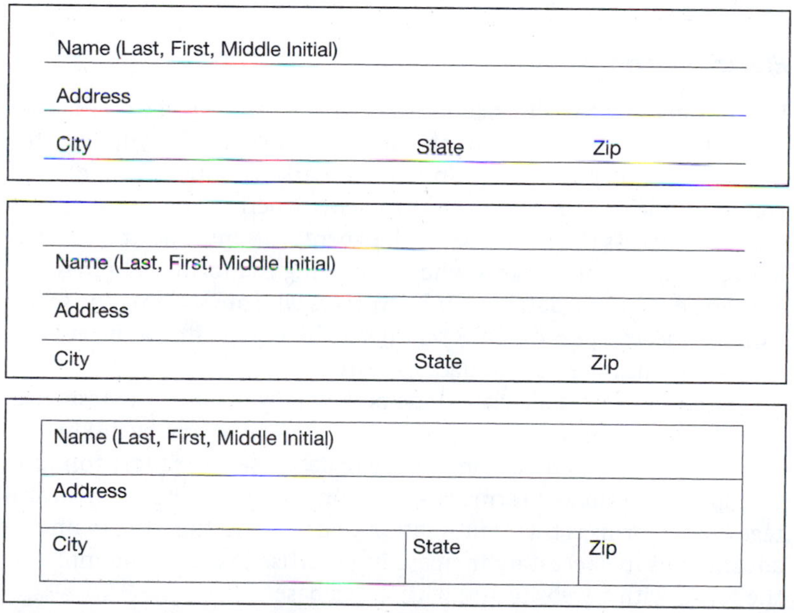

Prompts on lines

Prompts below lines

Prompts "hanging" from top of box

Figure 9.28 Arranging prompts and responses.   Here are some options for creating relationships between the prompt and the response.

strongly that few wouldn't know where to put a response. But it requires more vertical space (so users can write beneath the prompt), and it creates a boxy-looking form.

Regardless of what design you choose, be sure to provide users with adequate space in which to enter their response. Some personal names and city names, for example, can be remarkably long; you must design the form to accommodate the longest entry possible but still fit the form within the design of the page and the format of the document.

As for option fields, most printed forms use check mark boxes, although some might use a short blank line instead. The convention for check mark boxes is remarkably strong, and most Western users will recognize the box as a place in which to make a mark.

TEST FORMS

Test your forms with real users before you send out the forms into the world.

Be sure to *test* your forms with real users before you send out the forms into the world. A frustrating, misleading, or inaccurate form can cause significant headaches to many people, including users who try to fill out the form, secondary users who try to use the resulting (usually faulty) data, and everyone else who has to mend bridges and clean up afterward.

Even a short usability test will give you valuable insights into how well users respond to your form, allowing you to solve problems *before* they get out of hand. For more information on conducting usability tests, see Chapter 10.

Electronic Forms

Paper forms have two distinct disadvantages. First, they rely on the clarity of users' handwriting, which can be illegible or idiosyncratic; too large or too small; or written in felt-tip markers, faint pencil, or even crayon. Handwriting can cause problems whether humans or OCR scanners process the forms. Second, paper forms must be processed by hand, either by the workers who are reading the form and physically entering data into a database or by workers who are sending the forms through sheet feeders on OCR scanners. These steps are inefficient and lead to significant errors in data capture.

Electronic media alleviate these problems by making user responses more legible (to people and especially to computers) and by linking the form more directly and automatically to databases. The most common example of automated forms is a form on a website. The main advantage of web forms is their automation of data collection; the main disadvantage is the necessary increase in expertise to create and integrate the forms with a website and with a database.

Web forms add one significant new element to forms: a set of buttons for users to submit the form to the database or cancel their entries. The **submit button** takes the place of instructions on a paper form for submitting the form by hand, fax, or mail. The submit button also authorizes the form, taking the place of the signature on a paper form. For this reason, submit buttons almost always appear at the bottom of a form. It's also a good idea to include a **cancel button**, which resets the form and allows the users to begin again if they've made a mistake.

Most web forms share many visual conventions with paper forms, and as a result, the same principles apply to their visual design. The complexity arises in making the automated links between the form fields and the database fields, which requires expertise in computer scripting languages, database design, and web design. Perhaps this is why many web forms are often badly designed, relying on the basic visual default settings of HTML and common web browsers.

In addition, some forms are designed to be filled out on a computer and then printed out for traditional submission. Adobe's Portable Document Format (PDF) allows for the creation of such forms, with alphanumeric fields in which a user can type and option entry fields on which a user can click to set a check mark or radio button. All other areas of the form (layout, prompts, introduction, instructions) are protected from user input. Microsoft Word provides a similar functionality.

Of course, this kind of electronic form must still be processed just like traditional paper forms. But they can be very convenient in situations where only a few dozen or several hundred forms must be processed, or when the organization would like to distribute the form by e-mail.

Exercises

1. Talk to a researcher at your university who uses survey forms as part of her or his scholarship. Consider asking these questions:

   a. In what way can the design of the form affect responses?

   b. What particular problems do you frequently see in form designs?

   c. Have you ever had an experience where the design of the form interfered with or affected your results?

2. Find three forms on the Web and critique their visual design. How do these forms share the conventions of print forms? How do they differ from print forms? Are there features common to print forms that are counterproductive for web environments?

3. Choose a small employer or manufacturer in your community and imagine you work there as a personnel manager. You've used traditional paper job application forms for years. Given your situation and resources, would your company be best served by sticking with the traditional paper forms or shifting to an online application system? What are the advantages and disadvantages of each approach to gathering data about prospective employees?

4. Imagine that you work as a design consultant for a movie theater chain, and you're designing a more successful movie listing for its theaters to place in local newspapers. Given the client's desire to draw moviegoers and the moviegoers' desires to find a movie to see, how would you advise listing the movies in a newspaper? In an unordered list? In an ordered list? If the latter, in what order? Most recent to oldest? Alphabetical? What are the ramifications of your choices?

Work Cited

Bagin, C. B., and A. M. Rose. "Worst Forms Unearthed: Deciphering Bureaucratic Gobbledygook." *Modern Maturity* (February–March, 1991): 64–66.

Further Reading

Barnett, Robert. *Forms for People: Designing Forms That People Can Use.* Portland, OR: Business Forms Management Association, 2005.

Meyer, Joachim, Marcia Kuskin Shamo, and Daniel Gopher. "Information Structure and the Relative Efficacy of Tables and Graphs." *Human Factors* 41.4 (1999): 570–87.

State of Ohio. "Visual Communication for Forms Design." Forms Management Paper No. 3. Online: <gsdprint.das.ohio.gov/Forms/visual.pdf >.

W3C. *Cascading Style Sheets.* Online: <www.w3.org/Style/CSS/>.

Zimmerman, Beverly B., and Jessica R. Schultz. "A Study of the Effectiveness of Information Design Principles Applied to Clinical Research Questionnaires." *Technical Communication* 47 (2000): 177–94.

CHAPTER 10

Projects

In the spring of 2006, a team of collaborators that included scholars, graduate students, editorial board members, library staff, and potential users began work on a big document design project: an online edition of a nineteenth-century magazine that scholars and students all over the world would be able to use. The team faced typical technological and editorial challenges, but the most difficult part was coordinating the efforts of so many people.

The first thing they had to do was *get organized*. Working with all the project stakeholders, the team conducted research and developed a plan. Figure 10.1 is a Program Evaluation and Review Technique (PERT) chart of the critical first four months of the project. It shows how the project managers divided into four teams (Training, Editing, Technology, and Administration) and how each team's tasks were coordinated. (For more information on PERT charts, see Chapter 7.) The chart and the planning process that led to it helped team members understand what to do, when to do it, and how their efforts contributed to the whole project.

Like this project, all design projects are complex activities, requiring us to juggle a lot of variables. As a designer, not only do you need to think about the principles of design and make decisions about format, medium, color, and typography—some of the concepts you read about in Units One and Two—but you also have to keep in mind big questions like these:

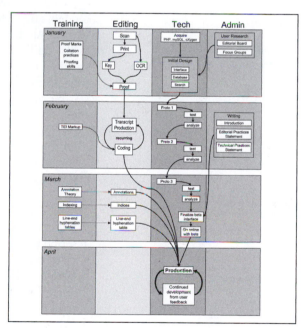

Figure 10.1 A Program Evaluation and Review Technique (PERT) chart.   This PERT chart shows the project management of a document design project. Organization and planning are critical to the successful management of large projects.

- Who are the clients? Why do they want us to create this document? What are their particular requirements, needs, and agendas?

- Who are the users? What are their needs and situations?

- When does the project have to be finished? How much will it cost? Or from another perspective, how much time and money do we have to work with?

- Who else will be working on this project? What are their responsibilities? What is their schedule?

- How will the design team track our progress on the project so we can know if we're on task and on schedule?

All of these questions are issues of **project management**. In practical terms, they center around how you're going to *do* a design project. To deal with these issues effectively, it's absolutely necessary to approach design projects with a good set of project management skills. Even if you're not the project manager yourself, understanding project management techniques will help you work successfully within a project team.

In this chapter we discuss two common project management models and then introduce a model that combines the best of both worlds. Along the way, we'll discuss some of the project management skills you'll need either to manage a design project yourself or to work within a project that is managed by someone else. These skills include scheduling projects, conducting user research, performing usability testing, working with design teams, and documenting your plans and progress.

Project Management

Project management is the collective term for the techniques we use to *define*, *control*, and *assess* work on a project. Because many documents respond to specific situations and problems, it's easy to understand why they're often thought of as *design projects*. Design and project management go hand in hand—particularly when a design project is large enough to require the coordination of complex factors to bring a document to reality. The most important of these factors are people, time, and money.

- *People:* All document design projects involve clients, users, and a designer, but large projects typically include a design team whose members have various responsibilities for creating content, conducting research, and creating the design. Project management coordinates the efforts of a design team.

- *Time:* Projects take place in a finite period of time, from initial concept to final execution. Project management helps determine how much time is required to do the job, as well as how to break up the time and tasks into reasonable, manageable, and measurable units. Project management also estimates how much personnel time is necessary for a design team to complete a project.

- *Money:* Design projects take place in a real world where people and resources cost money. Project management helps to predict or estimate project costs. Even small projects that require little production cost might require considerable personnel costs.

Project management will help you evaluate and control the development of your design projects. Without conscious project management efforts, you risk creating unsuccessful finished documents.

Working with Design Teams

As a document designer you might work alone on a project, particularly if it's a small-scale or a low-level design project. In those situations, you'll have to think and act quickly and assume all the roles of project management yourself. But more often you'll work with a *team* of people, all focused on creating a successful document.

This design team might include people with a variety of roles:

- Document designers
- Writers or content contributors
- Illustrators
- Editors
- Subject matter experts (SMEs)

The structure of the team might range from hierarchical to egalitarian, but typically all of these people will work under the direction of a project manager who coordinates the team's efforts and serves as the client's primary contact person. As the document designer, you might also be the project manager yourself, or you might work for a project manager. Each member of the design team is an important contributor to creating a successful document. Ideally, each is an expert in his or her own area and has valuable insights and vital skills to offer to the project.

Communicating with Your Design Team

Anytime a group of people is involved in a project, clear communication is absolutely essential. Even if the design team includes members working remotely, most teams have at least one face-to-face kickoff meeting to begin a design project. Your team might need to have regularly scheduled meetings or meetings scheduled at important stages of the project. Plan on attending all team meetings and keeping good notes about what was discussed. Document your progress and efforts so everyone knows what you're up to and what you've accomplished. If everyone does this, the entire team should have a good sense of the team's progress.

Especially if members are working remotely, consider setting up an e-mail distribution list or listserv. Doing so allows members to send a message to one e-mail address, which then broadcasts the message to the rest of the list members.

Your team also might consider starting a team **blog**, **wiki**, or **content management system (CMS)** in which to track your project online:

- A blog is a web-enabled diary in which people can report their progress, ask questions, and share information. A project blog can serve as an ongoing progress report for the project, making more formal progress reports less necessary. Free blog services include blogger (<www.blogger.com>) and wordpress (<www.wordpress.com>).

- A wiki (from the Hawaiian word *wikiwiki*, meaning "quick") is a rapid web page–building system that allows team members to create new pages or contribute to established ones quickly, with little or no coding. Wikis can become a useful dynamic space in which to build a team knowledge base or to archive design prototypes. Free wiki hosting services include pbwiki (<www.pbwiki.com>) and wikidot (<www.wikidot.com>).

- A CMS is a web-enabled space that allows members to upload and organize documents such as progress reports, drafts, and content provided by SMEs. A CMS usually includes an e-mail distribution list and calendar functions, making it a good choice for project management. For student group design projects, a useful free CMS is Yahoo!Groups (<groups.yahoo.com>).

Your employer might also have invested in dedicated project management software, which helps teams organize and document their efforts. Whatever your situation, look around for ways to communicate better with your project team and take advantage of whatever tools you find.

Models of Project Management

Each project requires its own unique approach. But most project managers agree that there are two main schools of thought in project management. The *waterfall model* tries to control project development by creating a formal plan and set of specifications for the document before any drafting or visual design actually takes place. The plan and specifications govern the allocation of people, time, and money to the project. The *iterative model* of project management begins to create prototype documents at the beginning of the project and solicits user feedback to help control the direction of the project. In the sections that follow, you will see how each approach has its own strengths and weaknesses.

The Waterfall Model

In the waterfall model, project managers organize a project as a linear series of sequential phases from initial research and planning through delivering the finished product. This is called a *waterfall* because each stage is considered relatively unitary; like water cascading from one rock to another, the project completes one phase before going on to the next.

The waterfall model organizes each project around the same general design process. JoAnn T. Hackos, a well-known proponent of a waterfall model for technical communication project management, suggests that this process has five stages (28–29; see Figure 10.2):

- *Information planning:* The project managers gather all possible information about the project and users and then write planning documents that describe the project in detail, create a project timeline, define the deliverables to be created, and assess what personnel will be needed.

- *Content specification:* The project managers create a document detailing the proposed contents for the deliverables proposed in the information planning stage.

- *Implementation:* The project team creates the deliverables specified in the content specification stage, taking them through several drafts.

- *Production:* The project managers see the deliverables through production, often through a professional printer.

- *Evaluation:* The project team looks back over the project to learn from its successes and mistakes.

Figure 10.2 The waterfall model of project management. In the waterfall model of project management, the design process is mapped out linearly; each phase is completed before moving on to the next.

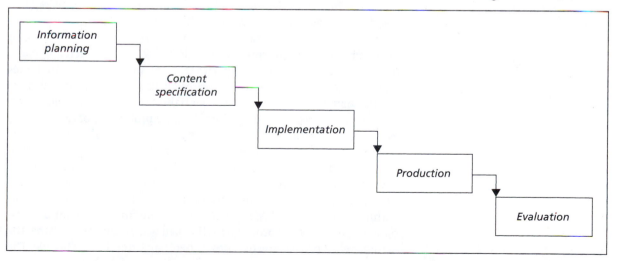

This model gives considerable control to the project manager. The planning and specification stages allow for accurate estimations of time and costs. The staging, with its clear milestones and project documentation (such as the planning documents, the specifications document, and periodic progress reports), helps the project manager assess whether the project is on track, on time, and on budget. The extensive project documentation also promotes good communication between the project team and the client. And the evaluation at the end gives the project team an opportunity for reflection and learning so their next project will be more successful than the last.

However, Hackos acknowledges that the waterfall model has some limitations, mostly when it comes to meeting client and user needs accurately and quickly. Organizations that are less careful in their management of document design are likely to skimp on planning, but planning shortcuts often lead to a content specification that doesn't accurately respond to users' needs or the client's objectives. The result could be wasting a lot of time and money on something that doesn't work (40). Even with good planning, the lack of user input early in the process can lead to inadequate specifications. Waterfall models also assume a relatively long development process. Hackos uses the example of a six-month, 1,000-hour project. The length of this process means waterfall models can have trouble delivering a product quickly and responding to rapidly changing user needs.

The Iterative Model

If we look at how they actually work, most design teams push forward a bit, look back to see where they've come from, then push forward a bit more. This gradually progressing series of actions and reflections, known as **iterations**, is often called **post-process** because it recognizes creative work as cyclical rather than linear (Figure 10.3).

The iterative model takes advantage of the tendency to work in cycles, gradually progressing toward a desired goal. One such approach, **Rapid Application Development (RAD)**, was first proposed by James Martin as an alternative to the waterfall model in software design. Rather than spending time on sequential stages of research, planning, and specifications, RAD jumps into creating prototypes of the product, which are then shown to prospective users or even released as introductory or **beta** versions of the product. The users' feedback then guides the development of the final product. Whereas the waterfall approach usually assumes that a project will take several months, RAD provides a product that meets most users' most urgent needs within 60 to 90 days. RAD uses a rigidly finite time frame for a development project: if the project isn't finished within that time frame, the designer eliminates some features rather than extend the schedule. The

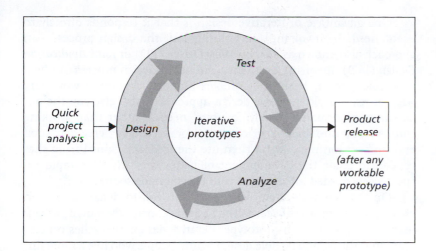

Figure 10.3 The iterative model of project management.   Each prototype is designed and tested. After the team analyzes the test, they feed the results back into the development of the next prototype.

resulting product may be incomplete or imperfect, but it can be refined in later versions. Iterative approaches such as RAD are particularly popular in the open-source software movement, and some companies have taken iterative design as their primary project development model. Google, for example, often releases beta versions of its software years before rolling out a "final" version, which still undergoes continued development.

In document design terms, iterative design projects typically start with a quick analysis of the rhetorical and practical situation surrounding the project and then develop a series of rough and incomplete prototype documents to show to users. These prototypes might start with sketches on paper (also known as *paper prototyping*), conceptual models, or mock-ups of page or screen designs, but the goal is to produce better prototypes with each iteration.

For each prototype, the designers gather user feedback to guide the development of the next prototype. Users might be asked merely to comment on certain aspects of a prototype, either individually or in a *focus group*. Or they might be asked to do basic tasks with the prototype, in a process known as *usability testing* (for more information, see "Usability Testing: Getting User Feedback on Prototypes" on page 332).

This process might involve omitting features that the design team had planned to include. For example, the designer might think that color would be a nice addition to a document but find through testing a black-and-white prototype that color isn't necessary to fulfill users' immediate needs. The designer could then decide whether to wait until a later version of the document to include color. Or in a website design project, the designer might initially plan to include a web forum for users but decide that there isn't time to implement this feature within the initial project timeline.

One advantage of iterative design is that it responds directly to users' needs by involving users throughout the design process—an approach also known as *Participatory Design* (PD) or *Joint Application Design* (JAD). Involving users throughout the design process can help you avoid creating beautiful, complex products that don't work very well for real people. Iterative design approaches also give you the opportunity to respond quickly to users' needs. Rather than working through an entire linear development process, you can create a "good enough" version rapidly and then use the feedback gained from that version to guide the development of better versions. This rapid response gets needed information into users' hands sooner.

On the downside, iterative design can lead to dynamic or even chaotic design projects because the target is constantly moving as you learn from testing each prototype. Iterative design also relies on creative, innovative, and flexible design teams; people who like a more linear approach often feel uncomfortable with the uncertainties of responding dynamically to user input. Management can also feel out of control with iterative design, since the model doesn't rely on the strict scheduling, milestones, and reporting of the waterfall model. Iterative design also makes estimating costs and deliverables more difficult because it is hard to predict users' responses to a prototype. Finally, by jumping into the design process without much planning, iterative design projects sometimes wallow around in uncertainty long enough for the project to lose momentum.

Planned Iterations: A Mixed Approach

Clearly, the waterfall model and the iterative model are opposing approaches to project management. The waterfall model is controlled, methodical, and consistent, whereas the iterative model is dynamic, creative, and changeable. You may work in organizations that favor either of these developmental models.

But the models can also be complementary. A growing number of projects develop a compromise approach, maximizing the strengths and minimizing the weaknesses of both models. For example, Hackos suggests that "the publications-development life cycle has the flexibility to fit into the rapid-prototyping model" (40), but nesting the iterative model within the waterfall model works just as well.

The *Planned Rapid Document Development* model (PRDD; Figure 10.4) retains some of the staging of the waterfall model, while placing iterative prototyping within a finite development stage. It also retains the project documentation common in the waterfall model, thus promoting clear communication between the project team and the client.

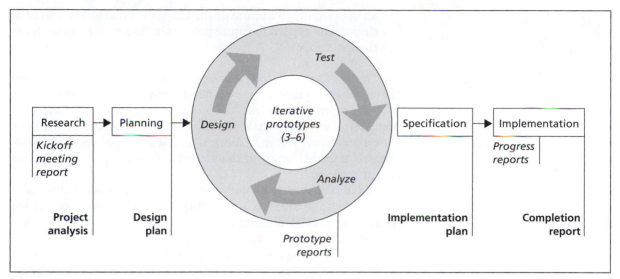

Figure 10.4 The Planned Rapid Document Development (PRDD) model for project management. Planned Rapid Document Development combines the approaches of the waterfall and iterative methods to project management. Formal reports are in bold; informal reports or team documentation are in italics.

PRDD includes five stages. Each stage is accompanied by a series of either formal or informal reports to document the design process and ensure clear communication between the design team and the client:

- **Stage 1: Research.** The project team meets with the client for a kickoff meeting about the client's agendas and expectations for the project, writing up the results in an informal *kickoff meeting report*. The team then conducts user research to build a clear understanding of the project and uses this research to write a formal **project analysis report**.

- **Stage 2: Design planning.** In this relatively short stage, the design team writes a planning document, specifying for the client and the team the iterations planned for stage 3, including a schedule for usability testing.

- **Stage 3: Iterative prototyping.** Within a strictly bounded time frame, the project team creates a series of three to six prototypes and conducts focus groups and usability tests to get user feedback. The goal of these iterations is to build toward a firmer idea of the document's design and contents. After each prototype cycle, the team writes an informal **prototype report** to codify its findings and recommend directions for further development.

- **Stage 4: Specification.** The team finalizes the document's design and contents, writing a formal **implementation plan** to guide stage 5.

- **Stage 5: Implementation.** The team implements the design finalized in stage 3. This stage includes a formal **completion report** as an opportunity to document the lessons learned in the project so they can be applied to future projects or future developments of the same project.

The PRDD approach retains some of the advantages of the waterfall model while gaining some of the advantages of the iterative model. It breaks down projects into reasonable stages with clear project deliverables: a set of reports that help the client and the design team understand where you're heading. It also sets aside a specific stage for research at the beginning of the project and provides a major product rollout at the end.

At the same time, it involves users early in the process, through both user research and iterative prototyping, and it allows the design team to create a workable document rapidly. The process can also reiterate as often as necessary or as time allows, returning to the prototyping stage to improve the document in future versions. If time runs short, any workable iteration can be released as an introductory beta version, with further development to follow.

Of course, this is only a general model. Most projects will have some constraints or dynamics that might make you modify the model more toward iterative design or toward the waterfall model. If you're working on a small project, for example, you might consider replacing progress reports and testing reports with a project blog that serves the same purpose less formally. If you're working on a larger project, you might include more formal documentation, such as reports for each of your user research activities in stage 1. Overall, try to balance organization with flexibility; sometimes you must change your plans to meet new conditions.

In the sections that follow, we'll discuss how to conduct, complete, and document each stage of PRDD.

Try to balance organization with flexibility.

Stage 1: Research

The goals of the research stage are to understand the user and client situations and to determine what kinds of documents might meet user needs and fulfill client agendas. To do this, you will need to conduct some field research to find out as much about the user and client as possible within a reasonably small time frame.

Remember that the primary purpose of this stage is to get a relatively quick sense of the rhetorical situation of the project before moving into prototyping. Don't get stuck on this stage, but spend enough time here to get a good sense of the users' situations. In a typical 60-day project, you should spend about two weeks conducting initial research into clients and users.

CLIENT RESEARCH

Many design projects start with the client. Clients frequently approach designers with an idea — to create a brochure, a website, an informational sign, a kiosk application, a newsletter, or some other kind of document. Your first job as a designer, then, should be to talk to clients about their agendas and expectations for the design project.

The project kickoff meeting. Ideally, you should sit down face-to-face with your client for a project kickoff meeting to talk about the client's agendas and expectations. The meeting should include all members of the initial project team, as well as all stakeholders in the client's organization. If you can't meet in person, try a conference call or a web conference. As a last resort, an exchange of e-mails can suffice — although at these beginning stages of the project, e-mail can take a lot longer than face-to-face meetings and possibly lead to misunderstandings.

The main purpose of this meeting is for you to find out what the client wants and how the client envisions the project. During the meeting, encourage the client to be as specific as possible about their ideas, and ask careful questions to get a clear picture of the project. The kickoff meeting should include at least the following:

- Introductions of personnel and stakeholders
- Client's initial project description, including a description of anticipated users
- Client agendas
- Client expectations and project scope

At the meeting, it often helps to repeat what the client has said to make sure you understand what he or she is thinking: "So, if I understand you correctly, you want a leaflet that will encourage your customers to ask sales reps about the new product. Is that right?" Take careful notes. It's easy to hold a successful meeting, and then quickly forget what happened in it!

Client agendas. An *agenda* is what the client wants to *do* or to have *happen* as a result of the design project. Agendas are usually broader than the document itself. For example, a client might ask you to design a brochure, but to do that effectively you'll need to understand what the client wants the brochure to do, which could be many things. The client could have any of the following goals for the brochure:

- To promote a product or service
- To disseminate information to users
- To answer frequently asked questions, decreasing customer service demands
- To encourage users to contact the organization for more information

Ask specific questions of the client to understand the agendas as completely as possible. The answers might even lead you to suggest that another kind of document might be more suitable than the document initially envisioned. Keep a list of the agendas you identify in your discussion with the client.

Level of design. Discuss the level of design the client thinks will be appropriate for the document. As we discussed in Chapter 1, some documents are more important to the client's overall mission than others. You wouldn't want to spend the client's money unwisely by over-designing a document that's not really that important to the client's mission. On the other hand, you wouldn't want to waste time creating a document with too low a level of design — something that might embarrass the client in front of an important group of users.

To figure out the appropriate level of design, first discuss the client's sense of the document's potential users. The client often interacts with users regularly and has a good intuition of their situations and needs. The client will also have a good idea of how important the users are to the client's mission. If every user is very important and must be impressed with the document, then a higher level of design is warranted. If it's not particularly important to impress the users, a lower level of design might do the job just as well.

After discussing users, take your initial list of the client's agendas and work with the client to *prioritize* the list by dividing the items into three categories:

- *Mission critical:* The document must do these things and will fail if it doesn't.
- *Optimal:* The document will work better if it does these things.
- *Optional:* The document will probably still work okay without these things, but they'd be nice to have.

These prioritized agendas will help you fine-tune the level of design for the project.

Client expectations. It's also a good idea to ask your clients explicitly what their expectations are, both of you and of the design project.

Most clients have a variety of assumptions about what you will do for them in the project. These expectations often arise from the following issues:

- How long the project will take
- How much the project will cost
- How many people will be involved on the project team
- How much the client needs to be involved
- How and how much you'll communicate with the client about your progress
- How the project will be broken into stages
- What the deliverables will be — what you'll give the client at the end of the project

Some of the client's expectations about these issues might make a lot of sense; others might lie beyond what you can fulfill.

Making the client's *implicit* expectations *explicit* allows you to negotiate between what you can provide and what the client expects. It also gives you an opportunity to communicate clearly with your client about expectations. If the client knows what to expect from you, the client is less likely to be disappointed or frustrated by your work.

> Making the client's *implicit* expectations *explicit* allows you to negotiate between what you can provide and what the client expects.

The kickoff meeting report.   As soon as possible after your kickoff meeting, write up your notes in an informal report to the client. For small projects, even an e-mail to the client will suffice. Reiterate the information you gathered in the meeting, and ask the client to review the document for accuracy. This process will highlight more questions that need to be asked or areas that need clarification. This report also gives clients the opportunity to "take back" any ideas that they decide don't mesh with their agenda. If the project is going to change, it's best that it change during these early stages rather than after you've invested your time and effort.

USER RESEARCH

The client's sense of users' situations and needs is a useful starting point for understanding prospective users. But clients' intuitions about users might not always be accurate. User research tries to develop a more solid picture of users and their needs within their own contexts. Design teams conduct user research primarily by observing users working in their own contexts and by asking those users targeted questions.

Finding users to research.   One of the challenges of user research is finding users and getting their permission to observe or talk to them.

Many potential users are happy to talk to you about their situations, including what kinds of documents might make their lives more convenient or their work more effective. Your client might be able to point you toward potential users to observe. The client's customers might be happy to talk with you because they already have at least some interest in improving the client's products or services. If the project anticipates creating internal documents for the client's employees, you should have little difficulty finding people to talk to. For design projects at your college or university, you might ask friends or members of student organizations to help.

Members of the general public are the most difficult kind of users to find and observe. If your project anticipates a public user group, you might need to advertise for participants. Regardless of the context, try to find participants who are as close as possible to the anticipated users in demographics, background, and interests.

User research and ethics.   Of course, it wouldn't be ethical to observe people without their knowledge and explicit permission. Before engaging in any user research, ask potential participants to sign a statement that gives you permission to talk to them, observe their work, and use the results in your design project. You will especially need written permission if you intend to record participants on audio or video. Natu-

---

DESIGN TIP

A Checklist for Conducting User Research and Usability Testing

Before the research activity or test:

- Obtain the participants' permission in writing.
- Explain the purpose of the activity, and describe what you'll ask users to do.
- Assure users that their participation is voluntary and that they can stop participating whenever they like.

During the research activity or test:

- Observe carefully.
- Take notes.
- Consider recording users with audio or video (but only with their prior permission).

After the research activity or test:

- Thank the users for their participation.
- Consider providing the users with a small gift.

rally, you should avoid asking users to do anything they might find uncomfortable, unethical, or coercive.

Before conducting any user research activity, talk with the participants for a few minutes about the design project and about the activity in which they'll be participating. Let them know what to expect, as well as how long your observation and the ensuing discussion will take. Tell the participants how the data you gain will be used — particularly any video or audio recordings you make. Assure them that throughout the research activity, they are free to ask questions, decline to respond, stop participating, or even leave if they feel uncomfortable.

After conducting user research, it's customary to reward each participant with a small gift to thank them for their participation. A gift certificate to a local restaurant or coffeehouse, a nice pen, or a coupon for goods or services at the client's business can all work well. This step is less necessary if the participants are employees of your client or if you're working on a student design project for a college course, but even a few home-baked cookies will go a long way toward making your participants happy and cooperative. In all cases, thank participants for their time and effort in helping you design a better document.

User research can involve a variety of techniques, including site visits, shadowing, task analysis, individual interviews, and focus groups.

Site visits and shadowing.   Site visits involve actually going to the environment where the anticipated document will be used and observing user activities in that environment. Site visits can help you develop a general sense of the environment in which your document design will be used. You may be allowed to walk around by yourself, but it's more likely that you'll have a guide or host to show you around the site and introduce you to people. Take careful notes, and, if possible, get permission to take some digital photos to remind you of what you saw.

While you're at the user site, it can be a good idea to get permission to follow a specific user around for an hour or two to see how and where he or she works. This technique is known as *shadowing*. Shadowing helps you build an in-depth picture of a single user's activities and attitudes toward the situation the document you're designing will address. While shadowing, avoid interrupting the participant's work or getting in the way. Instead, focus mostly on observing the participant and taking notes about what questions to ask later. At the end of the visit, talk with the participant about what you observed and ask any questions you might have.

Task analysis.   Task analysis is a more intense kind of shadowing that focuses on watching a participant perform a specific task. It's particularly common in design projects where the expected deliverable is a set of instructions or a procedure. If your goal is to help other users perform the task successfully, you need to watch a user who already knows how to do the task. The more focused your observation, the more successful you will be in accurately reconstructing the instructions or procedure.

In some situations, you can have users perform the task in controlled conditions, such as a usability lab. But it's best to watch users perform the task where they normally would. Try to get their permission to videotape them as they perform the task. This kind of recording isn't absolutely necessary for a successful task analysis, but it is helpful to be able to review the task repeatedly afterward. Even if you are able to videotape, take careful and precise notes about your observations.

To conduct a task analysis, first ask the participant to complete the task on her own. Then ask her to repeat the task again and narrate what she's doing as she does it—a technique known as the **talk-aloud protocol**. Finally, ask if you can do the task yourself under the participant's direction. Take notes about your impressions during the task—particularly at points where you hesitated or got lost. Compare these repetitions of the task. You may find that the participant breaks down the procedure differently in narration than in any previous descriptions of the task. Or you might find in doing the task yourself that the participant has internalized steps he or she doesn't even consciously recognize anymore.

Interviews and focus groups.   Interviews and focus groups are the best ways to gain insight into users' needs, situations, and attitudes. An interview is usually conducted with only one other participant, whereas a focus group might have five to eight participants. As in task analysis, video or audio recording is helpful.

Interviews and focus groups should not be free-form conversations, however. Start by creating a relatively small set of discussion questions to ask the participants; about a half-dozen main questions are all you can hope to cover in an hour-long session. That means you must choose and sharpen your questions carefully before the session begins. Focus on the issues that are most important for you to understand about users and their situations. If you have short, basic questions to ask (such as demographic information), consider preparing a survey or form for participants to fill out *before* the session.

Keep your questions open-ended and non-leading. Rather than asking, "Do you have a positive impression of this organization?" you might ask, "What impressions do you have of this organization?" Also avoid leading participants into giving the answers you want to hear. The question "What do you like about doing this task?" would probably make participants focus on what they like, even if they might not like doing the task very much. Asking "How do you feel about doing this task?" will give you a much better sense of the participants' honest attitudes, positive or negative.

Keep in mind, however, that people don't always tell the truth in interviews and focus groups. Individual interviews are basically structured conversations with a stranger; participants sometimes wish to present themselves and their situations in a different light than what might be objectively true. Focus groups also involve group dynamics. Sometimes a focus group can be swayed by the opinions and attitudes of a single dominant or vocal member. At other times, peer pressure can make individuals tend to conform to the group, even when their opinions might differ markedly from those of the group.

WRITING THE PROJECT ANALYSIS REPORT

After you have conducted all of the client and user research you have time to do, write a project analysis report. This report should be addressed to the client and describe the project in terms of the findings of your research. The goal of the report is to create a good mental picture of the project, for both the client and the project team. The project analysis report also helps you to communicate with your client, explaining how you intend to proceed and asking for client feedback on your progress.

The project description is typically broken down into the following segments:

- *Introduction:* Introduce the report with a section that explains what this report will cover.

- *Initial project description:* Describe the project as the client described it to you, including the client's expectations.

- *Client goals and agendas:* Summarize the client's goals and agendas for the project, including the mission-critical, optimal, and optional objectives. (These first two sections can arise from the kickoff meeting report, incorporating any subsequent client feedback.)

- *User research:* Summarize the methodologies and results of your user research activities.

- *Initial deliverables recommendation:* Given what you have discovered about the client and the users, make an initial recommendation of what kind and scope of document or documents will best fulfill client agendas and user needs.

Of course, you should adapt this general outline to fit your own project. Submit a copy of the report to your client and ask for feedback.

Stage 2: Design Planning

Stage 2 probably won't take very long because it simply involves writing a planning document to guide the iterative design in stage 3. For shorter projects, this planning document might even be appended to the project analysis from stage 1.

The goal of this document should be to develop a workable schedule and tentative plan for the design iterations you'll create in stage 3. The number of design iterations will naturally depend on the level of design and time available for the project. Mission-critical and complex projects will probably benefit from more iterations so you can explore different approaches to the design, while less-critical or simpler projects might need fewer.

As much as possible, you'll also want to plan for what *kind* of iterations and testing you'll perform. Part of iterative design is that you will need to use each iteration to guide the development of the next, but you should have a general idea of what sequence of iterations you're planning to follow. Remember that you must plan sufficient time for usability testing of each iteration, as well as for analyzing and reporting the results.

Because this planning document explains what actions you'll take throughout the rest of the project, it's considered somewhat binding. Make sure that you promise only what you can deliver. Submit the planning document to your client and ask for feedback — now is the time to negotiate a shared idea of how the project should move forward.

Stage 3: Iterative Prototyping

As we said before, the objectives of iterative prototyping are to get something into users' hands quickly and then use their feedback to improve the product in future iterations. In PRDD, you'll move through three to six prototypes, advancing toward the completion of the document with each iteration. The number of prototype iterations you choose to go through will depend on a variety of factors, including the complexity of the project and the amount of time you have to release a workable document to users.

In stage 2 you should make a tentative plan for the number and type of prototypes you'll create in the project analysis report, but you can decide how many are necessary at any point during the prototyping process. If you run out of time after coming up with a prototype that does a basic, good enough job, you have the option of releasing it as a beta version. You can always develop this prototype later in more polished versions.

CREATING PROTOTYPES

Typically, iterative design moves from rough prototypes in early iterations to more finished ones later on. These prototypes are referred to in terms of their *fidelity*, or truth to the final intentions of the project, from *low-fidelity (lo-fi)* to *high-fidelity (hi-fi)* (Figure 10.5).

Fidelity can be measured vertically or horizontally, depending on *completeness* and *polish*. A *vertical prototype* is *polished* but not *complete*. It shows only a single working portion of the document. Examples of a vertical prototype would include a single section of a paper document that includes actual content or a single web page with all of the links activated (but with little or no content on the pages the links lead to). A vertical prototype works, as far as it goes — we can use the parts that the prototype includes but none of the other parts of the document.

A *horizontal prototype* is more *complete* but less *polished* than a vertical prototype. An outline or sketch of a document's entire structure is probably the most horizontal of prototypes, including all of the parts but no details. A highly finished page layout sketch with no real content would also be considered horizontal because it focuses on global design issues (the page design that will be applied to the whole

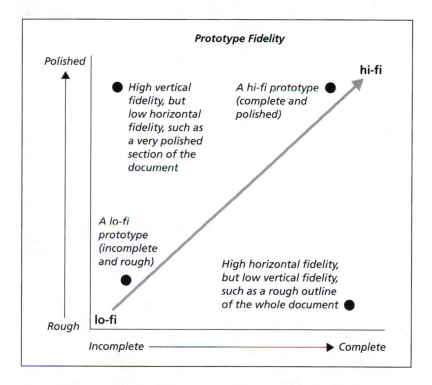

Figure 10.5 The fidelity of prototypes. The fidelity of prototypes can be measured vertically, from rough to polished, and horizontally, from incomplete to complete.

document) but no actual content. A horizontal prototype doesn't actually work, but it gives a good comprehensive picture of the entire document.

Both kinds of prototypes can be important in different iterations, depending on the goals of your project. If you need to iron out the whole structure of the document you're designing, horizontal iterations will help you meet that goal more quickly than a polished, vertical prototype. But if you need to get a mission-critical part of the document working right away, a vertical prototype might take priority.

Don't underestimate the value of lo-fi prototyping in either the horizontal or vertical dimension. Hi-fi prototypes might look more complete and polished, but they take longer to create than lo-fi prototypes, which can be created quickly and repeatedly. Lo-fi prototypes are particularly useful for defining general concepts, such as the overall structure of the document, and basic page layout concepts. Even a very lo-fi prototype can be incredibly useful early in a project; sometimes a simple sketch on paper or on screen will help you develop a global vision of the project's direction. Early lo-fi prototypes can also help you gain valuable user feedback quickly, which you can roll into the development of the next, higher-fidelity prototype.

> The most important goal of iterative design is to fulfill as many of the client's agendas as possible as early as possible, working from the mission-critical agendas first.

Ideally, a design project should work toward both horizontal and vertical fidelity—that is, a complete *and* polished version of the document. But remember that the most important goal of iterative design is to fulfill as many of the client's agendas as possible as early as possible, working from the mission-critical agendas first. You can always go back to fill in less important details and polish the design in subsequent iterations.

In the next three sections, we'll introduce some more specific kinds of prototypes that you may want to develop in your design projects. In general, you'll find three types of prototypes most useful. Moving from low-fidelity to high-fidelity, these types include conceptual prototypes, design sketches, and operational prototypes.

Conceptual prototypes.   Conceptual prototypes are typically very lo-fi explorations of potential concepts, such as the structure or navigational features of the document. Because they don't try to show anything close to a finished design, they're usually more horizontal than vertical.

One common early-conceptual prototype technique is **card-sorting**. The goal of card-sorting is to get users to help you organize a document in an order that makes sense to them rather than just to you. To conduct a card-sorting exercise, first brainstorm a series of potential concepts, topics, or sections the document might include. Write those concepts on index cards, one concept per card. Then ask a potential user to sort the cards into groups and place them within whatever order

---

DESIGN TIP

Version Control

As you develop sequential prototypes or drafts in a document design project, you must keep track of successive versions—a practice known as **version control**. Version control is particularly important when you're working on a design team on multiple iterations of prototypes. Otherwise, as several people work on the same project, it becomes easy to lose prototypes, overwrite prototypes, or develop competing prototypes. Some companies with large design teams even invest in version-control software to help them keep track of versions.

The simplest way to keep track of version control is to develop a consistent **naming convention** for your prototypes. For example, you might simply number the prototypes sequentially (1, 2, 3 . . .). If you're working with more than a few versions, however, you might want to have major and minor revision numbers (A1, A2; B1, B2, B3; and so on). Software revision numbers (0.5., 0.9, 1.0, 1.1, 2.0, etc.) can also work well. Numbers under 1.0 are usually considered beta versions, making it easy to see whether the version you're working with has already been fully released.

For paper prototypes, simply mark the version number on the back in pencil. For digital prototypes or textual drafts, add the version numbers to the end of the computer filename (for example, InformationPamphlet_0-8.indd, Information Pamphlet_0-9.indd, InformationPamphlet_1-0.indd, etc.).

Make sure everyone on your team understands and *uses* the naming conventions you've established for your design projects.

---

makes most sense. Finally, interview the user to ask why he categorized and ordered the cards as he did, taking particular note of what logical method he used to organize the cards. Because this takes only a few minutes, you can repeat the exercise with several users in a couple of hours.

Working from the results of a card-sorting exercise or from other ideas, you might create a *conceptual diagram* of the document you can use to structure an interview or focus group discussion. A conceptual diagram doesn't look anything like the finished document; rather, it's an abstracted version of a potential document. Figure 10.6 on page 330 shows a conceptual diagram used in the design of Chapter 4 of this book.

A conceptual diagram can also be a flowchart that shows a user how to go through a task using the document. Potential users can then give feedback on whether they would use the document to perform the task that way or some other way. In an even more conceptual mode, you might ask potential users to help you draw a conceptual diagram that models the structure or use of the document. For example, you might ask users to help you draw a site map that shows the structure of a website.

Design sketches.   Unlike conceptual prototypes, which focus on refining the structure or navigation of a document, *design sketches* help you refine the visual design of the document. As such, design sketches are often more vertical than horizontal.

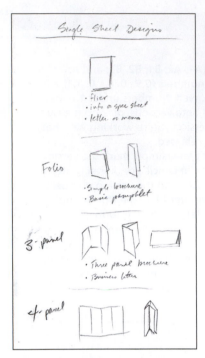

Figure 10.6 A conceptual prototype used in the development of this book.   Conceptual prototypes are a good way to get a lot of ideas on paper quickly. Don't worry about making them too neat!

Figure 10.7 Early design sketches for this book.   These design sketches represent our initial ideas about the cover and layout of this book. As with conceptual prototypes, speed is more important than accuracy. Get all your ideas down as quickly as possible, and then refine those ideas with further sketches.

Low-fidelity design sketches are often completed with those old standbys, pencil and paper. For example, in thinking about the design of this book, we created the design sketches in Figure 10.7.

Pencil and paper are cheap and fast, so they are a good way to try out a variety of designs quickly. You might want to use relatively large sheets of paper, subdivided into areas with about the same aspect ratio as your planned page or spread format. That way, you can see multiple sketch iterations on the same sheet for easy comparison. If you're designing for the screen rather than the page, however, it can be a good idea to use multiple sheets of standard 8½" × 11" paper: Turned sideways, they're very close to the aspect ratio of a typical computer monitor. Once you've created a few strong ideas with paper and pencil, you can branch out to colored pencils, crayons, or markers for more complete design sketches. If you're working collaboratively, a whiteboard or paper easel can be a great tool for sketching out design concepts. A bulletin board can be a useful place to tack up different iterations with pushpins so you can compare them all at once.

Use the sketching process to try out as many ideas as possible. Work quickly and creatively—there's little sense in making the sketches beautiful or perfect, since you'll discard most of them anyway. Once you see concepts or ideas you think work well, start creating more polished sketches that have a higher level of fidelity so you can show them to potential users and get some feedback.

After you've gone through a series of design sketches on paper, you might want to create some digital sketches on the computer. This will be more time-consuming, but digital design sketches will have a higher level of fidelity than paper sketches. Figure 10.8 shows a digital sketch of the layout for this book.

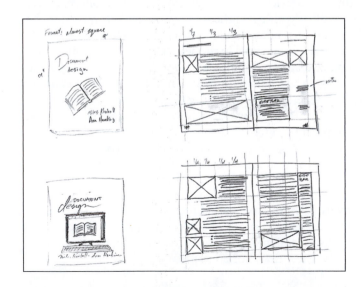

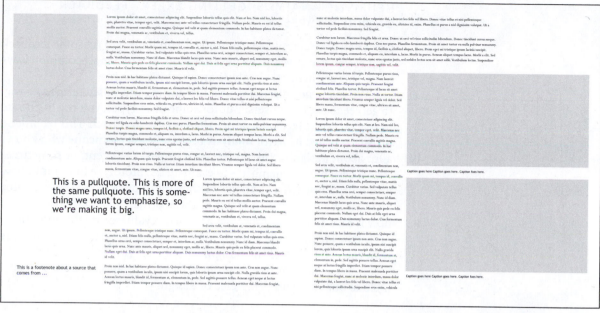

Figure 10.8 A digital design sketch for *Document Design*. This vertical prototype was created with a page layout program, so it's a relatively polished iteration of the design. The design evolved over time, but this vertical prototype was useful for getting feedback on more specific design ideas.

To create electronic sketches, start with whatever software is fast, easy, and available. Your goal is to test your ideas and get feedback, so at this stage, don't worry about getting just the right image or text. Placeholder text (*lorem ipsum*) and placeholder images can stand in for real content for the time being.

For later prototypes with more vertical fidelity, you might want to create design sketches in the program that you intend to use to produce the final version of the document. You also might want to start importing real content, both images and text.

Operational prototypes. **Operational prototypes** have a relatively high level of horizontal fidelity (completeness), although they might have less vertical fidelity (polish). The goal of creating an operational prototype is to determine how well the prototype fulfills user needs. Typically, that means that the prototype will need to have all of the features to fulfill mission-critical agendas. (Of course, if one of the mission-critical agendas is that the document should look very polished, then an operational prototype might have a high level of vertical fidelity as well.)

An operational prototype is particularly suited to usability testing, since it should have enough functionality for users to do something with it. Because they're relatively complete, operational prototypes are also close to being releasable, at least in beta versions.

HEURISTIC ANALYSIS: GETTING EXPERT FEEDBACK ON PROTOTYPES

Once you have completed a prototype, you'll need to get some feedback on it so you can develop the next iteration. The two most common ways to do this are heuristic analysis and usability testing.

We've already discussed usability testing in limited terms as a way to get feedback from users. But for some prototypes, you might choose to rely on *expert* feedback rather than on *user* feedback. This technique is usually called **heuristic analysis** because it asks someone who knows a lot about design or the project — an expert, the client, or sometimes even a design team member — to evaluate the prototype in terms of how well it fits a **heuristic**, or an established set of principles. The evaluator analyzes the prototype in terms of these principles, noting where and how it falls short. For example, an expert evaluator might note that a prototype lacks clear alignment of page elements, leading to problems with the coherence of the design.

For a document design project, those principles should probably include our standard principles of design:

- Similarity
- Contrast
- Proximity
- Alignment
- Order
- Enclosure

For website design, you might consider using Jakob Nielsen's "Ten Usability Heuristics" (available at <www.useit.com>).

Heuristic analysis is an organized way to get a quick sense of whether a prototype is on track. Rather than simply asking for an opinion about the prototype, you're asking *how well* the prototype meets generally accepted principles of design. The limitation of heuristic analysis is that although experts know general principles very well, they might not understand what it's like to be a real user of the document. Only users can give you that perspective.

USABILITY TESTING: GETTING USER FEEDBACK ON PROTOTYPES

After you've completed a prototype, you can use it to get feedback from real or at least potential users. You can use some of the techniques we've already discussed for user research, including focus groups and individual interviews. But the primary approach to getting feedback on prototypes is *usability testing*.

Usability testing might sound intimidating, but the general concept is simple: *to find out how usable a document is, ask some people to use it*. If you observe their use carefully, you can learn a lot about how to improve your next prototype.

Some corporations and universities have invested in expensive usability testing laboratories, but you can get good results less formally with a set of techniques known as *discount usability testing*, pioneered by usability guru Jakob Nielsen. Discount usability testing usually involves nothing more than a prototype (on paper or on the screen, as the project demands), a participant, and some means of recording the participant's actions and comments, such as video or audio recording. Discount usability testing doesn't require many participants. As Nielsen and Tom Landauer reported in their 1993 paper, the first few participants will find most of the problems with a prototype; later participants will find fewer and smaller problems, decreasing the return on investment in the testing process. Nielsen and Landauer suggest that the optimal number of participants is three to five people.

Usability testing techniques.   The most common techniques used in discount usability testing are scenario testing and the talk-aloud protocol. *Scenario testing* involves presenting participants with a prototype and a few small tasks to perform. For example, you might test a prototype website by asking the participant to order a product, find the customer service phone number, and find the answer to a frequently asked question. You might test a paper document by asking the participant to find a particular section, find the definition of an important term, or follow a set of instructions in the document.

The *talk-aloud protocol* involves asking participants to narrate what they are thinking and doing as they perform the requested tasks. This technique brings the participant's mental processes out into the open, where they can be observed, recorded, and discussed. Using the talk-aloud protocol, you can readily detect when users are confused, when they hesitate, or where they get stuck in the task. This information is invaluable for making sure that users can perform tasks successfully.

Fidelity and usability testing.   You can perform usability testing on low-fidelity or high-fidelity prototypes, as well as on vertical or horizontal prototypes. Low-fidelity testing is fast and cheap, and it can give you some great feedback early in the design process. With high-fidelity prototypes, however, you will probably be testing something closer to a draft of a document that might be near a beta release. You can even

> Usability testing might sound intimidating, but the general concept is simple: *to find out how usable a document is, ask some people to use it*. If you observe their use carefully, you can learn a lot about how to improve your next prototype.

do usability testing on a document that has already been released, gaining feedback on how to improve the next version of the document.

Creating high-fidelity prototypes takes more time, but it can result in higher-quality feedback in usability testing, since participants are using something closer to the final version of the document. For example, with a high-fidelity prototype, you can time how long it takes users to complete the tasks. This information can give you a precise sense of whether one iteration of your design improves over a previous iteration: if the participants can perform the task more quickly, you can conclude that the new design is more usable.

Planning and conducting usability tests.   Just as you did with user research (see page 321), be sure to get permission in writing from usability testing participants. Explain to the participants that they are not required to participate and that they can stop at any time. (See "Design Tip: A Checklist for Conducting User Research and Usability Testing" on page 322.)

When planning the scenarios for a usability test, think about two factors: the client's mission-critical agendas and previous user feedback. As you'll recall, the client's mission-critical agendas are what the document *must* do to be successful. These agendas can usually lead directly into the scenarios for prototype usability testing. For example, if one of the mission-critical agendas of a software manual is that users must be able to install the software successfully, then one scenario should probably ask users to install the software using a high-fidelity vertical prototype of the document section that includes the installation instructions.

Feedback from previous usability tests or user research can also help guide your development of scenarios. If you found in your user research that most users say they prefer a pocket-sized format for the document you're designing, you might ask the usability test participants to carry the prototype document around and use it for a while. If they stick it in their pockets, your earlier research was accurate; if they don't, you might consider changing the format.

To keep the test consistent between multiple participants, it's usually best to create a written plan for the usability test, known as a *script*. The script should specify what the observer should say to introduce the usability test, what the participant will be asked to do, what the test is for, and how long the test will take. It should also include the scenarios, written out either for the participants to read themselves or for the observer to read to the participant. This written script helps to keep the usability test consistent for all participants, giving you more reliable results.

While conducting the usability test, be sure to ask participants to talk aloud. You might even have to remind them while the test is in progress, since many people will forget while they're concentrating on the task. Let the participants know that if they get stuck on a task, they can ask you for a hint. But try not to take over the task and give the participant direct instructions, because the goal is to see how the prototype works on its own. At the end of the usability testing, be sure to thank participants for their help.

WRITING PROTOTYPE REPORTS

For each phase of prototype usability testing, write an informal report addressed to the client that summarizes the test and your findings. Use your best judgment to determine what counts as a *phase*. If you conducted several quick usability tests of a succession of paper prototypes in one afternoon, you might want to write one report on the results rather than multiple reports. For short or fast-moving projects, you might want to write your reports even more informally on a project blog or wiki.

Prototype reports should include at least the following sections:

- *Introduction:* Explain the purpose of the report, record the date of the usability test, and summarize your general recommendations.

- *Methodology:* Describe how you set up the usability test, including how you chose participants and determined the scenarios.

- *Results:* Summarize the results for the usability test.

- *Discussion:* Analyze the results and discuss their significance for further development of the prototype.

- *Recommendations:* Recommend what changes the testing indicates the team should make to the project's direction.

- *Appendices:* Include materials such as the test script, transcripts, and other raw data.

The goal of these reports is to record and communicate the results of the usability test and to recommend what actions to take in the next phase of prototype development. It's more important to write a concise report quickly and move on to the next phase rather than to write an extended report and hold up the iterative design process.

Stage 4: Specification

At the end of the prototype stage, you should have a good sense of what kind of document you'll be producing, including its medium, format, organization, page layout, typography, navigation, and para-textual features (tables of contents, lists of figures, indexes, appendices, glossaries, and so on). In the specification stage, you'll codify these features into a guide you'll use in the implementation stage. This guide, called the *implementation plan*, should be addressed primarily to the project team, with the client as a secondary audience. You'll need the client's feedback on and approval of your implementation plan, but the plan's main purpose is to guide the team's efforts as you bring the document to a releasable state.

Not all projects are big enough in scope to require a formal implementation plan. But all projects, no matter how small, require at least some informal specification to help you keep design features consistent throughout the design. Larger projects—particularly those that require multiple documents that will feature a consistent design—need a more formal guide that can extend across all of the deliverables. Large projects are also likely to involve more people on the project team, and those people will need the implementation plan so they can work in concert to create a unified design. The implementation plan usually includes two main parts: a style sheet (or template, for smaller projects) and an implementation schedule.

CREATING A STYLE SHEET OR TEMPLATE

To keep the design consistent throughout multiple-document projects, you'll want to create a style sheet that specifies the design of all the page elements, the page layouts, and the colors of the document. A style sheet might include the following information:

- Heading 1: Eras Bold ITC 16pt, 1p0 before, 0p2 after
- Heading 2: Eras Demi ITC 12pt, 1p0 before, 0p2 after
- Body text: Calisto MT 10pt, first-line indent 0p3
- Header: running, Eras Light ITC 10pt
- Color scheme: PMS 2695; PMS 542

The style sheet should also include a labeled diagram of the page layout, including information about margins, columns, gutters, and the position of headers and footers. For website design projects, the style sheet will probably be formatted as a CSS (cascading style sheet) file, which you can incorporate directly in the design.

Alternately, you may prefer to create a template instead of a style sheet. A template is simply a page layout file (or for a website, HTML and CSS files) that includes all of the preceding elements actually put into action. You can set up the page layout, including columns, margins, and gutters, as well as create paragraph or character styles for the different textual elements. In other words, the template serves as an empty shell for the design. After creating the template, you can simply "Save as" to create a new version into which to port content. Templates are particularly useful for design projects that have several deliverables with consistent designs, such as a project creating a series of pamphlets or a newsletter that will come out periodically.

CREATING AN IMPLEMENTATION SCHEDULE

The implementation plan should also include a schedule that specifies when each part of the design project will be completed. For example, it might include separate milestones for copy (text), copyediting, art, and layout. It should also specify when the document will be ready for production. If the deliverable is a paper document that will be printed professionally, be sure to include the print shop's milestones as well, including proofs (see Chapter 11). If the deliverable is an electronic document such as a website, specify when the site will go live on the Internet.

Stage 5: Implementation

The final stage of the PRDD model is implementation. In some ways, this is the simplest stage—you have merely to follow the implementation plan. But inevitably, problems and complications will kick in as you try to bring the document to the highest quality possible during the time available. So it's important to track your progress and communicate effectively with the client about any potential difficulties.

WRITING PROGRESS REPORTS

The best way to track and communicate your progress is to write an informal *progress report*. The purpose of a progress report isn't just to say, "Everything's going fine; here's what we've done so far." Instead, a progress report measures progress against the implementation plan. For example, if the plan specified that the graphics for the project were to be completed by November 15, a progress report should measure whether the graphics were in fact completed on time. If they weren't, the progress report will need to discuss what went wrong and how the team plans to get back on schedule.

Write your progress reports with the client as the primary audience. Communicating regularly about your progress will help both you and the client understand where the project stands and what to expect as the project continues.

On smaller or less formally managed projects, you might consider keeping a running blog of your progress rather than writing separate progress reports. Since blogs are online, you can broaden your concept of audience for progress information to include users, who might be very interested in how your project is going and when they can expect to see it complete or usable.

WRITING THE COMPLETION REPORT

Finally, design projects often end with a *completion report* addressed to the client. The completion report sums up the entire project and makes recommendations for future development of the deliverables. It should also describe the lessons learned through the project. These lessons are important organizational wisdom that can affect the development of new design projects.

If you're completing a student design project, the completion report is also a very good opportunity to absorb and reflect on everything you've learned while doing the project. Most of us learn a lot by doing, but if you can express what you have learned, you're more likely to take those lessons on to new experiences and greater successes in the future.

Exercises

1. Imagine that you're working on a project to design a new guidebook for international students at your university. The client—your university's international student center—envisions a brochure or handbook that includes information international students might not know about the school and community, such as how to open a bank account, where to get an ID card, how to use the local bus service, and so forth. The goal is to make international students' entry into the academic and local community go smoothly. What user research would you conduct for this project? What questions would you need to answer?

2. For a project that you're working on, create a PERT chart like the one on page 309. Using your understanding of the mission-critical elements of the project, be sure to distinguish between critical paths (absolutely essential steps) and optional paths. For example, you can use red lines for critical paths and dotted lines for optional paths. (Hint: The PERT chart was created in Microsoft PowerPoint. Try out the Connectors AutoShapes to create lines that stick to text boxes while you move the boxes around.)

3. For a project that you're working on, keep a journal that describes your impressions and thoughts as you go through the project. At the end of the project, look back on your journal and reflect on what you learned.

Works Cited

Hackos, JoAnn T. *Managing Your Documentation Projects.* New York: John Wiley & Sons, 1994.

Martin, James. *Rapid Application Development.* New York: Macmillan, 1991.

Nielsen, Jakob. "Guerrilla HCI: Using Discount Usability Engineering to Penetrate the Intimidation Barrier." Online: <www.useit.com/papers/guerrilla_hci.html>.

Nielsen, Jakob. "Ten Usability Heuristics." Online: <www.useit.com/papers/heuristic/heuristic_list.html>.

Nielsen, Jakob, and T. K. Landauer. "A Mathematical Model of the Finding of Usability Problems." *Proceedings of the SIGCHI Conference on Human Factors in Computing Systems,* 1993.

Further Reading

Barnum, Carol. *Usability Testing and Research.* New York: Longman/Allyn & Bacon, 2002.

Kuniavsky, Mike. *Observing the User Experience: A Practitioner's Guide to User Research.* San Francisco: Morgan Kaufmann, 2003.

CHAPTER 11

Production

Up until this point, we have discussed what happens *before* a document is produced — the process of researching, planning, and designing that ends with a completed prototype. The final stage, production, can be complicated, particularly for designs that will be printed by a commercial print shop like the one in Figure 11.1. Production includes the steps we need to take before we deliver a design to a print shop or prepare it for printing ourselves — a process known as ***prepress***.

Whether you're preparing a document for simple photocopying or sending it to a full-service print shop, you will design more successful documents if you understand production processes. Printing is a complex industrial process, and understanding that process will help you anticipate what the printer needs to produce your design. Understanding print production will also help you communicate effectively with printers, your partners in moving from a design to a real product.

Of course, production applies primarily to documents in paper, since electronic documents are essentially "produced" when the design is complete and made available to users. So in this chapter, we'll focus on the printing technologies that are commonly used today and a couple of new printing technologies that are gaining acceptance. Then we'll discuss some of the processes that happen after printing, such as folding, gathering, trimming, and binding. Finally, we'll cover some of the things you'll need to think about when communicating and working with professional printers.

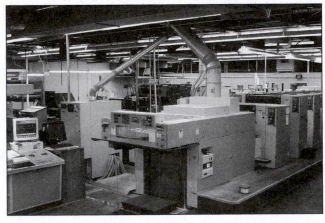

Figure 11.1 A commercial print shop.   Printing is an industrial process that requires special skills and expensive equipment, such as the six-head lithographic press and the digital operator's station shown here. Knowing a little about printing processes will help you communicate successfully with your commercial printer.

Printing Technologies

As a designer, you should know about six main kinds of printing technologies:

- Intaglio
- Relief
- Lithography
- Reprography
- Inkjet
- Commercial digital printing

We'll define each of these technologies, emphasizing those you are most likely to encounter as a document designer. This information should help you make good decisions about which printing technologies are best for your project. Although the sections to come provide the details, refer to the summary table on page 343 for a quick overview of the uses, strengths, and weaknesses of each of these technologies.

Precursors: Intaglio and Relief Printing

The primary difficulty in printing is how to get ink onto the paper where we want it, while keeping it out of the areas where we don't want it. Intaglio and relief printing do so with two complementary strategies: inking a *depressed* surface or inking a *raised* surface (Figure 11.2).

Intaglio and relief printing are rarely used today, but being familiar with the transmission from one technology to the next will help you understand some of the terms your printer uses and the options he or she provides.

Intaglio printing (also known as gravure) uses *depressions* in a metal plate to hold the ink that will later transfer to the paper. These depressions are created either mechanically, by *engraving* the plate, or chemically, by *etching* parts of the plate with acids. Both approaches leave the part to be printed lower than the surface of the plate. Ink is then rolled onto the plate and the excess wiped away, leaving ink only in the depressions. When the paper is pressed onto the plate with high pressure, the ink transfers from the depressions to the paper.

Intaglio printing requires highly skilled artists to engrave or etch the plates, and the plates are difficult or even impossible to correct if there are any mistakes. For a long time intaglio printing was the primary method for printing illustrations and maps. Today, it's mostly used to print currency and stock certificates because the highly artful

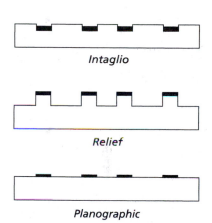

Figure 11.2 Intaglio, relief, and planographic printing methods in profile. Intaglio printing inks a *lowered* surface. Relief printing inks a *raised* surface. Planographic printing places the inked and uninked areas on the same plane.

nature of intaglio plate engraving makes it hard for counterfeiters to copy the plate.

Taking the opposite approach, *relief printing* uses a *raised* surface on which the ink can be spread, usually with a roller. Paper is then pressed onto this raised surface, transferring the ink to the paper. The earliest relief printing occurred in China in the eleventh century with large, carved wooden blocks. But the most influential application of relief printing appeared in the fifteenth century in Europe with Johannes Gutenberg's development of movable type for *letterpress* printing.

In letterpress printing—the primary relief printing technology from Gutenberg to the middle of the twentieth century—each letter of the typeface was molded in reverse on a small block of metal, with the area to be printed raised to take the ink. In a process called *composition*, a worker would choose pieces of type one at a time from subdivided drawers called *cases*. The lower case held the lowercase letters, and the upper case held the capitals and punctuation marks. The compositor arranged the individual pieces into lines separated by strips of lead, from which we get the term *leading*. After completing a whole page of type, he would tighten it into a frame using blocks and wedges. The printer placed this frame in the press and inked the raised surfaces of the type. He then used a printing press to press paper onto the framed page of type to receive the impression of the ink. At the end of the press run, workers took the type out of the frame and separated, cleaned, and distributed it back to the cases, one piece at a time.

This process became more efficient after the 1890s with the introduction of machines such as the Monotype, which molded individual pieces of type on demand and composed them into text, and the Linotype, which molded a whole line of type in one piece. But even with these advances, letterpress printing was labor-intensive and expensive. As a result, it fell out of mainstream use between the 1950s and the 1970s with the development of photolithography (which we discuss in the next section). But because people used letterpress printing for five centuries, the conventions developed by letterpress printers have become very closely associated with all printed documents, such as justified type, leading, and typefaces. In addition, most of the typefaces we use for documents today are based on Renaissance typefaces designed for letterpress printing.

Lithography

Intaglio and relief printing have a significant disadvantage: it's hard to create the depressed or raised surfaces needed to separate the inked areas from the uninked areas. Planographic printing, however, places

Printing Technologies: Uses, Advantages, Disadvantages

Printing Technology	Common Uses Today	Advantages	Disadvantages
Intaglio	Printing currency, stock certificates, and similar official documents	Beautiful and difficult to duplicate	Requires highly skilled artists Plates wear out quickly
Relief	Printing packaging materials (flexography)	Useful on flexible materials like plastics and cardboards	Imprecise Pooling at edges of inked areas
Lithography	Printing high-quality, complex color documents such as books, brochures, pamphlets, and reports	Inexpensive in large print runs Increasingly automated Flexible output in nearly any size and format	Industrial, requiring expensive machines and highly skilled personnel Expensive in short print runs Hard to fix mistakes
Reprography	Printing short runs of single-sided, black-and-white or sometimes color documents in standard paper sizes	Inexpensive in short print runs Fast desktop access Easy to fix mistakes Within control of designers	Expensive in long print runs Lower quality than lithography, especially in terms of color and images
Inkjet	Color proofing Quick printing on low-level designs Large-format printing (signs)	Relatively inexpensive equipment Commonly available	Very expensive consumables, especially for process color printing Poor print quality, especially for process printing
Commercial digital printing	Print-on-demand (POD)	Very fast Small print runs	Very expensive Lower quality than traditional offset lithography

both the inked and uninked surfaces on the same plane, neither raised nor lowered (see Figure 11.2, page 341).

The most significant planographic method is *lithography*, invented by Alois Senenfelder in 1798. To get the inked and the uninked surfaces on the same plane, lithography relies on the principle that oil and water don't mix.

Early lithography (which means "stone-writing") started with a smooth, flat stone. A printer or artist drew on the stone with an oily crayon, and the stone was wetted with a mixture of water and gum arabic (a thickening agent). The stone was then inked with oily lithographic ink, which would stick to the oily crayon marks but not to the water-soaked areas of the stone. Paper was then pressed on the stone at moderate pressure, and the ink was transferred to the paper. This early lithography was used increasingly throughout the nineteenth century to produce illustrated books, maps, and inexpensive art for decorating the home.

PHOTOLITHOGRAPHY

The manual process of lithography became more efficient with the development of *photolithography*, which came into common use in the 1950s.

Traditional photolithography begins with *camera-ready copy*, which requires treating type and images separately. For type, computerized typesetting machines are used to create the prototype blocks of text on paper at high resolution. For images, photographic prints are photographed again through a fine, grid-like filter called a *screen*. The screen allows light through its holes and blocks light with its lines. The result is a *halftone* image of the imposition, made up of tiny dots that blend together to simulate the photo. Until around 1980, the halftones and typeset blocks of text were then pasted with wax or glue onto a paper or clear plastic substrate in the proper arrangement for the page design. This assembled camera-ready copy was photographed once again to create a negative of the whole page or imposition. Finally, a positive plate of the image was created by shining a strong light through the negative onto the *plate*, a thin, flexible plate of metal coated with light-sensitive chemicals. The areas of the plate where the light shone through the negative underwent a chemical reaction that made them receptive to lithographic ink. The areas where the light was blocked remained unexposed; these areas were then wetted in the lithographic process to keep them from receiving ink.

Fortunately, this manual assembly or *paste-up* process is now managed digitally to make the plate. But basic lithographic printing happens in much the same way now as it did in the last century. At the press, the developed plate is attached to a roller called the *plate cylinder*. As the plate cylinder rotates, the press inks and waters the plate. The exposed portions of the plate receive the ink and repel the water, while the unexposed areas receive the water and repel the ink. Finally, a sheet of paper is rolled through the press between the plate cylinder and the *impression cylinder* (a drum against which the plate is pressed), and the ink transfers to the paper, creating a positive image of the page (Figure 11.3).

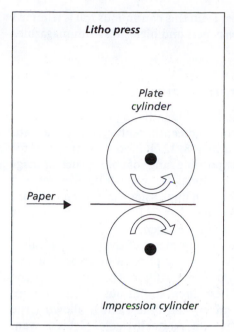 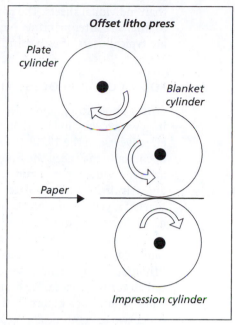

Figure 11.3 Side view of lithographic and offset lithographic presses.   The offset press introduces a blanket cylinder between the plate and the impression cylinder to make the plate last longer. The rubber blanket picks up the ink from the plate and presses it on the paper, keeping the abrasive paper away from the plate itself.

OFFSET LITHOGRAPHY

One disadvantage of this basic lithographic printing process is that the plates wear out quickly because they come into direct contact with the relatively abrasive surface of the paper. So around 1900, printers developed *offset lithography*, which protects the plate and makes it last longer. Almost all lithographic printing done today uses offset lithography.

Offset lithography puts a rubber-covered *blanket cylinder* between the plate cylinder and the impression cylinder. The inked plate cylinder presses against the blanket cylinder, which takes up the ink from the plate and then presses the ink onto the paper. Because the rubber blanket is nonabrasive, the plate lasts much longer—usually enough to print tens of thousands of impressions.

Motorized offset presses can print hundreds of sheets a minute this way, using a series of vacuum and roller feeds to pick up sheets, send them through the press, and collect them at the other end. Even faster are *web presses*, which take up the paper from a continuous roll rather than individual sheets. The paper from this continuous roll is trimmed to final size after printing. Newspapers and high-press-run magazines are typical users of web printing.

FOUR-COLOR PROCESS LITHOGRAPHY

Offset photolithography also lends itself easily to *process color* printing, which was invented in the eighteenth century but came into effective use in the 1920s (Griffiths 118, 127). Process color is used for documents that need the fullest possible range of colors, such as magazines, annual reports, and promotional materials. It involves making and printing from four plates for each impression — one each for cyan, magenta, yellow, and black, abbreviated as **CMYK**. (See Chapter 8 for a full discussion of CMYK and color management.)

Process color printing requires four plates of the page, also called *color separations*. Until recent years, these plates were created photolithographically using a series of camera filters (in addition to the screen for halftones). Each of these filters strains out one of the three additive primary colors, red, green, and blue (RGB), allowing the other two to combine and produce the subtractive color plates in cyan, magenta, and yellow (CMY). Finally, a grayscale filter produces the key plate (the *K* in CMYK), so called because it's usually the first plate printed, and the other three are matched up or *registered* to it. The key plate adds saturation, clarity, and darker shadows than CMY can produce on their own.

The resulting four plates are then printed one at a time onto each sheet of the print job, producing what looks like a full-color image. Many offset lithographic printing presses now also include more than one printing assembly, so a sheet can be printed in all four color impressions at one pass. Even more complex presses, called *perfecting presses* or just *perfecters*, can print multiple colors on both sides of the sheet simultaneously. In larger print shops, it's not uncommon to find perfecters that are able to print six colors (CMYK plus two spot colors) on one side and four colors on the other side, all in one pass of the paper through the press. (For more information about spot color ink, see "Spot and Process Inks," page 358.)

FURTHER REFINEMENTS IN LITHOGRAPHY: COMPUTER-TO-PLATE AND DIRECT IMAGING

Newer developments in lithography bypass the need to create and photograph camera-ready copy to make a plate. Today, the separation process typically takes place inside page layout or imaging software, where each separation is called a *channel*. Each channel can be manipulated and adjusted digitally, giving considerable control over the output.

With **Computer to Plate** (CTP) or **Digital Imaging** (DI), process color lithography is automated even further. CTP uses a machine called a **plate processor** to create the lithographic plate directly from a digital file rather than through photography. The plate can then be printed normally in a traditional offset lithographic press. DI extends this development by combining the plate processor with the press itself. Using DI, the press receives the digital file at one end and outputs printed material at the other, reducing manual intervention even further.

Both of these processes shorten the distance between the designer and the printed document by making the production process more streamlined. In essence, they allow a tighter integration between the digital files that designers submit to print shops and the resulting product that comes out of the press.

ADVANTAGES AND DISADVANTAGES OF LITHOGRAPHY

The greatest advantages of offset lithography are high quality and cheap per-unit cost for long print runs. The biggest single expense in doing a lithographic job is typically making the plates; once you've gone to that expense, offset lithography is relatively cheap per copy. As a result, the higher the volume of copies printed, the cheaper the price per copy becomes. If the plate costs $200 to make, then the first copy made with the plate will cost about $250 — the cost of the plate plus a bit more because the printer will waste some sheets of paper in setting up the press (a process called **make-ready**). But if we print a second copy, the plate and setup costs will be spread over twice as many copies, cutting the price per copy in half, to just a few cents over $125 (even one sheet of paper costs a bit). Print four copies, and the unit price goes to a little more than $62.50, and so on. Over thousands of copies, the cost of plate-making and make-ready is amortized until it's a very small part of the per-unit cost. Conversely, for short-run print jobs (anything fewer than several hundred copies), the expense of creating the plates makes offset relatively expensive per copy.

The biggest disadvantage of lithography also has to do with plates — namely, that *mistakes on lithographic plates cannot be corrected*. To correct a mistake after a plate is made, the print shop must make the correction in the camera-ready or digital copy and make a new plate, which doubles the plate cost. Other disadvantages of lithography arise from the highly mechanized nature of the process, which requires expensive equipment and highly trained personnel.

Reprography

Because printing technologies like lithography are so complex, innovators have long searched for ways to bring printing into the hands of less-skilled people. The Xerox corporation introduced a technology in the mid-twentieth century that allowed people to reproduce documents using a relatively simple machine that anyone could operate. The machine used a process called **reprography**, also commonly known as **photocopying**. Later, reprography was adapted to mesh with computers in **laser printing**. Reprography is a tremendously useful technology for document production—particularly with the kind of ephemeral documents many of us create each day.

THE REPROGRAPHIC PROCESS

The most common form of reprography is photocopying. Photocopiers use the principle that electrical charges attract their opposites. Here's how it works:

1. You place an original document on the photocopier's impression window and activate the machine.

2. A bright light scans across the original. Where the original is black (such as text or images), no light is reflected. Where the paper is white, light is reflected onto a positively charged rotating drum.

3. This reflected light changes the places on the drum where you *don't* want ink to a neutral charge, leaving a positive charge only on the areas where you *do* want ink.

4. The drum picks up a powdered, negatively charged plastic ink called **toner**. Because opposites attract, the negatively charged ink sticks only in the areas where the drum is still positively charged.

5. The photocopier picks up a sheet of blank copy paper and gives it a positive charge before sending it to the drum.

6. The negatively charged ink image on the drum transfers to the positively charged paper.

7. A heating element called the **fuser** melts the ink onto the paper.

This last step explains why paper always leaves a photocopier feeling warm.

Laser printers work very much like photocopiers. But instead of shining a bright light on an original, laser printers use a laser to change the charge on the drum. The laser is digitally controlled by the printer's computer processor to change the drum's charge to positive only in the areas where we want images or text to appear. The rest of the printing process works just like steps 4 to 7 in the photocopying process.

Color laser printers have recently become more common as their prices have fallen. As you might guess, color laser printers work by applying the four process-color inks (CMYK) to each page. They transfer the powdered ink to the page and fuse it there exactly the same way as a monochrome laser printer does—just with four repetitions using four separate drums.

ADVANTAGES AND DISADVANTAGES OF REPROGRAPHY

Reprography has significant advantages for document designers. The equipment is inexpensive and common enough that companies, organizations, and individuals can afford it. After half a century of development, the technology has become very easy to use. For short-run documents—from one to a few hundred copies—reprography gives control and flexibility to document designers, allowing us to create prototypes or finished documents from our desktops cheaply and on demand, rather than having to wait for a print shop to run an offset job. Mistakes in the document are also easy to catch and fix with reprography; you can print drafts cheaply and make corrections at any time.

Print shops or specialized copy centers benefit from reprography as well, using the technology to print short document runs cheaply and quickly. At these facilities, reprographically produced documents can also be folded, stitched, and bound just like more traditional offset documents. More recently, color reprography has even allowed printers to produce small runs of full-color documents on demand (see "New Printing Technologies," page 351).

However, reprography does have two significant disadvantages when compared to lithography: lower quality and higher per-copy cost. Reprography handles line-drawn images like logos and diagrams well, but it reproduces photographs and other halftone images poorly. The inks used in reprography can be dense and dark under the best conditions, but as anyone who has eked out a few too many printouts from a laser printer cartridge knows, it's common to get pale or streaky darks with reprography. Quality problems can also arise because laser printers and photocopiers are often kept in a dusty office corner, mistreated, and poorly maintained. Photocopies often have stray gray streaks on the white areas, which are caused by worn-out drums, inconsistent toner, or smudges and dust on the imposition glass.

In long print runs, reprography also costs more per copy than offset printing. As we discussed before, with offset lithography an economics of scale kicks in as print runs get longer; each copy made is cheaper than the last. But with reprography, every copy costs exactly the same, no matter how many you make. So while lithography is often cheaper for long print runs, reprography wins out for short print runs. There's also a point, usually somewhere around several hundred copies, where reprography and lithography cost about the same per copy. At that point, other factors such as quality and time come into play in the decision about which technology to use.

Inkjet Printing

The kind of printing you're probably most familiar with is performed by the printer sitting next to your computer. If you're like most computer users, that printer is probably an *inkjet*. Inkjets have become so common that they're often included when you buy a computer. And there are some good reasons to remember the humble inkjet in your document design work.

In some ways, inkjets are the simplest of modern printing technologies; they work by directly squirting tiny drops of ink onto the paper. More specifically, inkjet printers work by propelling drops of ink through a series of microscopic holes in the print head. The print head moves across the page in sequential rows, spraying out precise, computer-timed pulses of ink to create the printed image.

This technology also lends itself conveniently to four-color printing. Inkjet printers can print CMYK inks through four heads simultaneously. Some inkjet printers use a single combined ink cartridge with connected reservoirs for the four ink colors; others use four separate ink reservoirs and heads, so you can replace each color as it runs out.

ADVANTAGES AND DISADVANTAGES OF INKJET PRINTING

Inkjet printers are cheap and ubiquitous; you can readily find them in many stores. They've made color printing available to nearly everyone who has a computer, and they can also be useful for quick and dirty proofing of color print jobs.

But the per-unit printing cost of inkjet printing is high, primarily because of two factors: ink and paper. Inkjets go through ink cartridges like monkeys go through bananas, and the cartridges aren't cheap. Inkjet ink actually costs more per gram than gold. On lower-quality machines, a single new set of cartridges often costs more than the printer itself! And if you're printing in color, you'll need even more ink as the process colors are overprinted on top of each other. With cheap inkjet printers, it's common to get only 40 or so pages of four-color printing from a single set of CMYK cartridges. The cartridges also tend to run out at the most inconvenient time — like right in the middle of a page, leaving the rest of the printed pages with three process colors instead of four.

Paper also plays a role in inkjet print quality and expense. Although inkjets can disperse precisely metered drops of ink onto the paper, the quality of the paper determines whether the ink will stay where the printer put it. If the paper is porous or rough, it can allow the ink to bleed beyond its original spray area, effectively decreasing the resolution of the output. If you use a higher-quality and more expensive coated paper to avoid bleeding, you might run into problems with smearing: instead of soaking into the paper, the ink sits wet on the surface until it dries, just waiting for anyone or anything to touch it (see page 356–57 for more information about coated papers).

Finally, although manufacturers have made great strides recently in inkjet output quality, inkjet printers often provide an unmistakably streaky, pale, and poorly registered output. This comes from the sequential passes of the print head; as the printer wears out, the print head doesn't move as consistently as it should. Streaks and pale output can also arise from ink clogging as the print head becomes contaminated with gunky, dried ink.

For these reasons it's important not to depend too heavily on inkjet printers for accurate proofing work. They can give you a quick and relatively cheap sense of how your design might look when printed offset, but the output of inkjets usually differs remarkably from the output of process-color offset lithography. If you want more accurate color proofing, you might want to invest in a more expensive dye-sublimation printer or color laser printer.

Inkjets can also be used for final copies of very ephemeral documents — the lowest of low-design level work. Sometimes a quick flyer printed on an inkjet is just the ticket for advertising an office party. But be aware of the conditions in which the document will be used: inkjet inks are water-soluble, so documents printed with inkjets don't stand up well in humid or wet environments.

New Printing Technologies

As printing technologies have advanced in the past several years, a gradual coalescence of computers and printing presses has developed. In some ways, the goal of new printing technologies has been to use computers to automate the printing process so much that the industrial process of printing will move toward the convenience and flexibility of desktop printers — just on a larger scale and with higher quality. Broadly speaking, these new technologies can be called *commercial digital printing*, but there are several different technologies currently under development.

The goal of new printing technologies has been to use computers to automate the printing process so much that the industrial process of printing will move toward the convenience and flexibility of desktop printers — just on a larger scale and with higher quality.

Digital offset printing, for example, entirely eliminates the need to create a separate plate for each page. One iteration of this approach, developed by Hewlett-Packard, uses a *Photo Imaging Plate (PIP)* on a drum in place of the traditional metal lithographic plate (Hewlett-Packard 5). In a sense, the PIP combines the electrically charged impression drum of reprography with the mechanical processes of offset printing. The PIP can be altered with a laser to accept or reject an electrically charged liquid ink on the fly. The negatively charged liquid ink (much like the electrically charged reprographic toner) sticks to the PIP only where we want an image. The resulting ink-image is then transferred to a blanket cylinder and then to the paper, just like in traditional offset lithography.

The big advantage of this technology is that the PIP can change on the fly, even potentially with each impression. This allows each copy of the document to have different content — for example, we can insert a personalized name or address label for each copy that goes through the press. Because digital printing bypasses plate creation entirely, it's remarkably flexible and fast: a digital file goes in one end of the press, and finished sheets come out the other end.

Other similar approaches set aside the lithographic process entirely, using industrial-capacity laser printers or color laser printers to produce finished documents. The resulting *commercial reprographic printing* provides quick response and flexibility when producing small-run documents. The documents are produced faster and less expensively than those output from desktop laser printers or office photocopiers — and they usually have a higher quality.

This flexibility enables *Print On Demand (POD)*. Strictly speaking, POD is an approach to printing rather than a particular print technology. Since the input of digital printing is simply a digital file, it's possible to print very small print runs of documents as they're needed, just as you do with a desktop printer. The print shop can keep digital files for different documents on hand and then print out more copies when necessary — even if it's only one more copy.

Currently, POD is still considerably more expensive than traditional commercial printing, but the costs are decreasing as digital printing technology becomes more efficient.

Paper

Printing technologies are only one part of document production. The paper on which a job is printed is an important and often-overlooked element in itself. In this section, we'll examine the different types and characteristics of paper used in printing.

Types of Paper

Document designers enjoy a myriad of papers to choose from today—enough to make specifying paper for a print job a bewildering experience. Because we're always on the lookout for a new paper to make a document look distinctive or interesting, designers drive this variety by encouraging paper manufacturers to develop new paper products.

Despite this variety, printers make one broad but useful distinction in the types of paper they use for document production: book paper and cover stock. **Book paper** is designed to hold printed text and images. Book paper can come in many colors, but it's typically a relatively thin, white paper that takes ink well with minimal bleed-through (if the paper is to be printed on both sides). It can be as simple as standard photocopy paper or as complex as the specialty papers used for printing high-design documents like glossy sales brochures and annual reports.

Cover stock is typically a thick, stiff, hard-surfaced paper that folds well and holds up to handling and abrasion. Cover stock can also come in a wide variety of finishes, textures, and colors. As the name suggests, its most common use is in bindings that protect book paper, but it can be used for other documents or parts of documents, such as postcards, folders, bookmarks, reply cards, and so on. The thickness and quality of cover stock can have a significant effect on users' perceptions of the document and the client it represents.

Characteristics of Paper

Book paper and cover stock is a pretty broad distinction, so this section introduces some more specific terminology used to specify papers so you can accurately describe what you are looking for. Given the great variety of papers available, it's worthwhile to get samples before specifying a job—especially for high-design projects, which are more likely to require unusual papers. Printers also try not to keep large stocks of paper on hand, so they might need to order unusual stock from a wholesale paper supplier, which can take a day or two. Plan accordingly, and talk to your printer about paper early in the production process.

Paper for printing has several interacting factors that can affect specifications for print jobs:

- Size
- Grain
- Weight
- Thickness
- Opacity

Given the great variety of papers available, it's worthwhile to get samples before specifying a job—especially for high-design projects, which are more likely to require unusual papers.

- Finish
- Brightness
- Color

SIZE

The width and height of raw paper — the paper the printer must work from before it has been printed, trimmed, folded, or bound — can affect or even determine what sizes and shapes of documents we can design. Knowing the standard sizes of these sheets as they come from paper manufacturers will help you design documents to match these dimensions, resulting in jobs with less waste and accordingly lower costs.

Most document printing uses sheet-fed presses, which take up sheets of paper one at a time and send them through the print heads. Paper sheet sizes are specified by width and height — for example, 28" × 34". Either before or after printing, sheets can be trimmed on the edges, and larger sheets can be split into smaller sheets (see "Trimming and Bleeds" on page 362).

In the United States, paper sheet stock comes in dozens of standard sizes, ranging from 8½" × 11" to 54" × 77". The most common paper sheet size used for offset printing typical documents such as manuals, pamphlets, brochures, and reports is probably 25" × 38", but this can differ significantly, depending on the type of paper, the paper supplier, and the press capacity (some presses can accommodate bigger sheets than others).

European Union countries use paper sizes based on International Standards Organization (ISO) standards, specified in millimeters. Especially common ISO sheet sizes are in the A-series standard, based on an A0 (A-zero) sheet (see Figure 11.4):

- A0: 841mm × 1189mm (33⅛" × 46¹³⁄₁₆")
- A1: 594mm × 841mm (23⅜" × 33⅛"), half of an A0 sheet
- A2: 420mm × 594mm (16½" × 23⅜"), half of an A1 sheet, or one-quarter of an A0 sheet
- A3: 297mm × 420mm (11¹¹⁄₁₆" × 16½"), half of an A2 sheet, or one-eighth of an A0 sheet
- A4: 210mm × 297mm (8¼" × 11¹¹⁄₁₆"), half of an A3 sheet, or one-sixteenth of an A0 sheet

An A4 sheet, which is commonly used for business correspondence documents in Europe, is near the size of a U.S. 8½" × 11" sheet — just about one-quarter inch narrower and one-quarter inch taller.

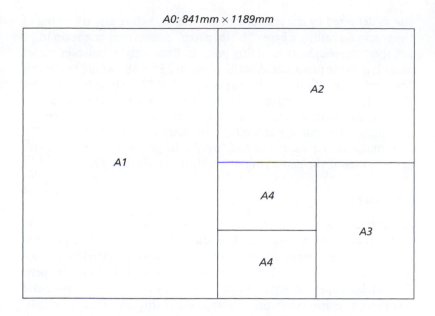

A0: 841mm × 1189mm

Figure 11.4 European paper sizes, based on the ISO A0 standard. Each size sheet is half the size of the next larger sheet: A1 is half of A0, A2 is half of A1, and so on.

GRAIN

Paper is made of fibrous materials such as cotton, flax, or wood pulp. In the manufacturing process for most papers, these fibers line up and interlock in one direction, known as the *grain*. Paper folds and tears more easily with the grain (in line with the fibers) than against the grain (across the fibers). Accordingly, printers take grain into account for any document that will be folded or trimmed into smaller pages.

Paper is usually cut so the grain runs in the long dimension of the sheet. Two different conventions can give you clues about which direction the grain runs in a sheet. Most commonly, the second dimension expressed in a paper size specification is usually the direction of grain, so 28" × 34" indicates that the grain runs along the long dimension, and 34" × 28" indicates that grain runs in the short dimension. As a less ambiguous alternative to this convention, sometimes the grain direction is underlined (28" × 34").

DESIGN TIP

Determining Paper Grain

You can recognize the grain in a sheet of paper in two ways:

- Fold the sheet gently in half without creasing it, first across its width and then across its height. Compare how stiff it is each way. The stiffer direction is against the grain because you're folding the fibers back on themselves.

- Tear a sheet. Paper tears straighter with the grain than against the grain.

WEIGHT

Two measurements of weight are common in printing: basis weight and grammage. The *basis weight* of paper is measured according to the weight in pounds of one ream (500 sheets) of the paper in its full sheet size as delivered by the manufacturer (that is, before any trimming at the press). So calling a paper "50 lb. paper" means that one ream in its full sheet size weighs around fifty pounds. Basis weight, however, varies according to the paper size. A 50 lb. paper in 25" × 38" would be a much "heavier" paper than a 50 lb. paper in 54" × 77", since in the larger sheet size, the same weight would be stretched over a greater area.

Because basis weight can be ambiguous, paper manufacturers increasingly use *grammage* as a more consistent measurement of weight. Grammage is the paper's actual weight in grams per square meter (g/m^2), even if the paper isn't available in sheets that size.

THICKNESS

Paper thickness is usually measured in thousandths of an inch. Thickness can affect both weight and opacity. But it's still an independent factor to consider, especially when specifying paper for a job that will involve folding because thicker papers fold less easily than thinner papers.

Thicker papers *can* have greater strength in terms of stiffness and resistance to tearing than thinner papers, but this isn't always the case. Paper towels are very thick, but weak and easily torn, while the thin papers used in reference works such as dictionaries can be quite strong.

OPACITY

Opacity is a subjective measurement of the amount of light blocked by the paper. Thickness, weight, and finish can have an effect on how opaque a paper appears.

Opacity can be an especially important concern in designs that are printed on both sides of the paper or that require a lot of ink, which might show through a less opaque paper.

FINISH

Paper stock can come in a wide variety of *finishes*, which refers to the texture, smoothness, and hardness of the paper surface. The most common finish specification is whether the paper is coated or uncoated. *Uncoated papers* typically have a matte, rough, absorbent surface. Standard copy paper is uncoated, as is the paper used for most books. *Coated papers* are covered with a layer of material such as clay, so they are shiny, smooth, and nonabsorbent. Coated papers are specified as either *C1S* (coated one side) or *C2S* (coated two sides). Coated papers are often used for process printing because they reflect light well and make colors seem more vivid; magazines and "glossy" final reports typically use coated paper. However, coated papers typically cost more than uncoated papers.

> **MORE ABOUT . . . PAPER FINISHES**
>
> Specialty finishes in today's papers, such as *vellum*, *linen*, *laid*, and *wove*, originally referred to the material or the manufacturing process for making the sheets. Vellum, also called parchment, was actually a prepared sheet of animal hide rather than paper; it typically offered a shiny surface and came in thick, individual leaves. Linen is made from fibers of the flax plant. Most papers between the Middle Ages and 1840 were made of linen. Today's vellum or linen papers are usually made from wood or cotton pulp pressed against a mold to create a surface texture similar to the original.
>
> *Laid* and *wove* also refer to the surface texture created by the mold used in papermaking. In most papers from the Middle Ages to the 1820s, papermaking molds were a grid of narrowly spaced horizontal wires held together at intervals by thicker vertical wires called "chains." The paper made in these molds was left with a pattern of narrowly spaced lines that typify laid paper. These patterns are artificially pressed into papers today to make them look old-fashioned.
>
> In the late eighteenth century, high-end papermakers developed a smoother finish by placing a fine woven mesh over the wire and chains to create a relatively smooth "wove" surface. Almost all papers manufactured today are wove papers.

Coated and uncoated papers also take ink differently. Ink soaks into uncoated papers, which can lead to fuzzy impositions and bleed-through to the other side of the sheet. Conversely, ink tends to sit on top of coated papers. This keeps impositions crisp and reduces bleed-through but can lead to smudging. Inks can also have different apparent colors when printed on coated or uncoated papers. A spot color ink on an uncoated paper might look significantly different from the same ink on a coated paper, since the coating changes the reflectivity of the paper (see "Ink," page 358).

One compromise between coated and uncoated papers is to use *calendered* papers, which are uncoated but mechanically smoothed or *burnished*. Like coating, calendering hardens the surface of the sheet, which cuts down on bleed-through and allows sharper impressions.

Paper can also have a variety of specialty textures, such as *vellum*, *laid*, *wove*, or *linen*. These finishes replicate the surfaces of older sheet-making technologies, so they're often used for designs trying to invoke an antique or old-fashioned feel. These qualities and terms are not standardized, so one paper manufacturer's laid paper can have a significantly different texture than another's.

BRIGHTNESS

A related characteristic to color is brightness, which refers to the reflectivity of the paper. White papers tend to reflect the most light, but some white papers are brighter than others. High-visibility colors (sometimes called *neon*) can also have high brightness — as much as or more than some white papers.

Bright papers provide the greatest figure-ground contrast between paper and black text, but they can be difficult to read from because the reflected light can fatigue the reader's eyes.

COLOR

Paper comes in a wide variety of colors and consistencies. Even the standard "white" paper we usually see used for business documents can come in a variety of shades or tints of white. Paper pulp can be bleached to remove the natural color of the fibers or colored with dyes to add color. In addition, sometimes paper manufacturers add visual features to the paper, such as bits of unbleached or dyed fiber, other plant materials, plastics, or preprinted patterns.

Paper color can significantly affect the design and printing of documents. Because the CMY inks used in process printing are translucent, process printing on a colored or even off-white paper can alter the intended color. Highly figured, colored, or decoratively patterned papers can also lead to insufficient figure-ground contrast between the paper and printed text. Some highly decorated patterned papers, such as marbled papers, are not meant to be used for printing at all — just for bindings or covers.

Ink

When it comes to moving from design to print, ink is just as important as paper. Lithographic inks in particular are worth knowing something about because there are so many to choose from.

Spot and Process Inks

Process inks are standardized translucent inks in cyan, magenta, and yellow, along with a key ink in a dense, opaque black. **Spot inks**, however, come in thousands of hues, tints, and shades, including metallic, pastel, and high-visibility inks for high-design or specialty print jobs.

As we mentioned in Chapter 8, spot inks are usually specified using the Pantone system. The most common reference tool for this system is a Pantone chip set, a series of sample color chips printed on strips of cover stock punched at one end and mounted on a ring so different chips can be held next to each other for comparison. The color chips are labeled with a Pantone number, usually in three or four digits. The chips are also printed on both uncoated and coated paper, since the paper finish can change the apparent color of the ink.

Total Ink

Four-color process printing overprints the same sheet with several different colors of ink—even more so if combined with additional spot colors. This over-printing risks adding so much ink to the page that the ink cannot adhere to the paper. In other words, there's a limit to the **total ink** that can be laid on a page without causing problems. One such problem is **picking**, where the ink laid down by one print plate (cyan, for example) sticks to the ink of subsequent plates, ruining the print job. Too much total ink usually occurs in places where three or four inks are overprinted in relatively equal quantities—in other words, in areas that are meant to be printed in gray.

But if the viewer is going to see gray anyway, why not just use black ink screened to gray? This idea is the basis of two techniques that address the problem of too much total ink: **Gray Component Replacement** (GCR) and **Under Color Removal** (UCR). GCR replaces CMY with screened black in areas where CMY would be overprinted in equal strengths. In other words, GCR replaces three overprinted inks with one ink, decreasing the ink density on the page. Rather than completely replacing CMY with screened black in gray areas, UCR simply removes one process ink and adds black to make up part of the difference. UCR retains a subtle hue in grays and shadows, while still reducing total ink.

Both GCR and UCR also have the advantage of increasing the apparent saturation of images, particularly photographs. You can specify GCR and UCR settings in Photoshop, InDesign, and similar programs.

Varnishing

Some projects require paper with special durability—for example, on the cover of a document that will get a lot of abuse. In those cases, you can specify **varnishing**, a clear lacquer or plastic coating that's added to the printed sheet like a final layer of ink.

Varnishing prevents smudging and makes the sheet less sensitive to abrasion or wear. The varnishing material can delaminate or peel away from the paper, however, so its adhesion to the substrate paper and ink must be taken into account. It also adds to the cost of the print job.

DESIGN TIP

Use Up-to-Date Chip Sets

Always refer to a current chip set for final ink specifications. Chip sets lose their accuracy as they fade with time, so they're stamped with an expiration date. Using a current chip set will help you specify spot inks accurately and consistently.

New chip sets can be expensive, so having an old chip set for desktop reference can be very useful. Sometimes a printer will give you an expired chip set—if you ask nicely!

From Design to Document

In this section, we'll discuss factors you need to understand about how printers get from document designs to finished documents. First, we'll discuss how items are arranged for printing (through imposition) and the issues one must consider when planning for printing (like numbers of pages and signature foldings). Then we'll move to how printed sheets are folded and assembled into documents.

Planning for Printing: Imposition and Signatures

While we usually encounter finished documents in single pages printed on what seem like individual sheets of paper, most documents are printed on much larger sheets of paper, with several pages arranged on both sides of each sheet. To make this work, the printer must arrange the pages so that they end up in the correct order when the sheet is folded and trimmed.

This arrangement of pages on the front and back of a sheet is called **imposition**. After printing, the large sheets are folded to make up **signatures** (an old term from the early years of printing when each folded unit was marked, or "signed," with a letter of the alphabet to indicate its place in the assembled book). Each signature, when trimmed, produces a group of individual **leaves**, and each leaf has two pages: the front page, which is known as the **recto** of the leaf, and the back page, which is called the **verso**. The most common signature foldings are **folio**, **quarto**, and **octavo** (see Figure 11.5).

Folio imposition

Quarto imposition

Octavo imposition

Figure 11.5 Folio, quarto, and octavo impositions. Sheets printed in these impositions are folded and trimmed to create final pages.

- A **folio** is folded only *once*—for example, for a short four-page/two-leaf newsletter. The outside pages 1 and 4 will be printed on one side of the sheet, and the inside pages 2 and 3 will be printed on the inside.

- A **quarto** is folded *twice*—once in half to make a folio, and then in half again across the first fold. A quarto can carry 8 pages and 4 leaves, twice that of a folio. Pages 1, 4, 5, and 8 are printed on one side of the sheet, and 2, 3, 6, and 7 on the other.

- An **octavo** is folded *three times*, by folding a quarto in half again across the second fold. An octavo can hold 16 pages on 8 leaves. For example, in the most common octavo impositions, pages 1, 4, 5, 8, 9, 12, 13, and 16 are printed on one side, and 2, 3, 6, 7, 10, 11, 14, and 15 are printed on the other.

Although people often think of folios as large documents and octavos as small ones, these terms have nothing to do with the size of the finished document. Depending on the size of the paper you start with, you can design a small folio or a large octavo: these terms refer only to how the sheet is folded.

You probably won't need to specify impositions and signatures yourself; the print shop will take care of this for you. But knowing about impositions and signatures is important because it affects how many pages can fit in a document most efficiently.

Signatures gather pages in 4-, 8-, or 16-page groups, so most documents are designed to be printed in some combination or multiples of those numbers. For example, a 48-page document can be printed in three 16-page octavo signatures ($3 \times 16 = 48$) or six 8-page quarto signatures ($6 \times 8 = 48$). Combinations of impositions are possible, as well: a 52-page document can be printed in three octavo signatures plus one folio signature, although the additional odd signature would increase the cost of printing.

Printing documents that don't match up easily with signatures is more difficult and expensive. For example, it's complicated to print and bind a 49-page document. With 47 pages, you could print a three-signature 48-page octavo and leave a blank page — perhaps the verso of the first leaf. But a 49-page document would require printing at least 52 pages and leaving three blank pages, which could look awkward and cost more. The only other alternative is to **tip-in** a single leaf that is printed on just one side and glue its edge into the spine somewhere in the document or to leave a tag on the spine side where it can be sewn in with the rest of the signatures. But tipping-in is labor-intensive and expensive. It's better to just design pages in multiples of fours, eights, or sixteens from the beginning.

Finishing

The final steps in the printing process are called **finishing**. These include folding, scoring, perforating, gathering, trimming, and binding (also known as stitching), and they all usually happen at one stage in the press facility. Today, it's increasingly common for one machine to perform all of these processes automatically, accepting printed sheets at one end and producing nearly finished documents at the other end. You should specify how you want your document to be finished when discussing the print job with the printer.

SCORING AND PERFORATING

Scoring and perforating are sheet processes that can be useful in some applications. Scoring puts a crease in a sheet without actually folding it. The cover of a perfect-bound (soft-cover) book or report is often scored about a quarter of an inch from the spine, making the cover easier to bend without breaking the spine. Perforating allows readers to tear out a sheet or part of a sheet easily. It's often used to encourage users to tear out, fill out, and return a sheet or card, such as a survey, subscription card, or RSVP.

FOLDING AND GATHERING

We've already discussed folding as it applies to large printed sheets that are folded into signatures. Most print shops have machines that fold and *gather* signatures automatically, placing them in the appropriate order for the final document.

TRIMMING AND BLEEDS

Trimming is performed with an electrical or hydraulic shear called a guillotine. Most guillotines can cut through between 500 and 1,000 sheets at one stroke, depending on the paper stock. Paper might be trimmed before printing to set it up for the press, but whole documents can also be trimmed after printing and before or after binding.

Because a signature results from one large sheet being folded to make a gathering of leaves, in most cases, the folds must be trimmed to open up the leaves. Trimming allows the leaves to separate but remain attached at the spine. A folio requires no cutting because its leaves are joined only at the one spine fold. A quarto is trimmed only on the *top-edge*. An octavo is trimmed on both the top-edge and the *fore-edge* (the edge opposite the spine). Although only these trims are necessary to release the leaves, sometimes the document will be trimmed on all edges except the spine, simply to square up the signatures before binding.

A final trimming issue arises when we want to print sheets to the edge of the page—for example, the cover of an annual report, a four-color flyer, or a quick reference card. This kind of printing is called a *bleed*. Printing presses require a small amount of paper they can grab, called a *gripper edge*, to send the sheet through the press. Presses can't print on the gripper edge, which is trimmed away at the end of the printing process (Figure 11.6).

As a result, printers must print bleeds on an oversized sheet and then trim the excess to make the sheet appear to have been printed on its entire surface. For example, printing an 8½" × 11" flyer might require designing for a 9" × 11½" sheet, leaving a narrow margin around the sheet that will be trimmed off so the ink will appear to go to the edge of the sheet. In these cases, designers use page layout software to place trim marks outside the printed area to indicate where the paper should be trimmed.

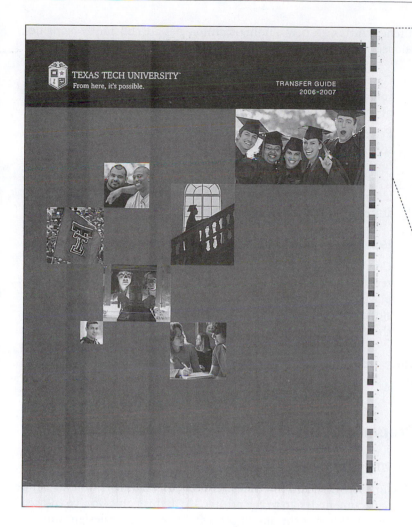

Detail of trim marks and bleed

Figure 11.6 Gripper edge and trim marks.
The printing press grabs the gripper edge
to pull the sheet through the press. The
gripper edge is later trimmed off at the
trim marks to leave the ink bleeding to
the edge of the page.

Texas Tech University, "Transfer Guide."

As we discussed in Chapter 4, you can also design for special edge
trimming in more complex patterns or shapes — anything from tabs on
the fore-edge to rounded corners. This kind of trimming is usually
called *die cutting* because it requires the use of a cutting head called a
die to make the special trim.

BINDING

After folding, signatures are bound. A single quarto or octavo signature
might be *stitched* (stapled) at the spine to make a booklet, or multiple
signatures can be glued or *sewn* together into a *codex* (a book). Documents printed in multiple signatures are typically bound rather than

stitched. Although new binding technologies are constantly being developed, the most common book bindings today are *case* and *perfect*:

- *Case bindings:* Signatures are sewn or glued together at the spine, trimmed, and then pasted into a hard-cover case made up of the front and back covers and the spine.
- *Perfect bindings:* Single sheets or signatures are glued into a soft-cover, square-backed binding made of cover stock. Perfect bindings are trimmed after the cover is attached.

In addition, a variety of techniques can bind individual sheets (rather than signatures of multiple pages). The most common are the following:

- *Wire bindings:* Individual sheets are drilled with small holes.
- *Comb bindings:* Individual sheets are punched with a row of rectangular slots near the spine edge. With a special tool, the plastic comb is held open and its teeth are inserted into the slots. When released from the tool, the comb closes and holds the sheets.

There are also many proprietary binding technologies you might consider; discuss options with your printer.

Preparing Designs for the Press

Communicating with Printers

Document designers sometimes get anxious when it is time to hand over a document design to the printer. Up to this point, you've enjoyed a lot of control over the design process. But once your design is in the print shop, the control shifts to a team of people with different priorities and pressures. Printers want to be your partner in creating a great document; one of their goals is to make you happy so you will bring more work to them. But it's easy to allow misunderstandings and mixed signals to undercut the smoothness of the experience or the quality of the finished product.

The key to avoiding problems is to communicate *early*, *frequently*, and *clearly* with your printer:

- *Communicate early:* Contact the print shop several weeks before you intend to deliver a job to them. They have other jobs to do, and yours must fit into their production schedule. The more complex the job, the earlier you should talk to the printer.

- *Communicate frequently:* Both before and during the printing process, check in with the print shop regularly — first to keep them apprised of your progress in getting the project into their hands on schedule and then to confirm and follow up on your specifications about the job.

- *Communicate clearly:* Communicate what you want *in writing* — e-mail is often fine — and ask for a written quote that specifies everything the printer will do. Be as specific as possible in describing what you want; printers can give you only what you ask for. Also try to use correct printing terminology. It's easy to dismiss this terminology as jargon, but think of it as a specialized vocabulary that allows for precise communication about a complex process.

Your printer has as much at stake in doing a good job as you do, so don't be afraid to ask questions if you don't understand something or need clarification. Printers are usually very happy to take the time to talk to you, since clarifying misunderstandings early saves time and money. If your printer won't talk to you or answer your questions, find another printer.

Getting Estimates

After you've communicated the specifics of the print job to the print shop, they will give you a formal estimate of the printing costs. This estimate will be based primarily on the specifics of the job, such as the number and type of pieces to be printed, the number of colors, finishing, binding, paper, and inks. If you have time and some flexibility, you can get competitive estimates from several print shops.

The estimate will usually include a charge for *make-ready*. As we discussed earlier, this term describes the waste sheets that the printer must use to set up the press before printing the actual run of your document. Some jobs require more make-ready than others, but setting up the press can increase the amount of paper the job requires by 10 to 15 percent.

If you aren't happy with the estimate, negotiate changes as soon as possible. You may want to change some of the specifications of the job to keep costs down. Ask the print shop for advice on ways to economize. They can tell you exactly where the unexpected costs are coming from.

DESIGN TIP

Printing Specification Checklist

Communicate the following information (as applicable) to the print shop so they can prepare your estimate:

- ❏ Your contact information
- ❏ Requested delivery dates
- ❏ Quantity of finished pieces
- ❏ Finished size
- ❏ Folds
- ❏ Number of inks on each side
- ❏ Types of paper for cover and interior
- ❏ Bleeds
- ❏ Finishing and binding specifications
- ❏ Mailing or delivery needs
- ❏ Billing information

Delivering Your Design to the Printer

This may sound very obvious, but make sure the materials you deliver to be printed are as correct and accurate as possible. After a certain point, mistakes in print jobs cannot be fixed without considerable added expense. If mistakes do arise and they are your fault, be prepared to pay extra to have them fixed. Sometimes an entire print run must be discarded and reprinted from scratch because of embarrassing mistakes or legal reasons. This effectively doubles the cost of printing.

Most print shops can give you detailed specifications for how they want you to deliver your design. These commonly include the page layout file formats the print shop will accept, the storage media they can access, and how to manage associated image files and fonts.

Make sure the materials you deliver to be printed are as correct and accurate as possible.

FILE FORMATS

Increasingly, print shops prefer to receive page layouts as Adobe Acrobat files (*.PDF), since these are common file types that can carry all of the page description and fonts. PDFs work particularly seamlessly with digital printing technologies. The print shop can make few changes or adjustments to a PDF, however, which means it's your responsibility to deliver a working design.

If you're not comfortable with that level of responsibility, ask if you can deliver your print jobs to the print shop as an application file. Most print shops readily accept a variety of page layout file formats, including those of the page layout software industry leaders, Adobe and Quark. For Quark, the file extensions are typically either *.QXD (QuarkXPress Document) or *.QXP (QuarkXPress Project). For Adobe, the file extensions can be *.INDD (InDesign), *.FM (FrameMaker), or *.PM (PageMaker). If there are small problems with the design, such as out-of-gamut colors or missing fonts, the print shop will be able to correct the problem (although big problems will probably incur an additional fee).

Few print shops like to work with home computer applications, such as Microsoft Publisher or Microsoft Word. These applications create severe limitations for preparing the design for printing. If at all possible, avoid using these applications for jobs that will be professionally printed.

LINKED AND EMBEDDED OBJECTS

Print shops will need not only your page layout files but also all of the associated files you used to make it, including image files and sometimes computer font files. The two ways to give the print shop all the files they need to create your document are linking and embedding.

With *embedding*, you actually insert the images in the page layout file. This makes a neat and tidy package, but it can create monstrously huge files. With *linking*, you simply insert a reference to the image files in the page layout file. When the page layout program renders the design on-screen, it retrieves these separate files and shows them where you've told it to. The advantage is that the page layout file stays much smaller. The disadvantage is that if the linked files are on another hard drive or computer, the page layout program can't access them.

Whether you link or embed, give the print shop all of the image files you used in the design, just in case the printer needs them to make a last-minute repair or modification. You will usually want to provide the files in TIFF or high-quality JPG format.

Be sure that you have used the CMYK mode in preparing your images, not RGB! The printer can replicate only CMYK colors; any RGB colors you specify might fall outside of the CMYK gamut. (See Chapter 8 for a discussion of color gamut.)

It's also a good idea to send along any unusual computer font files. Print shops usually have large libraries of font files, so they don't always need you to supply the font file with your print job. But if you specify an uncommon typeface, you might need to provide its font file to the print shop so they can load it temporarily on their system and print the job. Be sure to check out the terms of use, however—some typographers disallow copying their font files, even temporarily.

> **DESIGN TIP**
>
> ### Print Shop Delivery Checklist
>
> Provide at least the following items to a commercial print shop. The print shop might have other requirements, so be sure to follow their recommendations and specifications for delivering a job to them.
>
> - [ ] Printing specifications (see page 365)
> - [ ] Page layout files
> - [ ] Image files
> - [ ] Computer font files
> - [ ] Printed drafts
> - [ ] Mock-ups

DRAFTS AND MOCK-UPS

Finally, provide a good-quality printed draft of your document. Printers will use this printed version as a reference when they run across questions in the process of preparing your files for print. Make sure to print out the most recent version. It's often a good idea to print from the CD you made for the printer or from the electronic files you sent them. That way you can be sure that the printer's reference (your printout) is an exact replica of what you have provided electronically. If there are errors in the printer's version of the document, the printer will often refer to your hard-copy version to see if the errors are yours or theirs.

If your design involves any complex folds, die cuts, or other special features, include a *mock-up* of the design. To create a mock-up, use paper, scissors, tape, and glue to prepare a rough version of the finished document, including all of the folds and special features. This mock-up will give the printer a clear idea of what you have in mind for the design.

STORAGE MEDIA

Ask your print shop what media you can use to deliver your work to them. Most print shops happily accept CD-Rs, CD-RWs, or DVD-Rs. Smaller jobs might be e-mailed as attachments compressed in ZIP archives, or made available to the printer on an FTP server. For larger jobs, the printer might even accept a portable USB or Firewire hard drive — but be sure to ask for it back!

Responding to Proofs

When you deliver your document to the printer, confirm the expected production schedule, noting especially when you can expect to receive correction copies, or *proofs*, and the expected turnaround for returning those proofs to the press.

Most print shops will send you two sets of proofs: *first proofs* and *final proofs*. Make sure that you understand how you will receive the proofs (whether via e-mail, FTP, or hard copy) and where.

Proofreading

When the proofs arrive, make every effort to meet the return deadline that the print shop indicates. Since the shop has many clients with documents waiting to be printed, this deadline is typically firm. If you don't return the proofs as agreed, the shop will not delay the work of other clients because you didn't meet your obligations. Your job will have to be moved back to the next available opening in the printing schedule. If you're lucky, you will still be able to meet your project deadlines; if you aren't, you might find yourself with limited options and long delays.

Making Corrections

If you find errors made by the printer, the print shop will typically correct those without additional costs to you (although you should verify this during early discussions about the job). But most likely, any mistakes you find on the proofs will arise from the original material you supplied to the printer. In that case, you must pay for the corrections.

What you can change in proofs is very limited. Whatever changes you specify must be performed by the print shop personnel rather than by you, which makes changes expensive. In general, stick to correcting only factual errors, misspellings or grammatical errors, and statements that might have legal consequences, such as libel or copyright issues. Anything else that just doesn't appeal to you (clumsy sentences, bad

---

DESIGN TIP

Proofing Checklists

When reading proofs, do both linear proofing and layered proofing. For **linear proofing**, simply read the document all the way through with a fresh eye. Look especially for the following problems during linear proofing:

- ❏ Spelling errors (including especially proper names)
- ❏ Grammar errors
- ❏ Libelous statements
- ❏ Copyright infringement
- ❏ Errors in paragraph styles (sometimes the wrong style will get applied to a paragraph)

It's also a good idea to ask a colleague to do a linear proof. Someone who has not been intimately involved with the document might see problems that your eyes missed.

For **layered proofing**, go through the document again, one design element at a time:

- ❏ Titles
- ❏ Headers
- ❏ Footers
- ❏ Headings
- ❏ Art
- ❏ Captions
- ❏ Sidebars
- ❏ Pull-quotes
- ❏ Front matter (table of contents, list of illustrations, publication information, and so on)
- ❏ Back matter (appendices, index)
- ❏ Covers

During layered proofing, look not only at the correctness of all of these elements but also at their visual consistency. Each first-level heading should look like all the other first-level headings, all the captions should look the same, and so on. Be especially watchful for obvious errors. Sometimes the bigger the font size, the easier it is to miss a mistake.

---

line breaks, widows, orphans, unattractive typefaces, and so on) will have to remain if you wish to maintain your budget and the agreed-upon delivery date.

Any changes that affect the page layout of the document will be especially expensive. So avoid making any changes that will change the length of paragraphs or pages or the size of graphics. Adding a single word can sometimes make a paragraph one line longer—enough that it won't fit on the page, throwing off everything in subsequent pages of the document. And changing the size of a graphic can affect text wrapping, which can have a ripple effect on subsequent paragraphs or pages.

If you are working with content contributors who need to proofread the portions of the document they wrote, specify *exactly* what kind of changes they can and cannot make, as well as your deadline for receiving their corrections. Remind your contributors not to make stylistic revisions, deletions, or additions to the design or text of the document at this point. Set the contributors' deadline at least one day before the printer's deadline so you'll have time to collate their changes into a single set of instructions for the printer.

When marking proofs, use standard proofreading marks. You can find these in any style manual, such as *The Chicago Manual of Style*. In addition, follow the printer's guidelines for how to indicate corrections. Some printers prefer marked proofs, while others prefer a list itemized by page, paragraph, and line number. If you have questions about their preferences, ask if they can provide an example of the type of responses they prefer.

When you return your proofs, get a receipt or some other documentation. A simple e-mail message is sufficient, but it's a good idea to be able to confirm your date and time submission if it becomes necessary later to retain your place in the production schedule.

Conclusion

Sending a job to a commercial printer might seem intimidating. But remember that print shops are as interested in producing an excellent finished product as you are. Work professionally and responsibly with commercial printers, and they'll return the favor by bringing your designs successfully into existence.

Exercises

1. Go on a tour of a commercial print shop. Most large print shops will be happy to provide a short tour of their operations to potential customers and especially to students who might be customers for a long time to come.

2. Talk to a commercial print shop operator (either in conjunction with a print shop tour or at a separate time). Consider asking these questions:

   - What are the three most essential things I should do as a designer to make the production process run smoothly?
   - What three things should I most avoid doing?
   - What are your preferences for receiving print jobs?
   - How would you describe a successful client–print shop relationship?

   Write a short report describing what you learned from this conversation.

3. Find a fairly complex print document. Imagine that you are the designer of this document and are just about to send the design for commercial printing. Using the printing terminology discussed in this chapter and others, write a specifications list that describes this document to a commercial printer and communicates what the finished product should be like.

Works Cited

Griffiths, Antony. *Prints and Printmaking: An Introduction to the History and Techniques*. Berkeley: University of California Press, 1996.

Hewlett-Packard, Inc. *White Paper: Digital Offset Color*. Online: <http://www.infoworld.com/spotlights/hp/HP_Digital_Offset_Color.pdf>.

Further Reading

Gatter, Mark. *Getting It Right in Print: Digital Prepress for Graphic Designers*. New York: Harry N. Abrams, 2005.

International Paper. *Pocket Pal: The Handy Little Book of Graphic Arts Production*. 19th ed. Memphis, TN: International Paper, 2003.

Sanders, Linda. *47 Printing Headaches (and How to Avoid Them): How to Prevent Costly Printing Mistakes — A Solution Book for Designers, Production Artists, and Desktop Publishers*. Cincinnati, OH: North Light Books, 1991.

University of Chicago Press Staff. *The Chicago Manual of Style*. 15th ed. Chicago: University of Chicago Press, 2003.

About the Authors

Miles A. Kimball is an associate professor of technical communication and rhetoric at Texas Tech University, where he teaches document design, new media, and pedagogy. His scholarship includes work on visual design, visual culture, and visual rhetoric; the history of technical communication, including the development of information graphics; and online portfolios and other pedagogical tools. He is the author of *The Web Portfolio Guide* (Longman, 2003).

Ann R. Hawkins is an associate professor of English at Texas Tech University, where she teaches bibliography, book history, scholarly editing, and textual studies. Dr. Hawkins has held fellowships from the Folger Shakespeare Library and the Bibliographical Society of America, which named her a New Scholar in 2004. Her scholarship focuses on eighteenth- and nineteenth-century book illustration and visual culture. She has also taught at Rare Book School at the University of Virginia.

Acknowledgments, continued from p. iv

Fig. 1.2–1.4: Reprinted with permission of Amtrak. Painting by J. Craig Thorpe, Bellevue, WA. www.jcraigthorpe.com. Used with permission.

Fig. 1.7–1.8: © LeapFrog Enterprises, Inc. Used with permission.

Fig. 2.1: Reprinted with permission of Student Health Services, Texas Tech University.

Fig. 2.16: Reprinted with permission of EverNote Corp.

Fig. 2.17: © 2007 Inspiration Software®, Inc. Graphic created in Kidspiration® by Inspiration Software®, Inc. Used with permission.

Fig. 3.1: © 2004 The J. Paul Getty Museum. Used with permission.

Fig. 3.10: CBS-TV/UA/Gladysya Prod/The Kobal Collection. Used with permission.

Fig. 3.11: © Ashley Cooper/Corbis.

Fig. 3.15: Used with permission of Excel Industries.

Fig. 3.16: Shaun Inman Design & Development, Inc., www.haveamint.com.

Fig. 3.17: This image is provided courtesy of Wells Fargo Bank, N.A. and may not be reproduced in any form.

Fig. 4.1: Reprinted with permission of Mazda Motor Corporation.

Fig. 4.3: Reprinted with permission of Atmos Energy and Empire Designs.

Fig. 4.4: Catalog covers reprinted with kind permission of White Flower Farm. Photo credit for Spring 2004 catalog: Used with permission of Clive Nichols Co. Photo credit for 2003 catalog: Used with permision of Photos Horticultural.

Fig. 4.11: Used with permission of the International Cultural Center, Texas Tech University. Designer: Pat Maines; Photographer: Ashton Thornhill.

Fig. 4.15: "Time-Saving Ways to Buy Stamps & Send Packages" Brochure © 2005 United States Postal Service. All Rights Reserved. Used with Permission.

Fig. 4.18: Reprinted with permission of Atmos Energy and Empire Designs.

Fig. 4.19: Used with permission of the Denver Regional Transportation District, Denver, CO.

Fig. 4.20: Reprinted with permission of Palm, Inc.

Fig. 4.21: Used with permission of Citibus.

Fig. 4.27: Used with permission of Project Planet Corp.

Fig. 4.28: Accession Number 43.6. Edward Hopper, Ground Swell, 1939. Oil on canvas. 36½ × 50¼ inches. Courtesy of Corcoran Gallery of Art, Washington, DC. Museum Purchase, William A. Clark Fund.

Fig. 4.29: Used with permission of the Denver Museum of Outdoor Arts.

Fig. 4.30: © British Library Board. All rights reserved. Used with permission.

Fig. 5.1a: "Power in Numbers." Flyer created by Ben Zhu of Nucleus Studios, Inc. Reprinted with permission.

Fig. 5.1b: "David Garrick, A Theatrical Life." By permission of the Folger Shakespeare Library, www.folger.edu. Designed by Antonio Alcala, Studio A, www.thestudio.com.

Fig. 5.1c: "Countertops." © 2007 HOMER TLC, Inc. Used with Permission. All Rights Reserved.

Fig. 5.1d: Used with permission of Shaun Inman Design & Development, Inc.

Fig. 5.2: Used with permission of the Wrigley Company.

Fig. 5.4: Used with permission of AARP.

Fig. 5.5: Used with permission of the Campaign for Tobacco-Free Kids.

Fig. 5.6: Reprinted with permission of The National Trust.

Fig. 5.12: Exhibition Reverie and Reality: Photography by Rodney Smith, May 16–August 10, 2003, University of Virginia Art Museum. Catalogue design by Anne Chestnut. Reprinted with permission. Photography by Rodney Smith. Reprinted with permission of Rodney Smith.

Fig. 5.13: © The Art Institute of Chicago. Reprinted with permission.

Fig. 5.14: © The Art Institute of Chicago. Reprinted with permission.

Fig. 5.15: Brochure for the National Building Museum's exhibition Cityscapes Revealed: Highlights from the Collection. Used by permission of National Building Museum.

Fig. 5.16: Reprinted by permission of the Denver Office of Cultural Affairs. Design: Art & Anthropoly, Inc.

Fig. 5.18: © 2007 HOMER TLC, Inc. Used with Permission. All Rights Reserved.

Fig. 5.19: Used with permission of Alliance Boots.

Fig. 5.20: From America's 100th Meridian: A Plains Journey pamphlet, pp. 2–3. © 2006 Texas Tech University Press, 800-832-4042. Reprinted with permission. Photographer: Monte Hartman.

Fig. 5.22: University Human Resources, University of Virginia. Reprinted with permission.

Fig. 5.23: Reprinted by permission of UPS.

Fig. 5.27: Donna Seaman, "The People of the Book: Riding the Third Wave," American Libraries, May 2005, p. 53. Reprinted by permission of the American Libraries Association.

Fig. 5.28: The Portal reprinted with permision of Texas Tech University Libraries and Design Envy. Designers: John Raspberry and Donya Snead.

Fig. 6.1: Reprinted with permission of ArchiText. Design credit: TransPerfect, August 2006.

Fig. 6.3: Reproduced with permission of Yahoo! Inc. © 2007 by Yahoo! Inc. YAHOO! and the YAHOO! logo are trademarks of Yahoo! Inc.

Fig. 7.1: Reprinted with permission of Flying Dog Brewery LLC, Denver, CO.

Fig. 7.2: Used with permission of The Huntington Library, Art Collections, and Botanical Gardens.

Fig. 7.3: Reprinted with permission of The Huntington Library, Art Collections, and Botanical Gardens. Map illustration reprinted with kind permission of the artist, Lisa Pompelli.

Fig. 7.4: Reprinted with permission of Dickinson College.

Fig. 7.5: Used with permission from The Times, CSFB, and GfK NOK.

Fig. 7.6: Used with permission from the Texas Tech University System, College of Engineering and Applied Science.

Fig. 7.9a: The rendering of the Commonweal Theatre Company is used with permission of Holabird & Root.

Fig. 7.9c: Used by permission of DM Systems, Inc.

Fig. 7.12: Used with permission of Professor David Stotts.

Fig. 7.13: Reprinted with permission of the University of Colorado Discovery Learning Initiative.

Fig. 7.15: Reprinted with permission of Last.fm.

Fig. 7.17a: Cover for the Luce Foundation Center brochure, Smithsonian American Art Museum, 2006. Designed by Academy Studios, featuring Black Hawk Horse Weathervane Pattern, 1871–1872, attributed to Henry Leach. (Carved and painted wood, 22" × 34½" × 3⅜" Smithsonian American Art Museum, Gift of Herbert Waide Hemphill, Jr. and museum purchase made possible by Ralph Cross Johnson. 1986.65.358)

Fig. 7.17b: Used with permission from the American Academy of Allergy Asthma & Immunology (AAAAI).

Fig. 7.21: Photo: Jeff Stead/The Examiner. © The Examiner. Used with permission.

Fig. 8.1/Color Fig. 1: Reprinted with permission of Ethanol Promotion and Information Council (EPIC), www.drivingethanol.org.

Color Fig. 11: Used with permission of Shaun Inman Design & Development, Inc.

Color Fig. 12: By permision of the Folger Shakespeare Library, www.folger.edu. Designed by Andrea LeHeup, Soleil Design, www.soleilnyc.com.

Color Fig. 13: Used with permission of The Library of Congress.

Color Fig. 14: Reprinted with permission of the Shakespeare Theatre Company.

Color Fig. 15: Courtesy of the Freer Gallery of Art and Arthur M. Sackler Gallery, Smithsonian Institution, Washington, DC. Photo of Julia Coffey and Veanne Cox by Carol Rosegg.

Color Fig. 16: Reprinted with permission of Adobe Systems Incorporated.

Fig. 9.2: "Choose Any Time-Saving Tool" Brochure © 2005 United States Postal Service. All Rights Reserved. Used with Permission.

Fig. 9.8: Used with permission of Columbia Aircraft Manufacturing.

Fig. 9.23: Reprinted with permission of Leads.com.

Fig. 9.24: Reprinted with permission of the Avon Foundation.

Fig. 9.25: "Official Mail Forwarding Change of Address Order Form" reprinted with permission of the United States Postal Service. All Rights Reserved.

Fig. 11.6: Used with permission of Texas Tech University Office of Admissions.

Index